The Collected Works of
James M. Buchanan

VOLUME 13
Politics as Public Choice

Left to right: Ronald Coase, Duncan Black, James Buchanan, James Ferguson, Warren Nutter, Gordon Tullock, Leland Yeager. Thomas Jefferson Center, University of Virginia, Charlottesville, November 1962.

The Collected Works of

James M. Buchanan

VOLUME 13

Politics as Public Choice

LIBERTY FUND

This book is published by Liberty Fund, Inc., a foundation established to encourage study of the ideal of a society of free and responsible individuals.

The cuneiform inscription that serves as our logo and as a design motif in Liberty Fund books is the earliest-known written appearance of the word "freedom" (*amagi*), or "liberty." It is taken from a clay document written about 2300 B.C. in the Sumerian city-state of Lagash.

| 09 | 21 | 22 | 23 | 24 | C | 6 | 5 | 4 | 3 | 2 |
| 21 | 22 | 23 | 24 | 25 | P | 8 | 7 | 6 | 5 | 4 |

Library of Congress Cataloging-in-Publication Data
Buchanan, James M.
Politics as a public choice / James M. Buchanan.
p.   cm. — (The collected works of James M. Buchanan ; v. 13)
Includes bibliographical references and index.
ISBN 0-86597-237-0 (hc : alk.paper).—ISBN 0-86597-238-9 (pb : alk.paper).
1. Political science.   2. Social choice.   I. Title.   II. Series:
Buchanan, James M.   Works.   1999 ; v. 13.
JA71.B83   2000
320'.011—dc21   99-41676

LIBERTY FUND, INC.
11301 North Meridian Street
Carmel, Indiana 46032
libertyfund.org

Contents

3. Voters

4. Voting Models

5. Rent Seeking

6. Regulation

7. Public Choice and Public Expenditures

Foreword

James M. Buchanan is one of the founders of public choice theory and a longtime leader in the public choice revolution in economics and political science. This revolution was based on the expansion of economic methodology to include the study of government. After the revolution, government was no longer treated as a black box in public choice theory; it was analyzed with the tools and assumptions of modern economic theory. Public choice examines governmental institutions and actors on the assumption that behavior in markets and in government is essentially the same; that is, decision makers are animated by self-interest or by the idea of pursuing their goals effectively. Constraints on individual behavior may differ in government, but the actors themselves are the self-same individuals who populate market settings. Government agents are not seen as pursuing some nebulous idea of the "public interest"; they are seen, rather, as pursuing their individual self-interest in a governmental context.

This change of perspective probably seems simple in retrospect, but the fruits of this revolution have been plentiful. We now have a richer normative and positive understanding of how government can be improved and of how government actually works. Because of the public choice revolution, we immediately know more about voting rules, legislative decision making, bureaucracy, and many other aspects of government. We are also able to assess the realistic possibilities of government in a much wiser fashion. The lesson of public choice is that institutional alternatives must be assessed on a case-by-case basis and that the relevant choice is between imperfect markets and imperfect governments. While there is no automatic presumption that government interference in the economy is undesirable, there is also no automatic presumption that it is desirable. Selecting the "best" institutions becomes a critical problem in public choice theory. This important shift in emphasis and analysis has been one of the main results of the public choice revolution—a movement at the center of which Buchanan has been for his entire career.

One might ordinarily think that a collection of James M. Buchanan's essays on public choice would be mostly preempted by his contributions to this subject matter published in books such as *The Calculus of Consent* or *The Reason of Rules*, which appear elsewhere in his Collected Works.[1] Nothing could be further from the truth, as the essays in this volume aptly demonstrate. Originality and insight, as well as clear articulation of important theoretical principles, are the guiding themes of the papers in this volume. Moreover, many of these papers have had a significant impact on the subsequent literature.

Let us take a few examples. The paper "Voter Choice" (with Geoffrey Brennan), which appeared in the *American Behavioral Scientist*, has sparked a new approach to the problem of voter choice and voting behavior.[2] This new theory is called the *theory of expressive voting*, wherein the setting of democratic voting is analyzed as a low-cost environment in which to act, for example, altruistically. In such a way one might explain the emphasis on income redistribution policies that characterize most democracies. This fascinating approach to voter choice is gaining growing recognition in the literature of public choice and political science.

Buchanan has also made important contributions to the now popular theory of rent seeking. Buchanan's highly influential essay "Rent Seeking and Profit Seeking" appears in volume 1 of his Collected Works, *The Logical Foundations of Constitutional Liberty*. This paper served to educate a generation of economists about the nature and implications of the rent-seeking idea. Buchanan's contributions to the theory of rent seeking reprinted in this volume are also quite important. His paper "Reform in the Rent-Seeking So-

---

1. James M. Buchanan and Gordon Tullock, *The Calculus of Consent: Logical Foundations of Constitutional Democracy* (Ann Arbor: University of Michigan Press, 1962), volume 3 in the series; Geoffrey Brennan and James M. Buchanan, *The Reason of Rules: Constitutional Political Economy* (Cambridge: Cambridge University Press, 1985), volume 10 in the series.

2. Geoffrey Brennan and James M. Buchanan, "Voter Choice: Evaluating Political Alternatives," *American Behavioral Scientist* 28 (November/December 1984): 185–201.

ciety," for example, points out some of the basic difficulties in ridding the political system of the scourge of rent seeking.[3]

A final example of the originality and impact of the papers in this volume is the paper "Polluters' Profits and Political Response" (with Gordon Tullock).[4] This paper was reputedly written over a weekend in Blacksburg, Virginia, and it was the first paper to explain why social and environmental policies could be driven by redistributive rather than purely allocative considerations. As such, this paper has stimulated a modern literature that theoretically and empirically examines public policy in these areas with interest group models, and which stresses the importance of strategic behavior among firms in an industry in influencing the pattern and impact of regulation. The importance of this paper cannot be overstated.

While these three papers serve as an enticement to read the entire volume, the remainder of *Politics as Public Choice* makes for fascinating reading. Part 1 contains several retrospective and methodological papers on the public choice movement. Part 2 contains three papers that illustrate some of Buchanan's discontent with the modern development of public choice theory. Part 3 presents some of Buchanan's contributions to the theory of voter behavior. Part 4 presents some papers showing Buchanan's abiding interest in formal voting theory. Part 5 contains most of Buchanan's contributions to the emerging theory of rent seeking. Part 6 contains the "Polluters' Profits" and other papers on the subject of economic and social regulation. Finally, part 7 presents papers that deal with public choice aspects of the level and growth of public spending.

Read in conjunction with the other parts of the Collected Works, these papers offer the reader a fuller appreciation of the public choice revolution and its impact and prospects.

Robert D. Tollison
University of Mississippi
1999

3. James M. Buchanan, "Rent Seeking and Profit Seeking," in *Toward a Theory of the Rent-Seeking Society*, ed. James M. Buchanan, Robert D. Tollison, and Gordon Tullock (College Station: Texas A&M University Press, 1980), 3–15; "Reform in the Rent-Seeking Society," *Toward a Theory of the Rent-Seeking Society*, 359–67.

4. James M. Buchanan and Gordon Tullock, "Polluters' Profits and Political Response: Direct Controls versus Taxes," *American Economic Review* 65 (March 1975): 139–47.

PART ONE

General Approach

An Economist's Approach to "Scientific Politics"

The overall aim of this series of essays is that of forcing scholars outside of political science who look upon government and politics to tell what they may see. This aim is suggestive of the fable about the blind men and the elephant. The point that I should like to draw from this fable is not, however, the familiar one. It should be obvious that a group of reasonable blind men would compare notes, one with the other, and, upon so doing, they should, collectively, be able to put together a fair picture of the elephant after all. In matters of scientific import, we are all blind, although some of us may be blinder than others. And one way of living with our inherent blindness is that of getting together and comparing notes with others who we know have approached the common subject matter from different vantage points, through different windows, to use Nietzsche's appropriate metaphor. Of course, my inference here is valid only if we are somehow assured that we are all examining the same elephant, and when we substitute "government and politics" for the word "elephant," I am not at all certain that we are. There would be little point in the blind men comparing notes if some of them should be describing their contacts with an elephant and others with an ostrich.

As a very first step, therefore, let me define what it is that I shall be talking about when I use the words "government and politics," and when I try to discuss the approach to these that is taken, or may be taken, by the economist. Actually, as you will see, I shall discuss the approach that I think should be taken by the economist. Most scholars who now call themselves economists take an approach different from my own, and one that I consider to be

From *Perspectives in the Study of Politics*, ed. Malcolm B. Parsons (Chicago: Rand McNally, 1968): 77–88.

confused as well as wrong. In my vision of social order, individual persons are the basic component units, and "government" is simply that complex of institutions through which individuals make collective decisions, and through which they carry out collective as opposed to private activities. "Politics" is the activity of persons in the context of such institutions. These definitions perhaps seem simple ones, and you may find them broadly acceptable. Nevertheless, there are implications of these definitions which may not be so evident at the outset. In my vision, or my model, individual persons are the ultimate decision-makers, and if we want to discuss governmental decision processes we must analyze the behavior of individuals as they participate in these processes. We do not conceive government as some supra-individual decision-making agency, one that is separate and apart from the individual persons for whom choices are being made. In other terms, I stress the "by the people" leg of the Lincoln triad. Most modern analysts, including most economists, place almost exclusive emphasis on the "for the people" leg. Government is, presumably, "for the people," but people are rarely allowed to count in determining what is for them. Most economists, and, I suspect, most political scientists, view government as a potentially benevolent despot, making decisions in the "general" or the "public" interest, and they consider it their own social function to advise and counsel this despot, first, on the definition of this general interest and, second, on the means of furthering it. They rarely will admit all this quite so bluntly as I have put it here, but surely this is the honest way of stating the prevailing methodological orthodoxy. This position is, of course, a relatively happy one for the political economist. Once he has defined his social welfare function, his public interest, he can advance solutions to all of society's economic ills, solutions that government, as *deus ex machina*, is, of course, expected to implement. Politics, the behavior of ordinary men in this process, becomes tainted activity, albeit necessary in a begrudgingly admitted way. But politics should be allowed to interfere as little as is possible with the proper business of government. So runs the orthodoxy. You can add the illustrative refrains better than I can to this beginning verse.

The role of the social scientist who adopts broadly democratic models of the governmental process, who tries to explain and to understand how people do, in fact, govern *themselves*, is a less attractive one than the role that is assumed by the implicit paternalist. The social function is not that of improving anything directly; instead, it is that of explaining behavior of a certain sort which, only remotely and indirectly, can lead to improvements in the political process itself.

Now let me return to the initial question. If we should agree that what we are looking at is the complex set of institutional interactions among individual persons which is generated as a result of their attempts to accomplish mutually desired goals collectively, if this is what we mean by government, then my problem becomes: How does the economist view this set of institutions, and how does his own professional competence and prejudice affect his "vision"? And of what value can his interpretations of behavior be to the political scientist?

This leads me once again to basic methodological definitions. What is economics all about? And here, as I suggested, I find myself a heretic, for I do not think that most economists know. I think that they are hopelessly bogged down in methodological confusion, a confusion that threatens to destroy the whole discipline. Economics is about the economy. We can all agree on this. But what is the economy? We are back where we were with government. I define the economy in precisely the same way that I defined government. It is that complex of institutions that emerges as a result of the behavior of individual persons who organize themselves to satisfy their various objectives privately, as opposed to collectively. Thus, the economy and the government are parallel sets of institutions, similar in many respects, and, of course, intersecting at many separate points. In neither case is it appropriate for the analyst, the scientist if you will, to do more than explain the working of these institutions. It is wholly beyond his task for the economist to define goals or objectives of the economy or of the government and then to propose measures designed to implement these goals. The economist who claims professional sanction to say that protective tariffs are bad is on all fours with the political scientist who claims sanction to say that the Congress is an inefficient decision-maker. Both are wholly outside their appropriate professional roles. This kind of confusion dominates both disciplinary fields.

The economist, then, observes people as they behave in the institutional structure that, for convenience, we refer to as the economy, and he then attempts to explain this behavior. It would be fair to ask at this point whether or not I am proposing a return to the institutional economics that was propounded by a group of scholars in the United States in the 1920's, notably by

Veblen, Mitchell, and Commons. My answer is an ambivalent one. The institutionalists were broadly on target in many of their criticisms of orthodoxy; but their whole effort was largely wasted because of their scorn of theory, of analysis. Their methodological naiveté caused them to think that observation and description somehow automatically gives rise to predictive theories, to hypotheses, when, in fact, we now know that almost the reverse holds. What I am calling for, as the proper function of economists, is institutional theory or institutional analysis, which involves in many cases the use of highly rarified and abstract models, the implications of which can be checked by real-world observations. Much of modern economic theory can be made to fit the disciplinary pattern that I am outlining. We first try to create a logically consistent theory of individual behavior in the marketplace and then we try, as best we can, to test the implications of this theory against real-world observations. In this way, after much trial and error, we make, I hope, some scientific progress.

My professional and methodological prejudices suggest that the study of government should be approached in the same way. We should try to derive a theory of individual behavior in the political process, and then we should try to check out the implications of the theory against the facts. When I looked around at all this, some dozen years ago, I was surprised to find that a theory of individual behavior in political process did not exist, and that only a few scattered attempts had ever been made to create one. This demonstrated, to me, that there was at least this one rather profound difference between the development of economic and political "science," and it also suggested that there was, perhaps, a function for the economist who was willing to shift his emphasis from market processes to political processes. Since that time, since 1954 roughly speaking, I have been, in the on-and-off manner of academic custom, working within this broadly defined area of research. That is to say, I have been exploring, along with various colleagues and co-workers, some of the aspects of a theory of individual behavior in political choice.

My focus has been dramatically different from that of the orthodox political scientist who looks first at government as the entity, and then discusses its formation, evolution, and operation. To develop any theory of individual behavior, by contrast with this, we must look first at the individual person, at his private behavior as he participates in collective decision-making with his fellows. If we are to move beyond description here, however, if we are to derive any theory worthy of serious consideration, we find it essential to invent simple models of the whole political process. Only in this manner does it become possible to select, to reduce the complexity to manageable, discussable proportions, to abstract from the inessential elements while concentrating on the essential ones. Accepting the overall vision of government that I have mentioned above, the appropriate model within which to begin to examine individual behavior seemed to be that of pure democracy, in the town-meeting sense. In my first paper on this subject, therefore, I tried to contrast the behavior of the single individual in the marketplace and in voting under pure democracy.

I should mention that I was directly stimulated to think about all this, an economist thinking about politics, not by some independent discovery on my own part, but by an intuitive dissatisfaction with the book by Kenneth Arrow, published in 1951, and entitled *Social Choice and Individual Values*.[1] In this justly praised little book, Arrow employed the tools of modern symbolic logic and mathematics to show that the construction of a consistent and reasonably acceptable social welfare function from a set of unchanging individual preference orderings was logically impossible if the political decision rule should be that of simple majority voting. That is to say, Arrow demonstrated that majority voting could not be depended upon to produce a consistent set of social decisions. The paradox of voting was not, of course, new with Arrow; it had been known for decades by a small group of specialists who had concerned themselves about the theory of voting, notably Lewis Carroll, and it had been discussed more recently by Duncan Black, about whom more will be said at a later point in this paper. But Arrow was the first to place the paradox of voting in a broader context, in his case that of theoretical welfare economics, and his work did serve to draw the attention to scholars, both in economics and in politics, to the paradox.

As I said, I was unhappy with the Arrow book, and more importantly, with all of its reviewers, for a failure to sense what was, to me, a very significant aspect of constitutional democracy. Arrow, and all of his reviewers, seemed unhappy with his general conclusion; they seemed to feel that things would

---

1. Kenneth Arrow, *Social Choice and Individual Values* (New York: John Wiley and Sons, 1951).

have been so much nicer had his proof turned out the other way. It would have made for a more satisfactory social science if only majority voting could have been shown to produce a set of wholly consistent choices. Consistency in *social* choice seemed to be the criterion that was overriding in the general commentary. This suggested to me that neither Arrow nor his critics were talking about the same elephant that I thought about when I conceived government or politics, or majority rule. It appeared to me, and still does, that decisions made by voting majorities are acceptable, tolerably so, only to the extent that these majorities are shifting and unstable. If we had a majority voting rule that would, in fact, produce internally consistent choices in the Arrow sense, we should, indeed, have a tyranny of the majority. From all this, I concluded[2] that despite the fact that his whole structure of analysis was based on individual preference orderings, Arrow did not conceive governmental process as emerging basically from individual values.

In any case, I began to look somewhat further into the developments in theoretical welfare economics from the vantage point of a specialist in tax and expenditure decisions. Modern welfare economics owes its stimulus to Pareto, who developed a criterion, admittedly a very restricted one, which enables social situations or positions to be classified into non-optimal and optimal sets without requiring that interpersonal comparisons of utility be made, or external ethical norms be introduced. Pareto's criterion is simply that which defines a position as optimal if no changes from that position can be made without making at least one person in the group worse off. Admittedly, there are an infinite number of such positions, but the criterion does at least allow for the classification of all possible positions into the two categories. It does not, of course, provide any assistance at all in selecting from among all the optimal positions that which is somehow globally best. Economists who wanted to say a lot about public policy issues were not at all happy with the Pareto criterion. Therefore, they re-introduced interpersonal comparability in the form of an externally defined social welfare function, which they admitted to be dependent on explicit ethical norms. But, of course, there are as many social welfare functions as there are people to de-

---

2. James M. Buchanan, "Social Choice, Democracy, and Free Markets," *Journal of Political Economy* 62 (April 1954): 114–23.

fine them; in this sense, the notion is equivalent in all respects with the political scientists' conception of the public interest.

My own inclination was, and is, to throw out the whole social welfare function apparatus, which only confuses the issues, and to see what the full implications of the Pareto criterion might be. If we are willing to use the Pareto criterion where it is applicable and simply to admit our inability, as scientists, to say anything where the criterion cannot be applied, some worthwhile content remains in welfare economics. But this raises another question of fundamentals. How are we, as external observers, to know when a person is, in fact, better off or worse off? Here there admits of only one answer. We can judge the better offness and worse offness only by observing individual choices. If a man is observed to choose situation A when he could have remained in situation B, we say that he is better off in A, as revealed to us by his own actions. This is not, of course, to say that individuals do not make mistakes or that they always know with certainty which of a set of alternative outcomes will make them better off *ex post facto*. The implication here is only that the individual, observed to make his own choices, is a better judge of his own better offness than is any external observer of his behavior. This implication amounts to an explicit value judgment, admittedly so, but it is the value judgment upon which Western liberal society has been founded.

Starting with nothing more than this, how far can we go in analyzing political behavior? Two separate lines of advance seem to be suggested. First of all, commencing with a set of individual preferences along with a given rule for reaching group decisions, we may examine and analyze the results. That is, essentially, the route taken in the pioneer works of Duncan Black, whose theory of committees and elections[3] continues to be unduly neglected, both by political scientists and by economists. As Black suggests, this is pure theorizing about politics, and, as such, it is wholly devoid of normative content. Black is concerned exclusively with the prediction of the outcomes of certain rules for the making of group choices, specifically with majority rule, given a set of individual preference patterns.

Almost always, however, pure analysis has some normative implications,

3. Duncan Black, *Theory of Committees and Elections* (Cambridge: Cambridge University Press, 1958).

if not immediate normative content, and even Duncan Black, in his purely theoretical works, was motivated to search for alternatives to simple majority voting in order to surmount the obstacles posed by the paradox, by the cyclical majority, by the probability that no majority motion would be located. His work on the various schemes of Lewis Carroll, Borda, and Condorcet stands unique in the literature. Lying close to the surface of Black's work has been his implicit value position to the effect that, if it could be located and if it did exist, the majority motion or the majority solution *should* be the one adopted. Note that the underlying judgment is, in many respects, similar to that which can be criticized in relation to Arrow's work.

My own thinking has proceeded along a second, and alternative, path. In my own set of value judgments, there is nothing even remotely sacrosanct about the will of a simple majority of voters in an election. Influenced strongly by the thinking of Knut Wicksell,[4] a famous, if eccentric, Swedish economist, and coming to an analysis of politics out of a background of public finance, the rule of unanimity seemed to me to possess qualities that have largely been ignored. This, rather than majority rule, seemed to be the base, the reference point from which further discussion and theorizing about political choice must begin. If we reject the notion that there must exist a public or general interest apart from that of the participants, we are necessarily led to the conclusion that only upon unanimous consent of all parties can we be absolutely assured that the total welfare of the group is improved. As applied to politics, the rule of unanimity is equivalent to the Pareto criterion for judging a potential change to be optimal. Not only does majority voting lead to paradoxes, to cycles, but also, majority voting, under familiar institutional conditions, leads to a wastage of economic resources, as Gordon Tullock first demonstrated.[5]

At this point, the direction of analysis of political institutions seemed to be that of trying to reconcile, if at all possible, the widely observed use of majority and plurality devices for reaching group choices with the demonstrably inefficient results, in a resource allocative sense, that these devices

---

4. Knut Wicksell, *Finanztheoretische Untersuchungen* (Jena: Gustav Fischer, 1896).

5. Gordon Tullock, "Some Problems of Majority Voting," *Journal of Political Economy* 67 (December 1959): 571–79.

surely produce. This led Gordon Tullock and me to ask the simple question: Why should an individual, if he were given the opportunity, ever choose to be governed by the majority voting of his fellows? Once we had posed the question, and almost before we knew it ourselves, we found ourselves in an economic theory of the political constitution. If one begins to approach the study of political institutions in this way, that is, from the reference position of the single individual in the group, one begins soon to see that a "logical" explanation of the political constitution can be derived. In a very preliminary way, such an explanation was advanced in our book *The Calculus of Consent*, published in 1962.[6]

What I have done is to outline, in a shorthand sense, the way that one economist has looked, and looks, at government. Now let me turn to the second part of my task. I have talked almost exclusively about how an economist's approach to government, to political process, can be helpful, how this may be able to lead to fruitful explanation. I have not yet talked about how the extension and application of the economist's frame of reference can be helpful in analyzing politics in its most general sense. Politics is concerned with the behavior of politicians, not with the behavior of individual voters, and in real-world institutions, persons vote for or against politicians normally, not for or against proposals, as is assumed in the simple town-meeting models implicit in the general theory of committees and of constitutions. Also, politicians, in some more general sense of the word, inhabit the bureaucracy, and their behavior in this role also requires analysis. How can the approach of the economist be of assistance in analyzing the behavior of politicians?

Again, the more or less natural proclivity of economists is to look at individual behavior, at individual choice, and this has led, and is leading, to useful results. Anthony Downs, in his book *An Economic Theory of Democracy*,[7] analyzes the operation of a party system of government in terms of the attempts of party politicians to maximize votes, analogous to the behavior of

---

6. James M. Buchanan and Gordon Tullock, *The Calculus of Consent* (Ann Arbor: University of Michigan Press, 1962).

7. Anthony Downs, *An Economic Theory of Democracy* (New York: Harper and Bros., 1957).

businessmen in attempting to maximize profits. Somewhat more generally, Gordon Tullock applied the approach that may be called that of methodological individualism to the whole structure of political relationships, including specifically bureaucratic hierarchies. He commenced the analysis of bureaucracy by looking directly at the set of rewards and punishments that confront the bureaucrat, as he finds himself situated in the hierarchy. This seems a simple starting point, but it is one that traditional scholars in administration have rarely taken, and it is one that, when once taken, opens up whole areas of interesting research and analysis, including hypotheses that can be empirically tested. Tullock's formidable work on this subject, *The Politics of Bureaucracy,*[8] although just formally published in 1965, through its preliminary version, privately circulated in 1959, had already made its impact on thinking about bureaucracy. In this treatment of the "politics of the lower order," he compares the different worlds of bureaucrats and professional politicians. He analyzes their role perceptions and their interactions. The impact came, however, not through any influence on the thinking of those who have worked within the traditional methodology of administration but, instead, through its influence on those few economists who, being generally responsive to the Tullockian approach, have been willing to shift their attention to bureaucracy as an object of analysis.

Thus it is that Anthony Downs, an economist now with the RAND Corporation, has been recently engaged in what is possibly the most interesting research on bureaucracy that is under way anywhere. His *Inside Bureaucracy* proceeds from the assumption that all bureaucrats, to some extent, act in their own self-interest. From this and related assumptions Downs develops a theory of organizational behavior which encompasses a range of activities including bureau life cycles, types of bureaucrats, problems of communication, goal-consensus, and the relationship between individual freedom and the increasing bureaucratization of modern society.[9] He has worked closely at RAND with Roland McKean who, having applied an approach similar to Tullock's (which he developed independently) to town planning in Great

8. Gordon Tullock, *The Politics of Bureaucracy* (Washington: Public Affairs Press, 1965).

9. Anthony Downs, *Inside Bureaucracy, How Large Organizations Behave* (Boston: Little, Brown and Co., 1967).

Britain, is now analyzing the structure of the national defense establishment in the United States.[10]

This whole area of investigation, i.e., that which is devoted to an analysis of the behavior of the politician in bureaucracy, is now only on the threshold of its development. It is an exciting field. It is one which allows the analyst to bring theoretical models into contact with institutional reality, to test his hypotheses against observable facts.

You may be prompted to ask: Why do I claim so much here? How does the economist's approach to politics and government differ from that which the habitual political scientist adopts? As I have tried to indicate, the shift in thinking is a simple one. It involves only the shift from the organizational entity as the unit to the individual-in-the-organization. Instead of trying to examine the institutions of politics as organizations, the whole approach involves trying to examine the interactions among individuals as they carry out assigned roles within these institutions.

I am probably more vulnerable if you should object that I claim too much for the economist, as such, in developing the approach to government and politics that I have broadly outlined. Certainly, as economics is currently conceived by most scholars who call themselves economists, there is no particular contribution of the sort mentioned that emerges necessarily out of their concentration on governmental processes. The great majority of modern economists do not really think much about the process of government, and when they do, they adopt implicitly the same broad conceptions that the orthodox political scientist adopts explicitly. Hence, when I submit to you that there has been exciting work done recently on government and politics, and that this work has been mostly done by economists, I am really talking about a small group of mavericks, a few odd-balls, a few eccentrics, who have not yet commanded much attention, even among economists, and certainly not among many political scientists. But the ranks of this small group are gradually swelling, the list of books grows longer year by year, and recognition is being granted. I speak, of course, out of personal prejudice here, but I think that an exciting and new field of theoretical inquiry is emerging on the borderline between two disciplines. This new field does not as yet have

10. Roland N. McKean, "Divergencies Between Individual and Total Costs Within Government," *American Economic Review* (May 1964).

an appropriate descriptive name, and certainly the rubric "scientific politics" that I have rather boldly used in the title to this paper is not wholly suitable. Professional political scientists are beginning to work in this area along with the few economists, and the concentration promises to attract more and more young scholars in the decade just ahead.[11]

The approach is scientific in a genuine meaning of this term, something which the approach of traditional political science can scarcely claim. If, in fact, a pure theory of politics or a genuinely scientific politics is to be developed, the individualistic model that I have discussed here will be an important element in its source. To make this claim does, I appreciate, make traditionalists rise up in anger, and it is admittedly presumptuous on my part to advance it. Indeed, as a recent friendly critic put it, my tone here may seem messianic, and I suppose that it is. I am, personally, both involved in and excited about the contribution that the new scientific politics can make to our overall understanding of both government and politics. And I find it personally satisfying to participate directly in what is surely an emerging area of research and scholarly emphasis.

In partial apology, however, I should stress that I claim for my approach to the new scientific politics no exclusive domain. While I am convinced that it can be helpful in explaining real-world political phenomena, I know that many other models of analysis, such as statistical decision theory, game theory, communications theory, and others, can also be fruitful. Hence, I say only that here is an additional and supplementary set of tools which I hope more and more students of government and politics will learn to use. To return once again to the fable of the blind men and the elephant, the supplementary set of tools that this approach to scientific politics offers is just one more blind man added to the circle; that is all. But, by adding its own contribution to the collective discourse, to the collective wisdom of the existing world of scholarship, which, in effect, involves only a continuing comparing of notes, a somewhat better, although still imperfect, picture of the elephant may be drawn.

11. A paper by William C. Mitchell, "The Shape of Political Theory to Come: From Political Sociology to Political Economy" (mimeographed, 1967), which was delivered at the 63rd Annual Meeting of the American Political Science Association, September 1967, is extremely encouraging in these respects.

The Public Choice Perspective

1. Introduction

On several different occasions in recent years, I have offered my interpretation of the history, development, and content of public choice.[1] What I want to do here is something different from the earlier efforts. The very word "perspective" is helpful in allowing me to get some focus on the very general comments I want to make.

Let me start by indicating what the public choice perspective is *not*. It is not a *method* in the usual meaning of the term; it is not a *set of tools;* it is not a particular application of standard tools with standard methods, although we are getting somewhat closer with this last statement. Public choice is a *perspective* on politics that emerges from an extension-application of the tools and methods of the economist to collective or nonmarket decision-making. But this statement, in itself, is inadequately descriptive, because in order to attain such a perspective on politics, a particular approach to economics is required.

In these notes, I shall refer to two separate and distinct aspects or elements in the public choice perspective. The first aspect is the generalized *catallactics* approach to economics. The second is the more familiar *Homo economicus*

From *Economia delle scelte pubbliche* 1 (January–April 1983): 7–15. Reprinted by permission of the publisher.

1. See my "Public Finance and Public Choice," in *National Tax Journal,* 1975, 383–94; "From Private Preferences to Public Philosophy: Notes on the Development of Public Choice," in *The Economics of Politics,* ed. Arthur Seldon (London: Institute of Economic Affairs, 1978), 1–20; "Politics Without Romance: A Sketch of Positive Public Choice Theory and Its Normative Implications," Inaugural Lecture, Institute for Advanced Studies, Vienna, Austria, *IHS-Journal, Zeitschrift des Instituts für Höhere Studien, Wien* 3 (1979): B1–B11.

postulate concerning individual behavior. These two elements, as I shall try to demonstrate, enter, with differing weights, in the several strands of public choice theory, inclusively defined.

2. Catallaxy, or, Economics as the Science of Exchanges

My 1962 Presidential address to the Southern Economic Association in the United States was published in 1963,[2] and, incidentally, about the same time that Gordon Tullock and I founded what was to become the Public Choice Society (it was initially organized under the rubric "Committee on Non-Market Decision-Making"). In 1979, by way of a special celebration, several of my papers on methodology were published in a volume under the title *What Should Economists Do?*[3] which was directly taken from the title of my 1962 essay, which was included in the volume. In June 1982, I had occasion to rethink my general position in response to this old question I had posed on the occasion of an address in Gießen, Germany.

"What Should Economists Do?"—my 1962, as well as my 1982, response to this question was and is to urge that we exorcise the maximizing paradigm from its dominant place in our tool kit, that we quit defining our discipline, our "science," in terms of the scarcity constraint, that we change the very definition, indeed the very name of our "science," that we stop worrying so much about the allocation of resources and the efficiency thereof, and, in place of this whole set of ideas, that we commence concentrating on the origins, properties, and institutions of *exchange*, broadly considered. Adam Smith's propensity to truck and barter one thing for another—this becomes the proper object for our research and inquiry.

The approach to economics that I have long urged and am urging here was called catallactics, the science of exchanges, by some 19th-century proponents. More recently, Professor Hayek has suggested the term "catallaxy," which he claims is more in keeping with proper Greek origins of the word. This approach to economics, as the subject matter for inquiry, draws our attention directly to the *process* of exchange, trade, or agreement, to contract.

2. "What Should Economists Do?" in *Southern Economic Journal*, 1964, 213–22.
3. Indianapolis: Liberty Fund, 1979.

And it necessarily introduces, quite early, the principle of spontaneous order or spontaneous coordination, which is, as I have often suggested, perhaps the only real "principle" in economic theory, as such.

I could, of course, go on with an elaboration and defense of this approach to economic theory, but such is not my purpose here. You may well be asking what has this methodological argument to do with the public choice perspective, which *is* my assignment. My response is straightforward. If we take the catallactics approach seriously, we then quite naturally bring into the analysis complex as well as simple exchange, with complex exchange being defined as that contractual agreement process that goes beyond the economists' magic number "2," beyond the simple two-person, two-commodity barter setting. The emphasis shifts, directly and immediately, to all *processes of voluntary agreement* among persons.

From this shift in perspective on what economics should be all about, there follows immediately a natural distinction between "economics" as a discipline and "political science" or "politics." There are no lines to be drawn at the edges of "the economy" and "the polity," or between "markets" and "governments," between "the private sector" and "the public sector." Economists need not restrict their inquiry to the behavior of persons within markets (to buying and selling activities, as such). By a more-or-less natural extension of the catallactic approach, economists can look on politics, and on political process, in terms of the exchange paradigm. So long as collective action is modelled with individual decision-makers as the basic units, and so long as such collective action is fundamentally conceived to be reflective of complex exchange or agreement among all members of a relevant community of persons, such action or behavior or choice may readily be brought under the catallaxy umbrella. There is no "economists' imperialism" as such, in this inclusion. There remains a categorical distinction between "economics as catallaxy" and "political science" or "politics." The latter, i.e., politics as an academic-research discipline, is then assigned the whole realm of *nonvoluntary* relationships among persons, those relationships involving power or coercion. Interestingly enough, this dividing line between the two areas of social science inquiry is the same as that proposed by some political scientists and sociologists, e.g., Talcott Parsons.

Almost any observed empirical relationship among persons will incorporate some catallactic and some power elements. The idealized setting of perfect competition is defined in part for the very purpose of allowing a description of a situation in which there is no power of one person over another at all. In the world where each and every buyer of each and every commodity and service confronts many sellers, among whom he may shift costlessly, and where each and every seller of each and every commodity or service confronts many buyers, among whom he may shift costlessly, there is no power of one person over another. In such a setting, "economic power" becomes totally without meaning or content.

As we depart from this conceptualized ideal, however, as *rents*, actual or potential, emerge in the relationships between and among persons, elements of power and potential coercion arise, and behavior becomes amenable to analysis by something other than pure catallaxy.

I do not propose to elaborate the myriad of institutional variants in which both exchange and power elements coexist. I make the categorical distinction largely to suggest that the perspective of economics-as-catallaxy, with its quite natural extension to institutional settings in which persons interact collectively, offers one way of looking at politics and governmental processes, a "different window," to use Nietzsche's metaphor. And, in a very broad sense, this is what the public choice perspective on politics is about, a different way of looking at political process, different in kind from that way of looking which emerges from the politics-as-power perspective.

Note that in applying the catallaxy perspective to politics, or in applying public choice, to use the more familiar term, we need not, and indeed should not, make the mistake of implying, inferring, or suggesting that the power elements of political relationships are squeezed out as if by some methodological magic. The public choice perspective, which does model politics ultimately in the exchange paradigm, is not necessarily offering an empirically refutable set of hypotheses to the effect that politics and political process is exclusively or even mainly reducible to complex exchange, contract, and agreement. It should be evident that elements of pure rent, and hence of power, emerge more readily in settings of complex than those of simple exchange, and hence more readily in many-person than in two-person relationships, in political than in market-like arrangements. Hence, an appropriate division of scientific labor would call upon the discipline of "political science" to concentrate more attention to political arrangements and for that of economics to concentrate more attention on market arrangements. There are, nonetheless, major contributions to be made by the extensions of both perspectives across the whole spectrum of institutions. In this sense, the public choice perspective on politics becomes analogous to the economic power perspective on markets.

There are important normative implications to be derived from the public choice perspective on politics, implications that, in their turn, carry with them an approach to institutional reform. To the extent that voluntary exchange among persons is valued positively while coercion is valued negatively, there emerges the implication that substitution of the former for the latter is desired, on the presumption, of course, that such substitution is technologically feasible and is not prohibitively costly in resources. This implication provides the normative thrust for the proclivity of the public choice economist to favor market-like arrangements where these seem feasible, and to favor decentralization of political authority in appropriate situations.

Even without the normative implications, however, the public choice perspective on politics directly draws attention to an approach to reform that does not emerge from the power perspective. To the extent that political interaction among persons is modelled as a complex exchange process, in which the inputs are individual evaluations or preferences, and the process itself is conceived as the means through which these possibly diverging preferences are somehow combined or amalgamated into a pattern of outcomes, attention is more or less necessarily drawn to the interaction process itself rather than to some transcendental evaluation of the outcomes themselves. How does one "improve" a market? One does so by facilitating the exchange process, by reorganizing the rules of trade, contract, or agreement. One does not "improve" or "reform" a market-like exchange process by an arbitrary rearrangement of final outcomes.

The *constitutional* perspective (which I have personally been so closely associated with) emerges naturally from the politics-as-exchange paradigm or research program. To improve politics, it is necessary to improve or reform the *rules*, the framework within which the game of politics is played. There is no suggestion that improvement lies in the selection of morally superior agents, who will use their powers in some "public interest." A game is described by its rules, and a better game is produced only by changing the rules. It is this constitutional perspective, as it emerges from the more inclusive public choice perspective, that brings public choice closest into contact with current policy issues in the 1980s. I have, as an economist, always felt very uneasy about proffering advice on particular policies, e.g., this or that proposed change in the tax law. On the other hand, and by contrast, I do feel it to be within our potential competence to analyze alternative constitutional regimes or sets of rules and to discuss the predicted workings of alternative constitutional arrangements. Hence, as you might suspect, I have been personally, both indirectly and directly, involved in the various proposals for constitutional change that have been made in the 1970s and early 1980s. I refer, of course, to such proposals as Propositions 1 and 13 in California in 1973 and 1978 respectively, the one unsuccessful the other successful; or to Proposition 2½ in Massachusetts, or Proposition 6 in Michigan; and, at the federal government level, to the proposed balanced-budget amendment, and to the accompanying tax limit or spending limit proposals, as well as to proposed changes in the basic monetary regime.

Let me backtrack to the suggestion made above to the effect that the public choice perspective leads directly to attention and emphasis on rules, on constitutions, on constitutional choice, on choice among rules. The Buchanan-Tullock "classic" book, *The Calculus of Consent*,[4] was the first attempt to derive what we called an "economic theory of political constitutions." It would, of course, have been impossible to make that effort without the methodological perspective provided in economics-as-exchange or catallactics. The maximizer of social welfare functions could never have written such a book, and, indeed, even today, the maximizer of such functions cannot understand what the book is all about.

I have identified the first element or aspect of the inclusive public choice perspective as the catallactics approach to economics; the economics-as-exchange paradigm. I referred to 19th-century economists who urged the catallactics framework for emphasis. I should be remiss here, however, if I should fail to mention that, for me personally, the acceptance of the catallaxy framework for economic theory emerged, not from inquiry into economic methodology directly, but rather from the constitutional public choice perspective that I got from Knut Wicksell. I have often remarked that Wicksell is the primary precursor of modern public choice theory. Wicksell warned, as early as 1896, against the presumption that we, as economists, give advice

---

4. Ann Arbor: The University of Michigan Press, 1962.

to the benevolent despot, to the entity that would, indeed, try to maximize a social welfare function. Wicksell stated that, if reform in economic policy is desired, look to the rules through which economic policy decisions get made, look to the constitution itself. This "politics-as-complex-exchange" notion of Wicksell was the stimulus, for me, to look more closely into the methodological presuppositions of economics itself, presuppositions that I had really not questioned independently.

3. *Homo economicus*

The second element or aspect embodied in the inclusive public choice perspective that I identified in the introduction is the behavioral postulate familiarly known as that of *Homo economicus*. Individuals are modelled as behaving so as to maximize utilities subject to the constraints they face, and, if the analysis is to be made at all operational, specific arguments must be placed in the utility functions. Individuals must be modelled as seeking to further their own self-interest, narrowly defined in terms of measured net wealth positions, as predicted or expected.

This behavioral postulate is, of course, part and parcel of the intellectual heritage of economic theory, and it has indeed served economists well. It stems from the original contributions of the classical economists themselves, whose great discovery was that individuals acting in pursuit of their own interests may unintentionally generate results that serve the overall "social" interest, given the appropriate framework of laws and institutions. Since these 18th-century roots, economists and economics have relied on the *Homo economicus* postulate to analyze the behavior of persons who participate variously in markets, and through this, to analyze the workings of market institutions themselves.

No comparable postulate was extended to the behavior of persons in their political or public choice roles or capacities, either as participants in voting processes or as agents acting for the body politic. There was no such postulate stemming from the classical economists or from their successors. There was no "economic theory of politics" derived from individual choice behavior.

We might, in retrospect, have expected such a theory to be developed by economists, as a more or less obvious extension of their *Homo economicus* postulate from market to collective institutional settings. Once economists turned their attention to politics, they should, or so it now seems, have modelled public choosers as utility maximizers. Why did they not do so? Perhaps the failure of the classical economists, as well as that of their 19th-century successors, to take this step might be "excused" by their implicit presumption that collective activities were basically unproductive and that the role of the state was limited largely to what has been called minimal or protective functions. These economists simply could not conceive that much "good" or "goods" could be generated by collective or governmental action.

But why did their 20th-century descendants fail similarly, despite some suggestive models as advanced by Wicksell and the Italian public finance scholars (de Viti de Marco, Puviani, Pantaleoni, and others) in the waning years of the 19th century? My own interpretation of the modern failure is that 20th-century economists had been converted to the maximization-scarcity-allocation-efficiency paradigm for their discipline, a paradigm that is essentially at variance with that which classical economics embodies, and which draws attention away from individual behavior in exchange-contracts and toward some presumably objectifiable allocative norm that remains conceptually independent of individual choices. Economic theory, by the third decade of this century, had shifted to a discipline of applied mathematics, not catallaxy. Even markets came to be viewed as "computing devices" and "mechanisms," that may or may not secure idealized allocative results. Markets were not, at base, viewed as exchange institutions, out of which results emerge from complex exchange interaction. Only in this modern paradigm of economic theory could the total absurdity of the idealized socialist structure of Lange-Lerner have been taken at all seriously, as indeed it was (and, sadly, still is) by practicing economists. We may well ask: why did not economists stop to ask the questions about why socialist managers should behave in terms of the idealized rules? Where are the economic eunuchs who can be found to operate the system?

Or, to bring the discussion somewhat further forward in time, why did the economists of the 1930s, 1940s, 1950s, and into the 1960s take the Keynesian theory of policy seriously? Why did they fail to see the elementary point to the effect that elected politicians will seek any excuse to create budget deficits?[5]

5. On this point, see James M. Buchanan and Richard E. Wagner, *Democracy in Deficit: The Political Legacy of Lord Keynes* (New York: Academic Press, 1977).

It all seems so simple in retrospect, but we should never underestimate the difficulties, indeed the moral costs, that are involved by a genuine shift in paradigm, in the very way that we look at the world about us, whether this be economists looking at politics or any other group. It was not easy for economists before the 1960s to think of public choosers as utility maximizers in other than some tautological sense. In part, the intellectual blockage here may have stemmed from a failure of those who did advance self-interest models to incorporate the politics-as-exchange paradigm in their own thinking. If politics is viewed only as a potentially coercive relationship among persons, at all levels of conceptualization, then the economist must be either courageous or callous who would model public choosers (whether voters or agents) as net wealth maximizers. Few want to reap the scorn that Machiavelli has received through the ages. Such a world of politics is not at all a pretty place. And analysis based on such a model and advanced as "truth" becomes highly noxious. The very unpleasantness of these models of politics may have been the root cause that explains the neglect of what now appear to be clear precursors of this element in the public choice perspective. Some of the early Italians, and notably Pareto, who were themselves perhaps influenced importantly by Machiavelli, and in the middle of this century, Schumpeter, seem to have had little or no impact on the thinking of modern social scientists about political process.

It is only when the *Homo economicus* postulate about human behavior is *combined* with the politics-as-exchange paradigm that an "economic theory of politics" emerges from despair. Conceptually, such a combination makes it possible to generate analysis that is in some respects comparable to that of the classical economists. When persons are modelled as self-interested in politics, as in other aspects of their behavior, the constitutional challenge becomes one of constructing and designing framework institutions or rules that will, to the maximum extent possible, limit the exercise of such interest in exploitative ways and direct such interest to furtherance of the general interest. It is not surprising, therefore, to discover the roots of a public choice perspective which contains both elements here identified are to be found implicitly in the writings of the American Founders, and most notably in James Madison's contributions to *The Federalist Papers*.

In a very real sense, I look on *The Calculus of Consent* as the first contribution in modern public choice theory that combined and balanced the two critical elements or aspects of the inclusive perspective. And this combination might well not have occurred but for the somewhat differing weights that Gordon Tullock and I brought to our joint venture in that book. I think it is accurate to say that my own emphasis was on modelling politics-as-exchange, under the acknowledged major influence of Knut Wicksell's great work in public finance. By comparison (and interestingly because he was not initially trained as an economist), Gordon Tullock's emphasis (stemming from his own experience in and his reflections about the bureaucracy) was on modelling all public choosers (voters, politicians, bureaucrats) in strict self-interest terms. There was a tension present as we worked through the analysis of that book, but a tension that has indeed served us well over the two decades since initial publication.

In the 1960s, 1970s, and early 1980s varying contributions have represented differing weighted combinations of the two central elements in the inclusive public choice perspective. Works on the theory of bureaucracy and bureaucratic behavior and on the theory of regulation have been weighted toward the *Homo economicus* element, whereas works on constitutional analysis have been more derivative from the politics-as-exchange paradigm.

These two wings of modern public choice theory are not mutually inconsistent. Even if politics and political process are ultimately modelled in an exchange paradigm, simple and direct observation suggests that politicians and bureaucrats are inherent components. And these persons act no differently from other persons that the economist studies. Recognition of this simple point followed by a positive analysis of the working out of its implications in the institutional settings of modern politics are essential inputs into the more comprehensive comparative analytics that must precede any discussion of constitutional reform. It is precisely because of the insights of the modern theories of bureaucracy and regulation that there has emerged the increasing awareness of the need for new institutional constraints.

Toward Analysis of Closed
Behavioral Systems

This book contains several applications of the "theory of public choice." This theory represents an attempt to close up the analysis of social interaction systems. In this respect it may be compared and contrasted with the familiar "open" system analyzed in traditional economic theory. The latter is a highly developed theory of market interaction. Beyond the limits of market behavior, however, analysis is left "open." The "public choices" that define the constraints within which market behavior is allowed to take place are assumed to be made externally or exogenously, presumably by others than those who participate in market transactions and whose behavior is subjected to the theory's examination. The limitation of analysis to open behavioral systems can be helpful if the objective itself is comparably restricted to that of making predictions about a few variables. If the behavioral elements that are neglected remain genuinely external, little can be gained by closing the system analytically. As applied to orthodox economic theory, this would suggest that the formation of "public choice" may be left out of account, provided that the objective of the theory is limited to making positive predictions about market structure and nothing more. Such a limitation would, of course, greatly restrict the usefulness that economic theory might have in policy discussion. Political economy or welfare economics could not represent a natural extension of the positive theory in this context.

The observed behavior of economists does not conform to such a consistent and narrowly restricted role for their discipline. Many economists have examined the complexities of market structure on the assumption that economic motivation is pervasive. Utilizing such results, they have isolated and identified market failure. Much of modern welfare economics owes its origin to Pigou, whose primary contribution involved an emphasis on the possible divergence between private and social marginal product (cost). Almost without pause, Pigou and the economists who have followed him assumed that the behaving individuals in market process are motivated exclusively by private values, defined economically, and that social effects of their actions are neglected. This procedure represents a consistent extension of the behavioral assumption that is implicit in standard theory. Criticism becomes justified only when the "failures" of market process identified in this way are presumed to be correctable by political or governmental regulation and control. This last step represents an arbitrary and nonscientific closure of the behavioral system and, as such, cannot be legitimate. The critically important bridge between the behavior of persons who act in the marketplace and the behavior of persons who act in political process must be analyzed. The "theory of public choice" can be interpreted as the construction of such a bridge. The approach requires only the simple assumption that the same individuals act in both relationships. Political decisions are not handed down from on high by omniscient beings who cannot err. Individuals behave in market interactions, in political-governmental interactions, in cooperative-nongovernmental interactions, and in other arrangements. Closure of the behavioral system, as I am using the term, means only that analysis must be extended to the actions of persons in their several separate capacities.

I. The Elitist Model: An Open Behavioral System

Economists who have talked about "market failure" under the assumption that persons behave as automatons in market interaction have blithely, indeed almost blissfully, seemed willing to turn things over to the corrective devices of the politician-bureaucrat. What is the reason for this? Have the welfare economists assumed that persons are so much influenced by their institutional-environmental setting as to make ordinary men "socially conscious" when they take on political or bureaucratic roles? Some of the so-cialist romantics may have reflected this attitude, but this is not characteristic of those who have participated actively in sophisticated policy discussion. The practicing (and preaching) welfare economist does not really consider crossing the bridge. He does not think of the man who behaves in the mar-ketplace, and whose behavior he examines, as the same person who either does or should make collective or public decisions for the whole community. This explains my usage of the term "open system." The implicit assumption has been that someone else, someone other than the participants in the mar-ketplace, lays down the rules for collective order.

This limited and essentially open behavioral model can be made logically consistent and self-contained. The classical Italian scholars in public finance, such men as de Viti de Marco, Puviani, Einaudi, and Fasiani,[1] deserve credit for recognizing the necessity of defining specifically their assumed models of political order. Several of these scholars, and notably de Viti de Marco and Fasiani, developed parallel structures of analysis. On the one hand, fiscal phenomena were examined in a model where the producers-suppliers of collective-governmental "goods" are simultaneously consumers-demanders. This closure of the behavioral system is equivalent to that which "the the-ory of public choice," as presented in this book, embodies. Merely to define this interaction system (which was called "democratic," "cooperative," or "individualistic" by different writers) forces analysis of behavior of persons in separate capacities. On the other hand, and in sharp contrast, fiscal phe-nomena were examined in a model where collective-governmental deci-sions, effective for the all-inclusive community, are made by an elite or rul-ing group (members of a winning majority coalition, a party hierarchy, an aristocracy, an "establishment," a ruling central committee, a dictator). This model concentrates attention on the behavioral reactions of persons in the larger community, reactions to the set of collective decisions that are imposed externally upon them. To make this model complete, however, the behavior of the members of the elite in choosing the decision set must be

---

1. For a general discussion of the contributions of these scholars, along with appro-priate bibliographical references, see the essay "The Italian Tradition in Fiscal Theory" in my *Fiscal Theory and Political Economy* (Chapel Hill, 1960).

analyzed. Different persons act in different roles. As I have suggested, this is a consistent model and it contains implications that can be tested.

The criticism that may be lodged against those who have worked in the tradition of modern welfare economics is not that they have employed this ruling class or elitist model of analysis. Quite the contrary; had they done so, or had they expressed a willingness to do so, their work would have exhibited an internal coherence that has been largely absent. This lack of coherence warrants the legitimate criticism that is implied in the "theory of public choice," whether directly or indirectly. The social theorist remains and should remain free to select his own model, and this selection should be informed by those aspects of reality which the theorist expects to explain more adequately. What the theorist should not be allowed to do is to work uncritically without being forced to look at the internal behavioral structure of his model. If the individual actors in the economic process are assumed to be divorced from the decision-making structure that defines the constraints on their behavior, the openness of the system must be acknowledged. A "science" that is limited to an analysis of reaction patterns can, of course, be constructed. This may be of value to those who do participate in rule-making. It is unacceptable, however, for the practitioner of this "reaction science" to infer "failure" or "inefficiency" if the latter are measured against criteria that are themselves derived from the valuation of the individuals who are reacting, and then to imply that such "failure" either will be, can be, or should be removed by some change in the behavior of others, namely those who participate in the establishment of the constraints. Before this can be done, a plausible "theory" of the behavior of the members of the ruling elite must be developed. Until midcentury, such a theory was almost wholly neglected by social scientists, with the Italian public-finance scholars again providing a notable exception. Some of the elements of such a theory are now emerging, and important contributions have been made by some of the same scholars who have worked in the theory of public choice.[2] The development of an acceptable theory of bureaucratic behavior can be interpreted as bridging the gap through an explicit recognition of dual decision structures.

---

2. I refer to such works as Anthony Downs, *Inside Bureaucracy* (Boston, 1967); Gordon Tullock, *The Politics of Bureaucracy* (Washington, D.C., 1965).

II. Public Choice and Private Choice

The "theory of public choice" rests instead on a single decision structure. It involves the explicit introduction of a "democratic" model, one in which the rulers are also the ruled. The theory examines the behavior of persons as they participate variously in the formation of public or collective choices, by which is meant choices from among mutually exclusive alternative constraints which, once selected, must apply to all members of the community. In acting or behaving as a "public choice" participant, the individual is presumed to be aware that he is, in part, selecting results which affect others than himself. He is making decisions for a public, of which he forms a part.

This characteristic feature of "public choice" distinguishes it sharply from "private choice." We may typify the latter by individual behavior in an idealized market setting: If a person acts, say, as a buyer or seller in a fully competitive market, he has no sensation that his own behavior modifies the environment of other persons. He acts as if he generates changes in his "private" economy only. Despite the analyst's recognition that each economic act influences, even if infinitesimally, the conditions confronted by all market participants, the participant himself is not cognizant of this.

It is precisely in the domain of welfare economics that this idealized behavior which I have called "private choice" becomes impossible. When a person is able to modify the economic environment of others through his own behavior, and when he can recognize this, the welfare economist refers to "externality." This is formally equivalent to the divergence between marginal private and marginal social cost or product, mentioned earlier. It is clear that when personal behavior generates externality, whether this be positive or negative, it must take on characteristics of "public choice," even if the actor does not explicitly acknowledge his role as a decision-maker for the relevant community of persons (small or large) that are affected. In one sense, individual behavior in an externality relationship may be interpreted as a sort of halfway house between the idealized "private choice" typified by buying and selling in competitive markets and the idealized "public choice" typified by voting in purely democratic referenda. It is not surprising, therefore, that several of the contributors of essays in this book have approached their subject matter through the technical analysis of externalities. By contrast, it remains surprising that Pigovian welfare economists, in general, have failed to sense the internal contradiction between their models of economic interaction where external costs and benefits become criteria for market failure and their models of political behavior where such externalities are presumed to be corrected.

There is, of course, a difference in the institutional-environmental setting for personal behavior in the market and in the political process. The individual whose private economic behavior pollutes the air and imposes external costs on others in his community (a classic example of an external diseconomy) may be partially unaware of the effects of his actions on others. Even if he is aware of these effects, he may treat as "his own property" the atmosphere elements (air) that others claim in common, implicitly or explicitly. By comparison, consider the individual who votes in a political referendum and who, say, supports the imposition of taxes on all persons in a well-defined political community. He is exerting an external diseconomy on others, and he may be fully aware that he is affecting their potential economic positions. But the voter claims no "property right" in the selection of the tax system, as such. His behavior may be tempered by his understanding that, in subsequent referenda on taxes and on other constraints, he will find himself in losing rather than winning political coalitions. On some such grounds as this, a plausible case can be made out that "political pollution" is subject to somewhat more intensive internal behavioral constraints than "economic pollution." The implications of such an argument should, however, be kept in mind. Once the welfare economist accepts such a defense of his orthodoxy, he is already partially in the "public choice" camp. He is, willy-nilly, being forced to close up his behavioral system.

At the current stage of development in social and behavioral science, this would represent significant progress. Whether or not and to what extent men behave differently under varied institutional-environmental constraints deserves much more inquiry and investigation. Some research along these lines will be carried out in due course. But the bridge has been crossed once it is so much as acknowledged that the same men are involved in the several decision processes.

III. The Economic Model of Behavior

This section introduces both the main strength and the main limitation of the "theory of public choice," as developed and applied in the papers in this book and by scholars elsewhere. This theory has been developed almost exclusively by scholars who are professional economists. As Gordon Tullock discusses in his essay in this book, the theory of public choice might be taken to reflect economic imperialism, interpreted as efforts by economists to expand the boundaries of their own discipline so as to make it applicable to more and more aspects of human behavior. As they have done so, it should have been expected that the explanatory potential of the strictly economic model of behavior would be gradually eroded, as indeed most of its users will readily acknowledge. The model has been demonstrated to retain surprising strength, however, even when applied to behavior that might initially have seemed to be almost wholly noneconomic. Methodologically, the economic model remains singular in its ability to generate conceptually refutable hypotheses regardless of its particular application.

The economic model of behavior is based on the motivational postulate of individual utility maximization. This postulate, in itself, remains empirically empty until further restrictions are imposed on the definition of utility or, technically, on the utility function. Once this step is taken, once the "goods" that the individual (in some average or representative sense) values are identified, the way is open for the derivation of hypotheses that can be tested against observations. The economic model is almost entirely predictive in content rather than prescriptive. The actors who behave "economically" choose "more rather than less," with more and less being measured in units of goods that are independently identified and defined. This becomes a prediction about behavior in the real world that the economist carries with him as a working professional scientist. As such, the economist neither condemns nor condones the behavior of those whose behavior he examines. He has no business to lay down norms of behavior for the consumer, producer, voter, or for anyone else. In its pure sense, economic theory is devoid of valuation at this normative level.

Failure to understand the descriptive and predictive content of economic theory along with a proclivity to interpret all social "science" in prescriptive terms has caused many critics to deplore the "dismal science" and to rail against the "crass materialism" that economic behavior allegedly represents. The appropriate response of the economist to such criticism should be (but perhaps too rarely has been) that he is wholly unconcerned, as a professional scientist, about the ethically relevant characteristics of the behavior that he examines. To the extent that men behave as his model predicts, the economist can explain uniformities in social order. To the extent that men behave differently, his predictions are falsified. It is as simple as that.

The criticisms of the economic model of behavior, and of the science that embodies this model, have been long-continuing and pervasive even when the model has been limited in application only to the behavior of persons in well-defined market processes. These criticisms need not concern us here. But it should be apparent that when attempts are made to stretch the central predictive model beyond these confines, when the economic approach is extended to "public choice," the criticisms stemming from nonpredictive and nonscientific sources should be intensified. For precisely to the extent that the model loses some of its predictive content, its use to the nonscientist seems to become more and more suspect in some prescriptively relevant sense. A single example illustrates this point. The nonscientist may accept the use of an economic model of behavior, and he may acknowledge its explanatory power in relation to the price-making and price-taking by buyers and sellers of groceries. He may not condemn the economist out of hand for advancing the prediction that buyers will purchase more beans when they are cheapened relative to potatoes. By contrast, the same nonscientist may object, and strenuously, if the economist expands his horizons and uses essentially the same behavioral model to predict that the bureaucrat will increase his awards of public contracts to the prospect that sweetens the personal package of emoluments allowable within the legal constraints. Here the bureaucrat is, like the buyer at the corner grocery store, predicted to demand more of that "good" that is relatively cheapened in price. Because of the predictive-prescriptive confusion, however, the economist becomes suspect; he is interpreted as replacing the "is" by the "ought" in circumstances where prevailing moral principles make strict economic behavior partially or wholly unacceptable.

IV. Noneconomic Models of Behavior

Because of the predictive-prescriptive confusion, however, along with its subsequent creation of reluctance in noneconomist social scientists to undertake rigorous positive examination of behavior patterns, the extension of orthodox economic models to nonmarket behavior seems to fill an awesome gap in social analysis. Precisely because other approaches than the economic have been prescriptive, the latter appears initially to be more important in yielding predictive hypotheses about nonmarket behavior than it would be were alternative models also used in a positive or predictive manner. This latter would require that the noneconomic models be transformed. The traditional prescriptive norms *for* personal behavior would have to be converted into predictive hypotheses *about* personal behavior. The "ought" would have to be replaced by the "is." If this transformation can be effected, noneconomic models can be extended to many aspects of behavior, including an invasion of the domain traditionally commanded by the economists. If the theory of public choice and related work represents "economic imperialism," the way is surely open for the noneconomists to turn the tables and extend behavioral models of their own into the realm of market interactions. All social scientists should applaud the emergence of competing means of closing up the analyses of behavioral systems. And, even in the strictly defined market process, there are surely important unexplained residues that may be examined against alternative behavioral hypotheses.

Consider first, and briefly, the dominant ethical system in the history of the West, Christianity. This system has been almost exclusively discussed and elaborated as a set of prescriptive norms for personal behavior, a set of "shoulds," "commandments," "precepts." Nonetheless, it is possible to convert this ethical system into hypotheses about behavior. We may do so by beginning with individual utility functions as methodologically helpful starting points even if they remain empirically empty. In its starkest form, Christianity is represented by an individual utility function in which "goods" attributed to others are valued equally with "goods" attributed to the person whose function is being defined. Furthermore, there can be no discrimination among the large set of "others" in the pure predictive model of Christianity. For predictions to be made, "goods" must be identified, but, once this is done, hypotheses may be derived and subjected to observation. Do individuals in some average or representative sense behave as the Christian model predicts? Casual empiricism alone suggests that the central hypothesis has at least some explanatory potential. We do observe individuals giving up "goods" to others, including the set of "others" where the individual units remain unidentified to the donor and wholly outside meaningfully drawn boundaries of personal relationship (funds are freely given for the feeding of starving children in Biafra). Research should be extended and carried forward to determine the explanatory limits of this strict Christian hypothesis. In this respect and at this point, the efforts of Kenneth Boulding should be especially noted. Almost alone among social scientists, and once again from a professional background in economics, Boulding has drawn attention to the explanatory potential of what he called the "integrative" system of interaction, which is essentially his version of what I have called here the Christian hypothesis. Other scholars, many of whom have also worked in the theory of public choice, have joined Boulding in developing an "economics of charity." Such men as William Vickrey, Gordon Tullock, Earl Thompson, David B. Johnson, and Thomas Ireland have made contributions in this obvious attempt to include all forms of human behavior in a framework of positive analysis.[3]

Conversion of the prescriptive norm of Christianity into a predictive hypothesis in its pure or pristine form immediately suggests an intermediate approach, one in which the utility function attributes positive values to the "goods" of others, but where the "others" are personally identified, either as individuals or as members of groups embodying certain descriptive characteristics. This approach yields a whole set of possible behavioral hypotheses, the working out and testing of which may be summarized in such various rubrics as "the economics of the family," "the economics of marriage," "the economics of clubs," "the economics of ethnic groups," and so forth. In each case, the word "economics" suggests only that the positive analyses in each case remain largely in the hands of professionally trained economists. But my point of emphasis here is only that work in each of these areas reflects an attempt to accomplish what I have called here the closing of the whole behavioral system.

3. See Kenneth Boulding, "Notes on a Theory of Philanthropy," *Philanthropy and Public Policy*, ed. Frank G. Dickinson (New York, 1962); William Vickrey, "One Economist's View of Philanthropy," *Philanthropy and Public Policy*, op cit.; Gordon Tullock, "Information Without Profit," *Papers on Non-Market Decision-Making*, Vol. 2 (Charlottesville, Virginia, 1967); Thomas Ireland, "Charity Budgeting" (unpublished Ph.D. dissertation, Alderman Library, University of Virginia, 1968); David B. Johnson, "The Fundamental Economics of the Charity Market" (unpublished Ph.D. dissertation, Alderman Library, University of Virginia, 1968); Earl Thompson, "Do Freely Competitive Markets Misallocate Charity?" *Public Choice* 4 (1968), 67–74.

V. The Kantian Generalization Principle Treated as an Explanatory Hypothesis

A more interesting approach, and one that seems hardly to have been explored at all, lies in converting the prescriptive norm of Kantian ethics into a predictive hypothesis about individual behavior. Like the more restricted but comparable Christian hypothesis, this could be treated as a complete model which may have more or less explanatory potential under different behavioral environments. Prescriptively, the Kantian principle instructs a person to consider as a duty that form of behavior that will, when generalized to the whole community of persons, generate results that are desired in some noninstrumental sense. Predictively, the Kantian hypothesis states that when behavior is recognized to affect others, these effects will be taken into account and behavior adjusted as appropriate. The interests of others than the actor are included, however, not out of "love" as in the Christian ethic, but out of a form of enlightened self-interest which is based on a generalized recognition of the reciprocity of social interaction. Translated into utility-function terms, the "goods" that are positively valued by the individual are those attributed to or assigned to himself and not to others. The utilities of others, generally or specifically, do not enter the utility function in any directly interdependent fashion. The interdependence that seems to be inferred from the results arises because the "goods" that the individual values are more inclusive and less instrumental than those upon which the orthodox economic models have concentrated attention.

Clearly, something akin to the Kantian hypothesis describes many aspects of human behavior. Large areas of social life are, and must be, organized essentially on anarchistic principles. Individual property rights are not well defined, yet "pollution" is kept within reasonably tolerable limits by self-imposed constraints on behavior which can only reflect adherence to something like a generalization principle. And, indeed, this hypothesis offers some prospect for methodological reconciliation between the economist's analysis of market behavior and the noneconomist's analysis of nonmarket behavior. It may be plausibly argued that the Kantian hypothesis would yield predictions about market behavior that are identical to those produced by the more restrictive models of economic theory. The individual buyer or seller in a fully competitive market does not influence the position of others than himself.

Hence, he may behave in strict accordance with Kantian precepts when he acts as the automaton of economic theory.

The two hypotheses may diverge only when externalities characterize the economic interaction process. If the Kantian hypothesis should be dominant, there may be no need for policy makers to express concern about environmental or atmospheric pollution or erosion arising from personal behavior, and there might be no inefficient congestion of available publicly used facilities. Similarly, there should be little concern about the narrow and possibly self-seeking behavior of political representatives and bureaucrats. If the Kantian hypothesis about individual behavior should be generally corroborated, individuals who participate in "public choice" would be acting in the genuine "public interest," as defined by the widespread adherence to the generalization principle.[4]

It should be apparent that what is needed is considerably more research to ascertain the explanatory power of competing behavioral hypotheses, any one or any combination of which will allow a closure of the social interaction system. One result of such research will surely be that the relative applicability of the competing hypotheses will vary from one institutional-environmental setting to another. And indeed a central part of the research may be the identification of those institutional characteristics that seem to exert an influence on personal behavior. In a paper that is not included in this volume, I examined the possible influence of the sheer size of the interacting group on the individual's willingness to behave in accordance with the Kantian precepts.[5] Charles Goetz has responded to my challenge, and he has demonstrated that under certain conditions that involve the joint sharing of a collectively provided "good" the directional influence of numbers may be more than offset by the change in payoff differentials consequent on changing sizes of the group.[6] There are other apparent, and less "economic," char-

---

4. Individuals may, of course, disagree as to what the "public interest" is, and conflicts may arise even when each and every person behaves in accordance with Kantian precepts. Resolution of such conflicts raises interesting problems, but the source of conflicts here would be quite different from the more familiar private interest–public interest dichotomy.

5. "Ethical Rules, Expected Values, and Large Numbers," *Ethics* 76 (October 1965), 1–13.

6. Charles J. Goetz, "Group-Size and the Voluntary Provision of Public Goods," Working Paper 24 (Blacksburg, Virginia, November 1968).

acteristics of interaction settings that may be examined for their influence on personal behavior patterns. The influence of the family, the tribe, the church, the local community, the political party, the civic club, the team, . . . all of these and more can be important and can affect overall social stability. Effective research seems only in its very early stages.

VI. We Cannot Have It Both Ways

In conclusion, I should emphasize the relevance of seeking closure of the behavioral systems in our analyses by returning to the comparison and contrast between the position taken by the post-Pigovian welfare economists and that taken by those who have contributed to the "theory of public choice," as represented variously in this book. Neither group should be allowed to operate in an open system of analysis. As I have stressed earlier, the post-Pigovian should not be allowed to generate excitement and ultimately to modify social policy by his alleged discoveries of "market failures" without, and at the same time, acknowledging the comparable "failures" of his proposed political-governmental correctives. The discovery of market failures is normally based on the usage of a narrowly constrained utility function which describes individual market behavior in terms of narrow self-interest. If, in fact, individuals behave in such a manner in the marketplace, the inference should be that they will also act similarly in other and nonmarket behavioral settings. The burden of proof must rest on the discoverer of market failure as he demonstrates that the behavioral shift into a nonmarket setting involves a dramatic widening of personal horizons.

The same restrictions should be imposed on those of us who have tried to extend the economists' model into nonmarket spheres of behavior. We should not be allowed to discover "political failures" because we have succeeded in isolating the self-seeking behavior of politicians and bureaucrats and, at the same time, be unconcerned about the "market failures" that show up because of externalities. Both the post-Pigovian welfare economists and the public-choice economists should be required to work within broadly consistent analytical models. Both groups work essentially with an economic model; neither group should be allowed to slip into its own version of some Kantian-like hypothesis when and if this suits ideological prejudices.

The post-Pigovian may rescue himself from contradiction by either one of two routes. He may, as indeed several eminent welfare economists have done, join the ranks of the public-choice theorists and look critically at "government failures" alongside market failures. The result will be the emergence of some ideologically neutral grounds upon which both the public-choice theorists and the reformed Pigovians can evaluate alternative institutional arrangements on what must be a case-by-case comparative analysis.

The second escape from contradiction lies in the explicit extension of some variant of the Kantian hypothesis to market as well as to nonmarket behavior. The social scientist who sees bureaucracy as something other than the self-seeking of individuals within their own career hierarchy can also begin to look on market behavior and on the workings of markets differently. And indeed there are indications that some analysts are taking this route; witness the increasing attention that has been given to the so-called "social responsibility" of business.

The "theory of public choice" is only one step in the direction of an internally consistent social science. It should be interpreted as such by its proponents as well as by its critics. Its explanatory power varies greatly from application to application, but the number and the variety of these that are contained in this book alone should be sufficient to suggest both the generality of the theory and the promise of continued work.

From Private Preferences to Public Philosophy
The Development of Public Choice

I. Introduction

I appreciate the opportunity afforded me by this invitation from the Institute of Economic Affairs to come to London and to open this seminar on the "Economics of Politics," or, as we prefer to call it, "Public Choice," which is really the application and extension of economic theory to the realm of political or governmental choices. I shall be talking here about material that is familiar to many of you, but it remains nonetheless true that "public choice" has been somewhat slower to attract attention in the United Kingdom than elsewhere in Europe. This body of ideas has been relatively neglected here, despite the presence of one of the genuinely seminal scholars in the discipline, Duncan Black, who has been, in one sense, a prophet without honour in his own country, or at least without appropriate honour.

I shall return to the position of "public choice" in the UK, but first let me say that the subdiscipline is currently thriving, not only in America, but in

From *The Economics of Politics* (London: Institute of Economic Affairs, 1978), 1–20. Reprinted by permission of the publisher.

Basic reference works in public choice are listed at the end of the paper. A more sophisticated survey of the discipline is in Dennis C. Mueller, "Public Choice: A Survey," *Journal of Economic Literature* 14, no. 2 (June 1976), 395–433. This survey paper is followed by Mueller's longer monograph, *Public Choice*, which should be published in early 1979. My survey paper, "Public Finance and Public Choice," *National Tax Journal*, December 1975, relates developments in public choice to public finance. An elementary treatment of the various topics in public choice theory will be found in Gordon Tullock, *The Vote Motive*, Hobart Paperback 9, IEA, 1976.

West Germany, in Switzerland, in Japan, and, most recently, in France, where
Henri Lepage has recently published a laudatory descriptive essay in *Réal-
ités* (November 1977), an expanded version of which has now appeared as a
chapter in Lepage's fascinating book *Demain le capitalisme* (1978).

History of neglect of "public choice" in UK

The relative neglect of "public choice" in the UK is traceable to factors that
extend back for two centuries. To the classical economists, the state was unproductive. As a result of this common presupposition, less attention was
paid to the analysis of state activity. Britain was also the origin of Benthamite
utilitarianism, which provided idealised objectives for governmental policy
to the neglect of institutional structure. Britain was also the home of idealist
political philosophy in the late 19th century, a philosophy that put up barriers against any realistic examination of politics. Finally, the very dominance
of Britain in the theory of the private economy, through the major influence
of Alfred Marshall, drew intellectual resources away from the theory of the
public economy. British and American analysis in public finance was a half-
century out of date by the onset of World War II; the seminal contributions
of the Continental scholars at the turn of the century and before were
largely ignored, notably those of the outstanding Swedish economist, Knut
Wicksell.

In Britain, you surely held on longer than most people to the romantic
notion that government seeks only to do good in some hazily defined Benthamite sense, and, furthermore, to the hypothesis that government could,
in fact, accomplish most of what it set out to do.

Your economists, and notably Lord Keynes, along with their American
counterparts, continued to proffer policy advice as if they were talking to a
benevolent despot who stood at their beck and call.[1] This despite Wicksell's
clear but simple warning in 1896 that economic policy is made by politicians

1. For a discussion of the political setting for Keynesian economics, see J. M. Buchanan, John Burton, and R. E. Wagner, *The Consequences of Mr Keynes*, Hobart Paper 78,
IEA, April 1978. An extended treatment with primary application to an American setting
is in James M. Buchanan and Richard E. Wagner, *Democracy in Deficit*, Academic Press,
New York, 1977.

who are participants in a legislative process, and that economists could not ignore these elementary facts. But British and American economists throughout most of this century continued to seem blind to what now appears so simple to us, that benevolent despots do not exist and that governmental policy emerges from a highly complex and intricate institutional structure peopled by ordinary men and women, very little different from the rest of us. The political scientists were, if anything, even more naïve than the economists, and they have not, even today, learned very much.

II. The Economic Theory of Politics

Why do we call our subdiscipline the "economic" theory of politics? What is there that is peculiarly "economic" about it? Here I think we can look to Duncan Black to put us on the right track. Black commenced his work by stating, very simply, that for his analysis an individual is nothing more than a set of preferences, a utility function, as we call it. Once this apparently innocent definition of an individual is accepted, you are really trapped. If you are to argue that individuals have *similar* preferences, you are forced into a position where you must explain why. And if you can think of no good reason why they should do so, you are required to acknowledge that preferences may *differ* among persons.

From these innocent beginnings, the economic theory of politics emerges as a matter of course. The theory is "economic" in the sense that, like traditional economic theory, the building blocks are *individuals*, not corporate entities, not societies, not communities, not states. The building blocks are living, choosing, economising persons. If these persons are allowed to have *differing* preferences, and if we so much as acknowledge that some aspects of life are inherently collective or social rather than purely private, the central problem for public choice jumps at you full blown. How are differing individual preferences to be reconciled in reaching results that must, by definition, be shared jointly by all members of the community? The positive question is, How *are* the differences reconciled under the political institutions we observe? This question is accompanied by the normative one, How *should* the differences among individuals in desired results be reconciled?

Even at this most elementary level, we must examine the purpose of the collectivity. I have often contrasted the "economic" approach to politics with what I have called the "truth judgement" approach. Individuals may differ on their judgements as to what is "true" and what is not, and it is possible that, occasionally, we may want to introduce institutions that essentially collect or poll the opinions of several persons in arriving at some best estimate of what is "true" or "right." The jury comes to mind as the best example here. The accused is either guilty or not guilty, and we use the jury to determine which of these judgements is "true." But for matters of ordinary politics, the question is *not* one of truth or falsity of the alternatives. The problem is one of resolving individual differences of preferences into results, which it is misleading to call true or false.

We can return to the parallel with standard economic theory. A result emerges from a process of exchange, of compromise, of mutual adjustment among several persons, each of whom has private preferences over the alternatives. Further, the satisfaction of these private preferences offers the *raison d'être* for collective action in the first place. The membership of a congregation decides, somehow, that the church-house is to be painted blue rather than green, but it is inappropriate to talk of either colour as being "true." The members of a school board decide to hire Mrs. Jones rather than Mr. Brown, but we can scarcely say that the successful candidate embodies "truth."

THE PARADOX OF VOTING

Let me return to Duncan Black's seminal efforts, as he faced up to the central problem. I am sure that the natural starting place for Black was with ordinary committees that are used to govern many kinds of collective activities. In this, Black was probably influenced by his own participation in the machinery used for making university-college decisions, much as Lewis Carroll had been influenced by his own share in the committee governance of Christ Church, Oxford. And it is through Duncan Black that we know that the UK's claim to early ideas in voting theory rests largely with Lewis Carroll, who joins the French nobleman Condorcet in making up the two most important figures in the "history of doctrine" before the middle years of this century.

How do committees reach decisions when agreement among all members is not possible? Simple observation suggested the relevance of analysing simple majority voting in formal terms. When he carried out this analysis Black was, I think, somewhat disappointed, even if not surprised, to find that there may exist no motion or proposal (or candidate) from among a fixed set of possibilities that will defeat all others in a series of one-against-one majority tests. There may exist no majority motion. If this is the case, simple majority voting will produce continuous cycling or rotation among a subgroup or subset of the available alternatives. The collective outcome will depend on where the voting stops, which will, in turn, depend on the manipulation of the agenda as well as upon the rules of order. The committee member who can ensure that his preferred amendment or motion is voted upon just before adjournment often wins the strategic game that majority rules always introduce. (It is interesting, even today, to observe the reactions of fellow committee members when a public choice economist observes that the outcome of deliberation may well be dependent on the voting rules adopted.) The "paradox of voting" became one of the staple ingredients in any subsequent public choice discourse.

ARROW'S "PARADOX OF SOCIAL (COLLECTIVE) CHOICE"

Only a short time after Black's early efforts, Kenneth Arrow (Nobel Laureate in Economics, now of Harvard University) confronted a somewhat different and more general problem, although he was to reach the same conclusion. Arrow tried to construct what some economists call a "social welfare function" designed to be useful in guiding the planning authority for a society. He sought to do so by amalgamating information about the separate preferences of individual members, and he was willing to assume that the individuals' preferences exhibit the standard properties required for persons to make ordinary market choices. To his surprise, Arrow found that no such "social welfare function" could be constructed; the task was a logical impossibility, given the satisfaction of certain plausible side-conditions. The paradox of voting became the more general and more serious paradox of social or collective choice.

Perhaps it is unfair to both, but I think that Duncan Black would have been happier if he could have discovered that majority voting rules do produce consistent outcomes, and that Kenneth Arrow would have been happier if he could have been able to demonstrate that a social welfare function could be constructed. Black was, and to my knowledge remains, dedicated to government by majority rule; Arrow was, and to my knowledge remains, an advocate of social planning. Black started immediately to look for the set of conditions that preferences must meet in order for majority voting to exhibit consistency. He came up with his notion of "single-peakedness," which means that if all individual preferences among alternatives can be arrayed along a single dimension so that there is a single peak for each voter, there will exist a unique majority motion or proposal (or candidate). This alternative will be that one of the available set of proposals that is most preferred by the median voter. In this setting, majority voting does produce a definitive result, and in so doing it satisfies voters in the middle more than voters at either extreme. For example, if voters on school budgets can be divided roughly into three groups of comparable size—big spenders, medium spenders, and low spenders—the medium spenders will be controlling under ordinary majority voting, provided that neither the low nor the high spenders rank medium spending lowest among the three budget options. The formal collective or social choice theorists, shocked by the Arrow impossibility theorem, have continued to try to examine the restrictions on individual preferences that might be required to generate consistent social orderings.

III. The Theory of Constitutions

It is at this point in my summary narrative that I should introduce my own origins of interest in public choice, and my own contributions, along with those of my colleague, Gordon Tullock. As did Duncan Black, I came to public choice out of intellectual frustration with orthodox pre–World War II public finance theory, at least as I learned it in the English language works of such economists as A. C. Pigou and Hugh Dalton in the UK, and Harold Groves and Henry Simons in the US. It made no sense to me to analyse taxes and public outlays independent of some consideration of the political process through which decisions on these two sides of the fiscal account were made. *Public finance theory could not be wholly divorced from a theory of politics.*

In coming to this basic criticism of the orthodoxy, I was greatly influenced by Wicksell on the one hand and by some of the Italian theorists on the other. One of my first published papers,[2] in 1949, was basically a plea for a

2. This paper, along with several other early papers, including my essay on the Italian writers, is reprinted in my book *Fiscal Theory and Political Economy*, University of North Carolina Press, Chapel Hill, 1960.

better methodology. My initial reaction to Arrow's impossibility theorem was one of unsurprise. Since political outcomes emerge from a process in which many persons participate rather than from some mysterious group mind, why should anyone have ever expected "social welfare functions" to be internally consistent? Indeed, as I argued in my 1954 paper on Arrow,[3] it seemed to me that, if individual preferences are such as to generate a cycle, then such a cycle, or such inconsistency, is to be preferred to consistency, since the latter would amount to the imposition of the will of some members of the group on others.

"POSITIVE PUBLIC CHOICE"

The next stage in my logical sequence came when Gordon Tullock and I started to analyse how majority rules actually work—what Dennis Mueller has called "positive public choice." Tullock developed his now-classic 1959 paper on majority voting and log-rolling in which he showed that a sequence of majority votes on spending projects financed out of general tax revenues could over-extend the budget and could, indeed, make everyone worse off than they would be with no collective action.[4] Tullock's example was spending on many separate road projects all of which are financed from the proceeds of a general tax, but the same logic can be extended to any situation where there are several spending constituencies that independently influence budgetary patterns. We came to the view that the apparent ideological dominance of majority rule should be more thoroughly examined. This in turn required us to analyse alternatives to majority rule, and to begin to construct an "economic theory of political constitutions," out of which came *The Calculus of Consent* in 1962. This book has achieved a measure of success, of course to our great satisfaction. We used ordinary economic assumptions about the utility-maximising behaviour of individuals, and we sought to explain why specific rules for making collective decisions might emerge from the constitutional level of deliberation.

To pull off this explanation, we needed some means or device that would enable us to pass from individually identifiable self-interest to something

3. Ibid.
4. Gordon Tullock, "Problems of Majority Voting," *Journal of Political Economy* 67, December 1959, 571–79.

that might take the place of "public interest." Unless we could locate such a device or construct, we would have remained in the zero-sum model of politics, where any gains must be matched by losses. We got over this problem by looking at how rules for ordinary parlour games are settled *before* the fall of the cards is known. Uncertainty about just where one's own interest will lie in a sequence of plays or rounds of play will lead a rational person, from his own interest, to prefer rules or arrangements or constitutions that will seem to be "fair," no matter what final positions he might occupy. You will, of course, recognise the affinity between this approach that Tullock and I used in *The Calculus of Consent* and that developed in much more general terms by John Rawls in his monumental treatise, *A Theory of Justice* (1971). Rawls had discussed his central notion of "justice as fairness" in several papers published in the 1950s, and, while our approach came, we think, independently out of our own initial attempt to look for criteria for preferred rules, we do not quibble about the source of ideas. Indeed, the basic ideas in the "justice as fairness" notion can also be found in the work of other scholars that predates Rawls's early papers.

Our book was a mixture of positive analysis of alternative decision rules and a normative defence of certain American political institutions that owe their origins to the Founding Fathers, and to James Madison in particular. We considered that our analysis did "explain" features of the American political heritage that orthodox political science seemed unable to do. Explicitly and deliberately, we defended constitutional limits on majority voting. In a somewhat more fundamental sense, we defended the existence of constitutional constraints *per se*; we justified bounds on the exercise of majoritarian democracy. In this respect, I would argue that America's political history has been "superior" to that of Britain, where neither in theory nor in practice have you imposed constraints on the exercise of parliamentary or legislative majorities comparable to those in America. For example, it would be difficult to conceive of an American cycle of nationalisation, denationalisation, and renationalisation of a basic industry merely upon shifts in the legislative majority between parties.

IV. The Supply of Public Goods

I now want to get some of the early public choice contributions into methodological perspective. Black's early work on committees, Arrow's search for a social welfare function, our own work on the economic theory of constitutions, the derivations of these works in such applications as median voter models—all of these efforts were what we should now call *demand*-driven. By this I mean that the focus of attention was on the ways in which individual preferences might be amalgamated to generate collective results on the presumption that the outcomes would be there for the taking. There was almost no attention paid in these works to the utility-maximising behaviour of those who might be called on to *supply* the public goods and services demanded by the taxpayers-voters. There was no theory of public goods supply in the early models of public choice that I have discussed to this point.

Origins of public goods supply analysis

To get at the origins of the supply-side models, we must go back to some of the Italian scholars, who quite explicitly developed models of the workings of the state-as-monopoly, analysed as being separate and apart from the citizenry, and with its own distinct interests. Machiavelli is, of course, the classic source of ideas here, but the discussions of Vilfredo Pareto and Gaetano Mosca about ruling classes, along with the fiscal applications by the public-finance theorists such as Antonio de Viti de Marco, Amilcare Puviani, and Mauro Fasiani all deserve mention in any catalogue.

From these writers, and independent of them, we may trace the development of rudimentary ideas through Joseph Schumpeter and then to Anthony Downs, who, in his 1957 book, *An Economic Theory of Democracy,* analysed political parties as analogous to profit-maximising firms. Parties, said Downs, set out to maximise votes, and he tried to explain aspects of observed political reality in terms of his vote-maximising models. Perhaps the most important theorem to emerge here was the tendency of parties to establish positions near each other in two-party competition and near the centre of the ideological or issue spectrum. William Riker (of the University of Rochester), in a significant 1962 book, challenged Downs's vote-maximising assumption, and argued convincingly that parties seek not maximum votes but only sufficient votes to ensure minimally winning coalitions.

Downs's primary emphasis was on the political party, not on the behaviour of the politician or bureaucrat. This gap in early supply-side analysis was filled by Gordon Tullock who, drawing on his own experiences in the bureaucracy of the US Department of State, published his *The Politics of Bu-*

reaucracy in 1965, although he had written the bulk of this work a decade earlier. Tullock challenged the dominant orthodoxy of modern political science and public administration, exemplified in the works of Max Weber and Woodrow Wilson, by asking the simple question, What are the rewards and penalties facing a bureaucrat located in a hierarchy and what sorts of behaviour would describe his efforts to maximise his own utility? The analysis of bureaucracy fell readily into place once this question was raised. The mythology of the faceless bureaucrat following orders from above, executing but not making policy choices, and motivated only to forward the "public interest," was not able to survive the logical onslaught. Bureaucrats could no longer be conceived as "economic eunuchs." It became obligatory for analysts to look at bureaucratic structure and at individual behaviour within that structure. Tullock's work was followed by a second Downs book, and the modern theory of bureaucracy was born.

PROPERTY RIGHTS AND BUREAUCRATIC BEHAVIOUR

As the theory of constitutions has an affinity with the work of Rawls, so the theory of bureaucracy has an affinity with the work of those economists who have been called the "property rights theorists," such as Armen Alchian and Harold Demsetz of UCLA, and Roland McKean of Virginia, who initiated analysis of the influence of reward and punishment structures on individual behaviour, and especially in comparisons between profit and non-profit institutions. To predict behaviour, either in governmental bureaucracy or in privately organised non-proprietary institutions, it is necessary to examine carefully the constraints and opportunities faced by individual decision-makers.

The next step was almost as if programmed. Once we begin to look at bureaucracy in this way we can, of course, predict that individual bureaucrats will seek to expand the size of their bureaus since, almost universally in modern Western societies, the salaries and perquisites of office are related directly to the sizes of budgets administered and controlled. The built-in motive force for expansion, the dynamics of modern governmental bureaucracy in the small and in the large, was apparent to all who cared to think. This theory of bureaucratic growth was formalised by William Niskanen, who developed a model of separate budget-maximising departments and subdepartments. In the limiting case, Niskanen's model suggested that bureaucracies could succeed in expanding budgets to twice the size necessary to meet taxpayers' genuine demands for public goods and services. In this limit, taxpayers end up by being no better off than they would be without any public goods; all of their net benefits are "squeezed out" by the bureaucrats. The implication is that each and every public good or service, whether it be health services, education, transport, or defence, tends to be expanded well beyond any tolerable level of efficiency, as defined by the demands of the citizenry.

Alongside this theory of bureaucracy, there have been efforts to analyse the behaviour of the politicians, the elected legislators, who seek opportunities to earn "political income." Attempts have also been made (by Albert Breton and Randall Bartlett) to integrate demand-side and supply-side theories into a coherent analysis.

V. Rent-Seeking

To this point, I have largely discussed what we might call established ideas in public choice, although this epithet should not imply that fascinating research is not continuing in some of the areas mentioned. But let me now briefly introduce an area of inquiry, "rent-seeking," that is on the verge of blossoming. You may, if you prefer, call this "profit-seeking," which might be descriptively more accurate. But "rent-seeking" is used here in order to distinguish the activity from profit-seeking of the kind we ordinarily examine in our study of markets.

Once again, we can look to Gordon Tullock for the original work on rent-seeking, although he did not originally use that term, and did not, I think, fully appreciate the potential promised in his 1967 paper.[5]

Tullock's work has been followed by papers by Richard Posner, of the University of Chicago Law School, Anne Krueger, of the University of Minnesota, who invented the term itself, and others, but my own prediction is that the genuine flurry of research activity in rent-seeking will occur only during the next decade.

5. "The Welfare Costs of Tariffs, Monopolies, and Theft," *Western Economic Journal,* June 1967.

What is "rent-seeking"?

The basic notion is a very simple one and once again it represents the extension of standard price theory to politics. From price theory we learn that profits tend to be equalised by the flow of investments among prospects. The existence or emergence of an opportunity for differentially high profits will attract investment until returns are equalised with those generally available in the economy. What should we predict, therefore, when politics creates profit opportunities or rents? Investment will be attracted toward the prospects that seem favourable and, if "output" cannot expand as in the standard market adjustment, we should predict that investment will take the form of attempts to secure access to the scarcity rents. When the state licenses an occupation, when it assigns import or export quotas, when it allocates TV spectra, when it adopts land-use planning, when it employs functionaries at above-market wages and salaries, we can expect resource waste in investments to secure the favoured plums.

Demands for money rents are elastic. The state cannot readily "give money away," even if it might desire to do so. The rent-seeking analysis can be applied to many activities of the modern state, including the making of money transfers to specified classes of recipients. If mothers with dependent children are granted payments for being mothers, we can predict that we shall soon have more such mothers. If the unemployed are offered higher payments, we predict that the number of unemployed will increase. Or, if access to membership in recipient classes is arbitrarily restricted, we predict that there will be wasteful investment in rent-seeking. As the expansion of modern government offers more opportunities for rents, we must expect that the utility-maximising behaviour of individuals will lead them to waste more and more resources in trying to secure the "rents" or "profits" promised by government.

VI. Empirical Public Choice

So much for a survey and narrative of the development of ideas in public choice theory. I have to this point said little about the empirical testing of these ideas or hypotheses. In the last decade, these empirical tests have occupied much of the attention of public choice economists. Indeed, to the Chicago-based group of scholars who talk about the "economic theory of politics," the ideas that I have traced out above amount to little or nothing until they are tested; their view is that empirical work is the be-all and the end-all of the discipline. Those of us in the Virginia tradition are more catholic in our methodology; we acknowledge the contributions of the empiricists while attributing importance to the continuing search for new theoretical insights. The empiricists, among whom I should list my own colleagues Mark Crain and Bob Tollison, in addition to the Chicago group, notably George Stigler and Sam Peltzman, have taken the utility-maximising postulates and derived implications that are subject to test.

The Chicago-based emphasis has been on economic regulation of such industries as transport, broadcasting, and electricity. What is the economic model for the behaviour of the regulator and, through this, for the activities of the regulatory agency? What does the record show? Stigler suggested that the evidence corroborates the hypothesis that regulation is pursued in the interests of the industries that are regulated. Others have challenged Stigler and have tried to test the differing hypothesis that regulation is carried out for the self-interest of the regulatory bureaucracy, which may or may not coincide with the interest of the industry regulated. Little or none of the empirical work on regulation suggests that the pre–public choice hypothesis of regulation in the "public interest" is corroborated. In the long run, this research must have some impact on the willingness of the citizenry, and the politicians, to subject more and more of the economy to state regulation, although the end does not seem yet in sight.

Crain and Tollison have looked carefully at the record for legislatures in the American states. They have used straight-forward utility-maximising models, with objectively measurable "arguments" in the utility functions, to explain such things as relative salaries of legislators among states, relative occupational categories of legislators, committee structures in legislatures, varying lengths of legislative sessions. They have developed strong empirical support for the basic hypothesis that politicians respond to economic incentives much like the rest of us.

POLITICAL BUSINESS CYCLES

A different area of empirical work that can be brought within the public choice framework is that on "political business cycles," i.e., the alleged attempt by politicians in office to create economic conditions timed so as to further their own electoral prospects. This research will be more fully discussed by Bruno Frey at the seminar (Paper 4). The results seem to be somewhat mixed, and I shall not attempt to offer any judgements on this research here.

VII. Normative Implications of Public Choice

As some of you know, my own interests have never been in the empirical tradition, as narrowly defined. I have been more interested in a different sort of research inquiry that follows more or less naturally from the integration of the demand-side and the supply-side analysis of governmental decision-making institutions.

As proofs of the logical inconsistencies in voting rules are acknowledged, as the costs of securing agreement among persons in groups with differing preferences are accounted for, the theory of rules, or of constitutions, emerges almost automatically on the agenda for research, as I have already noted. But my own efforts have been aimed at going beyond the analysis of *The Calculus of Consent*. I have tried to move cautiously but clearly in the direction of normative understanding and evaluation, to move beyond analysis of the way rules work to a consideration of what rules work *best*.

CONSTITUTIONAL FAILURE: THE LEVIATHAN STATE

In the last five years or so, my interest has been in examining the bases for constitutional improvement, for constitutional change, for what I have called "constitutional revolution." My efforts have been motivated by the observation that the American constitutional structure is in disarray; the constraints that "worked" for two centuries seem to have failed. The checks on government expansion no longer seem to exist. The Leviathan-state is the reality of our time. I state this for the US with certainty; I doubt that many of you would disagree concerning the UK.

My book *The Limits of Liberty* (1975) was devoted to a diagnosis of this constitutional failure, a step that I considered to be necessary before reform might be addressed. (In this context, I found Nevil Johnson's 1977 book *In Search of the Constitution*, with reference to Britain, to be congenial.) My current research emerges as a natural follow-up to the diagnosis. A first project has been completed. With Richard Wagner as co-author, we published *Democracy in Deficit* in early 1977, the theme of which is restated and applied to Britain with John Burton in the IEA's Hobart Paper no. 78, *The Consequences of Mr Keynes* (published on 28 April 1978). The book was an attempt to examine the political consequences of Mr. Keynes, and the central theme was to the effect that an important element of the American fiscal constitution, namely the balanced-budget rule, had been destroyed by the political acceptance of Keynesianism. Economists blindly ignored the asymmetry in application of Keynesian policy precepts, an asymmetry that the most elementary public choice theorist would have spotted. They naïvely presumed that politicians would create budget surpluses as willingly as they create deficits. They forgot the elementary rule that politicians enjoy spending and do not like to tax.

In *Democracy in Deficit*, Wagner and I called explicitly for the restoration of budget balance as a constitutional requirement. With Geoffrey Brennan, I am now engaged in an attempt to design a "tax constitution." We are examining ways and means through which the revenue-grabbing proclivities of governments might be disciplined by constitutional constraints imposed on tax bases and rates.

CAN GOVERNMENT BE CONSTRAINED?

These efforts, on my part and others', suggest that we proceed from a belief that governments can be constrained. We refuse to accept the Hobbesian scenario in which there are no means to bridle the passions of the sovereign. Historical evidence from America's own two centuries suggests that governments can be controlled by constitutions.

In one sense, all of public choice or the economic theory of politics may be summarised as the "discovery" or "rediscovery" that people should be treated as rational utility-maximisers in *all* of their behavioural capacities. This central insight, in all of its elaborations, does not lead to the conclusion that all collective action, all government action, is necessarily undesirable. It leads, instead, to the conclusion that because people will tend to maximise their own utilities institutions must be designed so that individual behaviour will further the interests of the group, small or large, local or national. The challenge to us is one of constructing, or reconstructing, a political order that will channel the self-serving behaviour of participants towards the common good in a manner that comes as close as possible to that described for us by Adam Smith with respect to the economic order.

VIII. The Wisdom of Centuries

I have described the economic theory of politics, or public choice, as a relatively young subdiscipline that has emerged to occupy the attention of scholars in the three decades since the end of World War II. If we look only at the intellectual developments of the 20th century, public choice is "new," and it has, I think, made a major impact on the way that living persons view government and political process. The public philosophy of 1978 is very different from the public philosophy of 1948 or 1958. There is now much more scepticism about the capacity or the intention of government to satisfy the needs of citizens.

At the start of my remarks, I stated that the ideas of public choice have been relatively slow to catch on in the UK. That statement is, I think, accurate, but I should be remiss if I did not end this paper on a somewhat different note. In one sense, public choice—the economic theory of politics—is not new at all. It represents rediscovery and elaboration of a part of the conventional wisdom of the 18th and the 19th centuries, and notably the conventional wisdom that informed classical political economy. Adam Smith, David Hume, and the American Founding Fathers would have considered the central principles of public choice theory to be so elementary as scarcely to warrant attention. A mistrust of governmental processes, along with the implied necessity to impose severe constraints on the exercise of governmental authority, was part and parcel of the philosophical heritage they all shared. This set of attitudes extended at least through the middle years of the 19th century, after which they seem to have been suspended for at least a hundred years. Perhaps they are on the way to return.

I could scarcely do better in conclusion than to introduce a citation from J. S. Mill's *Considerations on Representative Government* (1861):

> . . . the very principle of constitutional government requires it to be assumed, that political power will be abused to promote the particular pur-

poses of the holder; not because it always is so, but because such is the natural tendency of things, to guard against which is the especial use of free institutions.[6]

How much have we forgotten? Can modern man recover the wisdom of the centuries? Let us not despair. A start has been made.

BASIC REFERENCE WORKS IN PUBLIC CHOICE

Arrow, Kenneth. *Social Choice and Individual Values.* 2d ed. New Haven: Yale University Press, 1970.

Bartlett, Randall. *Economic Foundation of Political Power.* New York: Free Press, 1973.

Black, Duncan. *The Theory of Committees and Elections.* Cambridge: Cambridge University Press, 1958.

———, and R. A. Newing. *Committee Decisions with Complementary Valuation.* London: William Hodge, 1951.

Breton, Albert. *The Economic Theory of Representative Government.* Chicago: Aldine, 1974.

Buchanan, James M. *Fiscal Theory and Political Economy.* Chapel Hill: University of North Carolina Press, 1960.

———. *Public Finance in Democratic Process.* Chapel Hill: University of North Carolina Press, 1967.

———. *The Limits of Liberty: Between Anarchy and Leviathan.* Chicago: University of Chicago Press, 1975.

———. *Freedom in Constitutional Contract.* College Station: Texas A&M University Press, 1978.

———, and Gordon Tullock. *The Calculus of Consent: Logical Foundations of Constitutional Democracy.* Ann Arbor: University of Michigan Press, 1962.

———, and Richard E. Wagner. *Democracy in Deficit: The Political Legacy of Lord Keynes.* New York: Academic Press, 1977.

———, and Robert Tollison, eds. *Theory of Public Choice: Political Applications of Economics.* Ann Arbor: University of Michigan Press, 1972.

Downs, Anthony. *An Economic Theory of Democracy.* New York: Harper, 1957.

———. *Inside Bureaucracy.* Boston: Little, Brown and Company, 1967.

Niskanen, William A. *Bureaucracy and Representative Government.* Chicago: Aldine, 1971.

6. J. S. Mill, *Considerations on Representative Government* (1861), in J. S. Mill, *Essays on Politics and Society,* vol. 2, University of Toronto Press, Toronto, 1977, 505.

Olson, Mancur. *The Logic of Collective Action.* Cambridge, Mass.: Harvard University Press, 1965.

Riker, William. *The Theory of Political Coalitions.* New Haven: Yale University Press, 1962.

———, and Peter Ordeshook. *An Introduction to Positive Political Theory.* Englewood Cliffs, N.J.: Prentice-Hall, 1973.

Sen, A. K. *Collective Choice and Social Welfare.* San Francisco: Holden Day, 1970.

Tullock, Gordon. *The Politics of Bureaucracy.* Washington: Public Affairs Press, 1965.

———. *Private Wants, Public Means.* New York: Basic Books, 1970.

———. *Towards a Mathematics of Politics.* Ann Arbor: University of Michigan Press, 1972.

———. *The Social Dilemma.* Blacksburg: Center for Study of Public Choice, 1974.

Wicksell, Knut. *Finanztheoretische Untersuchungen.* Jena: Gustav Fischer, 1896. A major portion of this work is translated and published under the title "A New Principle of Just Taxation," in R. A. Musgrave and A. T. Peacock, eds., *Classics in the Theory of Public Finance.* London: Macmillan, 1959.

Note: References above are limited to books. A listing of article-length contributions would extend to many pages. See the Bibliography in Dennis Mueller's survey paper in *Journal of Economic Literature* 14, no. 2 (June 1976), 395–433.

Notes on the History and Direction
of Public Choice

By way of introduction, I call your attention to two papers. The first is Scott Gordon's "The New Contractarians,"[1] which was an extended review article on Rawls, Nozick, and Buchanan. The second is Milton Friedman's Nobel Prize lecture, "Inflation and Unemployment."[2] In the former, Gordon accused me of committing the "naturalistic fallacy," that of deriving an "ought" from an "is," of mixing positive analysis and normative precept. In the latter, Friedman argues that economics is, after all, a "science" like the natural sciences in the sense that it develops through the refutation of hypotheses.

You may appropriately ask what has all this to do with my title. Let me try to explain. I was not particularly disturbed by Gordon's accusation, since I have never worried very much about whether or not my own work falls within the methodological precepts laid down by others. I viewed my book *The Limits of Liberty*[3] as basically positive analysis, with ethical content squeezed to a minimum. I did not want explicitly to advance my own private values; I did not want to spell out, and I refrained from doing so, just how society "ought" to be organized. I think that my values count for no more in this respect than anyone else's. But we must all recognize, I think, that the ultimate purpose of positive analysis, conceptual or empirical, must

From *What Should Economists Do?* (Indianapolis: Liberty Fund, 1979), 175–82. Reprinted by permission of the publisher.

This chapter was initially prepared for panel presentation at the Public Choice Society Meeting, New Orleans, March 11, 1977.

1. "The New Contractarians," *Journal of Political Economy* 84, no. 3 (June 1976): 573–75.

2. Nobel Foundation, December 1976.

3. Chicago: University of Chicago Press, 1975.

be that of modifying the environment for choices, which must, in some basic sense, be normatively informed. The ultimate purpose is the "ought," no matter how purely we stick positively with the "is." Or to put a familiar statement of Pigou in context here, in social sciences it is the heat we are looking for, not pure light.

Let me take a single economics and public-choice example, the federal minimum-wage laws. Economists are almost universally agreed that the requirement of the uniform minimum wage creates a good part of the observed unemployment among teenagers, and notably teenaged members of minority groups (Ray Marshall to the contrary notwithstanding; Marshall really disqualifies himself as an economist by his position on such matters). This relationship between minimum wages and unemployment is perhaps as well established, both analytically and empirically, as any in the whole discipline of economics. But we do not observe some mysterious leap from this demonstrated "is" to the "ought" of the repeal of these restrictions. Why not? Public-choice analysts have provided part of the answer. They have looked straightforwardly at the self-interested motivations of certain groups in maintaining the minimum wage. Whereas many economists, locked in normatively to their notions of efficiency, would be quite willing to infer an "ought" from the "is" relationship here, public-choice theory allows us to demonstrate the future "is" proposition that explains why elected politicians pay so little attention to the economists' urgings. There is disagreement on the "ought," because the maintenance of the uniform minimum wage is to the interest of large groups of voters. And we are left with the "is" of observed policy, without a means of crossing the bridge to the "ought."

I shall return to this point later, but first let me trace out a bit of the "history" part of my remarks. Duncan Black was correct in labeling his theory one of "committees and elections" rather than a theory of democratic or governmental process. A small number of persons choosing among a small number of discrete alternatives—this is the idealized setting for the analysis of simple voting rules, surely one central part of public-choice theory as it has developed to date. But public-choice theorists have, perhaps too readily, transferred this analysis to the complex setting of political reality, where a few "candidates" become many "issues," where "issues" are prepackaged in platforms, where electorates number in the millions, and where there may be little correspondence between the simple choices confronted by the voter and the outcomes that may occur. The deficiencies of the demand-driven models of government, of an essentially passive supplier of public goods and services responding to the demands of median preferences—these deficiencies have come to be increasingly apparent, both because of our observations of real-world political behavior and because of analytical contributions represented in the theories of bureaucracy and application of monopoly models to governments. Increasingly, public-choice theorists now find common ground with some of the early Italian theorists who worked with ruling-class or establishment models of the state. The Leviathan that we observe today simply cannot be ignored.

In oversimplified terms we can look at the history of public-choice theory in this two-stage manner. First, there was the working out of voting-rule theory under demand-driven models of governmental process. Second, there was, and is, the working out of theories of transmission via organizational structures of government. In both stages, however, we can summarize public choice as a theory of "governmental failure," at least by comparison with the public-interest image inherent in the Wilsonian-Weberian conception of bureaucracy and the "truth-judgment" image of politics that informed so much of traditional pre-public-choice political science. Public choice is a theory of "governmental failure" here in the precisely analogous sense that theoretical welfare economics has been a theory of "market failure."

Let me return to Friedman's Nobel Prize lecture and to the "ought-is" question raised by Scott Gordon. Friedman suggests, implicitly, if not explicitly, that "science" is all, that the refutation of hypotheses is all that we are required to do, that a demonstration of the "is" must necessarily lead to some consensus on the "ought." Applied to the development of positive public-choice theory, the Friedman message is clear. By means of widely accepted demonstrations, both analytical and empirical, that governmental processes "fail" by comparison with alternative arrangements, our task is largely complete. The policy implications will, presumably, emerge from the "scientific advance" more or less automatically even if somehow mysteriously.

I suppose that my rejection of this view is evident. The "ought" of policy does not follow from the "is" of positive science in economics or in politics. I am on Hobbes' side of the argument here as in so many other places, for I recall that Hobbes is alleged to have stated that we should never have accepted the "truth" that two plus two equals four if it had been to the interest of any group to oppose this logic of the simple number system. To bring us forward more than three centuries to a 1977 example, can anything be more demonstrably self-evident than the superiority of the aggregate benefits of the TVA Tellico dam over the costs of eliminating the snail darter, which my informed biologist colleagues tell me is not an endangered species anyway? I hope that we shall not be so naive as to think that, because we have made progress toward some understanding of the way governmental processes actually function, improvements in design will follow, more or less as a matter of course. Would it were so!

Which brings me directly to what I have to say about the future developments and direction of public choice. Put bluntly, I think that we must become more *normative* in our efforts; we should use the results of our positive analysis in the discussion of policy reform. We must use the "is" to implement the "ought" which the "is" suggests, regardless of the methodological impropriety of this relationship, Scott Gordon to the contrary notwithstanding.

But let me clarify my position here. I am not, repeat not, proposing that we dirty our hands in day-to-day policy advocacy of the Brookings variety. I shall leave that to the Joe Pechmans of the world, although I do sometimes get a bit concerned about the one-sided progovernment, proregulation biases in such representation. But this aside, the sort of normative public choice that I support is far from such direct policy advocacy.

Again let me use an example. Public-choice analysts have no business telling President Carter or Jim Schlesinger just what energy policy "ought" to be proposed. Nor do they even have any role in delineating what would be an "ideal" policy mix. Positive public-choice analysts can tell us, however, and within broad limits, roughly the sort of energy policy that is likely to emerge from the collective decision-making institutions that we observe in operation. This is, and has been, our major contribution. And our predictions can tell us that the emergent results are unlikely to bear much relationship to those results desired, even by those who make the final normative decision as to the "ought." In a sense, public-choice analysts can take on a normative role in advocating some matching of policy proposals with the institutional realities of modern politics. We can talk meaningfully about the "best" rules, or the "nth best" arrangements, often quite independent of the ultimate policy targets. In other words, we can talk normatively about "process" or "procedure," while staying clear of normative discussion of "end-states."

Perhaps I should go further and say that public-choice theorists should begin to advance their own versions of the ideal constitution for society. In this, I may be doing nothing more than suggesting the way in which my own directions seem to lie rather than inferring this for the whole of the public-choice subdiscipline. But let me extend these remarks only a bit more to constitutionalism. I have argued, along with others, that we must have a genuine constitutional dialogue, and soon, if America is to remain a free society, if we are to escape the ravages of Rome (with some parallels forcefully brought home to me in a recent manuscript by Professor Silver)[4] and the British disease of our own century. There is still time. It is folly to think that "better men" elected to office will help us much, that "better policy" will turn things around here. We need, and must have, basic constitutional reform, which must of course be preceded by basic constitutional discourse and discussion. This is our challenge.

Public choice can claim to have contributed hugely to what can be the basis for such discourse and discussion. But there is also room for, indeed a necessity for, some intellectual entrepreneurship, some normative advocacy, in getting the dialogue going. The "science" does not create its own consequences.

Let us continue to scorn the petty bickerings of the partisan policy advocates; we should not be bothered at all as to whether or not mortgage interest is or is not a tax deduction, and we waste our time thinking about such matters. We should care, and we should think about, what the fiscal constitution for political democracy should look like, what sort of institutions should be most efficient in the workings of democratic politics. But we must do more than analyze what is. If we do not go beyond this, if we do not begin to suggest explicitly what "ought to be" in terms of these basic constitutional reforms of process, we can scarcely complain when we observe the continued drift into constitutional chaos. The several prisoners caught in a dilemma may all recognize their plight; but before escape is possible someone must take the step of changing his own behavior in an attempt to convince others that all can be made better off in the process.

In the final analysis, I refuse to think everything is hopeless, which strictly positive analysis without the accompanying Friedman faith might lead us to believe.

---

4. "Decline of Affluent Societies," mimeographed (New York: City College of the City University of New York, 1977).

Foreword to Gordon Tullock's
Politics of Bureaucracy

"It is not from the benevolence of the butcher, the brewer, or the baker, that we expect our dinner, but from their regard to their own interest." This statement is, perhaps, the most renowned in the classic book in political economy, Adam Smith's *Wealth of Nations*. From Smith onwards, the appropriate function of political economy, and political economists, has been that of demonstrating how the market system, as a perfectible social organization, can, and to an extent does, channel the private interests of individuals toward the satisfaction of desires other than their own. Insofar as this cruder instinct of man toward acquisitiveness, toward self-preservation, can be harnessed through the interactions of the market mechanism, the necessity for reliance on the nobler virtues, those of benevolence and self-sacrifice, is minimized. This fact, as Sir Dennis Robertson has so eloquently reminded us, gives the economist a reason for existing, and his "warning bark" must be heeded by those decision makers who fail to recognize the need for economizing on "love."

Despite such warning barks (and some of these have sounded strangely like shouts of praise), the politicians for many reasons have, over the past century, placed more and more burden of organized social activity on political, governmental processes. As governments have been called upon to do more and more important things, the degree of popular democratic control over separate public or governmental decisions has been gradually reduced. In a real sense, Western societies have attained universal suffrage only after popular democracy has disappeared. The electorate, the ultimate sovereign,

From *The Politics of Bureaucracy* (Washington, D.C.: Public Affairs Press, 1965), 1–9. Reprinted by permission of the publisher.

must, to an extent not dreamed of by democracy's philosophers, be content to choose its leaders. The ordinary decisions of government emerge from a bureaucracy of ever-increasing dimensions. Non-governmental and quasi-governmental bureaucracies have accompanied the governmental in its growth. The administrative hierarchy of a modern corporate giant differs less from the federal bureaucracy than it does from the freely contracting trades-man envisaged by Adam Smith.

This set, this drift, of history toward bigness, both in "public" and in "private" government, has caused many a cowardly scholar to despair and to seek escape by migrating to a dream world that never was. It has caused other "downstream" scholars to snicker with glee at the apparent demise of man, the individual. In this book, by contrast, Tullock firmly grasps the nettle offered by the modern bureaucratic state. In effect, he says, "If we must have bureaucratic bigness, let us, at the least, open our eyes to its inner workings. Man does not simply cease to exist because he is submerged in an administrative hierarchy. He remains an individual, with individual motives, impulses, and desires." This seems a plausible view of things. But, and surprisingly, we find that few theorists of bureaucracy have started from this base. Much of administrative theory, ancient or modern, is based on the contrary view that man becomes as a machine when he is placed within a hierarchy, a machine that faithfully carries out the orders of its superiors who act for the whole organization in reaching policy decisions. Tullock returns us to Adam Smith's statement, and he rephrases it as follows: "It is not from the benevolence of the bureaucrat that we expect our research grant or our welfare check, but out of his regard to his own, not the public interest."

Adam Smith and the economists have been, and Tullock will be, accused of discussing a world peopled with evil and immoral men. Men "should not" be either "getting and spending" or "politicking." Such accusations, and they never cease, are almost wholly irrelevant. Some social critics simply do not like the world as it is, and they refuse to allow the social scientist, who may not like it either, to analyze reality. To the scientist, of course, analysis must precede prescription, and prescription must precede improvement. The road to Utopia must start from here, and this road cannot be transversed until here is located, regardless of the beautiful descriptions of yonder. Tullock's analysis is an attempt to locate the "here" in the real, existing world of modern bureaucracy. His assumptions about behavior in this world are empirical, not ethical. He is quite willing to leave the test of his model to the reader and to future scholars. If, in fact, men in modern bureaucracy do not seek "more" rather than "less," measured in terms of their own career advancement, when they are confronted with relevant choices, Tullock would readily admit the failure of his model to be explanatory in other than some purely tautological sense.

When it is admitted, as all honesty suggests, that some individuals remain individuals, even in a bureaucratic hierarchy, Tullock's analysis assumes meaning. It provides the basis for discussing seriously the prospects for improving the "efficiency" of these bureaucratic structures in accomplishing the tasks assigned to them. There are two stages in any assessment of the efficiency of organizational hierarchies, just as there are in the discussions of the efficiency of the market organization. First, there must be a description, an explanation, a theory, of the behavior of the individual units that make up the structure. This theory, as in the theory of markets, can serve two purposes, and, because of this, methodological confusion is compounded. Such an explanatory, descriptive theory of individual behavior can serve a normative purpose, can provide a guide to the behavior of an individual unit which accepts the objectives or goals postulated in the analytical model. In a wholly different sense, however, the theory can serve a descriptive, explanatory function in a positive manner, describing the behavior of the average or representative unit, without normative implications *for* behavior of any sort. This important distinction requires major stress here. It has never been fully clarified in economic theory, where the contrast is significantly sharper than in the nascent political theory that Tullock, and a few others, are currently attempting to develop.

The analogy with the theory of the firm is worth discussing in some detail here. This theory of the firm, an individual unit in the organized market economy, serves two purposes. It may, if properly employed, serve as a guide to a firm that seeks to further the objectives specified in the model. As such, the theory of the firm falls wholly outside economics, political economy, and, rather, falls within business administration or managerial science. Essentially the same analysis may, however, be employed by the economist as a descriptive theory that helps the student of market organization to understand the workings of this system which is necessarily composed of individual units.

Tullock's theory of the behavior of the individual "politician" in bureaucracy can be, and should be, similarly interpreted. Insofar as such units, the "politicians," accept the objectives postulated—in this case, advancement in this administrative hierarchy—Tullock's analysis can serve as a "guide" to the ambitious bureaucrat. To think primarily of the analysis in this light would, in my view, be grossly misleading. Instead the analysis of the behavior of the individual politician should be treated as descriptive and explanatory, and its validity should be sought in its ability to assist us in the understanding of the operation of bureaucratic systems generally.

Once this basic theory of the behavior of the individual unit is constructed, it becomes possible to begin the construction of a theory of the inclusive system, which is composed of a pattern of interactions among the individual units. By the nature of the systems with which he works, administrative hierarchies, Tullock's "theory of organization" here is less fully developed than is the analogous "theory of markets." A more sophisticated theory may be possible here, and, if so, Tullock's analysis can be an important helpmate to whoever chooses to elaborate it.

Finally, the important step can be taken from positive analysis to normative prescription, not for the improvement of the strategically oriented behavior of the individual unit directly, but for the improvement in the set of working rules that describe the organization. This step, which must be the ultimate objective of all social science, can be taken only after the underlying theory has enabled the observer to make some comparisons among alternatives. The last half of this book is primarily devoted to the development of such norms for "improving" the functioning of organizational hierarchies.

Tullock's "politician" is, to be sure, an "economic" man of sorts. No claim is made, however, that this man, this politician, is wholly descriptive of the real world. More modestly, Tullock suggests (or should do so, if he does not) that the reference politician is an ideal type, one that we must recognize as being always a part of reality, although he does not, presumably, occupy existing bureaucratic structures to the exclusion of all other men. One of Tullock's primary contributions, or so it appears to me, lies in his ability to put flesh and blood on the bureaucratic man, to equip him with his own power to make decisions, to take action. Heretofore, theorists of bureaucracy, to my knowledge, have not really succeeded in peopling their hierarchies. What serves to motivate the bureaucrat in modern administrative theory? I suspect that one must search at some length to find an answer that is as explicit as that provided by Tullock. Because explicit motivation is introduced, a model containing predictive value can be built, and the predictions can be conceptually refuted by appeal to evidence. It is difficult to imagine how a "theory" of bureaucracy in any meaningful sense could be begun in any other way.

By implication, my comments to this point may be interpreted to mean that Tullock's approach to a theory of administration is an "economic" one, and that the most accurate short-hand description of this book would be to say that it represents an "economist's" approach to bureaucracy. This would be, in one sense, correct, but at the same time such a description would tend to cloud over and to subordinate Tullock's second major contribution. This lies in his sharp dichotomization of the "economic" and the "political" relationships among men. Since this book is devoted almost exclusively to an examination of the "political" relationship, it has little that is "economic" in its content. It represents an economist's approach to the political relationship among individuals. This is a more adequate summary, but this, too, would not convey to the prospective reader who is unfamiliar with Tullock's usage of the particular words the proper scope of the analysis. I have, in the discussion above, tried to clarify the meaning of the economist's approach. There remains the important distinction between the "economic" and the "political" relationship.

This distinction is, in one sense, the central theme of the book. In a foreword, it is not proper to quarrel with an author's usage, but synonyms are sometimes helpful in clearing away ambiguities. Tullock distinguishes, basically, between the relationship of *exchange*, which he calls the economic, and the relationship of *slavery*, which he calls the political. I use bold words here, but I do so deliberately. In its pure or ideal form, the superior-inferior relationship is that of the master and the slave. If the inferior has no alternative means of improving his own well-being other than through pleasing his superior, he is, in fact, a "slave," pure and simple. This remains true quite independent of the particular institutional constraints that may or may not inhibit the behavior of the superior. It matters not whether the superior can capitalize the human personality of the inferior and market him as an asset. Interestingly enough, the common usage of the word "slavery" refers to an institutional structure in which exchange was a dominant relationship. In other words, to the social scientist at any rate, the mention of "slavery" calls to mind the exchange process, with the things exchanged being "slaves." The word itself does not particularize the relationship between master and slave at all. Thus, as with so many instances in Tullock's book, we find no words that describe adequately the relationships that he discusses. Examples, however, serve to clarify. Would I be less a "slave" if you, as my master, could not exchange me, provided only that I have no alternative source of income? My income may depend exclusively on my pleasing you, my master, despite the fact that you, too, may be locked into the relationship. "Serfdom," as distinct from "slavery," may be a more descriptive term, especially since Tullock finds many practical examples for his analysis in feudal systems.

The difficulty in explaining the "political" relationship in itself attests to the importance of Tullock's analysis, and, as he suggests, the whole book can be considered a definition of this relationship. The sources of the difficulty are apparent. First of all, the "political" relationship is not commonly encountered in its pure form, that of abject slavery as noted above. By contrast, its counterpart, the economic or exchange relationship is, at least conceptually, visualized in its pure form, and, in certain instances, the relationship actually exists. This amounts to saying that, without quite realizing what we are doing, we think of ourselves as free men living in a free society. The economic relationship comes more or less naturally to us as the appropriate organizational arrangement through which cooperative endeavor among individuals is carried forward in a social system. Unconsciously, we rebel at the idea of ourselves in a slave or serf culture, and we refuse, again unconsciously, to face up to the reality that, in fact, many of our relationships with our fellows are "political" in the Tullockian sense. Only this blindness toward reality can explain the failure of modern scholars to have developed a more satisfactory theory of individual behavior in hierarchic structures. This also explains why Tullock has found it necessary to go to the Eastern literature and to the discussions in earlier historical epochs for comparative analysis.

Traditional economic analysis can be helpful in illustrating this fundamental distinction between the economic and the political relationship. A seller is in a purely economic relationship with his buyers when he confronts a number of them, any one of which is prepared to purchase his commodity or service at the established market price. He is a slave to no single buyer, and he need "please" no one provided only that he performs the task for which he contracts, that he "delivers the goods." By contrast, consider the seller who confronts a single buyer with no alternative buyer existent. In this case, the relationship becomes wholly "political." The price becomes exclusively that which the economist calls "pure rent" since, by hypothesis, the seller has no alternative use to which he can put his commodity or service. He is, thus, at the absolute mercy of the single buyer. He is, in fact, a "slave" to this buyer, and he must "please" in order to secure favorable terms, in order to advance his own welfare. Note here that the domestic servant who contracts "to please" a buyer of his services may, in fact, remain in a predominantly economic relationship if a sufficient number of alternative buyers for his services exist, whereas the corporation executive who supervises a sizeable number of people may be in a predominantly political relationship with his own superior. To the economist, Tullock provides a discussion of the origins of economic rent, and a theory of the relationship between the recipient and the donor of economic rent.

Tullock's distinction here can also be useful in discussing an age-old philosophical dilemma. When is a man confronted with a free choice? The traveler's choice between giving up his purse and death, as offered to him by the highwayman, is, in reality, no choice at all. Yet philosophers have found it difficult to define explicitly the line that divides situations into categories of free and unfree or coerced choices. One approach to a possible classification here lies in the extent to which individual response to an apparent choice situation might be predicted by an external observer. If, in fact, the specific action of the individual, confronted with an apparent choice, is predictable within narrow limits, no effective choosing or deciding process could take place. By comparison, if the individual response is not predictable with a high degree of probability, choice can be defined as being effectively free. By implication, Tullock's analysis would suggest that individual action in a political relationship might be somewhat more predictable than individual action in the economic relationship because of the simple fact that, in the latter, there exist alternatives. If this implication is correctly drawn, the possibilities of developing a predictive "science" of "politics" would seem to be inherently greater than those of developing a science of economics. Yet we observe, of course, that economic theory has an established and legitimate claim to the position as being the only social science with genuine predictive value. The apparent paradox here is explained by the generality with which the economist can apply his criteria for measuring the results of individual choice. Through his ability to bring many results within the "measuring rod of money," the economist is able to make reasonably accurate predictions about the behavior of "average" or "representative" men; behavior that, in individual cases, stems from unconstrained, or free, choices. Only through this possibility of relying on representative individuals can economics be a predictive science; predictions about the behavior of individually identifiable human beings are clearly impossible except in rare instances. By contrast, because his choice is less free, the behavior of the individual politician in a bureaucratic hierarchy can be predicted with somewhat greater accuracy than the behavior of the individual in the marketplace. But there exist no general, quantitatively measurable, criteria that will allow the external observer to test hypotheses about political behavior. There exists no measuring rod for bureaucratic advancement comparable to the economist's money scale. For these reasons, hypotheses about individual behavior are more important in Tullock's analysis, and the absence of external variables that are subject to quantification makes the refutation of positive hypotheses difficult in the extreme. For assistance here, Tullock introduces a simple, but neglected, method. He asks the reader whether or not his own experience leads him to accept or to reject the hypotheses concerning the behavior of the politician in bureaucracy.

Tullock makes no attempt to conceal from view his opinion that large hierarchical structures are, with certain explicit exceptions, unnecessary evils, that these are not appropriate parts of the good society. A unique value of the book lies, however, in the fact that this becomes more than mere opinion, more than mere expression of personal value judgments. The emphasis is properly placed on the need for greater scientific analysis. Far too often social scientists have, I fear, introduced explicit value judgments before analysis should have ceased. Ultimately, of course, discussion must reduce to values, but when it does so it is done. If the indolent scholar relies on an appeal to values at the outset, his role in genuine discussion is, almost by definition, eliminated.

The bureaucratic world that Tullock pictures for us is not an attractive one, even when its abstract character is recognized, and even if the reference politician of that world is not assigned the dominant role in real life. Those of us who accept the essential ethics of the free society find this world difficult to think about, much less to discuss critically and to evaluate. External events, however, force us to the realization that this is, to a large extent, the world in which we now live. The ideal society of freely contracting "equals," always a noble fiction, has, for all practical purposes, disappeared even as a norm in this age of increasing collectivization: political, economic, and philosophical.

Faced with this reality, the libertarian need not despair. The technology of the twentieth century has made small organizations inefficient in many respects, and the Jeffersonian image of the free society can never be realized. However, just as the critics of the laissez faire economic order were successful in their efforts to undermine the public faith in the functioning of the invisible hand, the new critics of the emerging bureaucratic order can be successful in undermining an equally naive faith in the benevolence of governmental bureaucracy. Tullock's analysis, above all else, arouses the reader to an awareness of the inefficiencies of large hierarchical structures, independent of the presumed purposes or objectives of these organizations. The benevolent despot image of government, that seems now to exist in the minds of so many men, is effectively shattered.

Genuine progress toward the reform of social institutions becomes possible when man learns that the ideal order of affairs is neither the laissez faire dream of Herbert Spencer nor the benevolent despotism image of an "economy under law" espoused by Mr. W. H. Ferry of the Center for the Study of Democratic Institutions. Man in the West, as well as in the East, must learn that governments, even governments by the people, can do so many things poorly, and many things not at all. If this very simple fact could be more widely recognized by the public at large (the ultimate sovereign in any society over the long run) a genuinely free society of individuals and groups might again become a realizable goal for the organization of man's cooperative endeavors. We do not yet know the structure of this society, and we may have to grope our way along for decades. Surely and certainly, however, man must cling to that uniquely important discovery of modern history, the discovery of man, the individual human being. If we abandon or forget this discovery, and allow ourselves to be drawn along any one of the many roads to serfdom by false gods, we do not deserve to survive.

Notes on Politics as Process

In Chapter 3, entitled "The Public Choice Perspective," I distinguished two related components that set public choice aside from orthodox approaches to politics. One is the extension of the economists' utility-maximizing framework to the behaviour of persons in various public-choosing roles. The second is the idealized conceptualization of politics as complex exchange. In this conceptualization the political process and the market process are analogous. In each process, individuals seek to further *their own* purposes, whatever these may be, by engaging in social interaction. There exists no purpose or objective over and beyond those of participating individuals. In the public choice perspective, properly understood, there simply are no such things as "social objectives," "national goals," or "social welfare functions."

This much is surely familiar ground to any modern public choice scholar. In these preliminary notes, however, I want to explore some of the implications of the politics-as-exchange conceptualization more thoroughly. I want to look closely at "politics as process."

The relationship to the Austrian and near-Austrian perspective on economics should be evident. For economists it is surely necessary to interpret the social interaction summarized as "the market" as a process before we can so much as commence to interpret politics similarly. If, by contrast, the market is viewed as a "mechanism," "device," or "instrument" for the furtherance of some independently existing objective—whether this be "efficiency,"

From *Liberty, Market and State: Political Economy in the 1980s* (Brighton, England: Wheatsheaf Books, 1986), 87–91. Copyright James Buchanan, 1986. First published in Great Britain in 1986 by Wheatsheaf Books Ltd., Brighton, Sussex. Reprinted by permission of Pearson Education Limited.

Material in this chapter was initially presented in a panel discussion at the Public Choice Society meeting in Savannah, Georgia, in March 1983.

"social justice," or the "glory of God"—there is no point in extending the argument prematurely to politics. That is to say, the required paradigm shift must have already occurred with respect to the conceptualization and understanding of the market before constructive dialogue can begin about politics.

Before getting into such dialogue, therefore, let me stay with the "market as process" and summarize what I mean and what I think that the Austrians mean, or should mean, when they make such reference. The market is an institutional process within which individuals interact, one with another, in pursuit of their separate individual objectives, whatever these may be. The great discovery of the eighteenth-century philosophers was that within appropriately designed laws and institutions separately self-interested individual behaviour in the market generates a spontaneous order, a pattern of allocational-distributional outcomes that is chosen by no one, yet which is properly classified as an order in that it reflects a maximization of the values of the participating persons. What these values are is defined only in the process itself; the individual values, as such, do not exist outside or independent of the process within which they come to be defined. In this sense, and in this sense only, can the order generated in the market process be labelled or classified as "efficient." Economists who presume some inherent ability to define that which is "efficient" independent of the behaviour of persons in the market process itself, a definition that is then utilized to evaluate the performance of the market as an institution, presume an arrogance that simply should not be countenanced.

Now let me return to two statements made above. I said that the market is an institutional process within which individuals interact, one with another, in pursuit of their separate individual objectives, whatever these may be, and that the great discovery of the eighteenth-century philosophers was that, *within appropriately designed laws and institutions*, separately self-interested behaviour in the market generates a spontaneous order. I then went on to say that this order reflects a maximization of individuals' values as these values are revealed in the process itself. What I want to emphasize here is that without the appropriate laws and institutions, which would include defined private property rights that are respected and/or enforced and procedures for guaranteeing enforcement of contracts, the market would not generate a spontaneous order embodying "efficiency" in any value-maximization sense, if indeed we could refer to "a market" at all. The spontaneous order of Hobbesian anarchy would not maximize individual values and presumably would come closer to value minimization. The point to be made here is that the behaviour of persons in any social interaction always takes place within a tension between at least two separately directed motivational pulls: between the furtherance of narrowly defined and short-term self-interest on the one hand and enlightened and long-term self-interest on the other, with the second behaviour described as embodying respect for the equal rights of others in the interaction process. (I shall leave other possible motivations, such as genuine altruism, out of account here.) That is to say, in any trade or exchange, the individual participant has a self-interested motivation to dissemble, to cheat, to defraud, and to default. Laws, customs, traditions, moral precepts—these are all designed and/or evolve to limit or control the exercise of such short-term self-interest. And the spontaneous order emergent from the market process maximizes separately conceived individual values *only* if these institutional constraints operate successfully.

Let me now turn to "politics as process" after the tour through what should have been familiar intellectual territory. The central point I want to make is that the complex exchange process of politics requires a much less familiar but precisely analogous set of institutional and/or moral constraints if the order emergent from such a process can be described as embodying any tendency at all towards the maximization of separately derived individual values. To think about this, return to the ever-present tension between narrow short-term self-interest and the enlightened self-interest that embodies respect for the rights of other participants in the interaction or exchange. Our ethos is such that the internal and external constraints on "deviant" self-interested behaviour in market exchange seem both natural and necessary. Honesty, as an attribute of exchange, is a quality that we acknowledge to be appropriately encouraged by internally applicable moral codes and by externally imposed legal sanctions. There is no comparable encouragement of a quality in political "exchange" that corresponds to "honesty" in market dealings. To be sure, there are both moral and legal sanctions against overt bribery and corruption, but these activities are miniscule in relation to the departures from what we might call "honesty" in political exchange in a sense at all comparable to that summarized under this rubric in connection with market behaviour. Many of the activities that are, by common interpretation, acceptable within the range of modern politics would be classified as predatory if carried out in markets.

In the market I respect the ownership rights of the person with whom I trade, and vice versa. I do not defraud my exchange partner, and I do not default on my contractual obligations. My exchange partner behaves reciprocally. At least this pattern of behaviour describes the idealization of the market process that we spend our time analyzing. In politics, as we observe it, ownership rights are not respected, if indeed such rights can be said to be defined at all. In certain conceptualizations of politics, the polity, the state, seems to lay claim to all values nominally held by its citizens, and, particularly, this putative claim is held to be "legitimate" if all citizens are somehow allowed access to equal voices in the ultimate determination of state decisions.

In Hobbesian anarchy there is no "mine and thine"; there are neither moral nor legal sanctions against my taking from you that value which I have the physical power to take. How is the modern state empirically any different? As envisaged by most modern political scholars as well as by practising politicians, there would be no discernible distinctions at this level. In such conceptualization, politics is not a complex exchange process, even in its most idealized perception.

Let me be clear that my concern here is not with politics as it operates as an observed institutional reality. My concern is with the idealization of politics, the basic model from which the empirical reality may be conceptually derived. What would be required if politics is to be appropriately conceived as complex exchange analogous to that which takes place in the idealized market?

Clearly, it is possible to conceptualize a contractual process in which many separate persons, each endowed with a set of valued claims (to person and property) that is acknowledged by all others in the group, enter into agreement to establish a political community, the agency of which will be charged with the task of enforcing the terms of the contract along with other contractually designated functions. As I tried to trace out in my book *The Limits of Liberty* (1975), each person gains in such a contractual process.[1] There are mutual gains from trade fully analogous to those emergent in the idealized

1. James M. Buchanan, *The Limits of Liberty* (Chicago: Chicago University Press, 1975).

market. And, indeed, some such political contract is a necessary precondition for the establishment of the constraining laws and institutions without which the market process itself cannot function.

In this most fundamental idealization, therefore, *politics is a complex exchange process* fully analogous to the market. But both as it is observed to operate and as it is justified in modern political discourse, politics is not constrained to ensure that mutual gains emerge from the exchange. There are no well-recognized limits to behaviour in politics that act to ensure that individual values are separately maximized.

Even if the requirement for such constraints should be fully recognized, however, designing them is not the straightforward task it may seem. To ensure mutuality of advantage over all parties to the complex exchange of politics, a Wicksellian rule of unanimity would seem necessary. But such an inclusive decision rule would of course make political action almost impossible. Some departure from unanimity must be accepted, by all contracting parties, as the Buchanan-Tullock analysis in *The Calculus of Consent* (1962) was designed to demonstrate.[2] Once such a departure is in place, however, there is necessarily an opportunity offered to those who would use politics for predation, who would leap outside of any boundaries defined by the range of mutuality of advantage. The only means of keeping the potentially exploitative polity from following its natural tendency in this respect lies in contractual-constitutional constraints that restrict sharply the range of state activities and functions. Politics that is confined to a few and well-defined tasks cannot be seriously predatory.

The American founders seemed to recognize this simple truth. Modern political scholars do not. Through their continuing refusal and reluctance to conceptualize politics as a complex exchange process, even in its ideal form, modern political scholars offer varying apologies, justifications, or rationalizations for the predatory politics that we all observe. Such predation tends to be obscured by all discourse that interprets politics teleologically, as if, in some ideal image, politics is aimed at the furtherance of some transcendent, extra-individual purpose or objective, whether this be "truth," "efficiency," "goodness," "social justice," or "the glory of God."

---

2. James M. Buchanan and Gordon Tullock, *The Calculus of Consent* (Ann Arbor: University of Michigan Press, 1962).

The Austrian insight of the market as process tends to undermine the teleological interpretation of economic interaction, although many who call themselves modern Austrians do not seem to have totally recognized the normative implications of the process interpretation. Public choice, in its Wicksellian-contractarian-constitutionalist variant or component that idealizes politics as a complex exchange process, tends necessarily to undermine any teleological interpretation of political interaction, although many public choice economists do not seem to have totally recognized the normative implications of the process interpretation.

PART TWO

Public Choice and Its Critics

Is Public Choice Immoral? The Case for the "Nobel" Lie

Geoffrey Brennan and James Buchanan

> Cynical descriptive conclusions about behavior in government threaten to undermine the norm prescribing public spirit. The cynicism of journalists—and even the writings of professors— can decrease public spirit simply by describing what they claim to be its absence. Cynics are therefore in the business of making prophecies that threaten to become self-fulfilling. If the norm of public spirit dies, our society would look bleaker and our lives as individuals would be more impoverished. That is the tragedy of "public choice."
>
> —Steven Kelman, "Public Choice" and Public Spirit[1]

Public choice analysis—the application of the theoretical method and techniques of modern economics to the study of political processes—has come increasingly to popular attention in recent years. The 1986 Nobel Prize in economics is both a reflection of that increased attention and an occasion for it. It is only to be expected that such attention would focus on the simpler and/or more controversial aspects of public choice theory. In a sense, this is

From *Virginia Law Review* 74 (March 1988): 179–89. Reprinted by permission of the publisher.

A much earlier version of this paper was presented at the 1982 Annual Meeting of the Public Choice Society in San Antonio, Texas. We have been directly motivated to publish this revised version in partial response to the challenge by Steven Kelman in 87 *Public Interest* 80 (1987).

1. 87 *Public Interest* 80, 93–94 (1987).

what "good press" is all about. It is more surprising, and to some extent regrettable, that some of the allegedly "academic" evaluations have been similarly focused.

It has to be conceded that public choice theory *is* controversial, and not just because some of its predictions are counterintuitive or its methods of analysis unusual; the controversy goes well beyond the "scientific" level. There is an apparent accompanying conviction on the part of many commentators that the whole enterprise is *immoral* in a basic sense. Steven Kelman's discussion reveals this position nicely, as the initial quotation suggests. But Kelman's position is by no means unique.[2] It merely takes up an anxiety that has been aired on and off by orthodox welfare economists and mainstream political scientists ever since the public choice revolution began.[3]

To some extent, this anxiety is based on a misconception. Public choice theory has been widely touted as being *defined* by the attribution of *Homo economicus* motivations to actors in their political roles. *Homo economicus*—the wealth-maximizing egoist—should be seen to play no more significant a role in public choice analysis than in the whole program of economic theory more generally. And it is simply wrong to conceive of economics as nothing more than egoistic psychology. Also, as we have argued, there may be good reason to believe that *Homo economicus* may be descriptively somewhat less relevant in the political setting than in economic markets.[4] The more appropriate use of the *Homo economicus* construction is to further the normative exercise of investigating the incentive structures embodied in various institutional forms[5] rather than the descriptive exercise of providing predictions as to the likely outcomes of political interactions.

2. For a more strident example, see John Foster's review note of our monograph *Monopoly in Money and Inflation*, in which he accuses us of providing "another small step on the road to fascism." Foster, Book Note, 91 *Economic Journal* 1105 (1981).

3. See, e.g., Samuelson, "The World Economy at Century's End," 34 *Bulletin of the American Academy of Arts and Sciences* 44 (1981) (remarks about the tax revolt movement and those whom he sees as spawning it); Gordon, "The New Contractarians" (Book Review), 84 *Journal of Political Economy* 573 (1976). In his review of J. Buchanan, *The Limits of Liberty* (1976), Gordon said that "Buchanan's reasoning eschews any moral considerations of duty or obligation." Gordon, supra, at 585.

4. See G. Brennan and J. Buchanan, *The Reason of Rules* 48–51, 145 (1985).

5. A point that we have reiterated consistently. See id. at 46–66; G. Brennan and J. Bu-

But definitions of public choice are, for the purposes of the argument here, somewhat beside the point. In fact, Kelman's anxiety is ultimately independent of whether political agents can be accurately described by egoistic motivations. Whatever the reality, the logic of Kelman's claim is that the responsible political analyst should err on the side of the heroic. If cynicism destroys politically useful illusions, then equally romanticism within limits *fosters* those illusions. This aspect of Kelman's argument is then not an argument for science but an argument for illusion. It is an argument designed to supply *additional* weight to, over and above any descriptive scientific critique of, the *Homo economicus* postulate.

To this substantive charge we must, of course, plead guilty at least to this extent: although we do not believe that narrow self-interest is the *sole* motive of political agents, or that it is necessarily as relevant a motive in political as in market settings, we certainly believe it to be a significant motive. This differentiates our approach from the alternative model, implicit in conventional welfare economics and widespread in conventional political science, that political agents can be satisfactorily modeled as motivated solely to promote the "public interest," somehow conceived. *That* model we, along with all our public choice colleagues, categorically reject.

In doing so, however, whatever the scientific imperatives, we have to reckon with the moral implications. That is our object here—to investigate the substance of the morally based critique of public choice. To do this properly, it is useful to set the empirical/scientific issues on one side: we shall take our critics seriously on their own terms, and examine the purely *ethical* case against public choice scholarship.

Two related questions seem relevant to this ethical critique. The first deals with the consequences of public choice models for the actual or imputed behavior of persons as they act in political roles. To the extent that public choice analysis influences the behavior of political agents, is this behavioral response desirable? There are, in turn, two distinct dimensions to this first

chanan, "Predictive Power and the Choice Among Regimes," 93 *Economic Journal* 89, 90, 97–104 (1983) [hereinafter "Predictive Power"]; G. Brennan and J. Buchanan, "The Normative Purpose of Economic Science: Rediscovery of an Eighteenth Century Method," 1 *International Review of Law and Economics* 155, 159–63 (1981) [hereinafter "Normative Purpose"].

question. One involves the behavior of politicians-bureaucrats—those who exercise discretionary power within the given political order. The other involves the attribution of legitimacy by the citizen to that political order, and leads to the more general question of its stability and possibly to the feasibility of any long-term political order at all. Beyond this, there is the second question of whether public choice may not be "immoral" simply by virtue of its dispelling illusions about the nature of the political order, quite independent of any of its political consequences.

The final section of the paper will be devoted to what we may call a "moral defense" of public choice. As we shall argue, however, this defense depends on a prior specification of the purpose of public choice analysis— one that may not be endorsed, even if it is understood, by all our professional colleagues in public choice itself.

I. The Behavioral Consequences of Public Choice

A. POTENTIAL EFFECT ON POLITICAL ACTORS

One of this century's scientific advances has been the recognition that what is being observed may be influenced by the fact of observation. Problems emerge from this source in *all* sciences; they appear in many guises and have many ramifications. In this respect, however, there is an important distinction between the human and nonhuman sciences.

In the nonhuman sciences, the interactions are restricted to those between the observer and observed. John Kagel and his colleagues must take into account how their own behavior might influence the behavior of the rats they study.[6] But they need not worry at all about the influence of their research on *the behavior of other rats*. Other rats do not read or understand economists' conversations about rats; the behavior of those other rats will remain totally unaffected by the reporting of the results of the experiments or by new analyses "explaining" such results to economists.

In the human sciences, no strict boundary between individuals who are observed and those who are not can be drawn for such purposes. Persons

6. See, as one example of their work, Kagel, Battalio, Rachlin, and Green, "Demand Curves for Animal Consumers," 91 *Quarterly Journal of Economics* 1 (1981).

read research reports; they listen to social scientists talk about experiments; they understand and interpret models of behavior imputed to others of their species. And this fact matters scientifically to the extent that the reading of such reports and the consequent changes in people's understanding of themselves influence human behavior. It matters *normatively* to the extent that those changes in behavior have morally relevant consequences.

Second, and somewhat more subtly, ideas may change values themselves. Two examples may help here. Suppose that some Kinsey-like report has revealed that, in fact, over seventy percent of married couples in the United States indulge in some sexual practice commonly believed to be decidedly eccentric and perhaps morally somewhat dubious. It seems plausible to suggest that the release of this information may serve to change sexual standards in the direction of this practice: the "facts" somehow serve to legitimize the practice. The charge that "everyone does it" is normally regarded as at least a presumptive argument in favor of "doing it" oneself. As a second example within social science itself, one might hazard the conjecture that economists (at least those with a strong "price theory" orientation) are more likely to act like the *Homo economicus* model they work with than are others not blessed with the "economist's way of thinking." This involves, in many cases, not only a greater attentiveness to the costs and benefits of alternative actions (particularly the financially measurable ones), but also a sort of cultivated hard-nosed crassness towards anything that smacks of the "higher things of life."

Suppose that we acknowledge this possibility—that analysis of social interactions in *Homo economicus* terms influences individuals towards behaving more in the way persons are *modeled* to behave. In the context of well-functioning markets, this prospect may be of little normative concern. Within the market, self-interested behavior, given the appropriate legal constraints, does not necessarily inhibit "social interest" and may indeed further it. In this institutional setting, any legitimizing of self-interest that economic theory provides need have no moral consequences of any significance.

In extending the application of the *Homo economicus* model to political contexts, however, any comparable response in the behavior of political actors may be of considerable normative account. Scientific enquiry—whether in the form of formal analysis or of the application of empirical tests to relevant hypotheses—may, in using the *Homo economicus* construct to "explain" the workings of political processes, tend to further the notion that the be-havior so modeled is the norm. To the critics, the very structure of enquiry here may serve to legitimize such behavior for those who exercise discretion-ary power in political roles. Voters, lobbyists, politicians, and bureaucrats may face reduced public expectations of their behavior—standards of public life will be eroded, and persons in these roles may predictably lower their own standards in response. Such moral constraints as do apply to political behavior will be reduced by the spread of the conception that most persons, when in such roles, seek only private interest, and that such behavior is all that can reasonably be expected. However, because there is no invisible hand operative in majoritarian political institutions analogous to that operative in the market setting, any lapse in political morality is of normative signifi-cance.

Even if the explanatory power of public choice models of politics is ac-knowledged, therefore, the moral spillovers of such models on the behavior of political actors may be deemed to be so important as to negate any purely "scientific" advance made in our understanding of how politics actually works. The maintenance of the standards of public life, it could be argued, may require a heroic vision of the "statesman" or "public servant," because only by holding such a vision can the possibility of public-interested behav-ior on the part of political agents be increased. The empirical evidence may suggest that any such vision remains decidedly utopian, yet the effects on the morality of those who occupy positions of political power may still be held to override all such factual evidence. Hence, so the argument would go, those who engage in the ideas of politics must preserve a calculated hypocrisy about the conduct of political affairs, and they must talk only in terms of "ideal types." They must explicitly eschew the dull "scientific" talk of sordid realities; they must lift their gaze to the "good, beautiful, and true." The con-sequences for a tolerably acceptable political life in failing to keep this essen-tial faith become potentially disastrous.

This argument deserves to be taken seriously, despite its apparent vulner-ability to caricature when viewed from the "scientific" perspective. More-over, we think that at some subliminal level, the force of the argument is well recognized. Suppose, for example, that a public choice economist or political scientist is asked to talk to a group of young persons in training for employ-ment in the bureaucracy. On what aspects of public choice would he or she focus? On explaining how to manipulate agendas? On showing how to maximize the size of an agency's budget? The public choice analyst would probably soft-pedal the cynical edges, and focus more on the prospects for institutional reform than on the maximization of career prospects.

More generally, consider the role of the public choice analyst in a setting where no change in the structure of political organization is considered to be possible. In this case, the only possible impact on policy outcomes lies in powers of persuasion over people who hold positions of political power. If all such persons are self-interested wealth-maximizers, the entire *raison d'être* of proffering policy advice collapses. Those who either actually or putatively offer advice to politicians must model their targets as something *other* than wealth-maximizers. We should hardly be surprised, therefore, when our political-establishment colleagues (indeed all those who do not understand, or have no taste for, the prospect of institutional reform) treat public choice as the heresy it is for their own church.

B. ILLUSION AND THE CITIZEN

To this point, we have focused on the possible feedback effects that public choice ideas may exercise on the behavior of "professionals" in the political process—effects that may well be judged undesirable by common normative standards.

The recognition of such consequences does not, of course, carry direct implications for the pursuit of scientific enquiry. But scientific enquiry embodies its own moral values—a belief in the value of knowledge for its own sake and predisposition towards the view that science is, on balance, "productive." In certain contexts, the importance of these values may be debatable.

We may agree that public choice analysis allows us to see politics without blinders. In that sense, we play the role of the boy who called attention to the emperor's nakedness. But the familiar story might be given quite a different twist if it went on to relate that the emperor fell into disgrace, that the nobles fought among themselves, that the previously stable political order crumbled into chaos, and that the kingdom was destroyed. The moral might then have been *not* that one should call a spade a spade, whatever the possible consequences, but rather that a sensitivity to consequences may require one to be judicious in exposing functionally useful myths.

In this argument, there are echoes of the Hobbesian concern about the precariousness of stable political order. Cynicism about the behavior of political agents, however empirically justified it may be, may wreak damage to the "civic religion." This is a danger that any enquiry into political arrangements must acknowledge. As scientists, we consider it our purpose to destroy myths. But we should recognize that the "myths of democracy" may be essential to maintenance of an underlying popular consent of the citizenry to be governed, in the absence of which no tolerable stable political order is possible.

The late-1981 action in which, by an amendment to a totally different piece of legislation, members of Congress substantially reduced their income tax liability[7] exemplifies the problem in a practical way. This action will surely induce ordinary taxpayers everywhere to become less moral in their own behavior vis-à-vis the Internal Revenue Service. In the United States, income tax arrangements continue to depend in large measure on taxpayer honesty—a dependence that makes effective income taxation infeasible in many countries. Public choice theory, in itself, does not induce politicians to behave as tax avoiders: it is not *responsible* for the recent tax change. But the theory does hold such cases up as being of the essential nature of political process, rather than an unfortunate and regrettable lapse. Public choice theory gives coherence and meaning to such events by providing an understanding of political process in the light of them. And this sort of understanding is not conductive to taxpayer honesty or to the good functioning of stable government, more generally.

As any good public choice theorist recognizes, *some* discretionary political power will remain in the hands of some political agents even under the best of feasible institutional arrangements: constraints are costly, and we must make the best of what we have. Economists are familiar with the proposition that not all "problems" are problems—that resources are limited, including "resources" of good will, altruism, honesty, and the like. In a world where political institutions were "optimal" in some sense, what useful purpose would it serve to destroy popular illusions about those institutions?

There is, of course, an aspect of the myth-destruction exercise that goes

---

7. See "Black Lung Benefits Revenue Act of 1981," Pub. L. No. 97–119, § 113, 95 Stat. 1635, 1641–43 (1981) (codified at I.R.C. § 280A [1982 & Supp. IV 1986]); see also *N.Y. Times*, Dec. 17, 1981, at B14, col. 3 (discussing passage of the provision that made it easier for members to deduct living expenses).

beyond the possible destruction of civic order. That is the more direct question of the ethics of destroying illusions—even when there is *no* behavioral response. As Eugene O'Neill's *The Iceman Cometh*[8] emphasizes, the destruction of illusion in and of itself without the offering of hope may be grossly immoral: it directly reduces individuals' perceived levels of welfare. The moral considerations involved in informing someone who has an incurable cancer of his condition, or in informing the recently bereaved and grieving widower that his wife had been having affairs for twenty years behind his back, do not obviously commend the virtues of "truth at all costs." Knowledge without hope, science without a conviction that it can lead to a better life—these are by no means unambiguously value-enhancing, and those who shatter illusions for the sheer pleasure of doing so are not so clearly to be applauded for their "work."

II. Public Choice in Constitutional Perspective

Public choice—the hardheaded, realistic, indeed cynical model of political behavior—can be properly defended on moral grounds if we adopt a "constitutional perspective"—that is, if the purpose of the exercise is conceived to be institutional reform, improvements in the *rules* under which political processes operate. This perspective requires that we shift attention away from the analysis of policy choice by existing agents within *existing* rules, and towards the examination of alternative sets of rules. Improvement, or hope for improvement, emerges not from any expectation that observed agents will behave differently from the way the existing set of incentives leads them to behave, but from a shift in the rules that define these incentives. The public choice theorist does not envisage his "science" as offering a base for "preaching to the players" on how to maximize welfare functions. His task is not the Machiavellian one of advising governors, directly or indirectly, on how they ought to behave. His task is that of advising all citizens on the working of alternative constitutional rules.

8. E. O'Neill, *The Iceman Cometh* (1940), Henrik Ibsen's play *The Wild Duck* (1884) deals with the same problem with a more consequentialist orientation. Edward Albee's *Who's Afraid of Virginia Woolf?* (1962) deals with a similar issue, though ultimately with a more optimistic "triumph-of-truth-in-spite-of-everything" sort of flavor.

We suggest that this methodological stance is that which informed both the classical political economists and the political philosophers of the eighteenth century.[9] Within such a perspective, the delusion that political agents are saints becomes costly folly. Politics can be reformed without depending on moral suasion of kings and princes. The burdens of politics can be minimized independent of agent motivation.

What is the appropriate model of man to be incorporated in the comparative analysis of alternative constitutional rules? In our response to this question, we follow the classical economists explicitly, and for precisely the reasons they stated.[10] We model man as a wealth-maximizer, not because this model is necessarily the most descriptive empirically, but because we seek a set of rules that will work well independent of the behavioral postulates introduced.

From our perspective, then, we agree that there is cause for some concern with public choice interpreted as a predictive model of behavior in political roles. Where public choice is used to develop a predictive theory of political processes in a manner typical of "positive economics"—that is, with the focus solely on developing an empirically supportable theory of choice *within* rules, and with the ultimate normative purpose of constitutional design swept away in footnotes or neglected altogether—then the danger is that it will indeed breed the moral consequences previously discussed.

The attainment of the "constitutional perspective" is by no means easy, surprising as that may be. It is somehow "unnatural" to many scholars, orthodox and otherwise. But what is intriguing in this connection is that the most intense resistance to public choice analysis arises from precisely those

9. For discussion of this hypothesis, see "Predictive Power," supra note 5, at 89; "Normative Purpose," supra note 5, at 163–64.

10. See, e.g., D. Hume, "On the Independency of Parliament," in 3 *The Philosophical Works* 117–18 (T. Greene and T. Grose eds. 1898 and photo. reprint 1964) (1742) ("[I]n contriving any system of government, and fixing the several checks and controuls of the constitution, every man ought to be supposed a *knave*, and to have no other end, in all his actions, than private interest."); J. S. Mill, "Considerations on Representative Government," in 29 *Collected Works of John Stuart Mill* 505 (J. Robson ed. 1977) (1867) ("[T]he very principle of constitutional government requires it to be assumed, that political power will be abused to promote the particular purposes of the holder; not because it always is so, but because such is the natural tendency of things, to guard against which is the especial use of free institutions.").

critics who cannot think in terms of constitutional alternatives. For such critics, it is apparently impossible to conceive of institutional arrangements within which political agents are constrained. They must then face a genuine dilemma: they must either model political man as he is and live with Schumpeterian despair, or model man as he "should be" and seek to make their dreams come true. Should we really be surprised that so many choose the second of these options?

Foundational Concerns
A Criticism of Public Choice Theory

I. Introduction

I have had difficulty in developing a coherent argument that would properly express my intuitions about some of the foundational principles of public choice, and particularly about some of the normative implications drawn from these principles. As I have tried variously to organize the argument here, differing issues of peripheral relevance have kept intruding, leading me off on tangents to the central set of ideas. Finally, I have come to the conclusion that I had best start with a statement of concern about the normative implications themselves and then work my way back through some of the foundational analytics. I shall do so, in part, by tracing out the route taken by my own thinking over a two-year period of inquiry.

Most inclusively defined, my concern is about "democracy," if this general form of political organization is taken to mean "majority rule." Specifically, my concern is about the understanding that "majority rule," as an institution through which collectivities select among alternatives that are binding on all members of the group, tends to generate results that are somehow expressive of median values, that it tends to compromise among potential extreme limits, that it does not, in its nature, allow for overt exploitation of one group by another.[1]

From *Current Issues in Public Choice*, ed. José Casas Pardo and Friedrich Schneider (Cheltenham, U.K.: Edward Elgar, 1995), 3–20. Reprinted by permission of the publisher.

I am indebted to my colleague professor Hartmut Kliemt of Duisburg, Germany, for helpful corrections in an initial draft.

1. Note that my concern is exclusively with the evaluation of majority rule *within* the public choice research program. I do not here include the more traditional interpretation of politics as the search for the "truth," an interpretation in which majority rule, or any rule, takes on a totally different meaning.

I think that this whole panoply of evaluative judgement about majoritarian processes is totally misguided. By its nature, majority rule means what it says: *rule by the majority*. And conversely rule by the majority means that the minority is ruled, is coerced into acceptance of states of affairs that its members do not prefer. This most elementary and central feature of majority rule has been obscured in formal public-social choice theory through the over-concentration of attention on the possibility that no political equilibrium exists. Little attention has been paid to the characteristics of majoritarian equilibria, as such, in situations where these positions do, in fact, exist. And, almost universally, analysis has proceeded on the presumption that the ultimate objects (motions, candidates, platforms, policies) among which selection must be made, are themselves exogenous to the process of selection itself. There has been an oversight of the elementary principle that majority rule, in itself, operates to define the set of alternatives among which collective "choice" is made.

II. Diagonals

Some two years ago I commenced playing with simple two-by-two game matrices as a novel way (for me) of approaching majority voting. Take the familiar prisoners' dilemma (PD) setting (Figure 1.1) in which the separate and

		B	
		W_2	W_1
A	W_2	I 3, 3	II 1, 4
	W_1	III 4, 1	IV 2, 2

Figure 1.1. Classic PD

individually rational choices made by two players produce a result that neither desires. The PD solution is Pareto-dominated by the jointly cooperative solution. In this setting, each player has an incentive to enter into a binding contract that will effectively enforce the mutually desired solution. A constitutional agreement to collectivize the activity in question seems dictated, along with the adoption of a rule of unanimity for actually making the choice of activity for each player.

Suppose, however, that the activities of the two players are collectivized as an initial step. Players can no longer make separate choices concerning their own activities. But now suppose that instead of a unanimity rule the collective choice over the activities of all players is to be settled by majority voting. The analogue to majority voting in the strict two-person setting is a coin toss to determine which player is allowed to make the choice for both. It is clear from the structure of the interaction that this rule will not generate the Pareto-superior outcome. This constitutional scheme will produce a result in one or the other of the off-diagonal cells, in each of which the level of activity of the two players differs along with the payoffs. The choice is no longer made as between two cells on the diagonal, where the activities are necessarily symmetric, but as among four cells, only two of which involve symmetry in behavior. And note that under this coin-toss (majority) rule one of the two players is actually placed in a position less desirable than in the initial PD solution. (This result is guaranteed by the ordering of the ordinal payoffs that generates the PD.) If there is uncertainty concerning prospects for in-period success and/or some risk-averseness, neither player would be likely to agree to collectivization under majority rule.

A distinction must be made, however, between the *domain* for collective action and the decision-making *rule* for selection of a position within this domain. The two-person matrix illustration (Figure 1.1) allows this distinction to be readily observed. If the domain for potential collective action is restricted to positions that incorporate behavioral symmetry between the two players, the decision rule becomes significantly less important. In the particular example shown in Figure 1.1, the two players are fully symmetrical in preferences. Hence if the domain for collective action is restricted to positions along the diagonal, the decision rule, *per se*, becomes irrelevant. A coin toss to choose the decision-maker for the group produces results identical to that which would be generated under a rule of unanimity.

If the participants (players) are not themselves symmetrical in preferences

	B	
	W$_2$	W$_1$
A W$_2$	I 3, 2	II 1, 4
W$_1$	III 4, 1	IV 2, 3

Figure 1.2. Non-dominance

(or endowments), the simple identity of results under differing rules will not hold. Consider the example depicted in Figure 1.2, with ordinal payoffs as indicated. Note that without symmetry in preferences in the two-person, two-strategy interaction the interaction is no longer that of the PD game. The separate and independent behavior on the part of the two players will generate, because of row and column dominance, the result in Cell IV. Suppose, now, that the interaction between the players is collectivized; no separate action on the part of either player is permitted; the collective "choice" involves the action to be taken by both players.

Consider, first, the coin toss to determine the decision-maker as an analogue to simple majority rule. The results are identical to those in the example depicted in Figure 1.1; the solution in either Cell II or III will be chosen; one of the two players will be maximally exploited, and the position for this player will be worse than that attained under individualized adjustment.

Consider, next, the possible operation of a rule of unanimity. In this case, note that there will not be convergence to agreement. All of the positions are Pareto-optimal. If anarchy is the starting point, the solution in Cell IV is present, and no change will be agreed upon by both persons. If any other position is the starting point, no unanimous agreement on change will be possible.

Suppose, however, that the parties agree, in advance, to a constitutional constraint on the domain of possible solutions. Suppose that only behaviorally symmetrical solutions are permissible; positions along the diagonal (Cells I and IV are the only ones that qualify). Now, with this constraint operative, think again of the coin toss for the choice of decision-maker, again treated as the analogue to majority voting. Here the position will be either Cell I or IV, depending on which player wins the toss. And in a series of such tosses, we could think of the collective solution rotating as between these two cells. Note that in this case the person who differentially prefers the anarchistic equilibrium to jointly cooperative action will never agree to a constitutional order that incorporates majority rule.

III. Increasing the Number of Behavioral Alternatives

SYMMETRY IN PREFERENCES

Consider a setting with two persons, as before, but now allow for three rather than only two behavioral options. Consider, first, a model with full symmetry in preferences, as depicted now in Figure 1.3. (As an illustration, think of two neighboring farmers in David Hume's example, with the behavioral alternatives described as inputs toward drainage of the swampy commons.)[2] Under anarchy, or individualistic adjustment, the solution in Cell IX emerges, generated by row and column dominance, as in the earlier models.

Suppose, now, that the interaction is collectivized under a coin-toss rule for selecting the decision-maker. In this case, a solution in either Cell III or VII emerges. And, if there is some constitutionally required "electoral" sequence, we should predict possible rotation as between these two extreme solutions. If the interaction is, by contrast, collectivized under a decision rule of unanimity, both parties may agree to shift from the individual adjustment equilibrium in Cell IX to the symmetrical payoff solution in Cell I.

Suppose, in another model, that the interaction is collectivized, as before, but that the constitution restricts solutions to those that embody behavioral symmetry on the parts of the two players; that is, all acceptable solutions

2. D. Hume, *A Treatise of Human Nature*, ed. L. A. Selby-Bigge, 2d ed., revised P. H. Nidditch (Oxford: Clarendon Press, 1978).

		B		
		W_2	W_1	W_0
	W_2	I	II	III
		6, 6	2, 7	−2, 7
A	W_1	IV	V	VI
		7, 2	3, 3	−1, 4
	W_0	VII	VIII	IX
		8, −2	4, −1	0, 0

Note: In cardinal utility units, the value of each unit of output (produced by a unit of input) is constant at 4 "utils"; the value of each unit of input is constant at 5 "utils."

Figure 1.3. Three-option PD

must lie along the diagonal in Figure 1.3. Suppose, further, that within this restriction, the rule is that of the coin toss to determine who is the decision-maker. In this case, the symmetrical solution in Cell I will emerge, regardless of which person "wins" the coin toss. Majority rule and the unanimity rule tend to generate identical outcomes.

NON-SYMMETRICAL PREFERENCES

This conclusion is changed if we drop the assumption of symmetry in ordinal preference rankings. Consider the ordinal payoff structure depicted in Figure 1.4. As before, the individual adjustment equilibrium is attained in Cell IX. Under collectivization with the coin toss to choose the decision-maker, the solution rotates between Cells III and VII, as before. But under collectivization with a unanimity rule there is no unique solution embodying behavioral symmetry, despite the fact that both Cells I and V are Pareto-superior to Cell IX.

But now consider collectivization with solutions constitutionally restricted to those along the diagonal, reflecting behavioral symmetry. Under the coin toss, a result in either Cell I or V will emerge, depending on the identity of the

B

		W_2	W_1	W_0
	W_2	I 6, 2	II 2, 7	III $-2, 8$
A	W_1	IV 7, -2	V 3, 3	VI $-1, 4$
	W_0	VII 8, -6	VIII 4, -1	IX 0, 0

Note: In cardinal utility units, values are the same for *A* as in Figure 1.3. The value of output for *B* is the same as in Figure 1.3. The value of the first input unit supplied is 5, and the second unit is 9.

Figure 1.4. Three-option PD, non-symmetrical

decision-makers, and, over a sequence of "elections," we should predict some rotation between these two outcomes.

Note, however, that in this two-person, three-alternative model, as depicted in Figure 1.4, both players will agree to collectivize the activity in question, even under the coin-toss procedure of choosing who makes the collective decision, provided that the solutions are constitutionally restricted to those that lie along the diagonal. Person *A* (or *B*) will expect to be better off under collectivization of the interaction, even if the decision rule is predicted to go against his/her preferences most of the time. (Recall that this conclusion could not have emerged in the two-alternative model considered above.)

Note also, however, that neither person would seem likely to agree initially to collectivization of the interaction under the coin toss unless the generality requirement is constitutionally guaranteed. Without such a guarantee, the potential loser would expect, in each period, to be made worse off than under the anarchistic equilibrium.[3]

---

3. If a single player anticipates that the gains from being the "exploiter" exceed the losses from being "exploited," given the probabilities of being in these two roles, along

B

	W_1 C		W_0 C	
	W_1	W_0	W_1	W_0
	I	II	III	IV
A W_1				M
	$2, 2, 2$	$-1, -1, 6$	$-1, 6, -1$	$-4, 3, 3$
	V	VI	VII	VIII
W_0		M	M	
	$6, -1, -1$	$3, -4, 3$	$3, 3, -4$	$0, 0, 0$

Note: In cardinal utility units, the value of unit of output is 3; unit of input is 7.

Figure 1.5. Three-person PD

IV. Three Players, Two Behavioral Alternatives

In this section, largely for analytical completeness, I shall revert to the two-alternative model, but now I shall increase the number of interactors from two to three.[4] The illustrative ordinal payoff matrix is shown in Figure 1.5. Many of the earlier results carry over. Symmetry in preferences is initially assumed, and the individual adjustment equilibrium is located in Cell VIII, by the dominance relationship. Collectivization of the activity under non-restricted majoritarianism will generate one of the solutions marked **M** in Figure 1.5, each of which will involve differential gains to two of the players at the partial expense of the third. Each of these **M** positions dominates the symmetrical payoff result in Cell I for two of the three players. If explicitly considered, such non-restricted majoritarianism is unlikely to secure constitutional authorization.

---

with assigned values for risk preference, he or she may prefer coin-toss collectivization to anarchy. But only with wildly divergent assessment of probabilities along with risk preference for both parties would agreement emerge on collectivization here.

4. This model has been used for a different purpose in my paper "A Defense of *Noblesse Oblige:* Reluctantly Offered" (Center for Study of Public Choice, George Mason University, Fairfax, Va., 1993, mimeographed).

	B			
	W_1		W_0	
	C		C	
	W_1	W_0	W_1	W_0
	I	II	III	IV
W_1				M
	$-1, -1, -1$	$-3, -3, 4$	$-3, 4, -3$	$-5, 2, 2$
W_0	V	VI	VII	VIII
		M	M	
	$4, -3, -3$	$2, -5, 2$	$2, 2, -5$	$0, 0, 0$

Note: In cardinal utility units, the value of inputs is constant at 7 "utils"; the value of output produced by each unit of input is constant at 2 "utils."

Figure 1.6. Three persons, no PD

Restriction of solutions to those that exhibit behavioral symmetry elimi-nates all of those shown in Figure 1.5 except Cells I and VIII. And, of course, the solution in Cell I will be chosen in this framework, regardless of the de-cision rule. And, clearly, all players are better off under collectivization with the proviso that solutions must lie along the diagonal.

A highly abstracted model such as that depicted in Figure 1.5 can also be used to demonstrate that unrestricted majoritarianism can produce undesir-able results even in those settings where collectivization of an activity is not indicated to be preferable on application of any Pareto norm. Consider Fig-ure 1.6, and note that the solution in Cell VIII now dominates that in Cell I for all three players. Further, the Cell VIII solution emerges from individual adjustment, as before. There is no dilemma-like "inefficiency" to be cor-rected. Note, however, that the operation of non-restricted majoritarianism will still produce one of the **M** solutions, since each of these dominates the Cell VIII result for two of the three players. Unless constitutionally restricted, majority rule will operate to introduce rather than to correct for inefficiency in the interaction process.

V. The Conventional Starting Point

We seem to have taken up much space without yet getting to the starting point for elementary public choice theory, which commences its analysis with the three-person, three-object model. I suggest, however, that the whole of the standard exercise is naive in the sense that it proceeds with analysis prior to any examination of that which is being analyzed. Quite literally, conventional public choice theorists do not know what they are talking about. In particular, they postulate objects among which collective choice is to be made, as if these objects exist "out there," separate and apart from the interaction process and from any behavioral input on the part of the participants. Once this critical step is taken, it is then relatively straightforward to assume that individuals can order the alternative objects, in which case the problem becomes one of combining or amalgamating these orderings into a coherent ordering for the community.

But how do the objects or alternatives for potential collective choice actually come into being? What, precisely, is being ordered by the participants?

The simplified models treated earlier are helpful in answering these questions. Consider, again, the standard PD game as an analogue to the political game under majority voting. The *four* possible solutions can be ordered by the two players, and the *status quo* is well defined as that equilibrium that emerges from the actions of individuals taken separately. The matrix form is helpful in suggesting that any of the outcomes, themselves defined in terms of payoffs to the players, is produced by the combined actions of *both* players, not by any single player acting alone. A collective choice of a position on the matrix must, therefore, be translated into a selection of two simultaneous courses of action, one on the part of each player. If there are two behavioral options for each player, it follows that there must be four possible solutions to the interaction process itself. Abstractly considered, therefore, the PD analogue becomes a two-person, four-object model.

The ultimate objects for collective choice, the separate outcomes as defined in the matrix cells, must be carefully distinguished from the behavioral actions available to each player. The standard PD game is a two-person, two-strategy interaction; each of the two players has available two separate courses of possible action.

Under what conditions will two persons face only two (or three) objects for potential joint or collective choice? If they are *technologically* locked into a setting where there is an either-or choice to be made, there are no independent behavioral actions possible for either player. Example: prospective room-mates must indicate to the landlord, in advance, whether the room is to be painted blue or green. There is no individual adjustment equilibrium as the initial *status quo*; the two persons are technologically trapped into a relationship that is necessarily collectivized. And, if preferences differ, one or the other must put up with the non-preferred alternative. A coin toss to determine the decision-maker (the two-person analogue to majority voting) is one means of generating a collective result, which, in this case, is equivalent to a coin toss to determine the result itself.

Note that in this setting the matrix construction is inappropriate because the players face no behavioral alternatives. By the technological nature of the relationship, all solutions must, in some sense, lie along the diagonal. Off-diagonal positions violate the technological constraints. One room-mate cannot live in a blue room while the other lives in a green room.

As the "technological publicness" model is dimensionally extended to allow for $n(n > 2)$ persons $n(n > 2)$ objects for choice, we enter the starting gate for elementary public choice theory. To modify our example, consider three room-mates, A, B and C, and three possible paint colors, *blue*, *green* and *red*. The familiar results are applicable. Majority voting, as a decision rule, tends to generate the result preferred by the voters whose preferences are median for the group, provided that all preferences can be arrayed so as to exhibit single-peakedness. In the absence of this latter condition, majority voting will not produce an equilibrium, and a cyclical pattern will emerge over a series of pairwise voting choices.

Simultaneous consideration of two or more technologically collective relationships makes the prospect for cyclical patterns under majority voting almost certain to emerge. But the generalized implications that majority voting tends to generate results that reflect median preferences of the members of the voting group remain.

VI. Non-publicness Dimensions

I suggest that the basic public choice exercise has been flawed by a failure to examine the objects for collective choice with sufficient care. As a result, the normative implications for the use of majority voting rules in narrowly defined settings of pure technological publicness have been inappropriately extended to other settings, where quite different implications should emerge. I submit that David Hume's example of neighboring farmers alongside the swampy commons yields more relevant insights than the room-mates faced with mutually exclusive choices among colors.

Politics in its more general sense is best conceived as a process of voluntary cooperation, in which individuals agree to join forces with the aim of accomplishing collectively those goals that are achieved only less effectively through private efforts. The boundaries for politics are determined by constitutional choices made by individuals rather than by some technological necessity. Technological considerations enter, of course, in any effort to choose rationally between the collectivized and the non-collectivized alternatives for the organization of activities. Even for those activities that exhibit pure or quasi-pure publicness (for example, drainage of the swamp), a collectivization decision must be made; some individualistic adjustment equilibrium describes the non-collectivized alternative.

Furthermore, even for those activities that involve pure or quasi-pure publicness, the achievement of any "social state" must involve actions on the part of persons that are "private." Even pure public goods must be produced, and production requires inputs which are private to those who supply them.[5] Recognition of this point suggests that there must exist behavioral options for each participant in the interaction that the activity represents. Once again, the two-by-two matrix of the PD analogue is helpful. Consider the individual adjustment equilibrium to be reached when neither of the two adjoining farmers takes action to drain the swampy common. For a specified input of effort on the part of each person, the mutually preferred solution in Cell I is reached. But the off-diagonal solutions are also possible, in each of which one of the persons is made worse off than in the independent adjustment equilibrium. These off-diagonal cells are described by differing inputs of the private "bad," namely, effort, even though the "good" (swamp drainage) remains purely public to both parties.

The presence of non-publicness, along any dimension, is the element that modifies dramatically the normative implications drawn from analysis of

---

5. James M. Buchanan, *Demand and Supply of Public Goods* (Chicago: Rand-McNally, 1968).

majority decision-making. To the extent that persons in a minority can be coerced by a dominant majority to take actions privately that are not also required for the members of the majority, the working of majoritarian processes may introduce consequences that are not preferred in a rational constitutional calculus, even by those who fully recognize that collectivization of a genuine publicness interaction might generate gains to all parties. Only if some requirement for generality in treatment is constitutionally enforced can it be predicted that majoritarian processes will work to increase rather than decrease social value.

VII. Numerical Illustration I: Symmetrical Preferences

I propose now to use yet another highly simplified numerical example to demonstrate the central thesis of this paper to those who remain unconvinced by the limitation of earlier analysis. In this section, I introduce a three-person model, one in which each person has available three possible courses of action: courses that may be chosen privately in the absence of collectivization or publicly (through the operation of a decision rule) under collective organization of the activity in question. I shall first present the model with fully symmetrical preferences among the three persons; in the following section, I examine the consequences of non-symmetrical preferences.

Figure 1.7 shows the numerical payoffs to each of the three persons, A, B and C, in each of the 27 possible outcomes or solutions of the interaction. For illustrative purposes, think of three farmers alongside Hume's swampy commons, with the separate behavioral alternatives, the Ws representing units of input supplied toward the production of the commonly shared or public good. The three dimensions of the interaction are collapsed into two dimensions by the inclusion within each matrix cell of three rows, each one of which represents a different course of action by the third player, C, ranging from no action (W_0) in the bottom row to the maximal provision of two units of input (W_2) in the top row. The payoffs in each triplet are arrayed in order for A, B and C.

The cardinalized numerical payoffs are computed from simple linear functions for the value of inputs (negative) and outputs (positive). Each person values each unit of input at 9 "utils" and values the output generated by each such unit at 4 "utils."

		B	
	W_2	W_1	W_0

A		W_2	W_1	W_0
	W_2	I **6, 6, 6** 2, 2, 11 −2, −2, 16	II 2, 11, 2 −2, 7, 7 −6, 3, 12	III −2, 16, −2 −6, 12, 3 −10, 8, 8 **M**
	W_1	IV 11, 2, 2 7, −2, 7 3, −6, 12	V 7, 7, −2 **3, 3, 3** −1, −1, 8	VI 3, 12, −6 −1, 8, −1 −5, 4, 4
	W_0	VII 16, −2, −2 12, −6, 3 8, −10, 8 **M**	VIII 12, 3, −6 8, −1, −1 4, −5, 4	IX 8, 8, −10 **M** 4, 4, −5 **0, 0, 0**

Note: In cardinal utility terms, each person values a unit of input supplied at 9 "utils" and a unit of output produced by a unit of input at 4 "utils." Rows in each cell reflect behavior of C, with Row 1 reflecting 2 units of W, Row 2 reflecting 1 unit and Row 3 reflecting 0 units.

Figure 1.7. Three-person, three-option PD

Under independent adjustment with no collectivization, no person will voluntarily supply inputs toward production of the shared good. The solution shown in Cell IX, Row 3 will emerge, again due to the dominance feature in the choice options faced by each player.

Assume, now, that the activity is collectivized; individuals no longer retain the option over the inputs to be supplied. The vector of inputs is now to be chosen by some collective decision process, and individuals must behave as this process dictates. Initially, assume that simple majority voting is the rule, and that there are no constitutionally imposed constraints on the range for majority action. In this situation, it is clear from inspection of Figure 1.7 that one of the three outcomes indicated by **M** will emerge, with the specific outcome being dependent on which coalition takes shape. Note that, in each of these possible majoritarian outcomes, one of the three persons, the minority member, is maximally exploited by members of the majority. This exploitation is made possible by the absence of constraints that prohibit differential or discriminatory treatment. In this setting, despite the acknowledged potential value of some action toward providing the commonly shared good,

persons at a stage of constitutional choice may find it rational to reject collectivization.

Consider now, however, the effects of a constitutional requirement that all
solutions embody generality in treatment among all persons, that all solutions lie along the relevant diagonal. There are three solutions that embody
full behavioral symmetry, those shown in boldface type in Figure 1.7. Note
that, as in the earlier models, with symmetrical preferences, the operation of
a majority voting rule and a unanimity rule will tend to generate equivalent
results. The solution in Cell I will be chosen and, further, under the generality restriction, the collectivization of the activity will tend to be supported
unanimously at the constitutional stage.

VIII. Numerical Illustration II:
Non-symmetrical Preferences

The decision rule becomes relevant when preferences are not symmetrical,
even if there are constitutional restrictions on differential treatment. Consider the payoff matrix in Figure 1.8. Again there are three persons, A, B and
C. Each person confronts four possible courses of action, indicated by the
matrix rows for A, the columns for B and the within-cell rows for C. As before, dominance insures that independent adjustment equilibrium is located
in Cell XVI, Row 4, in which no person supplies any input toward production of the commonly shared good. If the activity is collectivized and unrestricted majority rule is allowed to operate, one of the three solutions
marked by **M** in Figure 1.8 will emerge, each one of which involves maximal
exploitation of one person by the two-person majority. And, in some "electoral" sequence, a shifting among the three majoritarian outcomes might be
predicted to occur. (The single-peakedness requirement for equilibrium is
not strictly met.) Note that under many sets of probabilities about coalition
formation, individuals may never agree to collectivization of the activity if
given an initial constitutional choice, even though they fully recognize the
potentiality of securing the publicness benefits. The prospects for distributional exploitation under the operation of unrestricted majority rule may
more than offset the positively valued prospects for distributional and publicness gains. Note that, in this framework, majority coalitions, or political
entrepreneurs who put together and act for such coalitions, must propose

B

		W₃	W₂	W₁	W₀
		I	II	III	IV
	W₃	**9, 5, 2**	5, 14, −2	1, 19, −6	−3, 24, −10
		5, 1, 11	1, 10, 7	−3, 15, 3	−7, 20, −1
		1, −3, 20	−3, 6, 16	−7, 11, 12	−11, 16, 8
		−3, −7, 24	−7, 2, 20	−11, 7, 16	−15, 12, 12 **M**
A		V	VI	VII	VIII
	W₂	14, 1, −2	10, 10, −6	6, 15, −10	2, 20, −14
		10, −3, 7	**6, 6, 3**	2, 11, −1	−2, 16, −5
		6, −7, 16	2, 2, 12	−2, 7, 8	−6, 12, 4
		2, −11, 20	−2, −2, 16	−6, 3, 12	−10, 8, 8
		IX	X	XI	XII
	W₁	19, −3, −6	15, 6, −10	11, 11, −14	7, 16, −18
		15, −7, 3	11, 2, −1	7, 7, −5	3, 12, −9
		11, −11, 12	7, −2, 8	**3, 3, 4**	−1, 8, 0
		7, −15, 16	3, −6, 12	−1, −1, 8	−5, 4, 4
		XIII	XIV	XV	XVI
	W₀	24, −7, −10	20, 2, −14	16, 7, −18	12, 12, −22 **M**
		20, −11, −1	16, −2, −5	12, 3, −9	8, 8, −13
		16, −15, 8	12, −6, 4	8, −1, 0	4, 4, −4
		12, −19, 12 **M**	8, −10, 8	4, −5, 4	**0, 0, 0**

Note: The numbers in the payoff matrix indicate "utils." These numbers are derived as follows: (1) for all three persons *A*, *B* and *C*, the value placed on the output produced by a single unit of input (from any person) remains at 4 "utils" over the whole range of supply; (2) for individual *A*, a unit of input supplied is valued negatively at 9 "utils," which is constant over the whole range of supply; (3) for individual *B*, the first two units of input are supplied at a value of 9 "utils" each; a third unit is valued at 13 "utils"; (4) for individual *C*, the first input unit is valued at 8 "utils"; the second and third inputs are valued at 13 "utils" each.

Figure 1.8. Three-person, four-option PD

the **M** solutions for consideration. They cannot survive against potential competitors if they propose alternatives that are detrimental to members of their own coalition.[6]

Consider, however, the change in the model that might be produced by an enforceable constitutional prohibition on discriminatory treatment for mem-

6. James M. Buchanan, "How Can Constitutions Be Designed So That Politicians Who Seek to Serve 'Public Interest' Can Survive?" *Constitutional Political Economy* 4, no. 1 (Winter 1993): 1–6.

bers of the minority. In this case, the solutions must embody behavioral symmetry; the eligible outcomes must be located along the relevant diagonal. Only *four* of the possible 64 outcomes qualify for consideration under this restriction, those in boldface type in Figure 1.8.

Note that, because of the asymmetry in individual preferences, these four positions will be ordered differently by the three players. Individual *A* will prefer that solution in which each person supplies three units of input; individual *B* will prefer that each supply two units; and individual *C* will prefer that each supply only one unit of input to the production of the commonly shared good. A majority voting rule will, in this situation, generate the outcome indicated in Cell VI, that which is most preferred by individual *B*. Among the small set of possible outcomes that exhibit behavioral symmetry, this outcome is that which is median for the whole constituency. And, as depicted in the illustrative example here, all preferences are single-peaked. The outcome in Cell VI is a stable majority equilibrium. It seems also worth noting that, in the median outcome as generated from the majority voting process, as restricted, more of the public good is produced than in the cells of the non-constitutional majoritarian cycle. The effect of the generality requirement is to increase the production of the commonly shared good.

The conventional analysis of public choice theory re-emerges in this setting, but only after the constitutional generality requirement is in place. Some of those theorists who developed earlier models of majority voting may have, implicitly, assumed that the objects for collective choice did embody generality properties; for example, genuinely public goods financed by general taxes. The necessary distributional thrust of majority rule in the absence of the quite restrictive constitutional requirements indicated does not seem to have entered the early inquiries. The dynamics of the majoritarian voting process seem to be quite different in the non-constrained and constrained setting. In the latter, the small (relatively) set of fully symmetrical alternatives may be said to exist independent of the process of selection. In the non-constrained setting, by contrast, the critical stage is the formation of the majority coalition itself. Once a coalition is established, that alternative emerges which will maximize returns to its members.

Figure 1.8 is also helpful in suggesting that, if the constitutional prohibition of discriminatory treatment is in place, all parties may find it rational to support the initial collectivization of the activity, regardless of the subjective probabilities assigned to prospects for being successful in securing membership in majority coalitions.

IX. In the "Public Interest"

I acknowledge that the simplified numerical illustration of Section VIII is constructed deliberately to demonstrate my central thesis, which is that conventional public choice analysis of majority voting yields misleading normative implications. Unless it is constitutionally constrained in its operation by some semblance of a generality requirement, majority voting remains vulnerable to the distributional motivations of differentially interested members of political factions or coalitions. Any meaningful promotion of "public interest" is necessarily sacrificed in the process. I suggest that the elementary construction allows us to get some way toward a more meaningful definition of "public interest," while remaining within individualistic limits for evaluation. Under the constitutional requirement of generality in treatment, as between members of the majority and those of the minority, the considerations of alternatives for collective choice may be described as a search for "public interest." As the example indicates, persons may differ on the ultimate definition. Nonetheless, so long as the constitution guarantees symmetry in treatment, the argument can proceed without the intrusion of differential distributional interests, as such.

I also claim that the analytical models presented in this paper provide a more relevant introduction to what democratic politics is all about than those models used to introduce elementary public choice theory more conventionally. The organizing metaphor for my thoughts is that of Hume's swampy commons, in which persons face choices as to how many inputs to supply toward the production of the genuinely public good. The alternatives for collective choice do not exist without production; these alternatives are not analogous to the choice of paint colors for a room. "Publicness without cost" is not characteristic of the politics of democracy.

As presented in the models of this paper, I have presumed that the publicness feature, whether this be technologically or institutionally generated, applies to the positively valued or benefits side of the choice process. Generality in the availability of benefits from the commonly shared facility is assumed throughout. The potential for distributional differentiation lies wholly on the input supply side; different persons may be subjected to different treatment in their coerced and separated supplies of inputs. It is clear that the relationship between the two sides of the benefits-cost account could be reversed without difficulty. If generality is imposed on the cost side, differential distributional interests that satisfy majority coalition members may be promoted on the spending or benefits side of the political account. And, of course, generality may be violated simultaneously on both the benefits and the costs side; pork barrel spending projects may be financed by a differentially discriminatory tax structure.

X. The Meaning of Symmetry

It is easier to present an argument through the manipulation of abstract models than it is to make the further step that relates the analytical constructions to reality. It is straightforward enough to define what is meant by a violation of the generality norm in the previous illustrations. Symmetry in treatment is present when the separate actors in the game either voluntarily choose, or are coerced by a decision rule, to behave in the same way. I have used "behavioral symmetry" in the discussion as this term might be used in elementary game theory.

In the illustration depicted in Figure 1.8, the Ws represent supplies of inputs toward the production of the commonly shared good. Symmetry is present when different players offer the same quantity of inputs. But what if the different players are able to produce differing quantities of output with the same input, as measured in time units? Will equal inputs then satisfy or violate the symmetry norm?

We may relate this question specifically to the levy of taxes to finance a public good. Does symmetry require head taxes or flat-rate proportional taxes on income? In my view, an argument can be made to the effect that flat-rate proportionality meets the generality norm more adequately than the head tax. This conclusion does require resort to some base, such as time, as the ultimate measure for comparison. But, in any case, it is much easier to use the symmetry or generality criterion as a means of identifying violations than as a means of reaching a specific definition. Clearly, the elimination of some members of the polity from the tax rolls altogether violates the norm, as does the introduction of progressivity in the rate structure. Special benefit projects that secure their justification almost solely because of the make-up of the dominant majoritarian coalition equally violate the norm. And tariff or quota protection for particular industrial or product categories also fails the test.

The inability to be precise in the definition of equal or symmetrical treatment in the allocation of politically determined burdens and benefits should not be allowed to undermine the legitimacy of the principle of generality itself. At base, the cause for concern arises from the observed usage of the processes of majoritarian politics to promote the differential interests of members of majority coalitions at the expense of those in the minority. Departures from strict generality in treatment, on both sides of the account, may be permissible if such departures do not find their origins in commitments made during the process of coalition formation. But in the absence of enforceable constitutional constraints, majoritarian processes must, sooner or later, and to lesser or worse degree, succumb to distributional pressures.[7] And we should be under no illusions about distributional politics. As James Madison understood, the interplay among factions, each promoting its own interest at the expense of the common purpose of politics itself, is not compatible with liberal democracy.

As an end note, I can relate the analysis in this and other related recent papers to earlier works that were more directly inspired by Knut Wicksell.[8] The analytical starting point for the Wicksellian enterprise is the presumption that separate groups seek to further their own differential interests, and that, as a consequence, there is no relationship between majority voting rules and public sector efficiency, defined at either the public-private sector margin or within the public sector itself. Wicksell suggested that majority rule be

---

7. For an early treatment, see Marilyn Flowers and P. Danzon, "Separation of Redistributive and Allocative Functions of Government," *Journal of Public Economics* 24 (August 1984): 373–80.

8. James M. Buchanan and Gordon Tullock, *The Calculus of Consent: Logical Foundations of Constitutional Democracy* (Ann Arbor: University of Michigan Press, 1962); James M. Buchanan, *Public Finance in Democratic Process* (Chapel Hill: University of North Carolina Press, 1966); Buchanan, *Demand and Supply;* Knut Wicksell, *Finanztheoretische Untersuchungen* (Jena: Gustav Fischer, 1896).

replaced by a rule of unanimity or, in a practical setting, by a rule of qualified majority, up to five-sixths.

The Wicksellian proposal requires basic constitutional change in the voting rule. But the whole tradition of modern democracy elevates majority voting to center stage, and it is perhaps difficult to imagine that public attitudes would ever support the constitutional change required for a truly Wicksellian reform. If majority voting rules are recognized as institutional-historical parameters in the working of politics, the introduction of some version of the generality principle may serve as a substitute for more inclusive voting rules. And constitutional guarantees of symmetry in political treatment can be incorporated into the same general public wisdom that describes attitudes toward the comparable rule of law. In sum, my suggestion is that we extend to politics the same norm that has traditionally been extended to law.

Some "efficiency" is necessarily sacrificed by the imposition of any generality constraint. In some settings, asymmetry in treatment among separate persons and groups in the political community may be value-enhancing to all members, as might be evidenced by near-universal support—for instance, Sen's Lady Chatterley example.[9] But the slope becomes slippery indeed when the arms and agencies of politics are allowed to reward and punish particular groups on the basis of non-general criteria.

XI. Conclusion

I have subtitled this paper "A Criticism of Public Choice Theory." To present this criticism, I found it necessary to model the working of non-constrained majority rule, and to point toward the normative constitutional implications for reform. The majoritarian processes examined in the paper may seem to bear little resemblance to those that are found in conventional public choice analysis. In the latter, the alternatives for choice are not defined as outcomes that are produced by the provision of inputs by some or all of the participants. Instead, the "social states" from which choice is to be made are "out there," as mutually exclusive alternatives in some realm of potentiality, waiting to be evaluated in a calculus that cannot, due to the technology, be ex-

9. Amartya K. Sen, "The Impossibility of a Paretian Liberal," *Journal of Political Economy* 78, no. 1 (January–February 1970): 152–57.

tended explicitly to cover distributional attributes. Distributional elements may, of course, be relevant to such evaluations, but there exists no prospect for the deliberative action of political entrepreneurs, motivated by distributional consequences, to create new alternatives for collective consideration.

Conventional public choice theory proceeds as if the choice set is restricted to something akin to the positions on the diagonal, presumably owing to the requirements of technology itself. Dimensional complexities involve numbers of participants and numbers of separate collectivized activities that may be packaged for possible simultaneous consideration in a choice process. But nowhere is there explicit recognition that the set of relevant alternatives itself is created by the prior existence of the decision rule, as constrained or non-constrained by constitutional authority. Through its neglect of majoritarian exploitation as a principal feature of its basic analytical structure, conventional public choice (and social choice) theory loses much of its explanatory *raison d'être.*

The Achievement and the Limits of Public Choice in Diagnosing Government Failure and in Offering Bases for Constructive Reform

2.1. Introduction

I was asked to present a paper on the Public Choice approach to government deficiencies, and I want to use this occasion to go beyond orthodox analysis and to discuss some issues that have been at least partially neglected in the Public Choice approach.

It is useful to review the orthodoxy at the outset; this is attempted in Section 2.2. Section 2.3 summarizes the implications that may be drawn from the standard discussion. In Sections 2.4, 2.5, and 2.6, I explore methodological issues in the discussion from a perspective that is "beyond Public Choice" in one sense. In Section 2.7 I challenge the domain of *Homo economicus* with respect to individual behavior both in markets and in politics. In Section 2.8 I discuss the minimax principle for the design of institutional reform, and in Section 2.9 I relate this to Public Choice analysis. Conclusions are contained in Section 2.10.

From *Anatomy of Government Deficiencies*, ed. Horst Hanusch (Berlin: Springer-Verlag, 1983), 15–25. Reprinted by permission of the publisher.

I am indebted to my colleague Geoffrey Brennan for helpful comments.

2.2. Public Choice as a Theory of Government Failure

Theoretical welfare economics is properly labeled as "a theory of market failure." Analytical developments of the 1930s, 1940s, and 1950s, when the essential elements of theoretical welfare economics were articulated, first took the form of rigorous statements of the necessary and sufficient conditions required for efficiency in the allocation of resources in an economy, and, secondly, of definitions of relationships among economic variables that failed to satisfy such required conditions. There was relatively little institutional content, as such, in this welfare economics, but, by common acknowledgement, observed relationships in the capitalist economy were deemed such as to indicate "failure" in achieving allocative efficiency.

By implication almost universally, and by explicit statement in many instances, these "market failure" demonstrations of theoretical welfare economics were held to offer a *prima facie* case for corrective measures implemented through political-governmental means. There was no consideration given to the institutional structure within which such idealized corrective measures were to take place. To the theoretical welfare economists, markets "failed" in the allocative process; "ideal" government was assumed to be the alternative.

On several occasions I have referred to Public Choice, inclusively defined and as developed largely in the 1960s and 1970s, as "a theory of government failure" that offsets the "theory of market failure" that emerged from theoretical welfare economics. Just as the latter contains demonstrations that observed market processes fail to produce results that satisfy the conditions for allocative efficiency, Public Choice theory (once labeled as "welfare politics" by Paul Samuelson) contains demonstrations that observed political-governmental processes fail to satisfy the requirements for efficiency in the implementation of corrective measures.

At an elementary level of analysis, Public Choice theory does little more than to puncture the "benevolent despot" image or model of government and politics that theoretical welfare economics had incorporated as its standard of institutional comparison. At a more sophisticated level, Public Choice theory includes its own models of the processes of political decision-making, building in this respect on the economists' postulate of methodological individualism, with utility-maximizing actors in varying Public Choice roles.

Almost out of necessity, Public Choice theory has been somewhat more positive, or at least somewhat less normative, in content than theoretical welfare economics. As I have suggested, the thrust of the latter was to demonstrate that a particular institutional form, markets, fail. Against what? By comparison with what? Once this flaw in the normative implication of theoretical welfare economics was exposed, basically through an elementary but positive analysis of the alternative institutional structure, there is less emphasis on "failure." That is to say, Public Choice theorists have not duplicated the error or oversight of the theoretical welfare economists; they have not compared an actuality with an ideal. "Governments fail" against an ideal conception, but who might have expected any contrary finding? And Public Choice theorists have not held out some idealized market as the effective institutional alternative to politics.

2.3. Institutional Comparison

With some legitimacy, Public Choice theorists can claim to have advanced the discussion of comparative institutional alternatives. If we acknowledge that *both* markets and governments fail against idealized standards for operation, whether the objective be allocative efficiency, maintenance of individual liberty, distributive justice, or other desiderata, what is to be said about organizational structure? How should the interdependencies among persons in a society be institutionalized?

At the level of comparison between alternative organizational form for specifically designated sectors or "industries," the implication is that such a comparison can best be, and indeed must be, made on a case-by-case basis. For some "industries," the comparison may yield rather straightforward results. The efficiency-generating properties of a free and open market in the production-distribution of a partitionable good or service, say, shoes or plumbing, may outweigh any arguments for politicization, with the latter's inherent inability to embody incentives efficaciously. At the other extreme, the "publicness" or "commonality" properties of, say, national defense effort, may be such that the politicized institutional structure, despite its incentive-efficiency defects, may dominate serious consideration of market-like "privatization."

It is to be expected that, in any such case-by-case comparison, there will be numerous "industries" that fall somewhere near the margin of indifference, with the advantages and disadvantages of market-like and political organization roughly balancing each other. For this set of "industries," which may be called the "public utilities," we might expect to observe different organizational structures in different societies.

Public Choice theory, in its redress of the imbalance in the institutional comparisons informed by and inspired by welfare economics, has shifted the pendulum "rightward," so to speak. A comparison of market and governmental alternatives, both examined "warts and all," and without the "benevolent despot" blinders on, will necessarily produce a private sector–public sector mix less dominated by the public sector than that mix that might have been generated on the basis of prevailing ideas in, say, 1950 or 1960. Such a change in comparative results has nothing to do with any shift in the underlying ideology or nonideology of Public Choice, or of anything else. The change in question emerges strictly from a better-informed comparison of relevant alternatives.

Exclusive reliance on a pragmatic or case-by-case comparison of organizational structures, and without attention paid to the extension in the margins, however, is not acceptable procedure. Spillover or external effects may occur within the total organizational structure, effects that will tend to be obscured in any case-by-case, industry-by-industry comparison. The overall ratio of the value generated through the market sector, where individuals do adjust to private prices, to the value generated through the governmental sector, where private prices do not motivate behavioral adjustments on the part of individuals, may be of critical importance as an input into a properly conceived comparative evaluation for any single "industry." The differential weights assigned to allocative efficiency, to economic growth, to individual liberty, to political participation, and to distributive justice may affect the preferred degree or margin of politicization of the social order. At this level of comparison, normative principles enter the discussion, and Public Choice theory, as such, has nothing to offer beyond the clarification of the relevant trade-offs that are faced.

2.4. Utility-Maximization as a Logic of Choice

Up to this point, I have sketched in summary form what I suspect that the organizers expected me to present under the general title assigned to me. In remaining parts of this paper I want, however, to discuss some developing concerns that may, in one sense, seem to be "anti-Public Choice," at least in some of their implications. I want to look not at "government failure" or even at "market failure," but rather at what we might call analytical-methodological failure on the part of economists, and particularly Public Choice economists.

By "market failure" or "government failure," we refer to institutional-organizational structure. We analyze the predicted working properties of institutions, or rules, of constraints, and by adducing "failure" we imply that, if the rules could be changed, "better" results would be forthcoming. This institutional focus ignores or bypasses the characteristics of the persons who operate within the rules, who behave in accordance with the constraints that the rules define. The whole analysis, as I have noted, commences with utility-maximizing individuals.

There is no problem created by the utility-maximization postulate if we remain at the level of a strict logic of choice. That is to say, if we leave the arguments in individual utility functions unspecified and undefined, we can then use the utility-maximizing construction in analyzing processes of interaction. We cannot, however, operationalize the analysis so as to generate testable hypotheses or implications, even conceptually. In order to be able to generate such testable implications, the arguments in individual utility functions must be defined. And it is with this step of definition that major difficulties emerge.

2.5. *Homo economicus* and Market Failure

In their analyses of market relationships, economists have long relied on *Homo economicus*, old-fashioned economic man, who does have well-defined arguments in his utility function. In its least restrictive formulation, the *Homo economicus* construction requires only that objectively measurable economic value, designated in monetary units, enter as *one* argument in the representative person's utility function. In this version, the construction does not require that economic value be the only argument in the preference function or even that this argument be dominant in influencing behavior. But armed with this minimal, and widely accepted, model of behavior, economists are able to generate operational predictions. Quantities demanded increase as prices fall; quantities supplied increase as prices rise. Properly qualified, these predictions have been amply corroborated by empirical evidence.

It will be useful, however, to see precisely how this minimal formulation of the *Homo economicus* operationalization of economic theory bears on the market failure hypotheses that emerged from theoretical welfare economics. Consider one of the standard examples where markets are alleged to fail to generate efficient results, that in which externalities (spillover or neighborhood effects) exist. Take the classic example of the factory's smoking chimney that dirties the next-door laundry of the housewife. The Pigovian line of reasoning is familiar. The "true social costs" of the production that involves smoke generation should include the damages to the laundry. The factory owner does not incorporate these spillover damages as a part of his private costs which enter into his production decisions. The market fails; idealized efficiency norms would require an adjustment toward somewhat less smoke emission.

For purpose of discussion here I want to ignore the Coase-related possibilities that bargains may well be struck between the factory owner and the housewife to eliminate any inefficiency.[1] Even within the strict Pigovian setting, the conclusion that some corrective action is required to achieve efficiency depends critically on the assumption, and one that is rarely stated, that the factory owner disregards costs that he imposes on the housewife, that he acts solely and exclusively in his own narrowly defined economic interest, in this case, that he maximizes monetary profits. But note that this assumption embodies a much more restricted and circumscribed version of the *Homo economicus* construction than that which I outlined in the preceding discussion about the operationalization of market relationships generally. To assess market failure in the externality setting, we require the assumption that either economic value is the only argument in the utility function or this argument dominates all others in influencing behavior. Unless we make such

---

1. R. H. Coase, "The Problem of Social Cost," *Journal of Law and Economics* 3 (1960): 1–44.

a restrictive assumption, we cannot determine that the factory owner does not take into account the costs of the damages imposed in his own decision calculus, in which case there may be no basis for the claim that markets fail in generating efficient results. And there is no means empirically of determining whether or to what extent these external costs may be taken into account in the actual decision processes of persons in market relationships generally. The market-failure diagnosis is without clear empirical support.[2]

Note that I am not suggesting that there is no empirical content in the economic setting offered by the interaction between the factory owner and the housewife. We could predict, for example, that a tax imposed on smoke emission would reduce such emission. This prediction requires only that economic value be *one* argument in the factory owner's preference function, and it is a prediction that may be tested. What cannot be tested is whether or not the imposition of a tax (even one that ideally measures the costs imposed on the housewife) improves or decreases the efficiency of resource allocation in the economy that contains the factory and the housewife.

2.6. *Homo economicus* and Government Failure

I do not make the points above to suggest or to imply that markets do not fail in the sense sketched out in welfare economics. And I am not suggesting that persons take into account the full effects of their own actions on third parties who are not directly involved with them in economic interchanges. I make the points of the preceding section only as a way-station or bridge toward further discussion of the Public Choice diagnosis of "government failure."

As we know, the central methodological thrust of Public Choice is the extension of straightforward utility-maximization to explain the behavior of persons who act in Public Choice roles. Voters, bureaucrats, judges, legislators—these roles are filled by persons much like everyone else who seek to maximize their own utilities, subject to the constraints (rules) within which they operate. But let us examine some of the problems that emerge when we try to put operational content into the formal logical models. Let us try to

---

2. I have elaborated the argument of this paragraph in my *Cost and Choice: An Inquiry in Economic Theory* (Chicago: Markham Publishing Co., 1969).

employ our old friend *Homo economicus*, and suppose that persons who act in Public Choice roles proceed as if they are predominantly influenced by economic value. That is to say, let us adopt the *Homo economicus* model in its strong form, that which allows us to diagnose market failure from the presence of externalities.

Our effort runs aground immediately when we look at the behavior of individual voters. In large-number groups, there is a very small probability that any single vote will affect the majority-determined outcome. Hence, if the act of voting involves any cost at all, *economically* rational persons will not vote. This widely discussed paradox may, of course, be resolved by dropping the restrictive form of *Homo economicus* and by introducing other than net wealth arguments in the utility functions of voters, but the observed fact that persons do vote suggests that *Homo economicus* in the strict sense is not properly descriptive of behavior.

If this much is acknowledged, it is also necessary to acknowledge that the same problems arise with the "information failure" hypothesis that is subsidiary to the voter paradox and which is often cited as one of the basic sources of "government failure." The latter hypothesis states that, even for those persons in a large electorate who do vote, there is no economic incentive for them to invest resources in becoming informed about the choice alternatives that the group confronts. Since they do not individually bear the costs or reap the benefits, they have no privatized responsibility for making the choice. But, again, this hypothesis presumes that the strict *Homo economicus* model describes behavior. If this presumption is dropped, and if arguments other than net wealth are introduced in the individual's utility function, how can we conclude that there will be "information failure"? Just as in the case with "market failure" in the smoking chimney example, there is no direct empirical support for the hypothesis.

Again it must be noted that I am not suggesting that the analysis is drained of all empirical content. So long as a *Homo economicus* construction in its more limited, and surely more acceptable, sense is retained, we may still predict that more persons will vote if the costs of voting are reduced, that persons are more likely to become informed about the choice alternatives if the costs of information acquisition are reduced, and other like propositions. These offer empirically testable hypotheses, but they do not depend on the assignment of exclusive domain to *Homo economicus*.

We may extend analysis to the behavior of persons who act in other Public Choice roles. Consider the ordinary bureaucrat employed by government with an assigned set of duties to perform. It is plausible to model his behavior in the same way that we model the behavior of an employee in a private firm. In both settings, strict adherence to the more restricted *Homo economicus* construction suggests that the employee will seek to minimize work effort that is unpleasant to the extent that it is possible within the constraints that he faces. For the private-sector employee, however, these constraints may be more restrictive because behavior is more likely to be monitored carefully by the residual claimants to the firm's profits. In the governmental hierarchy, by contrast, supervisors of bureaucratic employees have no direct economic incentive for close monitoring of employee efforts, except insofar as such efforts impinge negatively on the rewards of the supervisors. There are no residual claimants in monitoring roles. Further, if bureaucratic rewards generally depend on size of agency, which in turn depends on the size of agency budgets, supervisors of bureaus will seek to maximize budget sizes, quite independent of any "demand" for the services actually provided. Unlike the owners of a private firm, bureaucrats are unable to capture rents or profits directly. They, therefore, seek to expand agency size beyond meaningful efficiency limits.

There are differing incentive structures in market and in governmental organization; these different structures allow us to predict differences in behavior, and these hypotheses may be empirically tested. But corroboration of these hypotheses does not legitimize the *Homo economicus* model for bureaucratic behavior, defined in the restricted sense that assigns the dominant role to net wealth maximization. There is no "proof" that bureaucracies "fail" in the sense that individual bureaucrats try to maximize budget size, that employees seek only private interest and shun their more traditionally conceived roles as promoters of "public interest."

When we extend the analysis to the behavior of elected politicians, to legislators, these are modelled as seeking almost single-mindedly to maintain the perquisites of office. Each legislator tries to "buy" the favor of voters by spending on the provision of services and transfers that cater directly to the particular coalition of voters selected exclusively on electoral grounds. It is not surprising that the strong version of *Homo economicus*, which incorporates net wealth maximization on the part of voters, bureaucrats, and legislators should produce demonstrations of "government failure." Indeed, if we accept this model, we may wonder that government works at all. There are self-evident paradoxes in the observations that some of the goods and services desired by citizens do get supplied by governments and that taxes are not at their strict revenue-maximizing limits.

2.7. The Relevant Domain of *Homo economicus*

I suggest that we cease and desist in any attempts to model man, *either* in his market *or* in his Public Choice behavior, as seeking exclusively or even predominantly to maximize the value of his net wealth. I suggest that we restrict ourselves methodologically to the more limited model of *Homo economicus*, one that allows the argument for economic value to enter into the individual utility function, in market or in Public Choice behavior, but to enter as only one among several arguments, and not necessarily as the critical influencing factor in many cases. There is, without doubt, an element of old-fashioned economic man in every one of us, and on the average this may be important for a lot of our ordinary behavior, but there are always other elements that operate alongside "old Adam." There are several "non-economic" men that live with *Homo economicus*, and it is folly to ignore their existence and their tempering influence because they are difficult to quantify.

As noted, it is indeed easy to diagnose "government failure" if we adopt *Homo economicus* as the all-encompassing explanatory model. In such a model, however, voters do not vote; those that do are ill informed; bureaucrats shirk their duties and use their discretionary powers to manipulate budget sizes and budget compositions to their own advantage; elected politicians seek to retain the perks of office and pander to the demands of minimally sized constituencies necessary for reelection; judges enjoy the quiet life and spend little time and effort in their duties. Considerations of "public interest" simply do not enter into the analysis at all.

It is hardly surprising that this model seems a caricature of what "politics" and "government" are all about from the perspective of the orthodox political scientist. It is, nonetheless, equivalent to that model for market behavior that the same orthodox political scientist is quite willing to adopt when he accepts the "market failure" diagnosis from the theoretical welfare economist, and uses this diagnosis to justify the extension of political controls over markets.

What I am suggesting in this paper is that *neither* markets *nor* politics can be appropriately modelled in the strict formulation of the *Homo economicus* construction. We must reckon on *other-than-economic* arguments in individual utility functions, both in market dealings and in political dealings. But we must also keep in mind that the *economic* argument always remains in utility functions as an important and relevant argument, in individual behavior, in markets and in politics. In a somewhat modest, but surely defensible sense, we can say that the methodological lesson to be drawn from Public Choice is nothing more than this admonition.

2.8. The Minimax Principle of Institutional Design

There are important implications for institutional design, however, that are contained in the ecumenical utility-function approach that I think we must adopt to make meaningful progress, both in diagnosing the performance of institutions and in organizing improvements. It was the genius of the 18th-century philosophers, and of Mandeville, Hume, and Smith in particular, to recognize that man's behavior in market institutions, even if wholly directed by the narrow pursuit of private interest, may, at the same time, indirectly and unintentionally promote what may be called the "public interest." These philosophers did not model man as being so narrowly focused, however; their interest lay in the design of institutions, and they sought to show that, even if narrow economic interest should dominate behavior, desired results might follow. By implication, therefore, market-like rather than government-like organization was to be preferred where possible, by a genuine minimax principle of choice. In politics, by sharp contrast with markets, there seemed to be no inherent structural linkage that could generate a correspondence between individual economic interest and the "public interest." We may, with Adam Smith, feel better if we know that our butcher is allowed to seek his own profits, because only in this way can we be sure that he will provide us with meat for supper. But we may, in sharp contrast with this, be quite displeased when we think that our bureaucrat may be also seeking his own economic interest, because we sense that he can do so only at our expense, rather than at our own improvement.

It is easy, for me at least, to understand the genuine intellectual excitement generated in the discoveries of classical political economy, discoveries of the efficacy of market coordination. The total and critical dependency of man upon the moral and ethical precepts of his fellows seemed to be at least partially mitigated. To the extent that markets were well designed and allowed to function in a constitutional-legal order, that men were allowed to follow the system of natural liberty in free and open competition one with another, there was less need to be concerned by man's failure to live up to the behavioral standards dictated by his bishop.

Many social scientists and philosophers of this century do not seem to understand and to appreciate the setting within which classical political economy was developed. Adam Smith did not construct his system of market order on any presumption that *Homo economicus* dominated all aspects of human behavior. Persons behaved in accordance with law and within the constraints of custom; perhaps exhibited "moral sentiments" one for another, which included sympathy and fellow-feeling. A legal order was a necessary part of the environment of a workable market economy. But, to Smith, the market did offer a unique setting within which men, acting in their own private interest, did not run squarely afoul of the like interests of their fellows. There seemed to be no political-governmental counterpart; to the extent that our affairs are subject to the decisions of persons in political office, be they bureaucrats, legislators, or judges, we necessarily depend on their willingness and proclivity to sublimate their own private interest to more "general interest" at least to some degree. It is little wonder that classical political economy came to be understood as a defense of the market and the market process, or by its critics as an apology for capitalistic institutions.

2.9. Public Choice and Institutional Reform

Why did the normative principles of classical political economy come to be forgotten in the late 19th and early 20th centuries? In what respects is it accurate to state that Public Choice amounts to an indirect "rediscovery" of these principles? A bit of history is helpful here, and in particular it is useful to recall that the late 19th and early 20th centuries were also described by the practical realization of the "democratic ideal," and specifically by the rapid expansion of the voting franchise. There was the new romance of electoral participation and the accompanying implicit faith that electoral controls were in themselves sufficient to keep the behavior of governments and governmental office-holders in bounds. These offered a fertile atmosphere for the promulgation and propagation of political-governmental nostrums for almost all conceivable social "ills," an atmosphere in which the motivational structure required for implementation was more or less totally neglected.

Public Choice has essentially brought this motivational structure to the light of day, after almost a full century of delusion. But, as I have emphasized, Public Choice economists reduce the normative impact of their own efforts if they advance their explanatory models as "strictly positive" theories of behavior of persons in Public Choice roles. Public Choice economists should take lessons also from the classical political economists; they should present the models that embody public choosers as maximizers of economic interest in the same sense that Adam Smith presented his models of man's behavior in markets. There need be no implication that such models fully or even primarily describe actual behavior. The models should, instead, be used normatively as bases for institutional design on the minimax principle noted. The objective should be that of designing institutions such that, if participants do seek economic interest above all else, the damages to the social fabric are minimized.

Within the structure of political-governmental organization, much can be done toward generating at least some rough correspondence between individual self-interest and the general interest. Dramatic changes can be made in the incentive structure within politics and government. Constitutional constraints can be imposed that will keep extreme patterns of behavior in limits.

The incentive structure of the political-governmental sector cannot, of course, become analogous to that of the market sector. As I have already noted, there is an argument for allowing the market order, which does channel individual self-interest in directions that correspond with the general interest, to organize as large a part of our interdependencies as is possible. And it is surely the case that, in 1980, there can be considerable "privatization" in most western economies. This result will emerge straightforwardly from a careful industry-by-industry comparative evaluation of the sort previously discussed. The movement toward deregulation in the United States reflects at least something of the flavor of this avenue for constructive reform.

The potential for improvement in the moral-ethical standards of conduct on the part of persons who act in positions of decision-making authority should never be neglected. Sir Dennis Robertson said we should always try to economize on love and try to find ways to do so institutionally. But this is not the same thing as saying that greed is better than love in those settings where dependence on the "good offices" of others is necessary. The balance here can, of course, be overdrawn. The moral zealot in positions of political power may well be less desirable than the private self-seeker who is on the take more or less openly. But within broad tolerance limits, it is better to have the career bureaucrat who is dedicated to his own conception of "the public interest" than it is to have the time-serving drone who minimizes effort. Economists in particular are likely to neglect the importance of ethical content in quite ordinary behavior, whether this be in market or non-market settings. There is a role for the moral teacher, "the preacher," that can be socially productive.

2.10. Conclusions

But can we unscramble the eggs? Can we get Humpty-Dumpty back together? This offers the challenge to our age. There are no lacunae in the normative theory, model, or conception of a social order in which persons can remain free, prosperous, and tolerant in a regime of law that constrains citizen and state alike. This ideal order has not, of course, ever been realized, but in the 18th and early 19th centuries, there seemed to be legitimacy in the hope that realization was on the way. Progress was visible and rapid, and persons believed in the possibility of progress. But Western man lost his way; he lost the wisdom of his forbears, and he unwittingly allowed the fruits of progress toward the ideal order to be dissipated. The advances in material well-being clouded retrogression in public philosophy and in the general understanding of the limits of social engineering. The healthy skepticism of the 18th century changed slowly but surely into the perfectionist naiveté of the early 20th century.

How can "public good" be produced by "private man"? This 18th-century question is with us still. But "public good" in the 1980s is surely to be defined in part by dismantling of the institutional apparatus that seems now to thwart our efforts and our liberties at every turn. But how was "public good" ever produced? How did the 19th-century world emerge from the mercantilist epoch? The historians have not told us a fully convincing story.

Those among our colleagues who insist that ideas of "public good" and of the "good society" cannot have consequences, and that the course of history is set by the determinate play of the forces of private self-interest, offer only despair at the fate that awaits us. As Professor Hayek has said, however, nothing is inevitable but thinking makes it so. For myself, I want "Public Choice" to merge with and to develop into "Public Philosophy," as a set of integrated ideas about the foundations of social order that will set us back on the high road.

PART THREE

Voters

The Political Economy of Franchise
in the Welfare State

3.1. Pareto-Optimal Redistribution

INTRODUCTION

In this paper I propose to examine carefully the implications concerning the voting franchise that are contained in the modern concept of Pareto-optimal income redistribution. This concept has been discussed at length in several papers in the late 1960s. I share some of the responsibility for generating this interest. In my early review of R. A. Musgrave's treatise,[1] I called explicitly for the derivation of a conceptual logic for redistribution that is on all fours with the logic for allocation in the public sector. It seemed inconsistent to me to adopt the stance of modern public finance theorists, exemplified by both Paul A. Samuelson and Musgrave in somewhat different ways, who attempt to derive criteria for public sector allocation from individualistic valuations but to reject these criteria for public sector redistribution.[2] Harold M. Hoch-

From *Capitalism and Freedom: Problems and Prospects*, ed. Richard T. Selden (Charlottesville: University Press of Virginia, 1975), 52–77. Reprinted with permission of the University Press of Virginia.

The author is indebted to both Winston Bush and Gordon Tullock for comments.

1. "The Theory of Public Finance," *Southern Economic Journal* 26 (Jan. 1960): 234–38.

2. In his now classic formulation, Samuelson defined the necessary conditions for allocative efficiency with public goods provision and then introduced a social welfare function to determine the final distribution. See Samuelson, "The Pure Theory of Public Expenditures," *Review of Economics and Statistics* 34 (Nov. 1954): 387–89. Musgrave was less willing to introduce external welfare norms to determine distributional outcomes, but his conceptual separation of the allocation and distribution branches of the budget suggested different normative principles. See Musgrave, *The Theory of Public Finance* (New York: McGraw-Hill, 1959).

man and James D. Rodgers, in their much-cited paper, and Edgar O. Olsen, independently, responded directly or indirectly to my suggestion. They attempted to construct a theory of income redistribution, or a theory of transfers, on the basis of individual utility interdependence.[3] This theory is open to either positive or normative interpretation, as explaining what is observed to take place through the fiscal process or as indicating what should take place under a regime characterized by utility interdependence of the sort postulated. Implicit in either interpretation, however, is the limitation of membership in the "fiscal club" of donors or potential donors. To the members of the donor group, whose utility functions contain arguments for the income or utility levels of other persons who are poor, the transfer of income to the latter group becomes a purely public good. And because of the jointness and nonexclusion attributes, a case is established, prima facie, for cooperative action, whether this is organized voluntaristically or politically.

If collective action takes its organizational form via political or governmental process, however, implications for the voting franchise are raised at the outset. If, in fact, the political decision mechanism is to serve, even to some remote approximation, as a surrogate for the idealized collective-cooperative fiscal club of potential donors, the voting franchise must be restricted to potential taxpayers, to those whose utility functions contain or might contain arguments for the income levels of poorer members of the larger community. Those persons to whom income transfers are to be made cannot be allowed to participate in the collective decision concerning the extent of this transfer itself since their own private interest will, of course, be unidirectional.

Elementary analytics

Consider a community of $n + 1$ persons, composed of n i's and a single j. Each of the i's $(i = 1, 2, \ldots, n)$ has the same utility function, which contains

---

3. Hochman and Rodgers, "Pareto Optimal Redistribution," *American Economic Review* 59 (Sept. 1969): 542–57; Olsen, "A Normative Theory of Transfers," *Public Choice* 6 (Spring 1969): 39–58. The Hochman-Rodgers paper stimulated several comments, both in criticism and in extension. See Paul A. Meyer and J. J. Shipley, "Pareto Optimal Redistribution: Comment," *American Economic Review* 60 (Dec. 1970): 988–90; R. A. Musgrave, "Comment," ibid., 991–93; R. S. Goldfarb, "Comment," ibid., 995–96; Hochman and Rodgers, "Reply," ibid., 997–1002; E. J. Mishan, "Welfare Economics and Pareto Optimal Redistribution" (typescript, June 1971).

an argument for the income of j, designated in an all-purpose consumption good which also is the numeraire,

$$U^i = U^i (Y^i, Y^j), \tag{3.1}$$

where the Y's represent all-purpose consumption goods. Since the Y^j enters the utility functions of all i's, and since it is nonpartitionable among the i's, it qualifies as a purely public good in the Samuelsonian sense. The necessary condition for efficiency is familiar,

$$\sum_{i=1}^{n} \frac{u_Y^{i\,j}}{u_Y^{i\,i}} = 1, \tag{3.2}$$

where the small u's refer to the partial derivatives of the utility function. This condition states that the summed marginal evaluations over all i's, evaluated in the numeraire, equals marginal cost, which is simply one, owing to the monetary dimensionality of Y^j.

The satisfaction of equation (3.2) may be but need not be accompanied by the fulfillment of equation (3.3),

$$\frac{u_Y^{i\,j}}{u_Y^{i\,i}} = \frac{1}{n} \text{ for all } i\text{'s.} \tag{3.3}$$

If equation (3.2) is met, the Pareto frontier is attained since there exists no means of shifting from this position so as to improve the position of any person without harming another. All gains from trade in the most inclusive sense are exhausted, and even allowing for full side payments at zero transactions costs, there is no proposal for change that could command unanimous agreement of all parties.

Note, however, that this seemingly straightforward application of the standard norm for public goods efficiency does not contain the evaluation placed on the income transfer by the potential recipient, j.[4] Since we are treating transfers of income or general purchasing power, it is clear that the

---

4. This has, of course, been recognized. Cf. W. C. Stubblebine, "Redistribution and Wicksellian Unanimity" (note, University of Virginia, 1962); George E. Peterson, *Welfare, Workfare, and Pareto Optimality,* Working Paper 1200-12 (Washington, D.C.: Urban Institute, Dec. 1970).

For simplicity, we assume that j is not concerned about the utility of the i's. That is, j's utility function is written $U^j = U^i (Y^j)$.

marginal evaluation placed on a dollar's additional transfer by j will, at all levels, be a dollar, or,

$$\frac{u_Y^{j,j}}{u_Y^{j,j}} = 1. \tag{3.4}$$

If we now incorporate this evaluation of j into the summation over all members of the community, the necessary condition for efficiency seems to become,

$$\sum_{i,j=1}^{n+1} \frac{u_Y^{i,j} j}{u_Y^{i,j} i} = 1. \tag{3.5}$$

But equations (3.2) and (3.5) are not satisfied at equivalent levels of income transfer to j. In order to satisfy equation (3.5), the summed marginal evaluations over the i's alone must equal zero, or

$$\sum_{i=1}^{n} \frac{u_Y^{i} j}{u_Y^{i} i} = 0. \tag{3.6}$$

When equation (3.6) is met, there is no utility interdependence at the margin. Note that both equations (3.2) and (3.5) describe positions on the Pareto welfare surface. These positions do not, of course, exhaust the Pareto set. Any level of income transfer at or beyond that which satisfies equation (3.2) will produce a result that qualifies as a Pareto-optimal position. Once attained, there will exist no means of changing or shifting from any such position under an idealized unanimity rule, when both the i's and the j's are franchised.

If the evaluation of recipients is included, note that equation (3.5) is not a necessary condition for Pareto optimality. Summed marginal evaluations need not equal marginal cost. This apparent paradox arises from the particular nature of pure income transfers, and this nonuniqueness in outcomes makes the application of the standard tools difficult. For purposes of comparison, consider the collective or public provision of a lighthouse-type purely public good. In this latter instance, absent transactions costs and income effect feedbacks, any departure from that allocation which satisfies the equivalent to equation (3.5) will set forces in motion that will return the system to the unique position where equation (3.5) is met.[5] No such equilibrating forces can emerge from pure income transfers because, despite a possible willingness of the donors, as a group, to offer amounts differing from a dollar for a dollar's change upward or downward in the amount of income transfer, such an offer cannot be accepted by the recipient(s) since this total, also, must be computed as part of the transfer. In one sense, therefore, the condition defined by equation (3.5) alone is meaningless because, operationally, it is not different from any other among a subinfinity of positions.

By contrast, for the i's treated as a group, the members of which evaluate the transfer of income to j as a public or collective-consumption good, condition (3.2) is fully analogous to the orthodox efficiency norm in public goods provision. Any change from that position defined or described by the satisfaction of condition (3.2) will set equilibrating tendencies in motion that will shift the outcome back to the equilibrium position, provided, of course, that the restricted assumptions about transactions costs and income effect feedbacks are maintained.

Public choice implications

The formal analysis is simple enough, but its implications for the problems of collective decision-making must be examined. Three quarters of a century have passed since Knut Wicksell admonished his fellow economists for their failure to relate economic policy norms to the political setting within which policy takes place.[6] He accused economists of assuming that policy is made by an "enlightened and benevolent despot," whose criteria are those provided to him by pure-minded professors. Wicksell's strictures are almost wholly applicable in the current professional and quasi-professional discourse on income redistribution policy. The pros and cons of the various in-

---

5. This is the collective or public goods equivalent of the Coase theorem. Cf. R. H. Coase, "The Problem of Social Cost," *Journal of Law and Economics* 3 (1960): 1–44. In the transactions costs rubric we must, of course, here include free-rider and preference revelation difficulties.

6. Wicksell, *Finanztheoretische Untersuchungen* (Jena: Gustav Fischer, 1896). Major portions of this work are published in translation as "A New Principle of Just Taxation," in *Classics in the Theory of Public Finance*, ed. R. A. Musgrave and A. T. Peacock (London: Macmillan, 1958), 72–118. The relevant passages are found on 82–87.

come maintenance plans, sometimes called negative income taxes, are discussed with little or no reference to the political choice process.[7] In this context, the preliminary attempts to develop criteria for politically implemented income redistribution from individual evaluations represent advance over the naiveté inherent in the invocation of external value norms. These attempts have remained seriously incomplete, however, because of the failure to relate the analysis directly to the political decision mechanism, either that which is potential or in being.

In order to discuss this relationship systematically, it is useful to digress briefly and summarize the elementary methodology of the Pareto criterion itself. An initial or existing state of the economy is described by an imputation (assignment, allocation, distribution) of goods (positive and negative) among persons in the relevant community. In the normal case, individualized shares in the total product are assumed to consist of full-fledged claims to the disposition of goods as their owners see fit, although behavioral limitations may be incorporated into the definitions without difficulty. Similarly, the goods are usually assumed to be fully partitionable among separate persons, although, once again, the existence of joint and common ownership rights may be embodied in the appropriate definitions. In all cases, however, the imputation defines a structure of rights or claims that is presumed to be known with certainty. If individuals are informed about the qualities of the goods assigned to them, and if they are assumed to be rational utility maximizers, the private behavior of each person carries him to what we may call the nonexchange utility possibility frontier. That is to say, all gains from internal trade will be exhausted in the private or presocial behavioral calculus of individuals.

The Pareto criterion, whether applied to a classification of final positions, described by imputations of goods among persons, or to a distinction among changes from one position to another, is rooted in interpersonal or social exchange, the central institution that is analyzed variously in economic theory. Given any imputation, the Pareto criterion enables us to classify it into the

7. There are notable exceptions to this generalization, among which are the contributions of both George J. Stigler and Gordon Tullock. See Stigler, "Director's Law of Public Income Redistribution," *Journal of Law and Economics* 13 (Apr. 1970): 1–10; Tullock, "Welfare for Whom?" *Il Politico* 33 (Dec. 1968): 748–61, and "The Charity of the Uncharitable," *Western Economic Journal* 9 (Dec. 1971): 379–92.

nonoptimal or the optimal set.[8] If it is nonoptimal, it enables us also to classify proposed moves or shifts as efficient or inefficient. The criterion can be applied positively to the observation of behavior as well as conceptually on the presumption that individual utility functions are known. Individuals, endowed with initial imputations, are presumed to engage in simple or ordinary trades that will shift the system in the direction of the Pareto frontier, exploiting the potentially available surplus obtainable. The Pareto norm can be utilized to assess the results of such trades, but its potential usefulness is found largely in the location and isolation of possible complex trading arrangements that may not emerge from the simpler trading processes. These complex trading prospects may, and normally will, involve simultaneous agreement on the part of more than two parties, and they may include trades in the form of agreements to change the rules or institutions within which orthodox trading can take place.

The donor cooperative or club. If this summary description of the Pareto criterion is provisionally accepted, what can be said about Pareto-optimal income redistribution? Commencing from some initial imputation, unilateral transfers in some numeraire good (income) might be observed to take place voluntarily if utility functions exhibit interdependence.[9] Some such transfers would take place under wholly independent behavior, but, as noted, there may exist both jointness and nonexclusion attributes that suggest superior results from joint or cooperative action. Potential donors would, in this setting, organize and join a voluntary cooperative for the purpose of making transfers to those persons designated as being eligible for charity. The latter would, however, remain external to the acting donor group or club, and these recipients would treat the transfers as purely gratuitous. They could scarcely be expected to participate in decisions concerning the amount of transfer they receive, and, of course, their evaluation of the transfer will not directly influence the decision of the donors.

Within the cooperative donor group or club, decisions must be made on

8. For background discussion, see Ragnar Frisch, "On Welfare Theory and Pareto Regions," *International Economic Papers* 9 (London: Macmillan, 1959), 39–92; and my "The Relevance of Pareto Optimality," *Journal of Conflict Resolution* 6 (Dec. 1962): 341–54.

9. Transfers of specific goods, income-in-kind, might also occur. These are not discussed in order to keep the basic analysis simplified.

the amount of transfer along with the distribution of the costs among individual members. In aggregate terms, the necessary condition for efficiency is that defined by condition (3.2) above. In a setting without decision-making costs, the group would operate under some effective rule of unanimity. Condition (3.2) would be satisfied, along with that defined in equation (3.3) for a set of equal i's. If members of the donor club should differ in preferences for income transfers, the equivalent of condition (3.3) would, of course, involve differing marginal costs among members. Decision-making costs exist, however, and these become significant where groups must reach agreement. Hence, even in purely voluntary donor clubs members might acquiesce in agreed-on, nonunanimity decision rules. Departure from unanimity removes any assurance that the aggregative marginal condition for efficiency, defined in equation (3.2), will be satisfied, or that the individualistic marginal conditions, defined in equation (3.3) or its equivalent, will be fulfilled. The voluntary nature of the arrangement embodied in the right of any member to withdraw unilaterally insures, however, that each person secure net gains from his participation. That is,

$$\int_0^T \frac{u_Y^j{}^j}{u_Y^i{}^i} \geq 1, \text{ for all } i\text{'s}, \tag{3.7}$$

where T measures the amount of income transfer to j by the fiscal club of the i's.[10]

In this more comprehensive setting that does allow for decision-making costs, the level of income transfer from donor groups to recipients under a regime of voluntary cooperative groups might appropriately be designated as Pareto optimal. Conceptually, this seems to have been the organizational model assumed by several of those who have participated in the recent discussion.

Governmental analogues to voluntary donor cooperative. The observed institutional framework for much income redistribution is not voluntary; it is political or governmental. The analysis somehow must bridge the gap between voluntary and coercive organizational structure. How can analysis based on voluntary exchange, and utilizing the Pareto criterion, be extended

---

10. In a regime of competing fiscal clubs each member must secure net benefits at least equal to that available to him from membership in any other club.

to apply to political or governmental structure, since the latter must be, in its nature, coercive?

There are three institutions that would allow governmentally determined income transfers to be brought under orthodox Pareto norms, and to be treated as if such transfers emerged from voluntary fiscal clubs with only minor variants. In each case, we make the preliminary and necessary assumption that decisions are made democratically through some voting process in which many persons participate, directly or indirectly. This rules out authoritarian decision-making on the part of governments.

Model I. In the first model, we can assume that a genuine rule of unanimity is operative, at least with respect to redistribution policy, and that all persons in the community have the voting franchise, both potential donors and potential recipients of transfers. The restrictiveness of unanimity may be relaxed sufficiently to allow for representative processes provided that the legislators selected represent all interests and that the unanimity requirement holds within the legislative assembly.

Commencing from an initial imputation of goods among persons, and with no voluntary redistribution, we may consider the results of an idealized decision process. It is clear that representatives of donors and recipients would agree on a level of income transfer that would satisfy condition (3.2) above. Proposals for additional income transfers beyond this level would be opposed by donor interests. Such extensions would, of course, be supported by representatives of recipient groups, as indeed would all proposals for additional transfers within meaningful limits. The political process would in this model accomplish essentially identical objectives as the cooperative or voluntary clubs organization discussed earlier. In practical fact, however, a political decision structure organized in that fashion would probably generate a lower level of total income transfer than the alternative regime of wholly voluntary fiscal clubs. In the latter, the voluntary participation feature would make individual donors more acquiescent in departures from effective unanimity as a means of allowing some reduction in group decision costs. In political organization, departures from unanimity would be more strongly resisted.

Model II. Consider now a second model in which politically determined income transfers might be discussed in an orthodox setting of Pareto optimality. If a regime of competitive governmental units exists, and if persons may shift membership among these at relatively little personal costs, each political unit may embody both an inclusive voting franchise and departures from an effective unanimity rule for collective choice while generating results that are akin to those broadly predictable under voluntary organization. This model is applicable, however, only in those situations where the utility interdependence, if such exists, involves members of the same local governmental jurisdiction. In this sort of setting, income redistribution takes on most of the properties of a localized public good, and a Tiebout-like adjustment process places severe limits on the possible inefficiency that can emerge regardless of internal political decision rules.[11]

Model III. A third model is one in which the voting franchise is specifically limited to those who are actual or potential contributors or donors in the income transfer system, that is, net taxpayers rather than net beneficiaries. In this model, those who receive income transfers are explicitly excluded from participation in the collective or governmental decisions that are concerned with either the level or the financing of the transfers. In this setting, income transfers to the poor, treated here as an external group, can be analyzed as a purely public good whose benefits and costs are shared among members of the potential taxpayer, and hence voting, group in the community. If, among this restricted set of persons, an effective rule of unanimity prevails for collective decisions, a regime closely analogous to that of voluntary clubs exists, with the differences previously noted. If the costs of decision-making suggest significant departures from unanimity, and if individual members of the group do not have available low-cost migrational alternatives, the moves or shifts in income distribution emerging from the political process may not be Pareto superior. If, for example, a majority coalition among the potential taxpayer group desires to redistribute substantial income to the poor outside the voting group at the expense of all potential taxpayers, the minority of the latter may suffer genuine fiscal exploitation. Nonetheless, the majority coalition need not act in such fashion, and the disenfranchisement of the transfer recipients removes the direct influence of

11. For further discussion, see Mark Pauly, "Income Redistribution as a Local Public Good," mimeographed (paper for COUPE meeting, Fall 1971); and my "Who Should Distribute What in a Federal System?" mimeographed (paper for Urban Institute Conference, March 1972).

those whose strictly private self-interest dictates extensions in transfers at all levels. Under such conditions, it seems plausible to treat observed political outcomes as indirect surrogates for something akin to genuinely voluntary transfers.

3.2 Property in Franchise

Observation tells us that none of the three models sketched briefly above describes the real world. What we do observe is politically determined redistribution of income at jurisdictional levels that guarantee high-cost migrational alternatives and under the operation of decision rules that are basically majoritarian rather than unanimitarian. We observe, furthermore, that transfer recipients are not excluded from voting and otherwise participating in politics, including the politics of transfer policy itself. In this realistic setting, either the Pareto criterion must be judged of relatively little value in analyzing transfers, or it must be modified substantially from its standard application.

Recall our summary of the methodology of the Pareto norm. Individuals in the social group are described in terms of an imputation or assignment of goods, with well-defined limits as to rights of disposition. The orthodox Pareto criterion assists in evaluating or in proposing changes that involve simple and/or complex trades in these assigned goods among separate members of the community. I now think that this traditional approach that has been taken by many political economists, including me, has been seriously deficient. The deficiency may be identified and discussed in terms of the problems considered in this paper.

NOMINAL AND REAL CLAIMS

In the distributional setting as observed in the real world, goods are not partitioned among separate persons (families) in the well-defined sense that is implicitly postulated in the standard analysis. To indicate this, I propose to distinguish nominal and real imputations or assignments over final goods, over rights to the use of goods. What we may actually observe, at any moment, is a set of nominal rights, which may be defined by an imputation, which may or may not accurately map the initial position or basis from which simple and complex trades among persons must commence. Along-side and accompanying the set of nominal claims over goods, there exists a membership right in the social group or community, which may or may not be accompanied by a voting right in group or collective decisions. Both the membership right and the voting right have economic value to the holders, an economic value that takes its meaning in terms of some contingent claim on the common fund of goods available in the whole community.

Membership rights and voting rights are separate, and in some cases the distinction is important.[12] But for purposes of this paper, these rights accompany each other; we simply assume that membership in the social group implies voting rights. What we observe, then, is a set of nominal claims, partitioned among persons and/or families in the group, along with universal and uniform voting rights (political equality) over all adults in the community. The latter rights take economic value in our model only through the indirect claims that they might represent over the total resource stock in the economy, all of which we assume is partitioned among persons in the nominal sense. For purposes of simplifying the analysis, we assume that there are no joint-consumption goods, no public goods of the standard variety.

CONSTITUTIONAL RESTRICTIONS

The value that a voting-membership right has for its holder depends on several things, including the allowable range for collective or political action. This will be defined by a political constitution, which may or may not be formally specified. We limit consideration in this paper to redistributional policy, and specify the effective constitutional requirements to be:

1. Income redistribution shall be general rather than discriminatory, and redistribution, if it occurs, must take the form of transfers from higher to lower income categories, with equalization as the limit.
2. No person in the recipient group who stands lower on the income scale

12. It is clear, for example, that open and free international migration would stimulate massive migration into nations even if migrants were wholly excluded from the voting franchise. It is precisely the claims that such migrants might make on the common funds of the community that provides one of the rational arguments against open migration. See Leland Yeager, "Immigration, Trade, and Factor Price Equalization," *Current Economic Comment* 20 (Aug. 1958): 3–8.

before political redistribution shall secure less in total transfer than another who stands higher on the scale.

3. No person in the taxpaying group who stands lower on the income scale before political redistribution shall be taxed by a higher amount than another who stands higher on the scale.

4. Collective decisions are reached through simple majority voting.

These requirements seem plausible on their own account, as well as realistic, if we confine attention to pure income transfer policy. Basically, these requirements state that arbitrarily composed political coalitions may not exploit minorities. Regressive and nondiscriminatory transfers as well as taxes are ruled out. Taken together, these requirements add stability to the expectations about redistribution policy, and they enable us to define more clearly the value of the membership-voting franchise.

No production — no utility interdependence

I assume initially that there is no utility interdependence of the sort adduced to explain observed income transfers under the orthodox Pareto constructions discussed in section 3.1. In the absence of collective action, therefore, each person (family) retains all the goods under his assignment in the nominal sense. I assume, further, that agreed-on laws against theft are enforced perfectly. Finally, I assume in this model that the initial assignment of goods falls as manna with a distribution that is unchanging from one period to the next. Goods are not produced by human effort.[13]

Under the restricted conditions postulated, simple majority voting will generate an amount and type of income redistribution determined by the median-income recipient acting to further his own position. His problem is one of simple maximization subject to the constitutional constraints imposed. In the no-production economy majority voting will tend to equalize all posttransfer incomes above and including the median and to equalize all positive transfers to persons below and including the median.

---

13. The model here, and indeed much of the discussion in this section, is influenced by my colleague Winston Bush. See his "Income Distribution in Anarchy," mimeographed (Virginia Polytechnic Institute and State University, Jan. 1972).

Figure 3.1 depicts family distribution in a community that resembles the United States with regard to distribution. The median is located at M. If, in fact, this pattern should describe a distribution in a no-production setting, and if the constitutional limits were those indicated, the posttransfer income distribution would be shown by the dotted curve. The transfer to the median family, measured by MM^*, would be maximized subject to the constraints suggested, including the necessity that the two shaded areas be equal in size, that is to say, that the transfer budget be balanced.

We may now look at the value of the voting franchise to a person along the income scale in this model. It is clear that the franchise has value only through its indirect influence on the location of the median voter. Disenfranchisement of, say, persons at the lower levels of income would shift M leftward on the diagram and the distance analogous to MM^* would be smaller. This would impose monetary costs on all transfer recipients, not only those who might suffer disenfranchisement as such. Similarly, disenfranchisement of persons at the upper end of the scale would shift the median rightward in the diagram. This would increase the amount of tax paid by each taxpayer, the number of taxpayers, the total amount of transfer, and the positive transfers received per recipient.

It may be noted from the construction of figure 3.1 that, in the conditions of this model, the median voter will be harmed by the disenfranchisement of

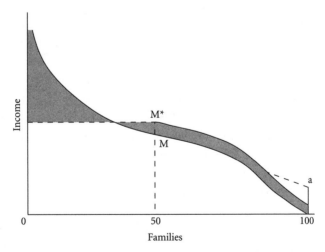

Figure 3.1. Constrained majority transfers in the no-production economy

voters at either end of the scale; he will suffer from any shift of the median. A shift to the right will equalize incomes at and above the new median, but this must be at a lower level. A shift of the median to the left will reduce the total tax revenue collections while simultaneously increasing the number of recipients. This must involve a reduction in the amount of transfer per recipient, and hence the amount received by the initial median voter. It will not, therefore, be to the direct interest of the established median voter, presumed here to be the median pretransfer income recipient, to extend or to limit the franchise asymmetrically. He will, of course, be indifferent to symmetrical changes.

No production with utility interdependence

The introduction of utility interdependence into this model will have less effect on the results than might have been anticipated. The preference of certain upper-income receivers for greater amounts of transfer than in the no-interdependence framework will have an effect similar to their own disenfranchisement. The effective median position shifts to the right, with the results indicated above. Note particularly that this sort of utility interdependence will not allow for the inverse discrimination represented by larger transfers to the lowest pretransfer income recipients so long as the effective median voter's preference does not exhibit a concern for the utility of those standing lower along the pretransfer income scale. There will be no flaring of the dotted curve upward as traced out by the extended segment shown by *a* in figure 3.1. If such a flaring is to be produced, this must arise because of utility interdependence of voters in median income ranges, at least if we confine analysis to this very simple political choice model.

Production without utility interdependence

The introduction of production will drastically change the model. Instead of goods being initially distributed as manna, we now assume that goods are produced exclusively by human effort, and that the initially generated distribution is the same as before. In this model, the amount of redistribution that becomes rational for the median-income recipient and median voter will be directly dependent on the incentive effects that taxation will exert on those from whom funds are to be exacted politically. It will clearly be inefficient to levy more than a revenue-maximizing tax on any person. Hence, we should predict that the posttax distribution of income will reflect some inequality throughout the scale under the constitutional restrictions previously postulated. Figure 3.2 depicts the situation. The heavy curved line indicates the pretransfer distribution of initially received incomes after income-earning adjustments to the transfers have been made. The dotted curve indicates the posttransfer distribution.

As in the no-production model, the median voter faces a constrained maximization problem. He will try to maximize the net transfer to him, shown by MM^*. Let us assume that the dotted curve over the net taxpayer group represents the strict revenue-maximizing locus. We want now to examine effects of a shift in the franchise as before. If persons at the lower extremities of the scale are disenfranchised, the median shifts to the left, as before, but note that this will have no effect on the total tax levied on those at the upper extremities of the scale. This is because these persons are, in all cases, being subjected to the revenue-maximizing tax. Shifts in the median will not, therefore, modify their final positions. In such cases, however, these highest-income recipients will be totally indifferent as to whether or not they

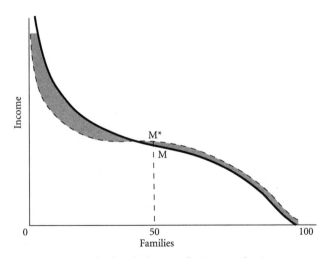

Figure 3.2. Constrained majority transfers in a production economy

exercise their own franchise. The vote will have no value to them, and they may be observed either to neglect the exercise of franchise or, more likely, to fulfill a presumed internal moral commitment by affecting to exhibit great concern for those at lower income levels.[14]

If this reaction on the part of the highest-income recipients is fully recognized by the median voter, however, this, in itself, will cause the latter to refrain from imposing taxes at the strict revenue-maximizing level. High-income recipients will be taxed at a level sufficiently below such limits as to insure their attention to the voting process. The potential upward mobility in the income scale that enters into the expectations of the median voter will also modify or mitigate against impositions of taxes at the revenue-maximizing limits.

In this model we should also note that changes in the location of the median voter along the income scale, brought about by voluntary voting abstention, utility interdependence, or explicit disenfranchisement, will not affect the net transfer to recipients at the lowest end of the scale nearly so much as in the no-production setting. Because the highest-income recipients are likely to be taxed at or near revenue-maximizing limits regardless of the location of the median, over broad middle ranges, this source of funds remains invariant. Shifts in the median will affect the transfer per recipient slightly, but the primary effect will be that of shifting the break-even position, where a person is changed from a net taxpayer to a net beneficiary of the transfer scheme.

DEMOCRATIC INCOME TRANSFERS AND PARETO NORMS

It is tempting to extend the majoritarian transfer models, to introduce further qualifications, and to modify the assumptions. All of this offers challenging subject matter for the application of the tools of public choice theory. My purpose here, however, is neither such elaboration nor defense of the particular models chosen. Rather it is to relate the basic majoritarian transfer process to the Pareto criterion framework within which income

---

14. This explanation of the apparent charitable impulses of the very rich is akin to that offered for other groups by Gordon Tullock in his paper "The Charity of the Uncharitable."

transfers were discussed in section 3.1. As noted, I now recognize a serious deficiency in the standard application of the Pareto norms, and I want to discuss this deficiency explicitly with reference to the models introduced above.

Orthodox procedure would classify the income transfers generated by the working of pure majority voting rules, or by any political process that may reasonably be described by this model, as being coercive in nature and, as such, clearly violative of the Pareto criterion as the latter is applied to changes or moves among positions. That is to say, a pure majoritarian transfer of income under the constitutional restrictions suggested would qualify as a non-superior move. I now think that this is an overly restricted usage of the Pareto norm, even as applied to changes. As I have noted at several places, the Pareto criterion, strictly speaking, is applicable only when the nominal imputation of goods among persons represents accurately the real set of claims or rights of persons over the final disposition of these goods. It is erroneous, however, to acknowledge a nominal imputation as real in a setting that allows for income redistribution under collective or governmental auspices.

Consider, for example, the position of a single high-income recipient. His nominal claim over the disposition of goods may be, relatively, very large indeed. But he secures (or earns) this nominal income in a polity (economy) that has extended universal and uniform suffrage to all its adult members. Furthermore, this recipient of the nominally high income cannot, by assumption, shift to alternative polities (economies) without undergoing major costs. In a very genuine sense, therefore, the high-income recipient does not possess a full-fledged property right to the goods over which his nominal income apparently gives him claim. By the very nature of their simple voting or potential voting membership in a polity (economy) that constitutionally allows income transfers to take place under collective aegis, all other members in the community hold a contingent claim on the goods purchasable by the nominal income of the person in question. Hence, to say that the recipient of a nominally high income actively opposes a majoritarian transfer policy that makes him a net taxpayer and that this behavior, in itself, reveals that the policy does not reflect a Pareto-superior move or change, tends to obscure the underlying nature or basis of the complex interaction that is involved here. The majoritarian transfer can be viewed merely as the working out of the real set of claims to income in the community, the revision in the nominal set of claims predictable under the political structure in being, which includes property rights in franchise. The observed opposition of the rich man to transfer policy is akin to that of the person who has to pay an obligation previously made. Since the nominal income is not his by any real rights of ownership in the first place, his opposition can hardly be adduced in evidence that the transfer is violative of a meaningful welfare norm. To the extent that such a transfer appeared to violate clearly the Pareto criterion, as applied in the orthodox sense, many economists have rejected the Pareto framework in application to the whole set of issues involving income redistribution. Having no alternative, many of those who reject the Pareto criterion have sought to introduce external ethical norms to apply to all redistribution policy.

My own work, as well as those who have advanced the analysis of so-called Pareto-optimal redistribution, has suffered in the opposite sense. Because political transfers seem to violate the standard Pareto norms, we have tended to opt out of any discussion and to say that nothing further can be constructed on the basis of individual evaluations. I now propose to modify this stance, and to do so in a substantial sense. Failure to carry out income transfer policy in a political setting such as that sketched out in the models above would represent a fundamental shift in the real assignment of rights, a shift in favor of those with the nominally higher incomes. Once the franchise has been extended to all adults, and once the constitution has allowed income transfers to take place collectively, the formal act of transfer becomes fully predictable from positive economic analysis. The basic property right inheres in the voting franchise, and the economic value of this franchise reflects the measure of the contingent claim to the incomes and wealth nominally imputed to individuals in the whole community.[15]

---

15. My own recognition of the basic point that the property rights assignment takes place when the franchise is granted was, so far as I can tell, influenced by two sources. First, the discussion of my colleague W. C. Stubblebine in a seminar on property rights made clear that the presence of others in the social group must modify the environment for Crusoe and this must be taken into account in any analysis. See his "On Property Rights and Institutions," mimeographed (Virginia Polytechnic Institute and State University, June 1972). Second, Nicolaus Tideman, of Harvard University, in a seminar discussion in Blacksburg, Va., on 19 May 1972 advanced a proposal for using posterior proba-

PARETO OPTIMALITY AND THE "STATUS QUO"

To this point, the income transfers from the nominally rich to the nominally poor that are predicted to occur under a democratic polity are derived from individual evaluations without normative content. The Pareto norms have not been utilized to evaluate these transfers, other than in the negative commentary suggesting their inapplicability. We may now, however, try to evaluate such redistribution in terms of the Paretian criteria. Is the institutional structure which embodies pure majoritarian transfers itself Pareto optimal? Does there exist a means of changing this structure that is Pareto superior; that is, does there exist any proposed change in constitutional-institutional rules that would, conceptually, command the assent of all members of the community?

At first glance, these questions may seem to reflect a return to the orthodox Pareto framework, which I have explicitly criticized. There is a major difference, however, which should be stressed. Paretian criteria have often been criticized because they lend support to the *status quo*. In a sense, this charge is correct, but my own response has always been that "we start from here," from the *status quo*, and, willy-nilly, this constrains our analysis. The error in my own earlier methodological position has been my initial definition of the *status quo*, or starting point, in terms of a presumed imputation of goods among persons that ignores the political process in being and the genuine claims to goods inherent in this process.[16] This is properly to be regarded as

---

bilities as a means of getting around the revelation of preference problem in public goods settings. In this discussion, Tideman explicitly referred to the notion that, once choice alternatives are introduced for a vote, the property rights of those who hold differing positions on the alternatives have already been modified.

16. This modification in my own position brings me close to that expressed by Musgrave in his "Comment" on the Hochman-Rodgers paper. Musgrave suggested that "primary" redistribution occurs as a result of the "social contract" within which political decision-making takes place. He did not, however, attempt to modify the applicability of the Pareto norms. Furthermore, Musgrave's position as expressed in this "Comment" seems at variance with the explicitly normative stance taken in his presentation of the three-part budget. In that part of their "Reply" relating to Musgrave's criticism, Hochman and Rodgers also take a position similar in many respects to that developed in this paper. However, they note, at one point, that "one cannot determine in welfare terms,

much a part of the *status quo* as is any strictly defined nominal imputation. Having redefined the *status quo*, we can apply the Pareto criterion in the standard manner.[17]

It seems clear that any restriction on the voting franchise, once this has been universally extended, is nonoptimal; such a shift would harm some members of the community. Under universal franchise, we may then ask whether any of the constitutional constraints can be modified to the advantage of all parties. If we limit attention to income redistribution alone, and leave other collective activity out of account, there seems no apparent change that would qualify as Pareto superior. If this is the case, the total regime as described can be classified as Pareto optimal.

3.3. Impure Redistribution

The whole approach of section 3.2 may be questioned, however, as regards its descriptive accuracy. Can the political process that we observe in the real world be approximated in such models, even if we accept the necessity of extreme simplicity and abstraction? Presumably, little distortion is created by the assumptions of universal suffrage. Effective majority voting rules, even when the complexities of actual political decision-making are acknowledged, seem broadly acceptable in the context of the discussion here. The presence of high-cost migrational alternatives can scarcely be challenged with reference to redistribution policy at the national government level.

---

whether the initial or market-determined distribution of income is satisfactory *until* Pareto optimal transfers have occurred" (p. 999). This inference is directly contrary to that which emerges from the analysis of this paper. Taking the property in franchise approach, one can say that the initial positions from which Pareto-optimal redistribution (defined in the Hochman-Rodgers sense) may take place cannot be established until the political or majoritarian redistribution has occurred.

17. In a discussion that is directly relevant to this paper, Alan T. Peacock and Charles K. Rowley criticize those who have developed models for Pareto-optimal redistribution on the grounds that the *status quo* starting point along with difficulties of securing unanimous agreement lend a conservative bias to the whole analysis, a bias that they consider contrary to liberal values. See "Pareto Optimality and the Political Economy of Liberalism," *Journal of Political Economy* 80 (May/June 1972): 476–90. Much of their criticism of the Pareto norms vanishes, however, under the reformulation suggested in this paper.

More serious issues may be raised concerning the specific constitutional restrictions imposed on redistribution policy itself. We do not observe much
pure income redistribution in the absence of collective provision of real goods
and services. When the allocative role of the political sector is included in
the analysis of distributional outcomes, quite different results may emerge.
A more acceptable and alternative model would allow tax funds to be used
(1) for financing publicly supplied or publicly subsidized real goods and
services; or (2) for financing pure income transfers. In this setting, it may
be to the advantage of the median voter-*cum*-income recipient to choose (1)
rather than (2). This offers a means of escaping from constitutional restriction on regressively discriminatory transfers in the numeraire. While it may
not be possible to discriminate in favor of the median voters by grants of
larger absolute amounts of money than those offered to persons standing
lower on the nominal income scale, the same purposes may be accomplished
by choosing for public or governmental supply that set of real goods and services which is most highly valued by median voters. Once supplied, these
goods and services may be available on equal terms to all members of the
community, but the actual distribution of benefits, as valued, may be skewed
dramatically toward middle income ranges.

This may be illustrated in figure 3.3. The curve Y_n, as before, depicts the
nominal income distribution, after behavioral adjustments but before trans-

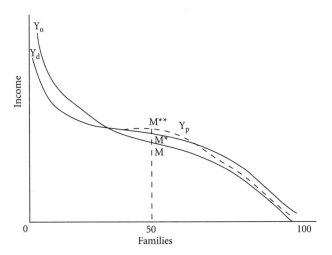

Figure 3.3. Unconstrained majority transfers

fers. The curve Y_d represents the most-preferred pure distributional scheme for the median voter under the constitutional restrictions imposed in section 3.2. The curve Y_p depicts the alternative curve of effective final distribution under the regime that allows for collective provision of real goods and services. Note that Y_p falls along Y_d over high income ranges and below Y_d over low income ranges.

This alternative model of impure redistribution is in accord with the hypotheses advanced by Aaron Director, George Stigler, and Gordon Tullock, which suggest that the major beneficiaries of transfer policies are those in the median income ranges rather than the very poor. In neither of the basic models here do the poor, as a group, possess decisive power via the voting process. Under a nondiscriminatory constitutional requirement, however, the very poor could do as well in terms of absolute pure transfers as median-income recipients. This outcome is circumvented to the extent that in-kind goods and services which are differentially valued by the median voters are offered governmentally. Public education, at all levels, seems to provide the example here.

3.4. Conclusions

Much of the confusion in the discussion of income redistribution stems from an inconsistency between our economic and our political attitudes. On the one hand, the ethics of capitalism suggest that the market earnings of resources become the property of the nominal owners, who may, presumably, dispose of these as they personally desire. They may, of course, elect to worry about their fellows, but in such an attitudinal framework charity is merely another consumption good. Any politically determined transfer of income above minimal limits involves a coercive taking. At the same time, however, the ethics of democracy suggest that restrictions on franchise are not to be tolerated. Few seem to have recognized the implications of the inconsistency between these value positions.

The inconsistency appears in its starkest form in redistribution policy, and it is the basis for the neoclassical dichotomy between allocation and distribution. Economists claim competence in defining and identifying allocative efficiency, using as inputs the revealed (actually or conceptually) preferences (values) of individuals. They stop short when faced with distribution, and they often pull in external and nonindividualistic norms which they acknowledge to be less "scientific" than those introduced for the theory of allocation. Efficiency in allocation is defined to characterize a position where all of the potentially realizable surplus has been squeezed out of simple and complex trading arrangements. Essentially, this procedure is to describe the end point of a process, and economists have not carefully considered the starting point. Implicitly, they postulate an initial distribution of endowments and/or capacities among persons, and it is presumed that this imputation can be mapped directly into a set of final imputations of goods on the Pareto welfare surface. As noted, efforts have been made to bring this basic Pareto efficiency framework into the evaluation of distribution but without much success, largely because, here too, economists have not escaped from the inconsistency noted.

In this paper, I have tried to reconcile the inconsistency by going back to the starting point, and to call into question the orthodox definition of that imputation from which trade commences. If membership in a sociopolitical community carries with it a valued right of participation, this value must be somehow incorporated into any exhaustive partitioning of potential goods among persons, even if it is fully recognized that such value can, at best, be only probabilistically estimated or determined. This procedure allows us, at least conceptually, to examine both allocation and distribution problems within a coherent analytical framework. The fact that the analysis, at all stages, becomes much more difficult, and perhaps less aesthetically satisfying, should not deter serious scholarship. Like it or not, we live in an environment where the workings and forms of capitalism are tempered by the workings and forms of majoritarian democracy.

Voter Choice
Evaluating Political Alternatives

Geoffrey Brennan and James Buchanan

Public choice theory is the application of the method and analytic apparatus of modern economics to the study of political processes. An integral part of this theory is the assumption that participants in political processes act "rationally"—that is, they act purposively to secure their particular individual ends. The object of this article is to show that such an assumption is highly problematic for a major group of participants in political processes—namely, voters in large-number majoritarian elections. The claim is such that the strict logical connection between preferences over alternatives and observed choices, characteristic of individual behavior in the market, is severed in majoritarian elections. In other words, basic rationality postulates applicable to market behavior are not sufficient to establish an a priori relationship between the way in which individuals vote and their preferences over political outcomes. Since the assumption that voters cast their votes rationally is the point of departure for virtually every public choice model in the literature, this claim represents a major criticism of public choice orthodoxy. Any predictive theory of voter behavior based on the assumption that voters vote in accordance with their "interest" is, at best, logically arbitrary. Furthermore, normative propositions based on the assumption of voter rationality must be treated very skeptically: Majoritarian decision making cannot be presumed to be a satisfactory device for reflecting the preferences of citizens over alternative electoral outcomes, for reasons quite different from those widely discussed in public choice orthodoxy.

From *American Behavioral Scientist* 28 (November/December 1984): 185–201, copyright 1984 by Sage Publications, Inc. Reprinted by permission of Sage Publications, Inc.

Our object in this article is to elaborate the argument advanced above. We begin with a simple analogy. The analytic core of the article is found in the two following sections, and the fifth section deals with the implications for public choice analysis—implications that undermine several of the most basic propositions in the field. A brief summary of the argument is offered in the final section.

A Simple Analogy

Each afternoon of every weekend of the various seasons, an enormous number of individuals watch sporting events, some on television, some directly at the scene of action. Many of these individuals appear to care who wins: They cheer for their respective teams and vociferously proffer advice (sometimes only to a television screen), and their spirits seem profoundly affected by the outcome. Indeed, those who do not really care who wins may, for the purposes of the exercise, "adopt" a team for the afternoon, taking on a partisan stance as a means of stimulating interest.

Even the most ardent of spectators would admit that intense psychological involvement in the game exercises no influence on the outcome. However precisely spectators would account for their interest and their expenditure of resources in indulging that interest, they would not claim that they watch a particular game because, in doing so, they help their team to win.[1]

Few economists would argue that the sports fan is "irrational." Economists would simply acknowledge that the spectators have a taste for watching their team play, and that would be that. Economists could, of course, use their technical tools to analyze spectator behavior. They could "explain" why when seat prices go up attendance declines, why when the weather is bad gate

1. There is some positive relation between a fan's support of his or her team and its performance: A team tends to perform somewhat better before an enthusiastic crowd; and, in the long run, good gates and good TV ratings allow a team to spend more on resources that contribute to its record. However, the relation here is simply too vague, too small, and too indirect to constitute a rationale for spectator behavior. A spectator is a booster because he or she wants to be—no more and no less. Although spectators care about the outcome, they do not act to determine it, and they do not conceive themselves to be so acting.

receipts are lower, why groups of teams will have an incentive to cartelize and restrict entry to the conference, and so on. But economists, presumably, would not find it necessary to explain attendance at events in terms of increased employment opportunities and higher incomes for supporters of the victorious team.

The analogy here with voting behavior is not entirely obvious. And, to be sure, the analogy is by no means perfect.[2] Yet, in some important respects, the activities of voting and watching sporting events are very similar. Voters do, in fact, participate in electoral processes, and they care about political outcomes. But there is no logical connection between these two facts, and the absence of this logical connection is crucial. It arises from the fact that the relation between how any individual voter votes and the outcome of the election is virtually negligible. We cannot, therefore, explain voter behavior in terms of preferences over outcomes: Voter behavior must be explained on its own terms. People vote because they want to—period. And they vote how they want to—period. And neither the act of voting nor the direction of a vote cast can be explained as a means to achieving a particular political outcome, any more than spectators attend a game as a means of securing the victory of their team.

The fact that any individual voter has a negligible effect on electoral outcomes in large-number electorates has long been recognized by public choice scholars. The implication that the act of voting cannot, therefore, be explained as a means of securing some desired policy change has also been recognized (though somewhat reluctantly in some cases). But there appears to be a widespread conviction that although we cannot explain why a person goes to the polling booth (except in the tautological terms that it must be utility maximizing for him or her to do so), we can explain how he or she will vote once there. The view seems to be that although people may go to the polling booth out of a sense of moral responsibility, or because they enjoy participating in political processes as a form of spectator sport, they can be presumed to cast their votes entirely on the basis of "economic interest." This claim is, we believe, essentially misconceived.

2. See, for example, H. Bowen, "An Interpretation of Voting in the Allocation of Economic Resources," *Quarterly Journal of Economics* 58 (1943): 27–48.

The Formal Analytics

It serves clarity in exposition to begin with a formal definition of voter "rationality" as used by public choice analysts. Accordingly, we offer the following:

> *Definition 1*: Let {S} be the set of all the outcomes on which any voter can exercise his or her vote. Then to say that the ith voter is "rational" means that he or she will vote for $s^* \ \varepsilon \ S$

$$\text{if } U_i(s^*) > U_i(s) \text{ for all } s \ \varepsilon \ S - s^n$$
$$\text{and only} \quad \text{if } U_i(s^*) \geq U_i(s) \text{ for all } s \ \varepsilon \ S - s^n,$$
$$\text{where} \quad U_i \text{ is the } i^{th} \text{ voter's utility function.}$$

This definition corresponds exactly to that of rational consumer choice among a set of alternatives {S}.

Clearly, the proposition that individuals vote rationally in this sense is quite a powerful one. To the extent that we can determine who benefits and who loses from particular policies, we can predict more or less precisely how particular individuals will vote. Furthermore, to the extent that electoral processes faithfully reflect the preferences of the vast bulk of the citizens, the quasi-utilitarian defense that is often offered of market processes may be extended relatively easily to the voting process (as tends to be done for the median voter theorem, for example).

Our claim, however, is that strict rationality on the part of the voter does not at all imply behavior according to Definition 1. The central element in supporting that claim is the observation that the object of choice in the election context is not the electoral outcome but, rather, the vote itself. More particularly, the expected return to any voter from exercising a vote according to the utility derived from the outcome is relatively small and, in many cases, negligible.

Consider, for example, an election in which there are exactly two options, a and b. The options in question may be two candidates for office, or yes/no votes in a referendum. The precise details are immaterial, provided the options are exogenously determined and fixed. We consider the rational calculus of some voter, i. Just as in the analysis of a market choice, we initially ignore any satisfaction that the individual derives from the act of voting per se: By assumption, the voter is taken to care solely about the outcomes of the election. Without loss of generality, assume that the ith voter prefers outcome a. Then the return to that voter of casting a vote for a will be as follows:

$$U_i(a) - U_i(b), \text{ if he or she is decisive, 0 otherwise}$$

Alternatively, the expected return, R, to the individual in voting for a is

$$R = h[U_i(a) - U_i(b)], \qquad [1]$$

where h is the probability that the ith voter will be decisive.

The parameter h is clearly crucial. It is the probability that there will be an exact tie among the remaining voters. Suppose, then, that there are $(2n + 1)$ voters, and for simplicity we can let this number be the entire population of enfranchised voters.[3] Let us initially suppose, further, that no voter has any idea how others may vote. Hence, the prior probability p that anyone will vote for candidate/option a is one-half, and, concomitantly, the probability that anyone will vote for b is one-half. Then, the probability of a tie between the remaining 2n voters (absent i) is as follows: The number of ways those 2n voters can be arrayed so that a will receive exactly n votes divided by the total number of ways those 2n voters might be arrayed across the two alternatives. That is,

$$h = \binom{2n}{n}/2^{2n}. \qquad [2]$$

More generally, if the probability p that others will vote for a is not one-half, then the probability of a tie occurring is

$$h = \binom{2n}{n}p^n(1 - p)^n. \qquad [3]$$

Using Stirling's approximation to simplify the calculation of equation 3, we have

$$h' = \frac{2^{2n}}{\sqrt{\pi \cdot n}} p^n(1 - p)^n, \qquad [4]$$

3. This reflects nothing other than the law of large numbers: The variance of the distribution of possible outcomes around p becomes very small as electoral size increases.

Table 1

Voting Population	Value of $[U_i(a) - U_i(b)]$ Required for R $= \$1$, for Various J			
(2n)	j = 0	j = .0001	j = .001	j = .01
2,001	56	56	56	62
20,000	177	177	179	481
200,001	560	566	619	12.3×10^6
10m.	4,000	6,533	60,000	~
100m.	12,500	1.9×10^6	6×10^{25}	~

and in the special case where p is one-half, this yields a corresponding approximation to equation 1:

$$h = \frac{1}{\sqrt{\pi n}}. \tag{5}$$

On this basis, we can now return to our central question: How large must the perceived difference in the value of alternative outcomes be in order for the expected return, R, to voter i in voting for a to be nonnegligible? To give a sense of the orders of magnitude at stake here, suppose we set R at $1. We take the dollar amount as a notional threshold, below which it is presumed that the expected benefit from voting for a rather than b is sufficiently small to be unnoticeable. Given this procedure, we can depict in the first column of Table 1 the values that $[U_i(a) - U_i(b)]$ must take for varying levels of electorate size in order for the purely instrumental return from voting to be exactly $1. Clearly, this is simply a convenient way of depicting values of h, as 2n varies: What is shown in Table 1 is the inverse of h. As an example, in a U.S. presidential election,[4] in which the electorate numbers roughly 100 million voters, candidate a would have to offer the voter approximately $12,000 more than candidate b before the expected economic benefit derived by the voter from casting a vote for a is as much as $1.

Furthermore, it is worth pointing out that the election involved in this case is a limiting case, in which the odds are exactly 50/50 that either candidate will win. If, instead, the prior probability that a randomly selected voter will vote for a differs from one-half, even very slightly, then the probability

---

4. This analysis discounts complications due to the electoral college system.

of an exact tie among the 2n voters falls drastically when the number of voters is at all large. Suppose, for example, that we define the unexpected majority, m, as the expected number of votes for a minus the expected number of votes for b (so m can be negative), and suppose m to be nonzero. Then the prior probability of any voter voting for a is

$$p = \frac{n + \frac{1}{2} m}{2n}. \tag{6}$$

Substitution into equation 4 yields

$$h' = \frac{2^{2n}}{\sqrt{\pi n}} \left(\frac{n + \frac{1}{2} m}{2n} \right)^n \left(\frac{n - \frac{1}{2} m}{2n} \right)^n$$

$$= \frac{1}{\sqrt{\pi n}} (1 - j^2)^n, \tag{7}$$

where j is the expected proportionate majority for a, m/2n. Clearly, even though j is small (and $[1 - j^2]$ very close to unity) the raising of $(1 - j^2)$ to the nth power makes $(1 - j^2)$ small when n is at all large. In Table 1, we depict for various values of electorate size (2n) and expected majority (j) the values that $[U_i(a) - U_i(b)]$ would have to take in order for the expected return (R) to be $1.

Consider again our presidential example. Suppose that the expected margin of victory for candidate a is 1 vote in each 1000. Then, in order for the expected return, R, to be $1, the value of $[U_i(a) - U_i(b)]$ would have to be of the order of 6×10^{25}, which doubtless more than exhuasts the world's total product.

Some care should be taken in interpreting such spectacular examples. When n is large, even a small deviation of p from 0.5 drastically alters the probability that a will win: For example, an expected majority of 1 vote in 1000 for a in an election of 100 million voters means that a is virtually certain to win.[5] This alerts us to the limited reliance of such examples. In almost all elections, even those that are not expected to be close, the odds in favor of the favored party do not suggest that the outcome is a foregone conclusion.

More generally, queries can be raised about the appropriateness of using the analogy with a sequence of random events to determine the probability

5. As n becomes large, the variance of the distribution becomes very small.

of a tie—even though this is the formulation that public choice theorists typically use.[6] We know full well that in most elections a substantial proportion of voters vote from habit, and that the corresponding proportion for whom outcomes might have weight is a significant subset of the voting population. The probability of a tie may be smaller or larger in such cases, depending on the proportions of habitual voters voting for each option. However, it must be explained why it is rational for voters to cast their votes habitually in this case, something that the traditional public choice model does not explain adequately.

In any case, the general point that emerges from all this is that in virtually all elections involving significant numbers of voters, the prior probability each voter might reasonably hold that he or she will be decisive is very small, possibly negligible. This seems entirely clear. The question at issue is what this fact implies for voting behavior. In order to indicate what is at stake, let us remove the assumption that only outcomes count in influencing voter behavior, and formulate each individual's utility function in somewhat more detail as follows.

We ascribe to each voter a utility function of the following form:

$$U_i = U_i[X_i; G; X_j; V; \ldots], \tag{8}$$

where

X_i is i's consumption of private goods (income)

X_j is the consumption of private goods (income) by other individuals,
$\quad j = 1, \ldots, i - 1, i + 1, \ldots, n$

G is the level of provision of public goods, and

V is the intrinsic consumption benefit from casting a vote in a particular way.

The formulation in equation 8 allows for two influences on i's behavior not allowed for in the conventional public choice model. The first is the possible presence of altruism, or concern for the welfare of others, as revealed by the presence of others' incomes in i's utility function. The second is the

---

6. See, for example, N. Beck, "A Note on the Probability of a Tied Election," *Public Choice* 18 (1975): 75–80, and W. Riker and P. Ordeshook, "A Theory of the Calculus of Voting," *American Political Science Review* 62 (1968): 25–42.

possibility that i will derive some satisfaction directly from the act of voting for one or another candidate per se, independent of the particular outcome that happens to emerge from the political process. We set aside at this point the plausibility of this formulation; it has the virtue of being a very general one and we do not, at this stage, rule out the possibility that some of the variables in the utility function will turn out to be of no importance (that is, the marginal utility will be zero with respect to some arguments).

On this basis, we can now isolate two distinct elements that are potentially relevant in the individual's decision to vote. Let A_i be the aggregate benefit measured in terms of dollars that i derives from voting for a rather than b. As our earlier analysis emphasizes, the "output-related" benefits of i voting for a are not dependent solely on how i votes, and will be so dependent only when i happens to be decisive in the election. By contrast, the satisfaction that i derives from the act of voting for some candidate per se is independent of the electoral outcome. That is:

$$A_i = h \cdot B_i + U_v^i,$$ [9]

where

  B_i is the benefit in dollars that i receives if a wins, and
  U_v^i is the money value that i places on the act of voting for a in and of itself.

Our interest here revolves not so much around explaining why i chooses to vote as around the relative significance of different elements in i's voting calculus. We seek to address the question of why, given that i does vote, he or she chooses to vote in the way he or she does. To make the implications of equation 9 for this question clear, it may be useful to offer a slight reformulation:

$$A_i = h \left[B_i + \frac{1}{h} \cdot U_v^i \right].$$ [10]

What equation 10 indicates is that considerations relating to U_v^i are 1/h times more important in explaining voting behavior than is the outcome-related parameter, B_i. And the values of 1/h are those numbers set out in Table 1 for various different electoral settings. If we are to explain voting behavior, therefore, there seems a very strong presumption that we ought to start with the U_v^i term, and not the outcome-related term: Even quite a modest preference for the act of voting for a (or b) becomes relatively important—in many cases, presumptively crucial—in explaining voting behavior.

If we take the assumption of rational behavior on the part of voters seriously, therefore, we must recognize that neither the act of voting nor the choice of whom to vote for can be explained solely, or even predominantly, by reference to voters' preferences over outcomes. When a voter i chooses to vote for a rather than b, it is a decision that in many cases will depend negligibly on the relation between the outcome-related terms, $U_i(a)$ and $U_i(b)$, in precise contradiction to the definition of rational behavior offered in Definition 1.

Market Choice, Revealed Preference, and Political "Choice"

The notion of rational behavior applied by public choice scholars to voting derives from a direct extrapolation of individuals "choosing," with a given budget, among consumption items in the market—the standard case of consumer choice. When an individual so chooses, he or she must recognize that the opportunity cost of taking more of one good (x) is the prospective utility of some of another good (y) forgone. The objects over which choice is exercised are direct or indirect arguments in the individual's preferences from the choices actually made. It is possible to speak of those choices "revealing the individual's underlying preferences." Economists are often skeptical of attempts to discern preferences through other means (such as questionnaires), because unless the preference is revealed in the context of actual choice, there is no real cost to the individual of revealing one set of preferences rather than another. Economics is firmly grounded on the methodological conviction that individuals act purposively and that their actions reveal those purposes.

Contrast this with the voter's choice in the polling booth as to which of two handles to pull.[7] Here we may presume that the ultimate arguments in

7. For an early attempt to compare individual choice in the two settings, see J. Buchanan, "Individual Choice in Voting and the Market," *Journal of Political Economy* 62 (1954): 334–43. Some of the points made here are hinted at in the treatment, though not explicitly articulated.

the voter's utility function include the objects of "political choice" (whether those be alternative policy packages or alternative candidates). That is, we may presume that the individual cares which outcome emerges from the voting process. But this does not permit us to presume that his or her choice in the polling booth reflects or corresponds with his or her preference over outcomes, for the voter is not choosing between outcomes: He or she is choosing between levers to pull (or marks to make on a card), and is exercising that choice in the full knowledge that the particular lever pulled bears only the most tenuous relation to the political outcome that finally emerges. When the voter pulls a particular lever, the opportunity cost of doing so is not a particular policy forgone, but simply the other lever or levers unpulled. There is, therefore, no necessary connection between the voter's preferences over outcomes (the things over which basic preferences are defined) and the action of pulling one lever rather than another. An individual may or may not vote for the outcome he or she prefers: He or she simply pulls the lever he or she prefers. In no sense, therefore, can we argue that the choice between levers—the act of voting—"necessarily reveals the voter's preference over the objects of collective choice" in the same way that an analogous market choice reveals a buyer's preferences over the objects of choice in the market. There is a logical wedge driven between action and preference in the voting process exactly equivalent to, and directly resultant from, the logical gap between action and outcome.

In this fundamental sense, consumer choice in the market and voter choice in the political mechanism are entirely unlike.[8] In the more formal language of the previous section, the considerations that predominate in voter choice (which of two levers to pull) are virtually absent in market choice. In market choice, even if there are considerations analogous to those captured by the U_v term in equation 10, they are not overwhelming as they are in the voting case. The analogous expression for market choice of some outcome A over B is as follows:

$$A_i = B_i + U_c^i, \qquad [11]$$

8. Certain sorts of market choice, in which the outcome is very uncertain, may be rather like electoral choice as here analyzed.

where U_c^i is the money value that i places on the act of choosing a in and of itself, and independent of whether the purchaser actually gets a.

We do not deny that U_c^i may be positive in the case of market choice. For example, an individual may like to think of him- or herself as the sort of person who supports the great classical literature of the culture. And, in some cases, this motive may be sufficient to induce the individual to buy books he or she will never read and perhaps does not really expect to read. But in the market, the individual must pay the full price of indulging such preferences: He or she has to choose a, not b. In the voting booth, by contrast, a voter can express a preference for a by casting a vote accordingly and yet recognize that he or she is not obliged to accept a, because that one vote alone is of relatively small significance in determining the final outcome. More specifically, in the market, \$1 worth of B_i is equivalent to \$1 worth of U_c^i; the terms of trade are 1 to 1. In voting, however, \$1 worth of U_v^i is, to the voter, worth 1/h dollars' worth of B_i—perhaps \$12,000 worth, perhaps rather more.

Implications for "Public Choice"

The implications of all this for the analysis of political processes depend, in part, on the purposes for which the analysis is undertaken. Within modern public choice theory, it is possible to discern two distinct strands—one concerned with providing a predictive science of politics essentially analogous to the predictive science of markets that conventional neoclassical economics purports to provide, the other concerned with the normative evaluation of alternative institutional arrangements and possibly the design of institutional arrangements that might generate superior social outcomes.

For many scholars the distinction between these two purposes need not be finely drawn. The understanding of the way in which political institutions actually work—in the sense of providing testable hypotheses that the data do not reject—is a crucial ingredient in the choice among alternative institutions. Positive analysis is viewed as a necessary precursor to normative conclusions, and all that is required for any normative exercise is to "tack on" additional evaluation criteria to the pure science. In other work we have attacked this sort of approach as unduly casual, and have argued for a more ruthless separation of political science, thus defined, from political economy in the classical sense (which we see as primarily concerned with the exercise of comparative institutional analysis and institutional "design").[9]

In spelling out the implications of our analysis, it is useful to draw this distinction quite sharply. For purely positive, predictive political science, it is clearly crucial to have some theory of why individuals vote as they do. What we have attempted to explain is that any theory that presumes that individuals vote according to their evaluation of political outcomes, much as they choose in market settings, is extremely problematic. Since the U_v^i term, and not the B_i term, is overwhelmingly predominant in equation 10, the choice of which candidate or policy option to vote for depends overwhelmingly on tastes for showing preferences as such, and hardly at all on the evaluation of outcomes. Voting behavior is then to be understood perhaps as "symbolic" or "liturgical" (rather like the choice of which team to support in an athletic spectacle) and hardly at all like the choice among alternative investments. We must therefore search for some theory like that which will predict why individuals support one team rather than another. In the process, we might consider the net wealth maximization hypothesis (or something like it) as a possible contender, but on the face of things any such hypothesis seems rather implausible.

The public choice theorist might, of course, respond that the U_v^i term mainly captures the individual's desires to exercise his or her vote, and is essentially independent of for whom the individual votes (i.e., $U_v^i[a]$ and $U_v^i[b]$ are virtually identical). Such a claim cannot be rejected on purely logical grounds, but it does not seem at all congruent with even the most casual observation. Individuals do seem to care as much for whom they vote as that they vote at all. The decision to vote is, after all, the decision to vote for someone, and if the decision to vote cannot be explained in outcome terms, then it would be surprising if the decision to vote for a particular candidate could be explained in such terms.

At the same time, one should be careful not to reject all public choice ex-

---

9. See G. Brennan and J. Buchanan, "The Normative Purpose of Economic Science: Rediscovery of an Eighteenth Century Method," *International Review of Law and Economics* 1 (1981): 155–66, and "Predictive Power and the Choice among Regimes," *Economic Journal* 93 (March 1983): 89–105, for a fuller discussion of the distinction involved here, and for a discussion of the analytic method appropriate to "constitutional analysis" in the classical political economy sense.

planations out of hand: Some important pieces of public choice theory are not affected in any significant way by the foregoing discussion. Positive public choice derives its predictions about the behavior of wealth-maximizing individuals in political institutions by appealing to two quite distinct mechanisms. One—the one that is relevant to the central point made here—depends on the action of political entrepreneurs who put together packages of public policies designed to secure electoral support from some majority of voters. To derive direct predictions about which particular policies will be selected requires both a means of determining the identity of the particular majority selected and a theory of what policies that majority will vote for. In the absence of the former means, the analysis may be able to make testable predictions about the pattern of outcomes, and perhaps say something of interest concerning the normative properties of those outcomes. But it could not develop a fully fledged predictive theory of public choice. However, it is the latter theory with which we are concerned here, and we have simply advanced the proposition that there can be no automatic presumption that voters will vote for policies that reflect their interests (however broadly those interests are conceived).

There is, however, a distinct mechanism by which wealth-maximizing individuals in political institutions interact—through lobbyists, who directly purchase particular policies from politicians-bureaucrats by direct graft, by payments in-kind, or by campaign contributions. Needless to say, hypotheses about the operation of political processes based on this mechanism remain totally unaffected by the basis on which individuals cast their votes. Purchase of policy outcomes in direct return for campaign contributions, for example, involves a more or less direct exchange of the familiar market kind. It is an exchange that has certain peculiar characteristics,[10] but there is no sense in which the contributor reveals anything other than his or her true preferences for policy outcomes. This dimension of positive public choice therefore remains entirely unscathed.

Furthermore, while it is true that voters do not necessarily vote in accor-

10. The growing literature on "rent seeking" deals directly with this type of transaction. See J. Buchanan, R. Tollison, and G. Tullock, *Toward a Theory of the Rent-Seeking Society* (College Station: Texas A&M University Press, 1980), for much of the relevant material.

dance with preferences over outcomes, we cannot reject the hypothesis that they in fact do so. The claim might plausibly be made that preferences over teams to support (the U_v^i term) in some measure reflect similar considerations to outcome evaluation (the B_i term). After all, voters may well be inclined to prefer candidates who redistribute in their favor (and otherwise reflect their interests). People are, one might argue, more ready to support a party that is "nice" to them than one that is not, on the same sorts of grounds that they prefer people who are nice to them as friends. The theory of behavior that underlies such a position is not the theory of contractual exchange, but the theory of reciprocal giving. A suitor, for example, does not buy the attentions of the object of his admiration when he makes her a gift: He simply symbolizes his affection and interest. She may reciprocate his gift to indicate a corresponding interest, or exhibit that interest in some other way. But there is no direct quid pro quo here, no contractual obligation of the sort we associate with conventional trade. Given this rendering, it may make sense to speak of politicians "wooing" votes, but not of "buying" votes, with policy changes. And one would surmise, as in the suitor analogy, that the magnitude of the "gift" is by no means the only relevant consideration in securing voter support, and in many cases is not an important one.

Based on this understanding, rational voting behavior (in the sense of Definition 1) becomes not a logical extension of underlying rationality postulates, but, rather, an "as if" proposition: If the predictions derived from such an assumption "fit" reasonably well, then the assumption of voter rationality (as in Definition 1) is justified by the "fact." The difficulty with such a stance is that it presupposes a great deal of knowledge as to what "the facts" are. The extent to which the interests of particular voters are totally reflected in easily identifiable things, such as subsidies received and income increases due to relative factor price changes, can easily be overstated. Normal economic interest also includes, for example, the consumption value to the individual of publicly provided goods consumed—a value that is not apparent from mere inspection. As revealed preference theory of consumer choice emphasizes, preferences generally cannot be known except to the extent that they are gratuitously revealed in the process of acting. Consequently, where the connection between action and preference is itself at risk, it is difficult to see how a decisive empirical test for that connection could be mounted.

Moreover, to the extent that political outcomes do appear to reflect constituent interests, this may be attributable not to electoral constraints on politicians' behavior but to constraints arising from the rational desire to maximize gains from lobbying and campaign contributions, which, as we have noted, is precisely analogous to ordinary market behavior.

Even the most enthusiastic defender of a method that presumes voters to vote preferences over outcomes must, therefore, acknowledge the possibility of an independent source of "noise," attributable to the logical gap between voter action and voter preference—noise that may, in particular instances, become thunderous. The pessimistically inclined may well despair of the possibility of developing any systematic theory of majoritarian electoral processes from an economic interest base. Public choice, as the political science counterpart to the neoclassical theory of market behavior, lacks the foundation of a purely logical a priori theory of voting behavior. By any reckoning, this is surely a major lack.

Once the notion that individuals vote their interests is seen to be at risk, then, clearly, so is the claim of any "efficiency" properties that might be construed to attach to political outcomes. Setting aside the peculiarities of majority rule as an "aggregation" device, of which standard public choice theory makes much ado, there remains the problem that the preferences so aggregated may bear little relation to the political outcomes that citizens would prefer to prevail. For example, even where the simple median voter theorem applies, and hence where there is no cycling, there can be no presumption that the median of revealed voter preferences will bear any systematic relation to the median of those voters' true preferences over policy outcomes. If voters cannot be presumed to vote for the outcomes they prefer, there seems to be widespread scope for electoral irrationality of the most basic kind. Clearly, such irrationality is a creature of the institutional setting within which voting occurs: It does not arise in analogous market settings. The familiar normative apparatus of modern welfare economics would, on this basis, indicate a presumptive preference for decentralized markets over majoritarian electoral processes.

Summary and Conclusion

The central proposition of this article is that the institutional setting within which preferences are revealed makes a difference in what is revealed. The

strict logical connection between individual choice and the individual's preferences over choice alternatives that exists in the market is essentially absent
in large-number majoritarian elections. Because no individual voter acts to
determine the social outcome (except in highly unlikely cases), voters cannot
be expected to choose among alternative outcomes in the manner they do in
the market. This implies that any simple extrapolation of voter behavior
from market analogues is misguided. The notion that voters vote according
to their preferences over alternatives is not an a priori truth emerging from
the basic proposition that agents are rational. At the very best, it becomes an
empirical proposition potentially subject to refutation. And, on the face of
things, it is by no means an overwhelmingly plausible proposition.

Public choice theory, in simply assuming that voters behave rationally and
in a manner analogous to that in which market agents can be presumed to
operate, is therefore at risk entirely on logical grounds. And, although pure
logic may not be sufficient to enable us to reject public choice propositions,
a great deal more in the way of empirical evidence would have to be amassed
before rational voting (in the public choice sense) could be presumed. What
logic and a priori theorizing can do is alert us to those considerations that
seem likely to weigh most heavily in voting behavior: On this basis, evaluation of the outcomes can be set aside as presumptively irrelevant.

Traditional political scientists may feel reassured by all this. To some extent, the ad hoc empiricism and casual theorizing of conventional political
science may seem to be vindicated by our analysis. But one of the major
thrusts of public choice theory—that the outcomes of majoritarian elections
may bear little relation to what citizens really want—reemerges in a rather
different form. Collective irrationality may occur, not so much because of
cycling problems and the like as because of the underlying irrationality of
voters' revealed preferences. Because ultimately such irrationality is a characteristic of the institutional setting within which voting occurs, simple majoritarian political processes must be recognized to be presumptively unsat-
isfactory, at least using any normative criteria in which voter preferences are
supposed to count.

Hegel on the Calculus of Voting

Public-choice theory attempts to derive conceptually refutable predictions about political outcomes from the rational behavioral calculus of individuals. A central problem in this developing body of analysis is that of explaining the voting act itself. Why do individuals vote? Since the value of a person's vote is slight, especially in large electorates, the existence of even small costs should deter voting participation. Alternative and essentially nonrational explanations have seemed to be necessary to explain voter turnouts.

The basic paradox of individual participation in elections owes its modern emphasis to Anthony Downs, who devoted considerable attention to measuring the value of an individual's vote,[1] and to Gordon Tullock, who characteristically presented the implications of Downs' analysis in their unwelcomed logical purity.[2] Discussions of the voting calculus and its implications for democratic process are found in almost all modern works on the public-choice bookshelf.[3]

There is little or no reference in these works to intellectual antecedents.[4]

From *Public Choice* 17 (Spring 1974): 99–101. Reprinted by permission of the publisher, Kluwer Academic Publishers.

1. Anthony Downs, *An Economic Theory of Democracy* (New York: Harper, 1957), especially Part III.

2. Gordon Tullock, *Toward a Mathematics of Politics* (Ann Arbor: University of Michigan Press, 1967), especially Chapter VII.

3. See, for example, A. K. Sen, *Collective Choice and Social Welfare* (San Francisco: Holden-Day, 1970), 195–96; Larry L. Wade, *The Elements of Public Policy* (Columbus: Charles Merrill, 1972), Chapter VII; W. H. Riker and P. Ordeshook, *Positive Political Theory* (Englewood Cliffs: Prentice Hall, 1973), Chapter III.

4. The only exception to my knowledge is found in Mancur Olson, *The Logic of Collective Action* (Cambridge: Harvard University Press, 1965). Olson carefully and correctly discusses the issue, which is, of course, a version of the free-rider problem in public goods theory, at several points, and (p. 164), he refers to a statement by Dr. Johnson as reported

As in other areas of modern social science, progress here may take the form of rediscovery, and it should not perhaps be surprising that the problem of the individual voting calculus should have been fully recognized by earlier writers. The purpose of this note is to call attention to Hegel's very clear recognition of the problem in its modern meaning. In his basic work in political theory, *The Philosophy of Right*, initially published in 1821, Hegel stated the problem clearly and recognized its implications for democratic process. I shall first present Hegel's statement in its original German, followed by the accepted English translation of the passage.

> Von dem Wählen die vielen Einzelnen kann noch bemerkt werden, dass nothwendig besonders in grossen Staaten die Gleichgültigkeit gegen das Geben seiner Stimme, als die in der Menge eine unbedeutende Wirkung hat, eintritt, une die Stimmberechtigten, diese Berechigung mag hinen als etwas noch so Hohes angeschlagen und vergestellt werden, eben sum Stimmgeben nicht erscheinen—so dass aus solcher Institution vielmehr das Gegentheil ihrer Bestimmung erfolgt, und die Wahl in die Gewalt weniger, einer Partei, somit des besondern, zufälligen Interesses fällt, das gerade neutralisirt werden sollte.[5]

> As for popular suffrage, it may be further remarked that especially in large states it leads inevitably to electoral indifference, since the casting of a single vote is of no significance where there is a multitude of electors. Even if a voting qualification is highly valued and esteemed by those who are entitled to it, they still do not enter the polling booth. Thus the result of an institution of this kind is more likely to be the opposite of what was intended; election actually falls into the power of a few, of a caucus, and so of the particular and contingent interest which is precisely what was to have been neutralized.[6]

It seems clear from the context of this passage that Hegel conceived the problem as it is now interpreted. The passage, in small print, is imbedded in

---

by Boswell. As cited, however, there is no indication in the statement that Dr. Johnson recognized the participation paradox at all, and, in fact, he seems to assume that voting is costless.

5. G. W. F. Hegel, *Grundlinien der Philosophie des Rechts*, Vol. 7 in *Hegel, Sämtliche werke* (Stuttgart: Frommanns Verlag, 1952), 421–22, or Section 311.

6. G. W. F. Hegel, *The Philosophy of Right*. Translated with Notes by T. M. Knox, Vol. 46, Great Books of the Western World (Chicago: Encyclopaedia Britannica, 1952), 104.

his defense of the representation of organized group interests in the legislative body as opposed to the open selection of individual legislators by individual voters who act separately.

The oversight of this important and early statement of the problem stems in part from the general neglect of Hegel's political theory.[7] More generally, we have here an example of the failure of those who have worked in modern public-choice theory to familiarize themselves with the masterworks in political theory. And, conversely, traditional political theorists, who do know the masterworks, have neglected the developments in public choice. All of which prompts a methodological recommendation. There is "gold in them thar hills" for both groups. Public-choice theorists can learn much from a careful reading and reinterpretation of the masters, and traditional political theorists can help greatly in this reinterpretation if they learn the working tools of public choice.

---

7. This neglect is on the way to being corrected by modern political theorists. See Shlomo Avineri, *Hegel's Theory of the Modern State* (Cambridge: Cambridge University Press, 1972). My attention was called to Hegel's statement by Avineri's book, which includes (p. 162) a portion of the passage cited above, and recognizes its importance. For another briefer, and more general, work on Hegel's political theory which does not, however, call attention to this statement, see Dante Germino, "Hegel as a Political Theorist," *Journal of Politics* 31 (November 1969): 885–912.

Public Choice and Ideology

It is impossible to deny that *public choice* has embodied a "theory of government failure" that is on all fours with the "theory of market failure" embodied in theoretical welfare economics. In saying this, I am *not* saying that public choice implies government failure *relative* to market alternatives. I am saying that relative to the images of government prevalent in the 1940s, public choice has embodied a theory of government failure. Public choice, along with complementary empirical observation, has defused enthusiasm for collectivist solutions to social problems. In this negative sense, public choice has exerted, and continues to exert, major ideological impact.

Public choice has also been important in opening up for inspection and evaluation previously sacrosanct aspects of social interaction. In so doing, it has become more difficult for intellectually self-respecting scholars to maintain mutually inconsistent standards for the evaluation of separate organizational alternatives. The economist who analyzes the distance between the market order that he observes and that which satisfies his formalized conditions for optimality cannot, by neglect, imply preference for the collectivist alternative. He can no longer act like the judge who awarded the prize to the second singer after he had heard the first. I am not here saying that my colleagues in economics have quit doing this. I am saying only that exposure to public choice makes it more difficult for them to do so.

It seems extremely difficult for anyone to adopt a socialist position and at the same time be familiar with and accept the analysis of public choice. Here I use *socialist* in the sense that this term was employed in the 1930s, when

From *What Should Economists Do?* (Indianapolis: Liberty Fund, 1979), 271–76. Reprinted by permission of the publisher.

This chapter was initially prepared for presentation in a panel discussion at the Public Choice Society meeting, New Orleans, March 1978.

Lange, Lerner, and others convinced so many of their colleagues that socialism could *work*. No more than a smattering of sophistication in public choice (or in ordinary common sense, for that matter) is required to suggest the absurdity in that position. Once any thought at all is given to the actual processes of collective decision-making, the claims for efficiency-generating properties of the socialist alternative collapse of their own weight.

Admittedly, my comment here applies to what has been called "market socialism," or, more generally, to what is still occasionally called "democratic socialism." The authoritarian socialist position is immensely stronger in terms of logical consistency. Democratic decisions cannot run a society, but perhaps the experts, the technocrats, the social engineers, the planners, can do so. What is there in public-choice theory that also gives the lie to the planning advocates? We need only return to the ancient Roman query: Who is to guard the guardians? Planners are also utility-maximizing individuals, and who could predict that planning decisions will be made contrary to the interests of those who make them?

Let me now shift beyond the ideological positions that might, in one sense, be classified as "economic," and examine the position I have sometimes called the "transcendentalist." In this position, politics is an activity that seeks "truth," and political process is a means of arriving at "truth judgments." There exist objectively defined "true" solutions to all political questions, and the task of politics and political scholars is to find them. This position captures the essence of classical political theory. It must be apparent that such a stance rejects the central organizing hypothesis of public choice, namely, the derivation of collective outcomes from the utility-maximizing behavior of individuals. Implicit in public-choice analysis is the notion that only individuals have values or preferences, that there are really no transcendent truths to be discovered by some mysterious process of political discourse. There are relatively few Straussians among us.

Let me move along in my array of philosophical positions or ideological stances that seem inconsistent with public-choice theory. We can, I think, dismiss the anarchist position readily, whether this be the romantic or the libertarian variety. Public-choice theory deals with persons as utility-maximizing beings, not as disembodied spirits full of love, or even as mindful of each other's "natural boundaries."

This leaves me with the Marxist position, which requires discussion at somewhat greater length. In some of his explanation of observed politics, the Marxist is closer to the public-choice theorist than either of them is to the "public-interest" theory of politics. Where the Marxist conception departs from the public-choice conception is in its failure to construct its analysis within an individualistic frame of reference. Persons cannot be rational utility maximizers and at the same time behave so as to further the interests of the social class in which they are located or to which they have arbitrarily assigned themselves. To say that class position dominates and drives behavior is fully analogous to saying that a person behaves always to further the public interest. After all, all of the members of the community are a "class." One model seems as empty of content as the other. Or as full.

So much for an array of those philosophical positions or ideologies that seem to be inconsistent with a considered internalization of the principles of public-choice theory. Let me turn briefly to consider those positions that seem broadly consistent. I group these into two sets, which I label the Panglossian and the meliorist. By Panglossian I refer to those views that imply, directly or indirectly, that there is really nothing that can be done to improve matters; hence, we live in the best of possible worlds. I am not quite sure that we can properly label these positions as "ideologies," but you will recognize them.

First, there is the pure Hobbesian, who asserts that everyone prefers order to anarchy and that only the sovereign can secure order. But there is no control over the passions of the sovereign. Relax and enjoy, if you can. My point here is only that this basic Hobbesian world view is compatible with public choice. All persons are utility maximizers. Much the same can be said for the Paretian world view, which is closely related to the Hobbesian. There always exists a sharp delineation between the rulers, the elite few, and the ruled. The elites may circulate, but there is no mythology of democratic control. Rulers rule in their own interest, and the ruled try to evade the rules to the extent that self-interest dictates. The task of the social scientist is to observe the uniformities, to identify the residues.

I should also put into the Panglossian category what I have defined as the social evolutionist position, which I associate with Oakeshott and Hayek. Efficient institutions tend to emerge through a spontaneous process of decentralized adjustment, akin to the common law, and attempts to design, lay on, or construct improvements must be self-defeating. I mention this philosophical perspective only to note that it is not, *per se,* inconsistent with the principles that drive the theory of public choice.

So much for the Panglossian varieties. Each of the world views described is broadly consistent with public choice because each can embody the presumption that individuals are rational utility maximizers in all capacities and roles.

Let me now turn very briefly to the meliorist position or ideology that is consistent with the principles of public choice, and you will not be surprised to learn that this is my own position. I refer, of course, to the constitutionalist-contractarian position, which is based in the recognition that individuals are utility maximizing and rational, and that they recognize that they are. Hence, there will be the need for "constitutions," for "rules," to constrain the behavior of persons, privately and collectively, and public choice offers the normative understanding necessary to lay down "better" rules. The Hobbesian scenario is rejected empirically; we observe that governments have been limited by constitutional constraints. We also reject the evolutionist view; we have observed designed or constructed social arrangements that work.

I have tried to suggest that certain positions are consistent with public choice while others are not. I am not implying in making this classification that everyone who works in public choice has a well-defined philosophical position. Many scholars do not. These scholars proceed in what they conceive to be their roles as "scientists," discovering many old wheels and a few new ones, with relatively little concern for the implications of "scientific findings" for a normative understanding of social order. To the extent that these social "scientists" among us really think that the problems of living together in organized community lend themselves to scientific solution, I think they are seriously deluded. But to discuss this point in detail would be both to repeat what many others have said and to go on far too long.

PART FOUR

Voting Models

What If There Is No
Majority Motion?

The Pure Majority-Voting Cycle

The theory of majority voting should occupy a central place in any volume celebrating the achievement of Duncan Black. In this paper, I propose to examine the results of majority-voting rules when the preferences of committee members are such as to produce the familiar cycle. Many investigators, from Duncan Black onward, upon discovering the logical possibility of the cycle, have turned their efforts toward narrowing the range for cyclical prospects on the one hand, and/or toward complementary or alternative rules on the other, rules that will make a unique selection from among the several potentially co-equal majority-vote outcomes. Duncan Black's discovery of the single-peaked preference theorem is an example of the first line of inquiry; the Borda method is perhaps the most familiar of the alternative rules designed to get around the majority-voting cycle.[1]

In order to eliminate all concern with these sorts of issues, I shall discuss the operation of simple majority-voting rules in an abstract model that is

From *Towards a Science of Politics: Essays in Honor of Duncan Black*, ed. Gordon Tullock (Blacksburg, Va.: Center for Study of Public Choice, 1981), 79–90. Reprinted by permission of the publisher.

I am indebted to my colleagues, and especially David Friedman, Nicolaus Tideman, and Gordon Tullock, for helpful suggestions made during a seminar presentation of this paper.

1. For a discussion along with a proposal for a sophisticated alternative rule, see I. J. Good and T. N. Tideman, "From Individual to Collective Ordering Through Multidimensional Attribute," *Proceedings of the Royal Society of London*, Series A, Vol. 347 (January 1976), 371–85.

highly idealized to produce a pure cycle. By "pure" I mean that neither simple majority voting nor any conceivable alternative procedure will make a definitive selection from among a finite set of specifically defined states or objects of choice. This idealization requires much more than the ordinal rankings minimally necessary to generate a cyclical result in a sequence of pairwise majority votes. The distribution of all voters over all of the preference rankings must be fully symmetrical. In addition, within the preferences of each voter, all differences among the choice options must be equal. If these additional restrictions are not imposed, we should have an "impure" cycle, which could be removed by resort to some alternative selection procedure.

Faced with such pure cycles, investigators have concluded that the group or committee cannot act consistently or coherently in selecting among the alternatives, that any outcome must be arbitrary. Such a conclusion is unwarranted in a general sense, and it depends on certain implicit assumptions or presuppositions about the "motions" that should at least be clearly enunciated. Precise characteristics of the choice set must be specified; in particular the temporal sequence of the pairwise votes among the separate choice options must be postulated. As I shall demonstrate, the attributes of the majority-voting cycle are quite different under different settings.

Predictability in the Cyclical Sequence

For purposes of expositional simplicity, we may work with a three-element choice set: A, B, and C. The elements may represent motions, candidates, or options. No elements outside this restricted set are considered to be possible. For additional simplicity, we may work with a three-person group. The three voters are labeled as: i, j, and k. The evaluations of the three alternatives are such as to generate the pure majority-voting cycle, as defined above.

The first of several straightforward logical points to be made concerns the directional form of the cycles that may exist among the separate elements of the choice set. Among the three elements, A, B, and C, there are only two directional forms of cycle that are possible, which I shall call the *clockwise* and the *counterclockwise*. These two forms are represented in Figure 1, with the arrows indicating the direction of movement in successive rounds of votes in the cycle.

It is clear from the figure that once the form of the pure cycle is identified

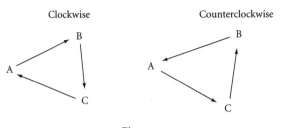

Figure 1

the precise pattern of the sequence of results is fully predictable. Any one of the motions can be majority-dominated by only one other motion just as the initial motion, in its turn, dominates only one other motion of element in the choice set. Hence, if any element of the set is defined as the starting point, or alternatively, if an initial pairwise majority vote is defined over any two of the three motions, the sequence of results in successive rounds of voting is fully predictable. From this regularity of pattern there follows the conclusion that the precise outcome is predictable if the number of votes is specified. The predictability that stems from the regularity of the cyclical sequence tends to have been obscured in the literature perhaps due to the usage of the words "inconsistency" and "incoherence" to apply to the majority cycle. But, as suggested, there is nothing that is inconsistent or incoherent in the operation of majority voting through a series of rounds, so long as the starting point is specified and the series is finite, given the implicit assumptions of unchanged preferences and the stability of the choice set.

Where Does the Cycle Start?

There are two distinct settings within which the majority cycle, even in its pure variety, may arise. If one of the elements in the choice set is the *status quo*, or, to use Black's term, "things as they are," the starting point is defined. The first vote in any sequence must be that between the *status quo* and one of the other options in the choice set. If the *status quo* wins in the initial pairwise comparison, there is no "start" to the cycle. If the *status quo* is defeated by majority vote, it must be paired against the single option that majority dominates it. We may call the vote that shifts the outcome to be an effective stage of the cycle. If A, among the three options in our example, is the *status quo*, the first effective vote in the cyclical sequence is that between A and B in the clockwise form of the cycle depicted in Figure 1, or between A and C in the counterclockwise form.

As Black indicated, however, the choice set may be made up entirely of elements that are nonexistent at the time of the initial vote. The group choice is to be made *de novo*, from among the several options that remain as prospects. With candidates, this is the setting where there is no incumbent. With policy options, each of three prospects may be assumed to dominate the existing state of affairs, the null or do-nothing option, for all three voters. In this choice setting, where does the voting begin?

There are two possible procedures. One of the options or motions could simply be selected, in some nonvoting fashion, as the initial position or as the option to be placed against the null option that is outside the cyclical set, and the sequence could then proceed just as if the arbitrarily chosen position were the *status quo* in the other setting discussed. Or, as a second procedure, any two of the three motions or options could be arbitrarily selected, and an initial vote between these two elements would then determine the direction of the cyclical flow. The selection of either one or two options from among the choice set must be arbitrary in the pure cycle. In the configuration of preferences that are postulated, no one of the alternatives is superior to any other under any conceivable procedure that assigns equal weights to the preferences of each voter. The inference must be that the group decision process, the voting rule, "should" reflect indifference as among all of the elements in the set. This essentially normative result suggests, in turn, that the initial selection be made through the use of some random device that will insure that each of the three possible outcomes is equally likely to emerge.

When Should the Cycle Stop?

As noted earlier, the sequence of outcomes in the pure majority cycle is predictable once a starting point is defined and the form of the cycle known. From this regularity, the specific result as of any effective stage of the cycle can be predicted. The starting point will not, of course, be decisive in determining a final outcome unless the stopping point is specified. Given any starting point, control over the number of rounds in the cycle can determine the outcome. Similarly, given any specified number of rounds of voting, control over the starting point can determine the outcome.[2]

One simple point to be made is that collective groups, committees, do make decisions, despite the widespread use of majority-voting procedures, and despite the possible majority cyclicity inherent in individual preference orderings. Ambiguity has been present in some discussion that suggests that, under majority cyclicity, the committee cannot reach decision; that the decision process is analogous to Buridan's ass, unable to choose among the alternatives confronted. This phenomenon would arise, however, only where the decision procedure evaluates the alternatives equally at each voting stage. With simple majority voting, and with pairwise comparisons between any two elements in the choice set, no such indifference or inability to reach a decision exists. (Ties are not possible in the pure cycle with an odd number of voters.) One of any two of the choice options always holds a decisive majority over the other. Indecisiveness is not a characteristic feature of the majority cycle.

This ambiguity may stem from failure to examine the temporal aspects of the choice setting. By inferring that the committee "cannot reach a decision," the analyst may suggest that, unless some arbitrary limit is placed on the number of votes, the process can go on forever. The "meeting" never ends; the cycle continues infinitely.

Empirically, cycles stop. But when "should" this point be reached? The introduction of this normative question requires resort to some criterion for determining the "best" rule for stopping the voting. I shall utilize a Rawlsian approach. We may ask the question, If a person is behind a veil of ignorance

2. Note should be made of the research by Charles R. Plott and Michael E. Levine on agenda manipulation. They have demonstrated that, by manipulating the agenda in a manner that does not seem biased, specific final outcomes can be made more likely to occur, even in the presence of the pure majority cycle. In the context of the analysis of this paper, Plott and Levine demonstrate that agenda manipulation is one means of selecting the starting point and the stopping point of the pure cycle in a nonrandom way. See Charles R. Plott and Michael E. Levine, "A Model of Agenda Influence in Committee Decisions," *American Economic Review* 68 (March 1978), 146–60.

concerning his own identification, when would he desire that the cyclical sequence be truncated? Assume that a person, at some constitutional stage where rules are chosen, could not know whether he will be in the position of i, j, or k, or what is the same thing, does not know what his ordinal preferences will be. What constitutional constraint would he prefer to impose on pure majority voting to insure that the "meeting" end short of forever?

To answer this question it is essential to be much more specific about the nature of the choice options than has been necessary to this point. A classification of choice settings must be attempted.

First, I shall discuss a setting in which the option, once chosen, is *permanent*. This permanence of result is important for the normative rule that is preferred. This feature refers to the length of calendar time that the decision, once made, is to remain in effect. Consider a simple illustration. Suppose that A, B, and C are three possible locations or routes for a new road that is to be constructed. Once a single route is selected and construction is complete, it will be extremely costly to relocate the facility. The decision, once made by the group, is essentially irrevocable.

In this situation, what is the preferred constitutional rule for stopping the majority cycle? If we assume either that voting itself is costly or that delay in reaching a group decision is costly, it is clear that the majority cycle here should be allowed to continue only so long as is minimally necessary to determine the regularity of the pattern over successive votes, or the symmetry of the pure majority cycle. After this point is reached, a random selection device should be introduced to settle the stopping point or, what is the same thing, to settle on one of the three choice options. If a computer is used, the preference rankings can be fed into it, and with the evidence of a pure and fully symmetrical majority cycle, the computer can be instructed to pick randomly from among the options with relatively little cost. The important point is that, to a person behind the veil of ignorance, any one of the three choice options is as good as any other. *Ex ante*, expected values of the outcome for the three voters or committee members can be equalized. No institutional procedure can equalize realized values *ex post*. Hence, any continuation of the majority-voting cycle as a process of choosing beyond minimal limits is inefficient.

NONPERMANENCE

Let us now examine a model where the decision made is not permanent but is, instead, limited in application to some finite period of calendar time. Perhaps the most familiar illustration is the election of a candidate who, once elected, will be in office for a fixed term. But it is not difficult to think of other illustrations where the choice is among motions or proposals that are comparably time-constrained. Initially, I shall assume that the length of the term, or application period, is exogenously determined, and that each successive or sequential period is of equal length.

How does this change in the model modify the choice of a preferred rule for stopping the majority cycle? In the case of risk neutrality, the use of some random selection procedure at the onset of each period or term will insure that the preferences of each person or committee member be accorded equal weight in the *ex ante* sense. If risk averseness is introduced, however, equalization of expected values at the constitutional stage may not be sufficient. Preferred rules may also involve some equalization in realized or *ex post* results, other things equal.[3]

If the costs of change in outcomes are not prohibitively high, a rule that allows only one pairwise majority vote for each period may accomplish the desired results. The preferences of each member of the committee are equally weighted in the regularly cycling sequence of outcomes over a number of periods. Under any positive discount rate, some advantage will necessarily be granted to those committee members whose preferences happen to be satisfied in relatively early periods of the cycle. If, however, the starting point of the cycle is randomly chosen, thus insuring *ex ante* equality in expected val-

---

3. Pauly and Willett make the distinction between *ex ante* and *ex post* equity, and they introduce several examples to suggest the applicability of each criterion for policy. See Mark Pauly and Thomas Willett, "Two Concepts of Equity and Their Implications for Public Policy," *Social Science Quarterly* 53 (June 1973), 8–19. Reprinted in *The Economic Approach to Public Policy*, edited by Ryan Amacher, Robert Tollison, and Thomas Willett (Ithaca: Cornell University Press, 1976), 300–312.

For a more general discussion that contains intriguing proposals for equalizing "political income" in an *ex post* sense, see Dennis Mueller, Robert Tollison, and Thomas Willett, "On Equalizing the Distribution of Political Income," *Journal of Political Economy* (March/April 1974), 414–22.

ues, the *ex post* criterion of equality is violated only by the higher discounting of the preferences of those members whose success in majority coalition formation falls late in the continuing cyclical sequence. In the case of candidates for office, a vote each period between the incumbent office holder and the opponent who can mount the effective challenge will insure continual rotation in office, which is precisely the result that may be most desired in this model.[4] An alternative rule that would generate essentially the same result would be one that assigned decision-making power to separate persons sequentially in each period.

How Long Should Majority Decisions Remain Binding?

To this point, I have examined two models with defined time dimensions. In the first, I have assumed that the group or committee choice is permanent and irrevocable. In the second, I have assumed that the time period over which the results of choice apply or remain in force is exogenously fixed at some finite length and that each successive choice binds the group for a period of equal length.

The next step in the analysis involves the normative issue concerning the efficient or optimal length of period, when this length is allowed to vary. If, at the constitutional stage, the term of office or period of applicability of a majority vote can be selected, what length is preferred? How long should a candidate be allowed to remain in office, once elected? Should office holders be required to stand for reelection monthly, annually, biannually, or at less frequent intervals? Should a city council's action on zoning ordinances remain valid one month, six months, a year, two years, a decade, or forever?

I shall not try to discuss these questions in general terms. I analyze them here only in the highly restricted setting of the pure majority cycle, as defined earlier, and I shall stay within the confines of the three-option, three-person model. I shall assume throughout the analysis that the chooser is risk averse

---

4. This is the model that I had implicitly in mind when I suggested in my review of Arrow's work that, if the preferences were such as to generate a majority cycle, the best result would, in fact, be some such continual rotation. See my "Social Choice, Democracy, and Free Markets," *Journal of Political Economy* 62 (April 1954), 114–23.

at the constitutional stage. This assumption insures that some attention will be paid to the variance in the results produced over the sequence of periods: equalization of expected values among the separate streams of payoffs at the constitutional level will not suffice as a criterion for evaluation of alternative arrangements. Under these conditions, if it is known or predicted in advance that the preference configurations of committee members or electors are such as to generate the pure cyclical sequence, what can we say about the length of term or period of application of a single pairwise majority choice? What are the variables that will determine the efficient term lengths in this model?

Three variables are immediately suggested: (1) the anticipated rate of discount or time preference of voters or committee members; (2) the costs of changing among the discrete choice options; (3) the differentials in the committee members' evaluations of the separate choice options. In the abstract setting for analysis here, I shall postulate that committee members or voters are equivalent with respect to these variables. That is to say, all persons are expected to have the same discount rate, to face the same net costs of change in choice options, and to exhibit the same differences in evaluation among their several choice options. The persons differ *only* in their rankings of the options available.

Discussion may be clarified by introducing the simple pure majority cycle depicted in Figure 2. Numbers in the cells represent cardinally measurable and interpersonally comparable evaluations of the options, A, B, and C, by committee members i, j, and k. The familiar majority cycle: $A_p B_p C_p A$ is generated.

Options \ Persons	i	j	k
A	3	1	2
B	2	3	1
C	1	2	3

Figure 2

Two parameters must be specified before we can further discuss the normative question of period length. In Figure 2, no time dimension is placed on the payoffs or evaluations. This ambiguity must be removed by defining relevant time rates. Assume for purposes of the analysis here that the evaluations are *daily rates*, that is, they are values or payoffs that will be generated *per day* of calendar time. Further, we assume that a day is the minimum length of period required for any payoffs to be realized by any committee members. Having set this parameter, we must also specify the length of the *planning horizon* that informs the calculus of the constitutional decision maker who is confronted with the prospective choice among the many possible term lengths that might be selected. For present purposes, assume that the planning horizon is *finite*, and that it is set at *N days*, with N being a very large number relative to the number of choice options.

RATE OF DISCOUNT

We may now examine the effects of the three variables on the selection of the efficient term length, with length of term or period of application being measured in days. Consider, first, the effects of the discount rate that the constitutional decision maker imputes to the committee members over the period of the cyclical sequences within the planning horizon.

Initially, assume that there is no time preference introduced. Values for differing time periods are weighted equally. In this extreme, if we allow for any costs of change above zero, the efficient minimal length of term or period over which the majority-voting choices are to remain valid is N/3 in the abstract example. Since there is no discounting, the delay in allowing any person's preferences to be more fully satisfied does not put such a person at a disadvantage. Since, by assumption, N is a very large number, this result suggests that the rules should, first of all, involve a randomized starting position, to be followed by one pairwise majority-voting choice each electoral period, but with very long periods, minimally of N/3 lengths.[5]

---

5. N/3 is the minimal length of period under the assumption here because, with very high costs of change, even longer periods, including infinite lengths, may be efficient. Even with risk averseness, the preferred constitutional arrangement may be one that does nothing more than equalize expected values *ex ante*.

Implicitly, the results suggested require that committee members live forever, or, at least, that they live for periods longer than the planning horizon, N days. If we allow persons to live finite lives, it is plausible to suggest that *ex ante* political equality could be attained only if the planning horizon is related to expected length of life. If we assume that life expectancy at birth is seventy-two years, and that twenty-five of these years are spent in childhood and/or dotage, a planning horizon of forty-eight years (17,520 days) might be considered maximal. In this case, even with a zero discount rate, the maximal length of the minimal term of application for any majority-voting choice would be sixteen years. Terms of this length would insure that the individual elector or committee member, over his adult life of forty-eight years, would find his first preferences met in one-third of these years, his second preferences met in another third, and his least preferred option selected in the remaining third.

The finite life model suggests, however, the basic absurdity of the no-discounting assumption. Even if persons place absolutely equal weights on the payoffs promised in differing time periods, each day or year that such payoffs are enjoyed, the mere fact that the actual length of life is determined stochastically to some degree implies positive discounting. That is to say, there is a necessary "biological time preference" in any rational behavior pattern. Once any positive rate of discount is introduced, the efficient length of time or period for the application or duration of majority-voting choice results is reduced, given normal ranges of values.

There is an additional reason why a positive rate of discount may need to be introduced into the constitutional selection of the optimal term length, quite apart from standard time preference. To the extent that the effects of the voting choice within any one period extend beyond the period itself, there is a rational basis for positive discounting, over and beyond the elements noted above. We are concerned here with the question of determining the optimal length of time the results of single-voting choices remain in force in the temporal cyclical sequence. We have assumed that the choice made in any one period is not permanent. But this assumption is not equivalent to eliminating all of the effects of a single-period action in later periods. It is necessary to examine the characteristics of the choice options, A, B, and C, even in the highly abstract models that restrict the analysis.

Consider an illustration in which the choice options take the following form: Suppose that the "community" owns a collective facility, say, a road. The alternatives confronted in each period are: (A) maintain the road, which will require an outlay of X dollars per day, *and* improve the road, which will take an additional X dollars of outlay per day; (B) maintain the road only, which requires a total outlay of X dollars per day; (C) allow the road to deteriorate at the physically defined rate of X dollars per day. The outlays per term length under each of the three options will be (A) 2X times the number of days of the term; (B) X times the number of days in the term; (C) and zero.

Assume that the payoffs or evaluations of the alternatives are defined, as before, as rates per day. Suppose that some randomized device selects option A for the initial period (some indeterminate number of days); this becomes the starting point for the cyclical sequence. Over the course of the first period, there will be net investment in the facility. At the end of the period, however, A will be defeated by C in a pairwise majority vote, and, during a second period of the same length, there will be net disinvestment in the facility. At the end of this time, C will be defeated in a majority vote by B, which will result in a policy of maintaining the capital value for the third period. And the cyclical sequence will continue.

It is clear from this illustration that the number of days included in the term or length of period for which the pairwise majority-voting choices are to be valid will determine the degree of bias introduced into the sequential results as a result of the initial randomized choice among the options. If, for instance, the length of period is limited to one day, the minimal allowed under our assumption about time rates of payoffs, the initial advantage granted to the person whose first choice is for the net investment alternative is weighted less over the whole sequence of results than would be the case should the period or term be, say, 10 days.

In our earlier discussion we noted that risk averseness was required to justify the continuing cyclical majority-voting sequence as opposed to the use of randomized selection at the onset of each period. In the consideration here, the presence of risk averseness also requires that the variance in the expected advantage given to those whose preferences are satisfied first in the cyclical sequence be minimized. This may be translated directly into the introduction of a positive discount rate, over and beyond that generated by positive time preference in some orthodox sense.[6]

THE COSTS OF CHANGE

The second major variable that will influence the selection of the preferred term length for a sequence of majority votes involves the costs of changing from one collective outcome or result to another. Again we can illustrate by taking an extreme case. If there are no costs of change, and if there is any positive discount rate at all, the optimal electoral period would be equal to the minimal time required for voters to recognize and attribute payoffs to results, which, in our example, we have assumed to be one day. A single majority vote would, in this setting, be allowed to remain in force for one day only, with each day's results being replaced during the next day by the option that wins out in an effective majority vote paired against the initial day's option.

As we introduce positive costs of change, the optimal period length is increased. The partial derivatives of optimal length of term with respect to the discount rate and to costs of change move in opposing directions over normal ranges. If the costs of change are very high (as in our initial road location example), the most efficient constitutional rule may involve some guarantee of *ex ante* fairness (equalization of expected values for each potential voter), along with explicit institutions designed to prevent the group from moving through a costly cyclical majority sequence. At very high costs of change, it may be wholly inappropriate to allow the relevant choice options to be brought up for the pairwise majority votes in successive periods, no matter how long such periods may be. At the constitutional level of deliberation, for

6. Objection may be made to the restrictions imposed implicitly by the three-option model in settings where there are essentially capital-investment or disinvestment aspects of single-period decisions. In the road-maintenance example, the average quality of road over the whole succession of periods will be different under differing patterns of the majority cycle, and it seems unreasonable, in one sense, to argue that individuals' preferences for road improvement, road maintenance, and road depreciation would be unchanged over changing levels of road quality. My concern is, however, not with the "realism" of the assumption of unchanging preferences, but rather with the normative implications for term length that can be variously derived while remaining within the unchanging preferences assumption, no matter how restrictive these might be in particular cases.

such choice options, it may be to the best long-term interest of each potential voter to prohibit the never-ending, period-by-period, majority cycle.

For other types of options, however, majority voting that would generate the cycle through subsequent electoral periods might be desired, provided the terms are sufficiently long to allow costs of change to be absorbed by the smaller variance in payoffs among the committee members or voters. In the illustration depicted in Figure 2, if each voter must undergo a net cost of 4 units under each change or shift of outcome, day-by-day voting would be less preferred than permanence of some randomized result. If, however, pairwise majority comparisons could be allowed over electoral periods of, say, 12-day lengths, the cyclical sequence might well be preferred to any single permanent outcome.

DIFFERENTIALS IN EVALUATIONS OF SEPARATE OPTIONS

There remains to be considered the third major variable that will influence the selection of the length of period. We have assumed that the valuations or payoffs of the separate voters or committee members are fully symmetrical over all options. We have not, however, done more than to specify an ordinal ranking over the separate choice options within the preferences of each voter. In the illustration contained in Figure 2, we may now assume that two zeroes are added to each three, one zero to each two, and nothing to the ones in the diagram. The cardinalized payoffs for each voter over the three separate choice options become (300, 20, 1) rather than the (3, 2, 1) of Figure 2.

It is evident that this simple change in the differentials among the three options, even if these are uniform over all voters, will modify the constitutionally preferred length of election period. At any given discount rate and with a given cost of change between any two options, an increase in the differentials will tend to reduce the length of the optimal period over which pairwise majority voters are allowed to remain valid. An increase in differentials is similar in effect to an increase in the discount rate, effectively increasing the weight given to the voter or committee member whose preferences are more fully met early in the cyclical sequence. Through this effect, the length of the optimal period of validity, considered constitutionally and behind the veil of ignorance, is reduced.

Conclusions

My purpose in this paper has been extremely limited. I have attempted to examine some of the properties of simple majority voting when the existence of what I have called the pure majority cycle emerges from the true configuration of voters' or committee members' preferences. An understanding of these properties allows certain normative inferences to be made concerning the efficiency of majority-voting procedures in differing choice settings. In particular, the analysis has implications for the question as to the optimal or efficient length of periods over which single pairwise majority-voting outcomes should be allowed to remain in force for the whole community, affecting majority and minority members alike.

I have made no attempt to go beyond the extremely simple model with three voters or committee members and three choice options. Such extensions should not prove difficult, and the central points are probably sufficiently outlined in the simple case. Extension in the number of voters can be accomplished readily, so long as persons with preferences identical to those of the three are added symmetrically to each group. Extension in the number of options involves no difficulty so long as the preferences over all options are fully symmetrical, which requires that the number of persons be at least as large as the number of options.

I have limited analysis to the pure majority cycle, largely in order to concentrate attention on the properties of the cyclical process itself rather than on prospects for alternative arrangements for selecting collective outcomes. In order to do this, I have assumed specific cardinal and interpersonal utility indicators in the model. The conclusions of the analysis do not, however, depend critically on these restrictions. To the extent that a majority cycle is predicted on the basis of ordinal preference rankings alone, but resort to alternative selection procedures is effectively forestalled, the normative implications of the analysis hold without significant change.

I have also implicitly assumed throughout the analysis that the group or committee has only the one choice on its agenda. It is assumed to have been assigned, potentially, the choice among A, B, and C, whether this choice be long-lasting in effect or made in each period. The group or committee is assumed not to face choices among, say, R, S, and T, or X, Y, and Z, along with the choice among A, B, and C. This sort of expansion of the choice set would allow for some trade-off as among the differing pure cycles, with the result that *ex post* equalization of realized payoffs might be more fully achieved.

The analysis has been based on the assumption of unchanging preferences. In this respect, there is no departure from standard economic analysis. But, in any treatment of political decision-making, such an assumption effectively denies the relevance of the whole process of political persuasion. One possible advantage of sequential majority voting, even if preferences may initially be such as to generate a pure cycle, might be the temporal change in voter attitudes that this institution allows to emerge and to modify the pattern of results.

The substantive methodological conclusion to be drawn from the analysis of this paper reinforces that which Gordon Tullock and I advanced in *The Calculus of Consent*.[7] A majority-voting rule is one among many possible institutions that may be used for the reaching of group or committee decisions. Majority voting has costs as well and benefits when viewed from the constitutional perspective of the potential voter or committee member whose own preferences are not yet identified. In some circumstances random dictatorship may be preferable to majority-driven and unending institutional change. In other situations, the efficient choice-making institution may well be the continuously changing period-by-period majority result. But the constitutional selection between these two institutions cannot be made rationally until the length of electoral term within the majority-voting sequence is itself efficiently chosen.

7. Ann Arbor: University of Michigan Press (1962).

Towards a Theory of Yes-No Voting

Roger L. Faith and James M. Buchanan

The formal theory of majority-rule voting has dealt almost entirely with the unique selection of a single candidate(s) or motion(s) from a set of alternatives greater than two. The analysis presumes that there is only a single group or collective decision to be made, a single "election," or a single "proposition."[1] This orthodox conceptual setting for collective choice is necessary to generate the possibility of the cyclically rotating, and hence disequilibrium, set of outcomes on the one hand and for the median-voter-dominated equilibrium outcome on the other. If the number of alternatives in the choice set is limited to two, simple majority-rule voting yields unambiguous results provided only that we assume an odd number of voters with each voter assumed to have strictly ordered preferences. In the orthodox voting-model setting, few problems of analytical interest seem to arise in the single pairwise choice between two alternatives, for example, between approval and disapproval of a proposition.

From *Public Choice* 37, no. 2 (1981): 231–45. Reprinted by permission of the publisher, Kluwer Academic Publishers.

We should like to thank our colleagues Geoffrey Brennan and Joseph Reid for helpful suggestions on earlier drafts of this paper, and Janet Faith, Richard Carter, and David Laband for their research assistance. Finally, we thank Akira Yokoyama of Josai University for saving us from some mathematical errors.

1. We use the term "proposition" here rather than "issue" in order to avoid confusion with the treatment of multi-issue space in public-choice analysis. In the latter, candidates, party platforms, and voters' ideal positions are described by vectors that employ several issue dimensions. But the analysis is directed toward the selection of a single candidate (a list), or platform, in a single election. Our analysis, by contrast, explicitly examines a bundle of "elections," or "group choices," each one of which is presented as a single yes-no proposition.

When the voting population is presented with a whole set of independent propositions, however, each one of which is to be resolved by simple "yes-no," "up-down," or "approve-disapprove" majority voting, questions of considerable analytical interest do arise. To our knowledge no one has discussed or investigated the analogues and contrasts between yes-no voting and the conventional, multi-alternative, majority-rule voting. The relative neglect of the properties of yes-no voting under majority rule is itself puzzling since many real-world collective choice institutions formally operate in this way. Examples that come to mind include zoning boards, referenda, and initiatives; in several states judges are re-elected on a yes-no basis.

1. The Basic Model

The institutional setting we wish to analyze is one in which there are several propositions to be settled by simple majority rule. The propositions are characterized by dichotomous choice—yes or no—and counterproposals are not permitted.[2] The propositions are independent in the sense that none, some, or all may be approved as a result of the voting process. There is no technological or consumptive complementarity or mutual exclusivity among propositions. With respect to voters, we assume they vote without strategic considerations. Vote-trading or other mechanisms by which differences in

2. One might interpret this as a setting of an agenda by an exogenous actor. The voters themselves do not offer new proposals for consideration. Some of the recent work on agenda manipulation where voters are presented with only two options may readily be brought within our framework of analysis. See, for example, T. Romer and H. Rosenthal, "Political Resource Allocation, Controlled Agenda, and the Status Quo," *Public Choice* 33 (Winter 1978), or R. J. Mackay and C. L. Weaver, "Monopoly Bureaus and Fiscal Outcomes: Deductive Models and Implications for Reform," in *Policy Analysis and Deductive Reasoning*, ed. G. Tullock and R. Wagner (Lexington, Mass.: D. C. Heath, 1978), and A. T. Denzau, R. J. Mackay, and C. L. Weaver, "On the Initiative-Referendum Option and the Control of Monopoly Government," *Papers of the Committee on Urban Public Economics*, Vol. 5, forthcoming.

An alternative interpretation is that the costs of communicating and enforcing compromise proposals are prohibitively high. This may particularly be the case when the issue is largely an emotional one such as the legalization of marijuana, the development of nuclear power, or the adoption of capital punishment. In other cases, the amount of wealth at stake simply may be insufficient to induce the affected party (or parties) to make expensive counterproposals.

preference intensities are resolved are precluded here. Each voter makes his or her own subjective evaluation of each proposition being voted upon. Note that this assumption does not preclude representation, where an individual voter acts as an agent or "representative" of some constituency or even for some special interest group.

For purposes of exposition let us initially consider a board of zoning appeals made up of three members. Their job is to vote, yes or no, on separate requests for zoning variances. Several requests are allowed to accumulate before any voting occurs, say, before the regular monthly meeting of the board. Suppose that six different, and independent, requests for zoning variances are placed on the agenda facing the three-person board.

As a first step, assume that the individual evaluations (or subjective benefit-cost computations) of the different requests for variance are such that all board members ordinally rank the six requests in the same way. This does not mean that evaluations for all six proposals are identical over all three members in some cardinal sense—the precise benefit-cost ratios need not be equal. If such a level of "objectivity" could be reached, no decision problem would arise, and all members would agree unanimously on the number and identity of proposals to be approved. Equivalence of ordinal rankings means only that if each member were asked to rank or array the six proposals according to his/her subjective estimates of benefits and costs, the three rankings would be the same. This assumption of equivalent ordinal ranking does not tell us anything about how many proposals are looked upon favorably or unfavorably by the individual voters. Two voters could have the same ranking, with one voter approving all proposals while the other voter approves none.

A hypothetical set of ordinal rankings is illustrated in Table 1 where the rows represent the six requests, numbered 1 through 6, and the columns represent the three voters, *i*, *j*, and *k*. The vote of each member is either "yes" (Y) or "no" (N) on each request as it comes under consideration.

2. Analogues and Contrasts to Conventional Majority-Rule Voting Models

The three board members, illustrated in Table 1, differ in the number of requests approved. Member *i* votes "yes" on two-thirds of the requests, *j* votes

Table 1

	i	j	k
1	Y	Y	Y
2	Y	Y	Y
3	Y	Y	N
4	Y	N	N
5	N	N	N
6	N	N	N

"yes" on one-half of the requests, and k votes "yes" on only one-third of the requests. Stated alternatively, the three voters or board members differ along what we might term the "proclivity to affirm" or "yea-saying" dimension.[3] If the six proposals are generically equivalent, e.g., all requests for zoning variances are to allow the development of separate and unrelated entrepreneurial projects, the underlying dimension might be classified on some scale of optimism-pessimism about the potential productivity of the projects. For other kinds of proposals, the underlying dimension might fall along ideological lines such as "liberal-conservative." Member i tends to evaluate benefits highly and costs minimally, while member k estimates costs highly and benefits minimally. Member j falls somewhere in between.

Under majority-rule voting, requests 1, 2, and 3 will be approved while requests 4 through 6 will fail to secure the requisite majority of "yes" votes. This set of outcomes, not coincidentally, is precisely that set of outcomes desired by member j. In a very real sense, j's decision-making status is the same as that of the median voter in conventional voting models where a single alternative is to be selected from a set of mutually exclusive alternatives and where individual preferences are single-peaked. In yes-no voting the analogue to the single-peakedness is the equivalence of the ordinal rankings of

---

3. This requires that propositions are defined such that "yes" has a consistent meaning. For example, a "yes" vote "to grant a zoning variance" is equivalent to a "no" vote "to not grant a zoning variance." We shall assume henceforth that propositions are worded so that affirmation is always denoted by a "yes" vote.

the separate propositions across all voters. The board member whose position is median on the "proclivity to affirm" dimension tends to dominate the results. The difference between this "median voter" and the conventional one is that here "median" is not defined with reference to the evaluation of a set of separate mutually exclusive alternatives from which one is to be selected. Rather "median" is defined with respect to the relative frequency of favorable votes cast in a set of independent proposals. The relationship between the "median-voter" construction in conventional models and that introduced here can be illustrated by a modification of our example. Consider a school board facing separate proposals for spending on six new schools, each costing $1 million. Voter i, in our construction, will approve four such proposals, voter j three, and voter k two. But note that this example might be translated into a single-election, conventional model by introducing the total budget dimension, in which case voter j, who prefers the $3 million outlay, will dominate the result.

It is, however, highly restrictive to assume that the ordinal rankings of the separate projects are identical over all board members, perhaps even more restrictive than to assume single-peakedness in preferences for all voters in the conventional majority-rule voting models. Since the benefit-cost calculus must in any case be highly subjective, it seems apparent that the ordinal rankings would probably differ across voters or board members. How would this affect our "median-voter" result? As we shall see shortly, interpersonal differences in ordinal rankings need not make our "proclivity to affirm" dimension lose all of its descriptive or predictive value.

Under nonidentical ordinal rankings, the comparisons of our model of yes-no voting with the model of majority-rule voting in the absence of single-peakedness are both interesting and complex. A characteristic feature of the latter voting model is the absence of any stable equilibrium. In contrast, our model of yes-no voting always yields a stable and unique voting outcome. Despite variation in the ordinal rankings across voters, one need only count up the number of "yes" votes cast on each proposal to see if a proposition is or is not approved. There will always be a definitive number of proposals approved; the voting process terminates. But will the median voter, the person who approves the median number of proposals, still dominate the proceedings? In general, the answer is negative. That is, there is an analogue between our model of yes-no voting on several issues and the cyclical-majority model in terms of the loss of direct correspondence be-tween the preferences of the median voter and the actual set of emergent outcomes.

Despite the fact that there will be a unique set of outcomes given *any* set of individual evaluations, one cannot predict, in advance, that these out-comes will correspond to those desired by the board member who is median in terms of our "proclivity to affirm" scale. However, the median voter does not lose all correspondence with the voting outcome, at least for a variety of different distributions of "proclivities for yea-saying" among voters. In the conventional model with a majority-rule cycle, by contrast, the voter with "median preferences" is no more likely to get his preferences satisfied than any other voter within the range of cyclical results. Median preferences are, of course, hard to define in the cyclical- or rotating-majority case, but for the sake of comparison we may say that along some dimension measured inde-pendent of the voting process, the "median voter" is defined as the one whose *first preference* is median with respect to the first preference of other voters. As the voting outcomes rotate among the possible outcomes, no voter is more successful than others in the relevant set of achieving his/her most preferred outcome.

3. Yes-No Voting Power Indices

Having claimed that in yes-no voting the person with median "proclivities to affirm" has, in most cases, a greater likelihood of having his/her preferences satisfied than his/her counterparts, the question of interest is Under what conditions is our claim valid? How likely is the median voter to have his/her preferences satisfied vis-à-vis other nonmedian voters?[4]

---

4. From both an empirical and practical viewpoint this question of correspondence of preferences with outcomes is interesting. Consider an individual board member. If every voting member had an established history or known frequency of voting "yes" or "no" on single issues drawn from a certain broadly defined set, then one might be able to pre-dict the probable outcome of each vote. For a hypothetical board member, such infor-mation would be important particularly if he were new to the board and were trying to figure out on which proposals his vote would be most highly weighted in the outcome (cf. W. W. Badger, "Political Individualism, Positional Preferences, and Optimal Decision-Rules," in *Probability Models of Collective Choice*, ed. R. Niemi and H. Weisberg) [Colum-

As mentioned above, given any pattern of ordinal rankings of propositions by the members of the voting group, a definitive set of outcomes results. And by association, some members' own preferences over the defined set of propositions correspond more closely with the set of outcomes than others. There is, of course, no reason to assume that the voter with the greater number of issues resolved in his/her favor is more "satisfied" in some utility sense. Such an implication would, of course, require an assumption about the intensities and interpersonal comparabilities of individual preferences.

We can, however, in some expected sense identify that voter who will have the greatest number of issues resolved in accord with his/her own preferences. (We shall, largely for purposes of expositional economy, refer to the relative positions of voters along such an "ability to get preferences satisfied" scale as "power," but the restricted meaning of this term should be kept in mind.) Consider again the example illustrated in Table 1. In order to ascertain voter i's chance of having his/her way on each of the six issues, we assume, without loss of generality, that the six issues are numbered in accordance with i's subjective benefit-cost ratios with issues 1 through 4 having benefit-cost ratios greater than one and issues 5 and 6 ratios less than one. We do not specify the ordinal rankings for voters j and k, but we retain the "proclivity to affirm" parameters for these two voters at one-half and one-third. Given any conceivable evaluation of the propositions by voters j and k, the probability of any given proposal securing majority approval *given that* i *votes "yes"* is .67. The probability of a given issue not passing *given that* i *votes "no"* is .83.[5] The *power index* for voter i can now be defined as the num-

---

bus, Ohio: Chas. Merrill, 1972]. By extension, a set of citizens searching for a person to represent them in some governmental body would want to know which of the candidates would have the most "power" to deliver legislation preferred by the constituency. In a rough sense, one might scan the voting proclivities of the current members of the legislative body and the proclivities of the candidates so as to decide upon the most effective candidate. The same may hold true within legislative bodies, like Congress, where newly elected representatives must be assigned to existing committees and subcommittees. In this case, the impact of one representative's purely random voting (a reasonable assumption if there is no prior information on the new representative) on the committee outcomes would be taken into account by the party leader in assigning legislators to committees.

5. If voter i votes "yes" on a proposition, then to secure majority approval it is required that either j or k or both vote "yes." The probability that j will vote "yes" on any given

ber of times i votes "yes" multiplied by the probability of majority approval plus the number of times i votes "no" multiplied by the probability of majority disapproval. Hence, in the current example the *power index* for i is $(4 \times .67) + (2 \times .83) = 4.34$. Similar calculations for voters j and k yield power indices of 4.67 and 4.34, respectively. Note that, as claimed earlier, voter j, the person with the median proclivity to approve propositions, has the highest power index.[6]

The most straightforward interpretation of the power index is that it measures the expected number of propositions to be resolved in a particular voter's favor. That is, over repeated votes taken on the same set of six propositions by the same three voters with fixed preferences, voters i, j, and k can expect to have 4.34, 4.67, and 4.34 propositions, respectively, resolved in accord with their preferences. In order to compare and contrast indices when the number of proposals vary, we can "normalize" by dividing the power indices by the number of propositions yielding power indices of .72, .78, and .72, respectively. These numbers are interpreted as the expected fraction of group decisions resolved in the three voters' respective favors.

To see how the power index changes and the effect on the median voter's influence when the parameters of the model change, we shall initially hold the number of voters fixed at three. Let N equal the number of propositions under consideration, and V_i, V_j, and V_k equal the number of "yes" votes that voters i, j, and k, respectively, are expected to cast when presented with N

---

proposition, that is for a randomly selected ordering of js preferences, is .5. For voter k this same probability is .33. As there are three pairs of votes from j and k which in conjunction with i's "yes" vote will result in a majority—yes-yes, yes-no, no-yes—the probability of approval is $(\frac{1}{2} \cdot \frac{1}{3}) + (\frac{1}{2} \cdot \frac{2}{3}) + (\frac{1}{2} \cdot \frac{1}{3}) = .67$. To obtain a majority "no," the necessary possibilities are yes-no, no-yes, and no-no; and the probability of majority disapproval given i votes "no" is $(\frac{1}{2} \cdot \frac{2}{3}) + (\frac{1}{2} \cdot \frac{1}{3}) + (\frac{1}{2} \cdot \frac{2}{3}) = .83$.

6. An alternative voting model is to allocate each voter a fixed number of "yes" votes to cast over all propositions in the set. The probability of a subsequent proposal passing given a prior proposal has passed will then decrease since some "yes" votes are "used up" in passing the earlier one. Calculating probabilities in such an analytical setting is extremely time-consuming. For example, if there are five voters and six propositions, to calculate the probability of the sixth proposal passing given the first five have passed for just one voter requires over 10 hours of computer execution time! Thus as a model with any empirical content along the lines suggested in note 4, this alternative formulation would be inappropriate. On the other hand, the probabilities discussed in the paper can be easily calculated.

independent propositions. Thus, V_i/N equals the probability of voter i voting "yes" on a given proposal. Further, assume that $V_i > V_j > V_k$. Generalizing the formulation presented above for the simple case, the power indices (PI) of the three voters can be written:

$$PI(i) = \frac{1}{N}[V_iV_j + V_iV_k - V_jV_k + N(N - V_i)],$$

$$PI(j) = \frac{1}{N}[V_iV_j + V_jV_k - V_iV_k + N(N - V_j)], \qquad (1)$$

$$PI(k) = \frac{1}{N}[V_iV_k + V_jV_k - V_iV_j + N(N - V_k)].$$

It follows that:

$$PI(j) - PI(k) = (2V_i - N)(V_j - V_k)/N, \qquad (2)$$
$$\text{and that given } V_i > V_j > V_k,$$
$$PI(j) - PI(k)\{\gtreqless\}0 \text{ if } V_i\{\gtreqless\}N/2. \qquad (3)$$

Further, it follows that:

$$PI(j) - PI(i)\{\gtreqless\}0 \text{ if } V_k\{\gtreqless\}N/2. \qquad (4)$$

From conditions (3) and (4) we see that the median voter has the highest power index if

$$\frac{V_i}{N} > \frac{1}{2} > \frac{V_k}{N}, ^7 \qquad (5)$$

Thus, in the three-voter case, the power of the median voter depends solely on the "proclivities to affirm" of the two extreme voters. The example illustrated in Table 1 where $V_i/N = .67$ and $V_k/N = .33$ satisfies the above condition, and, as we saw, voter j has the highest power index. It also follows from (3) and (4) that if either of the inequalities in (5) is an equality, the median voter shares the highest power index with that voter whose "proclivity to affirm" is not equal to one-half. For example, if $V_i = 3$, $V_j = 2$, and

7. This result is analogous to the "pairing off" condition for majority-rule equilibrium with the median preference dominating. See C. R. Plott, "A Notion of Equilibrium and Its Possibility Under Majority Rule," *American Economic Review* 57 (September 1967). However, as expression (5) shows, in our model median dominance also requires that the extreme voters do not both have proclivities greater than one-half.

$V_k = 1$, implying that $V_i/N = \frac{1}{2}$, the power indices of i, j, and k are 4.16, 4.83, and 4.83, respectively; while if $V_i = 5$, $V_j = 4$, and $V_k = 3$, implying that $V_k/N = \frac{1}{2}$, the power indices are 4.83, 4.83, and 4.16, respectively. Finally, it follows from (3) and (4) that if all voters have "proclivities to affirm" greater (less) than 1/2, the voter with the highest (lowest) proclivity has the highest power index. These relationships hold regardless of the absolute difference between any two voters' proclivity to "yea-say."

Before illustrating the effect of adding more voters, some simple comparative statics can be derived for voter i from conditions (1).[8] For greater generality we make no assumptions regarding the relative magnitudes of V_i, V_j, and V_k.

$$\frac{\Delta PI(i)}{\Delta V_i} = \frac{V_j}{N} + \frac{V_k}{N} - 1, \tag{6}$$

$$\frac{\Delta PI(i)}{\Delta V_j} = \frac{V_i}{N} - \frac{V_k}{N}, \tag{7}$$

$$\frac{\Delta PI(i)}{\Delta N} = \frac{V_j V_k - V_i(V_j + V_k)}{N^2 + N} + 1. \tag{8}$$

Equation (6) states an increase in one's own "proclivity to affirm" will increase one's power index if the sum of the affirming proclivities of the remaining voters is greater than one and contrariwise. If the sum of the other two voters' proclivities to affirm is greater than one, then, on average, these voters prefer that a proposal will pass. Thus, an increase in i's desire to see more propositions passed will be reinforced with an expectation of favorable votes from the remaining voters, increasing i's power index. On the other hand if the other voters on average tend to disapprove propositions, an increase in voter i's approval proclivity is a move away from the majority position and hence will reduce his power index. Equation (7) states that an increase in the "proclivity to affirm" of another voter increases (decreases) i's power index if the remaining voter is less (more) likely to vote affirmatively than the voter i. If voter i is more prone to voting "yes" than voter k, then

---

8. Since we are dealing with discrete changes in the parameters differential calculus is inappropriate for determining sensitivities. Thus, average rates of change are used where all changes in the independent variables are unit changes.

Table 2. Power indices—five voters and ten propositions

Voter	Proclivity to vote "yes"	Power index
i	.7	6.59
j	.6	6.89
k	.5	7.01
l	.4	6.89
m	.3	6.59

i's power index will rise with an increase in j's proclivity to affirm, which reinforces i's preferences relative to k's. If $V_k > V_i$ then an increase in V_j reinforces voter k's preferences relative to i's, and i's power index will fall. Finally, equation (8) states that an increase in the number of propositions increases or decreases one's power index depending upon the distribution of proclivities among the three voters.

Consider now an increase in the number of voters from three to five. The power index for each of the five voters is calculated in a similar manner as for three voters. In this expanded case, how does the median voter's power index compare to that of the remaining four voters?

For the sake of brevity, let us compare the median voter, voter k in the five-voter model, with the two voters who tend to be less prone to vote "yes" than k, voters l and m. In Table 2, we illustrate a hypothetical case of five voters voting on ten propositions, their respective voting proclivities, and resulting power indices. Note that once again the median voter is, in one sense, more "powerful," and because of the symmetric distribution of probabilities, the pairwise extreme voters on either side of the median voter have identical indices. Letting V_i, V_j, V_k, V_l, and V_m represent the expected number of "yes" votes to be cast on a set of N propositions for voters i, j, k, l, and m, respectively, it follows that:

$$PI(k)\{\gtreqqless\}PI(l) \text{ if } 2N(V_iV_j + V_iV_m + V_jV_m)\{\gtreqqless\}N^3 + 4V_iV_jV_m, \quad (9)$$

and

$$PI(k)\{\gtreqqless\}PI(m) \text{ if } 2N(V_iV_j + V_iV_l + V_jV_l)\{\gtreqqless\}N^3 + 4V_iV_jV_m. \quad (10)$$

A little arithmetic reveals some interesting properties. Suppose that voter m approves no proposition so that $V_m = 0$. Conditions (9) and (10) reduce to:

$$PI(k)\{\gtreqless\}PI(l) \text{ if } \frac{V_iV_j}{N^2} \{\gtreqless\}\tfrac{1}{2}, \tag{11}$$

and

$$PI(k)\{\gtreqless\}PI(m) \text{ if } \frac{V_iV_j}{N^2} \{\gtreqless\}\tfrac{1}{2} - \frac{V_l(V_i + V_j)}{N^2} + \frac{2V_iV_jV_l}{N^3}. \tag{12}$$

Assuming $V_i > V_j > V_k > V_l > V_m$, condition (11) says that the median voter's power index is greater than that of the relative negativist (voter l, as opposed to extreme negativist, voter m) if and only if the *product* of the relative and extreme affirmist's proclivities to affirm is greater than one-half. Consider the maximum value V_i can undertake, 10 (as there are only ten propositions). Then V_j must equal 6 or greater to give voter k, the median, a greater power index than l. This also implies via condition (12) that if $V_l = 0$ voter k dominates voter m. This result follows from our previous analysis of the three-voter case. If $V_i = 10$ and $V_m = 0$, then i and m cancel each other out leaving only three voters to determine the outcome.[9] In this case, voter j becomes the extreme affirmist and by our earlier result for three voters, the now-median voter dominates if V_j is greater than $N/2$, which is true when $V_j = 6$. Now suppose that $V_l = 1$ while $V_m = 0$. Condition (12) says if V_i assumes its maximum value, 10, V_j need only be equal to 5 for voter k to dominate voter m. Again, we can interpret this as saying voters i and m pair off. However, now that voter l is slightly more prone to vote "yes," his affirming counterpart, voter j, need not be as affirmative in order for the median to have the highest power index. Hence, whether the median will have the highest power index depends on the *aggregate* "proclivity to vote yes" of the pairs of voters on either side of the median voter. For example, in the case where $V_m = 0$ and $V_l = 0$, any sum of expected "yes" votes equal to or greater than 16 will give voter k the most power. When $V_l = 1$, this sum drops to 15. Finally, as in the case of three voters, if all voters have a probability of voting "yes" ("no") less than .5, then the absolute negativist (affirmist) dominates. These properties are illustrated in Table 3 where power indices for various distributions of voting proclivities are displayed. It should be obvious that if the orders of the distributions are reversed, the power indices will be in reverse order.

9. See note 7 above.

Table 3. Power indices—five voters and ten propositions

						i	j	k	l	m
Distribution of	10	4	2	1	0	1.24	4.89	8.59	8.78*	8.76
expected number	10	5	2	1	0	1.49	4.89	8.69*	8.69*	8.49
of "yes" votes	10	5	3	1	0	1.99	6.69	8.29*	8.29*	7.99
for voters i, j, k, l, m	10	6	2	1	0	1.76	4.89	8.79*	8.59*	8.24
	9	7	2	1	0	2.80	4.72	8.82*	8.56	8.16
	8	8	2	1	0	3.79	3.79	8.83*	8.55	8.14
	4	3	2	1	0	6.36	7.32	8.24	8.97	9.57*
	5	4	3	2	1	6.07	6.88	7.58	8.08	8.38*
	7	6	5	4	3	6.29	6.90	7.01*	6.90	6.29
	9	7	5	3	1	5.71	6.91	7.56*	6.91	5.71

*Indicates highest power index for a given distribution.

4. Generalized Information

Suppose that there is no information about individual proclivities to vote "yes," but there is general information about the whole group of voters. That is, only the proclivity of the *population* of voters to vote "yes" on a given proposition is known. Obviously, the notion of a particular voter with the "median" proclivity to vote "yes" vanishes. Some properties of the voting outcomes may, however, still be examined under these assumptions. For example, let there be a committee of seven voters casting "yes" or "no" votes on five independent proposals. Further, assume that the population proclivity to affirm is known, historically perhaps, to be .6 for the group. The probability of any proposal passing is the sum of the probabilities of getting exactly four "yes" votes, exactly five "yes" votes, exactly six "yes" votes, and exactly seven "yes" votes.[10] In the current example, this totals to .727. Notice the difference obtained here. The proportion of "yes" votes in the population over *all* issues in the set is .6. These votes, for lack of sufficient reason, can be

10. Letting L = total votes cast (voters times propositions), R = number of "yes" votes in L, D = number of voters, and k = number of "yes" votes in a random sample of D votes, the probability of getting exactly K "yes" votes on a given proposal is given by the hypergeometric probability:

Table 4. Probability of a given proposition passing for various numbers of voters and propositions and a group proclivity to vote yes of .67

Number of propositions	Number of voters			
	3	5	7	9
3	.773	.831	.871	.900
6	.755	.808	.847	.876
9	.748	.800	.838	.866
12	.747	.798	.836	.865

thought of as randomly distributed across the five voters and the five issues. The probability that any *given issue* will obtain a majority exceeds the population probability that a *given vote* will be "yes."

Table 4 shows probabilities of passage of a single proposition for alternative values of number of propositions to be voted on and number of voters when the general "proclivity" to vote "yes" is two-thirds. Fixing the number of propositions and the *proportion* of "yes" votes, an increase in the number of voters increases the probability of a proposal passing. On the other hand, increasing the number of propositions reduces (and apparently more slowly) the probability of any one proposition passing. Intuitively, as the number of voters becomes large given the number of propositions to be considered and the group "proclivity to affirm," the probability of any given proposal securing majority approval approaches 1(0) if the general "proclivity to affirm" is greater (less) than .5. This is because the random sample of votes drawn from the population approaches the population size and hence the expected number of "yes" votes in the sample will be close to the fraction of "yes" votes in the population. If this fraction is greater than one-half, a proposal will have

----

$$k = \frac{\binom{D}{K}\binom{L-D}{R-k}}{\binom{L}{R}}$$

See W. Feller, *An Introduction to Probability Theory and Its Applications*, Vol. 1 (New York: Wiley, 1957), 42.

Table 5. Probability of a proposition passing conditional
upon all prior propositions having passed—seven voters
and a group proclivity to affirm of .6

Proposition	Probability of passage
1st	.727
2nd	.687
3rd	.454
4th	.359
5th	.181

majority approval.[11] On the other hand, as the number of propositions becomes large given the number of voters and the average "proclivity to affirm," the probability of any given proposal passing approaches the average "proclivity to affirm" since one is drawing a sample of fixed size from an ever-increasing population.

An extension of this model is "casting lots" where there is a fixed number of "yes" votes in the group. There is no specific information on the number of "yes" votes held by each voter (cf. note 6). Assuming the "yes" votes are distributed randomly across voters and issues, the probability of any single issue passing remains the same as before. However, the probability of passage for subsequent proposals, contingent on the passage of prior propositions falls as "yes" votes, or lots, are "used up" in passing the prior propositions. For example in our seven-voter, five-proposition case where there was a .6 group proclivity to affirm, let there be a total of 21 "yes" votes randomly distributed through the population of votes. In this case, the probability of any one proposal passing is .727 as before. The probability of any second proposal passing given one proposition has already passed is .687, and the probability of any third proposal passing given two have passed is .454. Table 5 lists the conditional probability of passage for all five propositions. The average probability for the set of five propositions is .482 which can be interpreted as the expected fraction of propositions under consideration that

11. This result, in a somewhat different context, has been obtained by R. G. Kazmann, "Democratic Organization: A Preliminary Mathematical Model," *Public Choice* 16 (Fall 1973), and B. Grofman, "A Comment on 'Democratic Theory': A Preliminary Mathematical Model," *Public Choice* 21 (Spring 1975).

will pass given the voting scheme outlined above. Table 6 reports the expected fraction of propositions passed under the casting lots model for some selected voter-proposition combinations when 60% of the votes are "yes" votes. Table 7 reports expected fraction of propositions passed for the five-voter, five-proposition case given various percentages of "yes" votes in the total number of votes cast on all propositions.

As we saw earlier, the expected fraction of proposals passing, for a given percentage of "yes" votes in the population, rises with the number of voters and falls with the number of propositions. Not surprisingly, the expected passage rate increases with the percentage of "yes" votes in the population and appears to do so at an increasing rate.

5. Concluding Remarks

In conventional majority-rule voting models, a weakening of the information concerning individual voter preference orderings effectively rules out any analysis of the voting outcomes. In the model of yes-no voting presented

Table 6. Expected fraction of propositions passed when there is a .6 group proclivity to affirm

Voters	Propositions
3	.355
5	.429
7	.482
9	.491

Table 7. Expected fraction of propositions passed under various group proclivities to affirm given five voters and five propositions

Number (percentage) of "yes" votes in total votes cast on all propositions	Expected fraction of propositions passed
10 (40%)	.091
15 (60%)	.429
20 (80%)	.922

here, information assumptions can be progressively weakened without re-moving all of the model's predictive content.

We saw that when the rank ordering of the separate proposals are known and identical across voters, a unique outcome results and that this outcome exactly matches the median voter's preferred outcome. When ordinal rank-ings are assumed to differ among voters, majority-rule voting still yields unique and stable results while the equivalence between the outcome and the median voter's preferences is weakened but not lost. That is, when the only information available is each voter's probability of voting "yes," the voting outcome, under many circumstances, more closely corresponds to the pref-erences of the median voter than for any other voter. Finally, we considered the case where the only information is the voting group's aggregate likeli-hood to vote "yes." Here, the median voter has no meaning and all that can be said is that the expected number of propositions passed by the group de-pends on the number considered, the number of voters, and the group pro-clivity to vote "yes."

It should be pointed out that the results reported in this paper are pre-liminary. Our arguments have been made by reference to specific examples rather than by formal theorems and proofs. One possible way of generalizing our model is to construct a large-scale computer simulation of the model under various information assumptions in order to discover the properties of the model when there are large numbers of voters and issues.[12]

Elsewhere, we argued that the allocation of resources and the potential for economic growth will be affected differently when disputes over property are resolved privately or collectively by majority rule.[13] When such disputes are resolved by yes-no voting such as deciding upon zoning variances, our analysis of yes-no voting outcomes becomes both relevant and important. It is interesting to speculate on the reasons for the relative analytical neglect of the voting institutions discussed in this paper, which, as we have noted, are descriptive of frequently observed collective choice situations. Atten-

---

12. In a sense our efforts are at a stage analogous to that of G. Tullock and C. D. Camp-bell, "Computer Simulation of a Small Voting System," *Economic Journal* 80 (March 1970), who used simulation techniques to determine the probability of the occurrence of majority-rule cycles as the number of voters and number of candidates change.

13. J. M. Buchanan and R. L. Faith, "Entrepreneurship and Internalization of Exter-nalities," *Journal of Law and Economics* 24 (April 1981).

tion may have been concentrated on the single-election setting primarily because of the underlying motivation to answer questions concerning the "rationality" or "irrationality" of collective choice, questions that have been presumed to have normative or evaluative content. In straightforward yes-no majority-rule voting on a proposition, there is a unique result. The question of "collective rationality" that has preoccupied public-choice and social-choice theorists simply does not arise. But the absence of this particular "rationality" question does not make the positive analysis of yes-no voting either uninteresting or unimportant, perhaps even for normative questions of institutional-constitutional design.

Vote Buying in a Stylized Setting

James M. Buchanan and Dwight R. Lee

1. Introduction

At least since the early contributions of Downs and Tullock, public choice theorists have recognized the limits of rational behavioral models in explaining why some persons vote at all in large-number settings where outcomes are determined by majority rule, and, further, why those who do vote bother to become informed about the alternatives. Theories of rational abstention and rational ignorance have long been central in elementary public choice. More recently, and picking up an early discussion by Buchanan on the absence of individual responsibility in voting choice, Brennan and Buchanan have discussed in some detail the likely dominance of expressive elements in the psychology of the voting choice itself.[1]

These results all stem from the recognition of the relative impotence of the individual in being able to influence the ultimate result in the large-number majoritarian setting, where the simultaneous behavior of many persons in voting between alternatives generates a single outcome through the operation of the voting rule. In this paper, we propose to examine yet another implication of the probabilistic relationship between the potential

From *Public Choice* 49, no. 1 (1986): 3–16. Reprinted by permission of the publisher, Kluwer Academic Publishers.

We are indebted to Roger Faith, Arizona State University, for helpful comments on an earlier draft.

1. A. Downs, *An Economic Theory of Democracy* (New York: Harper, 1957); G. Tullock, *Toward a Mathematics of Politics* (Ann Arbor: University of Michigan Press, 1967); J. M. Buchanan, "Individual Choice in Voting and the Market," *Journal of Political Economy* 62 (1954): 334–43; G. Brennan and J. M. Buchanan, "Voting Choice: Evaluating Political Alternatives," *American Behavioral Scientist* 28 (November/December 1984): 185–201.

choice behavior of the individual voter and the ultimate collective outcome, one that has not, to our knowledge, been fully recognized. Our concern is with mutually advantageous opportunities for the buying and selling of votes that may emerge as the probabilities of influence over collective outcomes vary. The analysis is somewhat indirectly related to theories of coalition formation,[2] and also to Tullock's examination of rational behavior in rent-seeking.[3] There are also analogues between our analysis and the theories of markets for voting proxies in corporate takeover bidding.

We develop the analysis in highly stylized and abstract models. We do so without apology. We leave to others the discussion of whether or not our models have implications for the real world of politics.

2. The Basic Structure of the Model

First, consider a setting where a simple *Yes-No* or approval referendum is to be taken on a specific proposal for spending. Approval signaled by a majority authorizes the fiscal authority of the community to spend for a designated project and to levy the taxes required to finance the spending. We abstract from the problems of rational abstention, rational ignorance, and expressive voting. We assume that all voters go to the polls, and that all vote in accordance with their own identified interests, regardless of how miniscule the influence of a single person's vote on the ultimate outcome. Further, each voter

2. To our knowledge the analysis that most closely relates to that developed in this paper is contained in J. S. Coleman, "The Marginal Utility of a Vote Commitment," *Public Choice* 5 (1968): 39–58. Coleman is interested, however, in deriving values for individual vote commitments when the number of previously committed votes is directionally known and is allowed to vary. His analysis is more closely related to the theories of coalition formation than our own.

In the theories of coalition formation (see W. H. Riker and P. C. Ordeshook, *An Introduction to Positive Political Theory*, Ch. 6 [Englewood Cliffs, N.J.: Prentice-Hall, 1973], and references cited therein), emphasis is centered on the calculus of an individual in determining whether or not to join a protocoalition which involves probability estimates of the emergence of some ultimate winning coalition. The underlying game is zero-sum, whereas, in our models, the game may be negative-, zero-, or positive-sum.

3. In his paper "Efficient Rent Seeking," in J. M. Buchanan, R. D. Tollison, and G. Tullock, eds., *Toward a Theory of the Rent-Seeking Society* (College Station: Texas A&M University Press, 1980), Gordon Tullock analyzes the value of an incremental investment in rent-seeking activity under a variety of models.

is fully informed as to the consequences of the two possible outcomes (*Yes-No*) on his own economic position. Each voter's information about the probable voting choices of other voters is summarized in a single estimate of the "proclivity to vote *Yes*" assigned to each voter, and hence to the group.[4]

Our emphasis is concentrated on the value of participation to the individual voter, and on the possible willingness of a voter to sell his vote to a potential buyer. The central assumption of our model is that a voter will sell his right of participation, his vote, for anything above its value to him. That is to say, if the value of the voting act is, say, rX to individual i, then i will sell a proxy for his vote to anyone who offers a price that exceeds rX. (We may think of X as the differential in value between the two election outcomes to i, and r as the appropriate discount factor generated by the probability that i's vote will be decisive.) We assume that transactions are costless; neither moral nor institutional considerations inhibit the potential for perfect markets in votes.

In order to complete the general model, we need to examine the buyer's side of the market. If persons stand willing to sell votes for any value over and beyond the value of participation in the process rX, who will emerge as a potential purchaser?

The basis for a mutually beneficial trade stems from the prospect that a person with two votes, any person, has more influence on the ultimate outcome than a person with only one vote. That is to say, a person with two votes will value this two-vote package at some value above rX. The question to be considered is when and under what circumstances the two-vote package is valued more highly than 2rX. If the package is valued above 2rX, then there are mutual gains from trade; a vote purchaser, j, can offer to a vote seller, i, something more than the value of his "right to vote," which is rX, and still secure for himself some residual value above rX, his initial position.

All persons make the same estimates for the proclivities of persons in the electorate to vote *Yes* and *No*. We are not concerned with possible differentials in estimates of predicted voting outcomes. The proclivities remain, however, probability estimates: the individual knows only his own interest with certainty. Further, we postulate that all voters place the same differential

---

4. For a general discussion of *Yes-No* voting, see the paper by J. M. Buchanan and R. L. Faith, "Towards a Theory of Yes-No Voting," *Public Choice* 32, no. 2 (1981): 231–46.

in value as between the two alternatives, although the directions of evaluations must, of course, differ as between two possible sets of voters. Whether or not "the game" is negative-, zero-, or positive-sum depends, then, both on the direction of evaluation and the predicted voting proclivity.

Initially, we assume that the vote markets are blind on both sides in the sense that neither buyer nor seller knows the voting choice of his opposite number in the exchange. The prospective vote purchaser knows, of course, the direction of his own preferences or interest, but he does not know the interests of the vote seller, from whom he receives a proxy. The latter might have been a supporter or an opponent of the outcome supported by the buyer. Similarly, the person who sells the proxy does not know the voting preferences of the person to whom he sells. He may sell his proxy to someone who seeks to further the same interest as his own or to someone who will seek to further the opposing interest. The model is, literally, one of vote buying and selling; it is not a model of sale or purchase of directed voting support for one or the other of the alternatives.

As the subsequent discussion indicates, the very structure of the vote market may be such that a fully informed voter will know the identity of the person on the other side of a purchase or sale. This modifies the result only in the small-number example of Section 3 (see Note 5).

3. A Small-Number Example

Although misleading if the rationality assumptions are taken to be literally applicable, it will be analytically useful to begin with a simple case of three voters who must collectively decide on an issue that will provide a net gain (or prevent a net loss) of $1.00 to each of those on the winning side, and impose a net loss (or prevent a net gain) of $1.00 to the single loser. Each voter knows how he will himself vote, but he has only a probability estimate as to how others will vote, described in the single proclivity-to-vote estimate. The small-number model should be interpreted as a stylized and simplified representation of a large-number model rather than one that embodies predictive implications in its own setting.

Consider first the setting where individual 1 knows that he plans to vote *for* a proposal, but in which he assigns to each of the other voters a 3/4 probability of voting *against* the proposal. If 1 does nothing but vote his preference, namely *Yes*, he expects the proposal to lose, with probability 9/16 (3/4 × 3/4), with an expected loss to himself of $9/16. However, in this situation, if individual 1 should buy one vote, he could control the outcome. By insuring defeat of the proposal he can insure his personal gain of $1.00. Individual 1 will, therefore, be willing to pay as much as $9/16 for a single vote.

But what is the maximum value that voters 2 and 3 place on their own votes? Assume that each opposes the proposal, and, like individual 1, each places a 3/4 probability estimate on the opposition to the proposal by any voter. Each of the two voters, 2 or 3, then assesses the probability of the proposal being defeated in an untampered election as 1/16 (1/4 × 1/4). The expected value of the election to each of these two voters is, therefore, $15/16. (There is a 15/16 probability that a loss of $1.00 will be avoided in the electoral choice.) On the other hand, if, say, individual 2 should sell his vote, then the probability of his side winning, and the proposal being defeated, is seen to drop to 12/16. The expected value of the election has been reduced by $3/16. (There is a 1/4 probability that the purchaser of 2's vote will approve the proposal, and hence, impose the net cost of $1.00 on 2 by making up the majority in the election.) Vote selling will be attractive to individual 2 or 3 if a purchaser offers anything above $3/16. And, as the example demonstrates, individual 1 will be willing to pay anything up to $9/16. There are mutual gains from trade in the stylized vote market explained here.[5]

Similar logic shows the potential for trade for any voting proclivity other than 1/2. If, to consider a different case, the proclivity that any person in our three-person electorate will oppose a proposal is estimated to be 3/5, then the individual who favors the proposal will be willing to pay up to $.36 for another vote, and a person who opposes the proposal will sell his vote for anything greater than $.24. Only if the probability that any voter will vote for one

5. As noted, the small-number example is misleading in that the postulated assumptions may run counter to rational behavior by individual participants. In such a setting, the individual in the position such as voter 2 in the example would know, *from the structure*, that a prospective vote buyer would necessarily evaluate the alternatives differently from his own evaluation; that is, 2 would know that a sale of his vote would insure defeat of the alternative that he, personally, prefers. The assumption that the market is double blind is, in this sense, inconsistent with fully informed and rational behavior.

This inconsistency disappears in the large-number setting where the individual does not, even if he can identify the directional preference of the prospective vote buyer, by his own action substantially affect the probabilities of the ultimate collective outcome.

outcome is set at 1/2 will it be the case that the value of an additional vote is the same ($.25 in our numerical example) for all persons, and that gains from vote buying and selling are not possible.

Several points emerge in the three-voter example. First, vote buying does not depend on persons attaching differing absolute values to the differential gains and losses from the electoral alternatives. In the example, the differential in value between a favorable and unfavorable outcome was, for each voter, set at $1.00. Secondly, the closer the election is expected to be, the smaller will be the motivation to buy or to sell votes (the smaller the gains from trade). And when the two possible outcomes of the selection, in an expected value sense, are equally probable (the estimated proclivity for a vote for one of the alternatives is set at 1/2 for each voter), there are no gains to be realized from buying or selling votes. Finally, the example indicates that only those persons who favor the outcome assigned the lower probability of winning will find vote buying advantageous.

In the following section, we turn to the more general case to see how robust these conclusions are, and also to see if additional results can be uncovered.

4. The General Model

Given the structure of the basic model outlined in Section 2 above, we know that each individual will, in the absence of any purchase or sale of votes, place the *same* value on his own vote. This result follows from the postulates that all persons assess the voting proclivity identically and that all place the same differential value on the alternatives. In a large-number setting, this value of the individual vote will be very small indeed since the prospect that any vote will be decisive under simple majority voting is highly improbable. It is the smallness of this value that motivates the theorems of rational abstention, rational ignorance, and expressive voting. Our concern in this paper is not with computations of this value, which are well known to public choice theorists. Our concern is, instead, with the value of an *additional* vote to an individual since it is only this value that can possibly motivate a vote purchase.

Assume 2n voters who must decide either *Yes* or *No* on some exogenously presented proposal. Let p be the probability that any given voter will vote *Yes*, that is, in favor of the proposal, and q the probability he will vote *No*, that is, against the proposal ($p + q = 1$). Assume that each voter expects to gain (or avoid the loss of) $100 if his preferred alternative is selected. The question that needs to be answered specifically is, What is the value to any individual, say individual 1, of controlling one more vote than he is entitled to by right?

The answer to this question depends on the probability of a tie without the control of the extra vote. Individual 1 knows that he is going to vote in favor of the proposal; hence, he will assess the probability of a tie to be equal to the number of ways the remaining $2n - 1$ votes can be partitioned into ($n - 1$) *Yes*'s and n *No*'s, all multiplied by $p^{n-1} q^n$, or

$$\binom{2n - 1}{n - 1} p^{n-1} q^n = \frac{(2n - 1)!}{(n - 1)!n!} p^{n-1} q^n. \tag{1}$$

Multiplying the probability in (1) by $100, or

$$(\$100) \frac{(2n - 1)!}{(n - 1)!n!} p^{n-1} q^n, \tag{2}$$

gives the value 1 places on being able to control an additional vote. On the other hand, considering someone who is going to vote against the proposal, the value of controlling another vote equals

$$(\$100) \frac{(2n - 1)!}{(n - 1)!n!} p^n q^{n-1}. \tag{3}$$

Note that if $p < q$ then (2) > (3), and therefore the individual who favors the proposal is willing to pay more for an extra vote than the individual who opposes it. Individual 1 is, therefore, prepared to offer enough for a vote to make it attractive for someone to sell him one if he favors the low-probability outcome. The value of an *additional* vote exceeds the value of the single vote each person possesses initially.

If we assume that individual 1 has purchased one vote, the question then becomes, What is a third vote worth to him? Again, the answer is $100 times the probability that the election will end in a draw given that 1 casts his two votes in support of the proposal, or

$$(\$100) \binom{2n - 2}{n - 2} p^{n-2} q^n = (\$100) \frac{(2n - 1)!}{(n - 2)!n!} p^{n-2} q^n. \tag{4}$$

It can be seen that, for large n and $p < 1/2$, (4) > (2) [to get (2) you multiply (4) by $p (2n - 1/n - 1)$, which is < 1, since $(2n - 1/n - 1)$ is close to 2 when n is large], which means that having purchased one vote the vote buyer will place a higher value on the purchase of a second vote. The intuition behind this result is straightforward. As a voter who supports the minority position purchases control of more votes, the probability of a tie will, at least up to some point, increase.[6] This places a minority-position vote buyer in a categorically different position from that of a majority-position vote buyer. If someone favoring the majority position buys votes, he will know that he is reducing the probability of a tie, and therefore, with every vote he buys, reducing the value to him of the additional vote.

If the minority-position vote buyer manages to keep the extent of his vote buying known only to himself, then he will be the only one who knows how much the probability of a tie is increasing, and how much votes are worth. From his perspective, the ideal case is when each vote seller either is unaware that vote buying is taking place or, if his vote has already been purchased, believes that it is the only one that has been purchased. In this situation, the vote buyer will be able to purchase votes for a price that marginally covers the value an individual places on his vote in an untampered election. The vote buyer, in this case, continues to purchase votes until the value of the additional vote increases up to some maximum and then declines back to the constant supply price of votes.

Next we drop the double blind assumption, and consider a situation far less conducive to vote buying by assuming that the vote buyer does not know the implications which derive from the structure of the model. Specifically we assume that (1) the vote buyer knows nothing of the voting proclivities of those from whom he purchases votes, (2) minority-position voters not buying votes know exactly how many votes the vote buyer has purchased but do not know the voting proclivity of the buyer, and (3) majority-position voters know not only how many votes the vote buyer has purchased, but also how these votes will be cast.[7] Even under these conditions, there will still be a gain

6. Obviously, at some point enough votes will be controlled by the minority position so that it will become the majority position, and controlling additional votes in favor of the position will begin reducing probability of a tie.

7. Under these assumptions, the buyer will not be able to buy cheap, but to him worthless, votes from those who will vote the same as he. But because we have assumed that the buyer does not realize that he is buying only votes from the opposition, he will not value the additional vote as highly as he otherwise would.

from trade over some range between the vote buyer and voters favoring the majority position. Consider the value the vote buyer places on an additional vote, having purchased one, given by (4), and compare that value with that of an additional vote to a fully informed majority voter. Each majority voter knows that he will vote *No* and that a minority voter controls two votes which will be placed in the *Yes* column. With this information, the majority voter will assess the loss of selling his vote ($100 times the probability of a tie if his vote is not sold) as equal to

$$(\$100) \; \frac{(2n \; - \; 3)!}{(n \; - \; 2)! \; (n \; - \; 1)!} \; p^{n-2}q^{n-1}. \tag{5}$$

Notice that multiplying (5) by

$$\frac{2n \; - \; 2}{n} \; q \tag{6}$$

yields (4). For large n, and q sufficiently greater than 1/2, (6) will be greater than unity, and therefore (4) will be greater than (5). The vote buyer will be willing to pay more for another vote than the minimum amount our fully informed majority voter is willing to accept. Again, the intuition is straightforward. Since the majority voter knows his own as well as the buyer's position (the vote buyer knows only his own preference), the majority voter knows that the probability of a tie is less than that calculated by the vote buyer. Note, however, that once the buyer has amassed enough votes to go beyond the point that maximizes the probability of a tie vote, each individual who plans to vote *No*, and also knows that the vote buyer will cast all of his votes *Yes*, will see the probability of a tie to be higher than will the vote buyer who only knows how he is voting. In this case, when majority voters have full information on the vote buyer's activities, once the probability of a tie vote is maximized, they will no longer be willing to charge the vote buyer less for their votes than he is willing to pay.

Vote buying will occur in our model, therefore, under a wide range of informational assumptions. In the case where no one knows with certainty how any particular individual, other than themselves, will vote, and has no suspicions that vote buying is taking place on a large scale, then it will pay the vote buyer to purchase a sufficient number of votes to move into the range where the initial minority position he favors is known (by him) to be the most likely position to win. In the case where the vote buyer is not able to keep either his position or the total number of votes he has bought secret, it will still pay an initial minority-position individual to purchase votes up to the point where the probability of a tie is maximized (neither position has a probability advantage over the other). Other informational assumptions are possible, but vote buying will still occur over some range. For example, a vote buyer could know the voting propensity of those from whom he buys by recognizing that those who oppose the project place the lowest value on their votes. But this would simply make vote buying more attractive to the buyer over some initial range.

The most realistic assumption would be that a vote buyer could maintain some secrecy and arrange to buy votes from individuals with one seller being unaware of the existence of other sellers. This type of purchasing could be modeled after land acquisition schemes in which a large firm amasses a large block of land in an area by using several purchasing agents, each unaware of who the ultimate buyer is, to buy up small blocks of land.[8] This type of purchasing arrangement, of course, shifts the advantage to the buyer.

To this point, we have proceeded under the assumption that there is only one buyer. If anything, this assumption makes our results all the more striking. Our one buyer is motivated to act on behalf of all those who favor the initial minority position without any help or organized support. Receiving but a small fraction of the benefits that those on his side will receive if the initial minority position wins, our single vote buyer will, if his purchases remain clandestine, buy enough votes almost to insure that this position wins.[9] Furthermore, the result does not require that differential benefits accrue to supporters of a position.[10] Neither do we require concentrated benefits versus diffused costs to motivate action on behalf of the group receiving the benefits. In our model individuals in the benefiting group receive exactly the

8. In the early 1960s, Walt Disney purchased 43 square miles of land through several different law firms which were not aware that Disney was the buyer (see R. B. McKenzie, *Fugitive Industry* [Ballinger Publishing Co., 1984], 157).

9. That enough votes will be purchased to almost insure the alternative that began as the minority position will become clear from our example in Section 5.

10. M. Olson, *The Logic of Collective Action* (Cambridge, Mass.: Harvard University Press, 1965), has argued that individuals may take unilateral action on behalf of a group, but only if they receive larger benefits from successful action than do other members of the group.

same amount per person from successful action as those in the losing group lose.

There is no reason, of course, to expect that there will be only one vote buyer. If one voter sees advantage in buying additional votes, others will likely do the same. The only restriction our model implies in this regard is that vote buyers will be found in what is, at least initially, the minority position. Vote buying by multiple minority voters, of course, is completely consistent with the major result of this paper: that vote buying will take place and it will switch the advantage in the direction of what, in an untampered election, would be the minority position. And if several vote buyers organize into a collective effort, this result is likely to be reinforced. It should be acknowledged, however, that an organized vote-buying effort may be more difficult to keep secret and, therefore, may result in higher reservation prices on the part of vote sellers. This suggests the possibility that a single vote buyer, acting strictly on his own and in response to his own self-interest, may do more to advance the interest of a large group than will an organized group effort in which the free-rider problem has been overcome.

5. A Large-Number Example

In this section we illustrate the primary results derived from the general model with another example, this time with a relatively large, though computationally manageable, number of voters. It is assumed that the selection between two collective-choice options (*Yes* and *No*) is to be made by 800 voters in a simple majority vote. As before, it will be assumed that each voter stands to gain (or avoid losing) the same amount if the decision made is the one he favors. The probability that any given voter will vote *Yes* is .42, hence, .58 is the probability of any person voting *No*.

We first look at the value of incremental votes to a vote buyer who favors the proposal; i.e., supports the low-probability outcome, *Yes.* Letting X represent the value the vote buyer places on achieving his preferred outcome (and, by assumption, the value all voters place on achieving their preferred outcome), the value of the incremental vote is given by

$$X \frac{(799 - B)!}{(399 - B)!\ 400!}\ (.42)^{399-B}\ (.58)^{400}, \tag{7}$$

where $B = 0, 1, 2, 3 \ldots$ is the number of votes the vote buyer has already purchased. In words, (7) is equal to X times the probability that exactly 400 of the 799 − B votes the vote buyer does not control will be cast in opposition to the proposal, or that the election ends in a tie.

When $B = 0$, the probability of a tie is .00000105. For the sake of convenience, it will be assumed that $X = \$10,000$. With this individual payoff, the value realized from the first vote purchased equals 1.05 cents ($\$10,000 \times$ .00000105), barely over a penny. As explained in the previous section, once the first vote is purchased, the value of having an additional vote increases. With $X = \$10,000$, the value of (7) is 1.25 cents when $B = 1$. In Table 1 the marginal values of votes to the initial minority-position vote buyer are shown in Column 2 for intermittent values of B. There is a steady increase in the marginal value of a vote as more are purchased until $B = 110$, at which point another vote is worth $307.86. Further vote buying finds the marginal value of votes declining, with the additional vote worth barely over a penny when 203 votes have been purchased.

If our vote buyer can operate clandestinely, he is the only one who will realize that the value of a vote has been altered by his purchases. In this case, he will be able to purchase as many votes as he wants for slightly less than a penny each.[11] At a price of slightly under $.01, the rational vote buyer will, in our example, purchase 203 votes. This means that the vote buyer would control 204 votes which he will cast in favor of the proposal. Of the 596 votes outstanding, 42%, or 250, can be expected to be in support of the proposal. Under these circumstances, the probability of the total vote favoring the proposal is very close to unity.[12]

The assumption that the vote buyer is able to purchase votes with complete secrecy is, admittedly, a strong one that facilitates the buying of votes. We can, however, demonstrate that vote buying will occur even with full information on the part of those voters who are initially in the majority position. Assume, now, that all voters who initially oppose the proposal know

11. The actual value is .91 cents, as will become clear later in this section. This value is shown in Column 3 of Table 1.

12. For the vote to go against the proposal would require drawing less than 196 *Yes* votes from the 596 outstanding votes, or 54 fewer than expected. The standard deviation of a binomial distribution with 596 trails, $p = .42$ and $q = .58$, is approximately 11.93. So a loss would require drawing a sample in which the number of *Yes* votes was over 4 1/2 standard deviations below the mean.

Table 1

(1)	(2)	Vote buying secret (3)	Vote buying known (4)
B	Marginal value to buyer	Marginal value to seller	
0	$ .0105	.0091	$ .0091
10	$ .0560	.0091	$ .0489
20	$ .26	.0091	$ .23
30	$ 1.07	.0091	$ .96
40	$ 3.81	.0091	$ 3.46
50	$ 11.69	.0091	$ 10.76
60	$ 30.79	.0091	$ 28.73
70	$ 69.15	.0091	$ 65.42
80	$131.50	.0091	$126.13
90	$210.12	.0091	$204.39
100	$279.882	.0091	$276.08
109	$307.65	.0091	$307.49
110	$307.86	.0091	$308.15
111	$307.46	.0091	$308.20
120	$277.19	.0091	$281.53
130	$202.16	.0091	$208.40
140	$118.11	.0091	$123.61
150	$ 54.62	.0091	$ 58.04
160	$ 19.73	.0091	$ 21.29
170	$ 5.49	.0091	$ 6.02
180	$ 1.16	.0091	$ 1.29
190	$ .18	.0091	$ .21
200	$ .0209	.0091	$ .0240
202	$ .0130	.0091	$ .0191
203	$ .0102	.0091	$ .0150
204	$ .0080	.0091	$ .0093

that the vote buyer seeks the *Yes* solution; they also know when a vote is purchased, and, at any stage in the sequence, they know how many votes have been purchased previously. In this situation, the value each initial opponent of the proposal attaches to his vote is given by

$$X \frac{(798 - B)!}{(399 - B)!\ 399!} (.42)^{399-B} (.58)^{399}, \qquad (8)$$

where, as before, $X = \$10,000$ and B is the number of votes that have been bought. In words, (8) is equal to X times the probability that of the 798 − B votes that the potential seller does not know how will be cast, 399 will be cast in opposition. Therefore, (8) is the expected loss each person who prefers a *No* solution (and who has not previously sold his own proxy) attaches to his votes at any stage in the vote-buying sequence.

In the fourth column of Table 1, the value of (8) is given for different values of B. The important thing to notice is that, until the minority-position vote buyer has purchased 110 votes, the value of another vote to the buyer is greater than the minimum amount each majority-position voter is willing to accept for his vote. Once 110 votes have been purchased, the gains from trade have been exhausted, as is easily seen from Table 1. Notice also that once 110 votes have been purchased, the election is a toss-up. With 110 purchased votes, the vote buyer controls 111 votes in favor of the proposal. Of the 689 votes outstanding, the number expected to go in support of the proposal rounds off to 289 (689 × .42), for an expected total of 400. As argued in the previous section, once it is assumed that those in what was originally the majority position have full information on the activities of the vote buyer, vote buying will only proceed until the probability that the election ends in a tie is maximized.

6. Conclusions

As we noted in the introduction, we do not propose to discuss possible implications for the real world of democratic politics that may be drawn from the highly stylized models of vote buying that we have analyzed in this paper. To the extent that economic, legal, or moral thresholds prevent the emergence of the purchase and sale of votes among persons who initially possess property rights in the collective franchise, our whole analysis is simply inapplicable. If, however, such thresholds serve only to inhibit but not to prevent totally the emergence of such markets, there should be some value in an analysis that embodies the zero transactions costs assumption.

Democracy and Duopoly
A Comparison of Analytical Models

This paper is scientific arbitrage. I propose to summarize analytical models in the theory of two-party politics and the theory of duopoly. The similarities in these two theories have been widely recognized, but a more systematic treatment incorporating recent developments may be useful.

I. Duopoly Location in One-Dimensional Market Space

If a fixed number of customers is distributed uniformly along a line, say a road, and if each customer is assumed to purchase a fixed quantity of a good, marketed at a uniform price by either of two duopoly firms, with the choice between firms determined exclusively by distance, profit-maximization criteria will insure that both of the firms will locate at the center of the distribution. If the latter is not uniform over space, both will locate near the median customer. This clustering theorem of duopoly location was initially advanced by Hotelling, and it can scarcely be challenged, given the strict assumptions of the model.[1]

II. Party Platforms in One-Dimensional Issue Space

Many scholars, among them Hotelling, Black, Downs, and Tullock, have recognized that the basic clustering theorem on duopoly location has a precise

From *American Economic Review* 58 (May 1968): 322–31. Reprinted by permission of the publisher.
1. H. Hotelling, "Stability in Competition," *Economic Journal* (March 1929): 41–57.

parallel in two-party democratic politics.[2] If a fixed number of voters can be arrayed along a single line, that is, if the model can be meaningfully treated as unidimensional, each party, so long as it is motivated solely by a desire for electoral success, will offer a platform described by its estimate of the choices of the median voter. In such models, the implicit dimension is distance along the left-right spectrum.

III. Party Platforms in Two-Dimensional Issue Space

Political choice is normally too complex for meaningful analysis confined to one dimension only. Two-dimensional models seem minimal, and even these may be helpful largely as they reveal characteristic features of many dimensions. Once a second dimension is introduced, the cyclical majority problem arises.[3] Initially, this problem seems to reduce the generality of the clustering theorem. The party that succeeds in selecting a platform that mirrors the preferences of the median voter may find itself defeated, in a straight majority vote, by a party with a nonmedian platform.

The simple analytics are illustrated in Figure 1. Assume that there are three voters, A, B, and C, whose optimally preferred positions, defined in two dimensions, x and y, are shown at a, b, and c. Other relevant data about individual preference functions could be depicted by drawing in the standard indifference mappings. From this set of mappings, "contract" loci can be derived; these are indicated by the boundaries of triangular area in Figure 1. Lines of optima can also be derived for each person on each of the two-issue variables. These are depicted in the dotted lines of Figure 1. The

2. Duncan Black, *The Theory of Committees and Elections* (Cambridge University Press, 1958); Anthony Downs, *Economic Theory of Democracy* (Harper and Row, 1957); and Gordon Tullock, *The Politics of Bureaucracy* (Public Affairs Press, 1965).

3. The cyclical majority problem, the "paradox of voting," was discussed in detail by both Kenneth Arrow, *Social Choice and Individual Values* (John Wiley and Sons, 1951; rev. ed., 1963) and Duncan Black, *Theory of Committees*. The general model for this discussion was unidimensional. One way of defining a dimension, however, is in terms of observed results. If a cyclical majority is revealed, some members of the group must have preferences that cannot be arrayed so as to display single-peakedness. This amounts to saying that for these persons the issue space is at least two-dimensional.

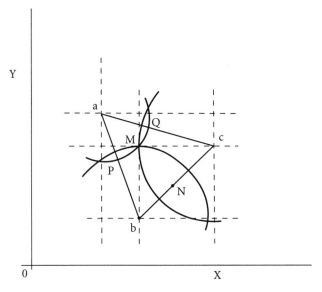

Figure 1

intersection of middle lines of optima determines the median position of each of the two issues, point *M* on Figure 1. The same person need not, of course, hold the median position on all issues.

If party 1 adopts platform *M*, however, party 2 can respond by offering platform *N*, *P*, or *Q* (or any platform described by a position within any one of the three lozenges formed by drawing indifference contours through *M*). Any one of these will secure a majority over *M*. The familiar cycle emerges, and unless adjustments are terminated by some arbitrary rule, the party platforms will tend to shift continuously. While there is a limited area over which platform changes will range, there is no tendency for these to settle at or near one median position.[4]

---

4. The basic geometry of two-dimensional issue space was developed by Duncan Black and R. A. Newing, *Committee Decision and Complementary Valuation* (William Hodge and Co., 1951), and, in quite a different context, by Ragnar Frisch, "On Welfare Theory and Pareto Regions, *International Economic Papers*, Vol. 9 (Macmillan, 1959), 39–92. For a recent, and more complex, treatment, see Charles Plott, "Equilibrium and Majority Rule," *American Economic Review* (September 1967): 787–806.

IV. Duopoly Location in Two-Dimensional Market Space

The cyclical majority has its counterpart in the locational indeterminacy of the comparable duopoly model. Figure 1 can be used to demonstrate this. The two dimensions now become spatial coordinates, and A, B, and C are now prospective buyers (or groups of buyers) whose precise locations are determined by *a*, *b*, and *c*. If one firm locates at *M*, a second firm can easily secure two of the three customers by locating at *N*, *P*, or *Q*, or at any point within any of the three lozenges. There is no location where the second firm could capture all three buyers from the firm at *M*. In response to the location of the second firm, the first firm could shift from *M* and recapture one buyer. The locational pattern of the duopolists will never stabilize under these conditions. Firms will not cluster at the effective center of the space, although the shifting of location will be bounded.[5]

V. Duopoly Location in Two-Dimensional Market Space, with Many Buyers

The parallel between the cyclical majority problem and the locational indeterminacy in duopoly has not been emphasized, primarily because one of the implicit assumptions of the duopoly model has been that the number of buyers is critically large. Most economists who have worked with the duopoly problem have, more or less intuitively and without careful analysis,[6] extended the clustering theorem to two-dimensional space. This extension

---

5. In order both to simplify the exposition and to make the comparison between the two models more meaningful, I have in drawing Figure 1 made a critical assumption. Following Gordon Tullock, "The General Irrelevance of the General Impossibility Theorem," *Quarterly Journal of Economics* (May 1967): 256–70, I have assumed that utility functions are symmetrical around the preferred positions. This means that the two variables are completely independent one from the other in individuals' preference functions. This device allows us to measure ordinal preferences in terms of distances from preferred positions. This assumption appears arbitrary in the party-platform model, but it is the standard one in location theory.

6. See, for example, E. H. Chamberlin, *The Theory of Monopolistic Competition*, 7th ed. (Harvard University Press, 1956), 260.

holds, as the following section demonstrates, only when the number of buyers becomes critically large.

VI. Party Platforms in Two-Dimensional Issue Space, with Many Voters

In relatively sharp contrast with duopoly theory, the theory of party-platform selection has been developed in small-number models. The paradox of voting has been almost universally illustrated in small-number examples, generally those with only three voters. This provided the basis for Tullock's specific extension of the analysis to a critically large number of voters.[7] If the electorate is expanded, the cyclical majority problem largely disappears because the internal space within which the cycle occurs becomes relatively very small. Given a sufficiently large number of voters, uniformly distributed over the two-dimensional issue space, the platforms of the two parties become almost identical. The full stability of the unidimensional model is not attained, but the area within which platform adjustments take place becomes small indeed. Practically speaking, the clustering theorem retains its validity.

VII. Duopoly Location in Two-Dimensional Market Space, with Many Buyers, and with Finite Threshold-Sensitive Response

Devletoglou has explicitly challenged the clustering theorem of duopoly theory.[8] In the context of a two-dimensional market space with many buyers, he has shown that profit-maximizing duopolists will locate at the center only on the presumption that buyers are hypersensitive to distance differentials. If buyers are assumed to respond only over a finite threshold, a minimum sensible dispersion rather than center-clustering will characterize locational patterns.

7. Tullock, "General Irrelevance."
8. Nicos E. Devletoglou, "A Dissenting View of Duopoly and Spatial Competition," *Economica* (May 1965): 140–60; Nicos E. Devletoglou and P. A. Demetriou, "Choice and Threshold: A Further Experiment in Spatial Duopoly," *Economica* (November 1967); and Nicos E. Devletoglou, "Threshold and Rationality," forthcoming.

The argument may be summarized briefly using the circular market space of Figure 2 to illustrate. Buyers are assumed to be uniformly distributed over this space, and each buyer is assumed to respond only if a threshold differential, rs, is crossed. Each person is indifferent as to which of the duopolists to patronize if these are located within rs distance of each other. Price, along with all other aspects of the product, are assumed identical for the two firms. It is apparent that, in this model, full center-clustering will make all buyers indifferent as between the two firms. This remains the case so long as the two firms locate closer together than rs. Some dispersion can, therefore, be predicted even in the model where buyers are assumed to be insensitive to changes in distance-costs and where firms are assumed to have no inventory costs.

Within the same basic model, where there is at least some distance-cost elasticity of demand, and/or where firms face positive costs of holding inventories, there will again be a specific profit incentive causing dispersion. As the two firms shift apart, beyond the minimum *sensible* range, say to R' and S', the market divides into three distinct regions or parts. All buyers in the left-

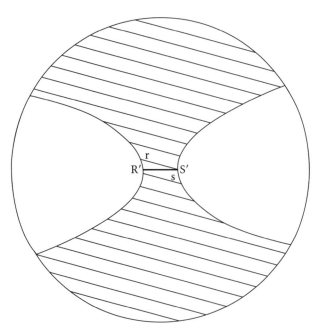

Figure 2

hand region attach themselves to r, the left-shifting firm; all buyers in the right-hand region attach themselves to s, the right-shifting firm; all buyers in the shaded area will remain indifferent as between the two sellers. For these, custom will depend strictly on chance elements. This construction makes it clear that if the total amount of the good purchased by a buyer increases as average distance is reduced and/or if firms find it advantageous to reduce the dependence of their own sales on chance, hence avoiding possibly violent shifts which make the carrying of large inventories necessary, some locational dispersion beyond the threshold distance will be generated by the profit-maximizing behavior of the duopolists.[9]

In his initial models, Devletoglou assumes that all buyers exhibit uniform thresholds of response to distance. As he shows, the basic conclusions do not require this rigid assumption. If all buyers are assumed to be threshold-sensitive, but the size of the threshold is assumed to increase proportionally with distance, an equally strong incentive is provided to the firms to disperse. Pressure for dispersion remains even when the size of the threshold varies among buyers, so long as the distribution is assumed to be roughly similar as among separate regions of the market space. As the proportion of all buyers who are hypersensitive increases, or as the size of the average threshold diminishes, the pressures on the firms to disperse will, of course, diminish.

VIII. Party Platforms in Two-Dimensional Issue Space, with Many Voters, and with Finite Threshold-Sensitive Response

The introduction of finite threshold-sensitive response in the models of two-party politics offers promise, and it may be argued that voters are more likely to exhibit such implied quantum jumps in choice behavior than buyers. Analysis that parallels Devletoglou's can be applied directly.

Assume that many voters are uniformly distributed over the circular issue space of Figure 2, with the location of a voter carrying the same meaning as

---

9. The specific locational pattern will depend on the strength of the various forces. The location of the firms will, in turn, fix the relative areas of the three regions, although the hyperbolic structure depicted in Figure 2 seems general given the central assumptions of the model.

that earlier discussed. The two issues are assumed continuously variable and are measured along the abscissa and ordinate. Using Tullock's examples, these can be thought of as appropriations for the Army and for the Navy.[10]

If a minimum *sensible*, a threshold of *rs*, is again postulated for each voter's choice behavior, party platforms would tend to cluster only to the extent limited by this range, even in the complete absence of voter disaffection and party requirements for voter loyalty. If the two parties select platforms near the center of the space and within this range of each other, all voters will be indifferent as between the two parties. The outcome of a majority voting process will depend on chance elements.

Some voter disaffection should be expected, however, as party platforms diverge from preferred positions. A reasonable assumption is, therefore, that the percentage of eligibles who actually cast votes will decrease as the distance from the nearest of the two platforms increases.[11] Analytically, this assumption in the political model is equivalent to that of positive distance-cost elasticity of demand in the spatial duopoly model. When such voter disaffection is plugged in, each party will find it advantageous to move slightly beyond threshold limits. By so doing, it can pick up a somewhat larger share of voters in the sector of the issue space toward which it shifts.

This pressure for dispersion is increased when considerations of party loyalty are allowed. If a political party is a permanent or quasi-permanent organization, it can scarcely depend on chance elements for its basic financial and canvassing effort. At least some minimal core of loyal supporters will be desirable. In order to insure this, a platform must be selected that for at least this minimum number of voters the threshold is crossed. This need for party loyalty is on all fours with the existence of positive inventory costs in the duopoly model. And, just as in the latter, this reinforces the pressure for dis-

---

10. Tullock, "General Irrelevance."

11. In a unidimensional model, Downs, *Economic Theory*, demonstrated the tendency toward platform dispersion that this assumption generates. The argument has more recently been elaborated by Gerald Garvey, "The Theory of Party Equilibrium," *American Political Science Review* (March 1966): 29–39. Gordon Tullock, *Toward a Mathematics of Politics* (University of Michigan Press, 1967), has extended Downs's analysis to the two-dimensional case.

person generated by voter disaffection. Party platforms will tend to differ to the extent that these elements prevail.

If the threshold of response is assumed to increase proportionally with distance, the tendency toward dispersion remains, just as in the comparable economic model. Somewhat interestingly here, as Devletoglou has shown, the issue space again tends to divide into three distinct areas of the shapes shown in Figure 3. The pressure toward dispersion of difference between party platforms remains even when the size of the effective choice threshold varies among voters. There are no distinctions in these respects between this and the duopoly model.

As noted in Section VI, full center-clustering is not attained with many voters in two-dimensional models, even without threshold-sensitive response. The cyclical majority problem arises to generate continuous platform adjustments, but these are confined to a limited area near the center, and, for some purposes, these may be disregarded. The introduction of the threshold would seem to add somewhat greater stability to the model in this respect. Minimal

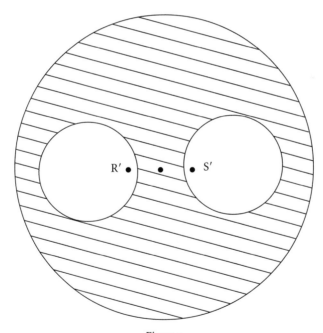

Figure 3

platforms adjustments become less productive to the parties, although the adjustments that are made will involve larger "jumps."[12]

The replacement of hypersensitive response by the threshold in the two-party model for political choice allows certain conceptually refutable hypotheses about institutional reforms to be advanced. Any change that reduces average voting costs—as, for example, the introduction of Sunday polling—should reduce the differences between party platforms. Similarly, any change that reduces party dependence on a core of loyal and financially able workers—for example, federal tax financing of presidential campaigns—should also reduce these platform differences.

IX. Welfare Implications

Only when the welfare implications of the two analytical models are compared does a significant difference emerge. To the extent that the duopolists are dispersed from the center of the market space, due to predicted threshold-sensitive response on the part of buyers, combined with distance-cost elasticity of demand and/or inventory costs, the average travel distance for all buyers in the space is reduced below that level which would be present under full center-clustering. If travel is not itself considered to be utility increasing, such a reduction can be taken to represent an increase in material welfare, in an admittedly limited sense. The dispersion from the center is, to this extent, therefore, welfare increasing.

This result is not forthcoming from the party-platform model, for the obvious reason that only one of the two competitors can win an election. Here it is as if the duopoly firms compete for mutually exclusive rights to sell to the whole market. Instead of reducing average distance, in this case between the voter's most preferred combination and the winning party's platform, the dispersion increases this distance relative to that which would be present under center-clustering. Any dispersion, any introduction of differences between party platforms, tends, therefore, to be welfare decreasing, given the setting of the model.

By the nature of politics, at least in some ideal sense, the issues that are

---

12. Intuitively, the effects of threshold-sensitive response on the stability of adjustment seem apparent. But I leave the formal proof to Devletoglou or others.

defined in party platforms represent proposals for general rules that are applicable for the whole community. Two competing governments, each of which is allowed to impose its own general rules, would seem to contradict the presumed necessity of such rules. When this is recognized, along with the possible welfare-decreasing effects of platform dispersion, effort directed at reducing threshold-sensitive response of voters by making them more aware of, and sensitive to, differences in party platforms seems socially productive. Relatively, such effort offers more "social" return than comparable effort in increasing the locational sensitiveness of market buyers. Inferentially, the analysis also suggests that there are potential welfare gains to be expected from measures designed to reduce the costs of voting itself and, also, from measures which tend to reduce the dependence of political parties on the establishment and maintenance of loyal groups of quasi-permanent supporters.

Insofar as threshold-sensitive response remains an important element in voter reaction, and, as a result of this and related factors, party platforms continue to differ measurably one from the other, the importance of party rotation in office is increased. The analysis allows this familiar principle of rotation to rest on a firm welfare basis. As noted above, by the very nature of political choice, one party and only one wins an election. It is thereby empowered to impose the general proposals contained in its platform upon all voters in the community, not only those who supported it in the election. Rotation provides the political analogue to the dispersed location of the two duopoly firms, each one of which caters to the specific market area determined by its location. If genuine rotation of two competing parties could be insured, some dispersion might be deemed welfare increasing even in politics, provided that welfare is measured in some dynamic sense.

X. Conclusions

None of the welfare implications or the policy suggestions inferred from these should be overemphasized. They were presented here primarily to indicate the potential usefulness of the analytical models. The main purpose of the paper has been that of simply tracing the parallels between two bodies of analysis. In both cases, the models remain highly abstract. Subsequent developments and extensions are apparent. In duopoly theory, a more systematic extension of the analysis to allow for an additional number of firms, perhaps moving from duopoly to triopoly to oligopoly generally, thence to n-firm competition, offers great promise even if the analytical barriers are formidable. An extension of the political models to allow for multiple parties is also suggested, although, again because of the mutual-exclusion aspects of political choice, this extension is less relevant than in the comparable economic models.

There is also a need to expand and to extend both models to include additional dimensions. In duopoly theory, spatial location introduces only two of an almost limitless number of dimensions worth exploring, the single most important additional one being, of course, price itself. Similarly, with politics, party platforms embody proposals on many more than two issues. As the dimensions of the models are expanded, a geometry of hyperspaces becomes necessary, and some shifting to less representational mathematics is indicated. With threshold-sensitive response models generally, there remains a gap between the aggregative constructions and those derivable by stages from analysis of individual choice behavior.

Majoritarian Logic

Abstract: The analogues to Pareto dominance and Pareto superiority, *majority dominance* and *majority superiority,* allow restriction on the domain of outcomes for majority-rule choices.
The logical structure of the argument extends and confirms the
proposition that the effective alternatives for collective choice
are *endogenously* determined by the existent rule for making
choices. Orthodox public choice theory has, explicitly or implicitly, presumed that the choice alternatives are exogenous to the
rule through which choices are made.

1. Introduction

The relationship between the normative structure of Paretian welfare economics and the Wicksellian normative criterion of unanimity in collective
choice has long been recognized.[1] In this paper, I propose to examine anal-
ogies to the concepts of Pareto dominance and Pareto superiority in a collective choice setting with a majority rather than a unanimity rule for decisions.

My central proposition may be stated prior to any analysis, as such. The
analogues to Pareto dominance and Pareto superiority, which I call *majority*

From *Public Choice* 97 (October 1998): 13–21. Reprinted by permission of the publisher, Kluwer Academic Publishers.

I am indebted to Geoffrey Brennan, Hartmut Kliemt and Yong J. Yoon for helpful
comments and discussions.

1. J. M. Buchanan, "Positive Economics, Welfare Economics, and Political Economy,"
Journal of Law and Economics 2 (October 1959): 124–38; P. Hennipman, "Wicksell and Pareto: Their Relationship in the Theory of Public Finance," *History of Political Economy* 14,
no. 1 (Spring 1982): 37–64.

dominance and *majority superiority*, allow us to restrict the domain of outcomes for majority-rule choices. The logical structure of the argument extends and confirms the proposition that I have advanced in earlier papers: The effective alternatives for collective choice are *endogenously* determined by the existent rule for making choices.[2] Orthodox public choice theory has, explicitly or implicitly, presumed that the choice alternatives are exogenous to the rule through which choices are made.

2. A Pareto Primer

Consider the inclusive set of all possible social states. The Paretian classification divides the set of all social states or positions into two subsets: (1) those that are Pareto optimal and (2) those that do not meet the criterion for optimality.[3] A state or position is defined to be Pareto optimal when there exists no change to another position that is possible without reducing the utility of at least one member of the relevant community. This set of Pareto optimal positions, the Pareto set, is referred to as the set of nondominated imputations, with domination referenced to the utility payoffs for all persons in the community.

The relationship between components of the set of nondominated positions (the Pareto set), both among themselves and with components of the set of dominated positions (the nonoptimal set) must be carefully specified. By construction, no position within the Pareto set dominates any other position in the set, and no position in the set is, in turn, dominated by any other position in the set, with domination again referenced for all persons in the relevant group. On the other hand, any position in the non-Pareto set is dominated by *at least one* position in the nondominated (Pareto) set. Note particularly, however, that there is no necessary relationship between any specifically selected position in one set with components of the other set. A position in the Pareto set does not dominate all positions in the nonoptimal

2. J. M. Buchanan, "Foundational Concerns: A Criticism of Public Choice Theory," in *Current Issues in Public Choice*, ed. J. Casas Pardo and F. Schneider (Cheltenham, U.K.: Edward Elgar, 1996), 3–20; J. M. Buchanan, "Rule Feasibility and Rule Dominance," Working Paper, Center for Study of Public Choice, George Mason University, Fairfax, Va., 1996.

3. R. Frisch, "On Welfare Theory and Pareto Regions," *International Economic Papers* 9 (1959), 39–92.

set, and, conversely, a position in the nonoptimal set is not dominated by all positions in the Pareto set, only by some.

These relationships can be clarified by introducing the Pareto classification of changes, moves or shifts among positions or social states. If a position is classified as within the Pareto set, there is no change away from this position that may be classified to be *Pareto superior*. On the other hand, if a position is classified within the nonoptimal set, there must exist at least one change to another position in the Pareto set. But there is no implication that any change away from a nonoptimal position need be Pareto superior. Changes from nonoptimal positions must be classified into two sets—those that are Pareto superior and those that are not.

To this point, the whole exercise is almost exclusively classificatory and taxonomic. We approach political relevance to an extent by making the Wicksellian move which relates the formal Pareto scheme to constitutional structure. If we acknowledge that individuals' preferences for collective alternatives can be revealed only through agreement, the Pareto norm translates readily into the rule for unanimity in making collective choices. If a position is, in fact, nonoptimal by the Pareto classification, there must exist at least one change that will secure unanimous agreement by all parties to the interaction. If there is no change upon which agreement can be reached, then, by definition, the initial or status quo position is to be classified within the Pareto set.[4]

3. From Unanimity to Majority

I propose now to move beyond the Pareto construction, even as extended by the Wicksellian implications for the critical relevance of the unanimity rule, and to work backwards, so to speak. I propose to commence analysis with the presupposition that collective choices are to be made by simple majority rule and to explore the possible efficacy of Pareto-like classificatory schemes. As noted, I propose to examine particularly those concepts of dominance and superiority, as applied to positions and moves respectively.

The exercise is straightforward, at least in a formal sense. Again consider

---

4. Wicksell used this construction to evaluate the prospects for fiscal reform. He suggested that any collective spending project that increases utility can be financed by tax share allocations that would secure unanimous acceptance. See K. Wicksell, *Finanztheoretische Untersuchungen* (Jena: Gustav Fischer, 1896).

the universe of all possible social states or positions. The requirement that all collective decisions be consistent with the satisfaction of the revealed preferences of a majority, any majority, of the community allows the inclusive set of all social states or positions to be classified, as before, into two subsets: (1) those positions that may be defined to be nondominated and (2) those that may be defined to be dominated. The procedure here is fully analogous to the Pareto-Wicksell construction. A position is classified to be in the nondominated set (the majority set) if there exists no change from such position that will increase (not decrease) utility payoffs to members of the majority that is decisive.

Think of the simple example—a three-person community (A, B and C) where A and B make up the majority coalition, and where the promised payoffs from one collective alternative X are measured in the payoff imputation (3, 2, 1), with payoffs to the three persons listed in sequence. If there should exist another social state or position Y that yields the imputation (4, 3, 0), the first alternative fails to meet the nondominated test. Both members of the majority coalition, A and B, find their payoffs increased by a shift from imputation X to Y. Note that nothing more is involved here than a redefinition of the set of persons or participants who are classified to be relevant for the application of the Pareto-like norm. Under the construction here, the model operates simply as if those persons outside the confines of the majority coalition do not exist, save as elements in the natural environment.

The set of dominated positions is defined analogously to the definition under Paretian analysis. A position is dominated if there exists at least one change to another position that will increase (not decrease) utility payoffs to all members of the minimal majority coalition that is decisive. Or, in terms of superiority, a position is in the dominated set if there exists at least one change that will secure the agreement of all members of the existing majority coalition. The relationships between components of the two sets are fully analogous to those traced out for the Pareto construction earlier.

4. The Pareto Set and the Majority Set

Both criteria of domination, the Paretian and the majoritarian, allow us to divide the set of all possible social states into two subsets. What is of interest here is the precise relationship between the two classificatory schemes. In the presence of certain empirically plausible conditions, the set of nondominated positions defined by the majoritarian criterion is a subset of the set of nondominated positions by the Pareto criterion.[5]

It is clear that positions that may be nondominated in the Pareto sense may remain dominated for a majority of persons in the inclusive community. Consider the simple example where the imputation $Z(3, 3, 3)$ is a feasible alternative in a three-person community; this imputation is majority dominated by $W_1(4, 4, 0)$, $W_2(4, 0, 4)$ or $W_3(0, 4, 4)$. Note, however, that the converse relationship does not hold. Any position in the majority set of nondominated positions also qualifies under the Paretian criterion. Consider an imputation that meets the majority requirement for nondomination. By definition, no improvement is possible for members of the majority in possession of choice authority. Utility payoffs for members of the minority are residually determined by actions of the majority. If members of the minority could suggest an improvement, or change, within the feasibility set that would improve the situation for members of the majority, the initial position would not have met the requirement for majority nondomination in the first place.

The differentiation in the Pareto and the majority set constructions does not lie in the domination relationship as such. The differentiation lies in the translation of the classification scheme into an evaluative standard for assessing changes or moves from one position to another. Recall that in the simple Paretian construction, the classification of a position in the nonoptimal or dominated set directly suggests that there exists at least one change that would meet with unanimous agreement. The construction does not imply, of course, that *any* change would be unanimously approved.

Again, the analogy with the majoritarian construction is relatively straightforward. But confusion arises because moves that might qualify as *majority superior*, and hence approved by all members of the ruling majority, might, at the same time, be *Pareto nonsuperior*, whether made from an optimal or nonoptimal position in the Pareto sense. Consider an example where initially there is a free and open market that basically meets the Pareto criterion as applied to its results. A majority coalition then restricts some markets so as to improve the payoffs of members of the effective coalition, thereby dam-

---

5. These conditions involve the interdependence between the positions attained by members of the minority and the majority. The members of the majority must ordinally prefer that persons in the minority secure the highest payoffs consistent with maximal payoffs to members of the majority.

aging members of the minority. Economists tend to classify the results of the restricted economy to be dominated in the Pareto sense, but, in this example, these results seem to be nondominated for the effective majority. Such a classificatory exercise is misleading, however, unless there is some presumption that side-payments remain possible such that members of the majority can secure higher utility levels than they secure under market restriction. In a world of zero transactions costs, such side-payments always exist; in which case, any market restrictions imposed by the majority coalition will produce results that are majority dominated by a set of straightforward transfers from members of the minority to members of the majority.[6] If side-payments prospects are ruled out, then any position that remains nondominated for a majority will also remain nondominated for the inclusive membership of the community.

5. A Distributional Example

Consider a simple setting in which six discrete units of value are to be distributed among three persons (A, B, C). In this pure distributional game, all imputations are Pareto optimal; all are in the nondominated set with reference to the preferences of all members of the group. Given the nonpartitionability of units, all possible imputations are listed in Table 1, with the assignments of payoffs as indicated sequentially.

We know that in this distributional setting there is no majority-rule equilibrium. Any position or imputation can be majority dominated by one or more selected alternatives. This familiar result seems to suggest that the majority nondominated set would be empty. Note carefully, however, just what the familiar voting theory logic involves here. The construction indicates that any imputation in the set is, indeed, dominated for an *alternative* majority. In the definition of majority dominance that was introduced in Section 3 above, however, a position or imputation was defined to be nonmajority dominated if any change would reduce the utility to any member of the *majority in authority*.

The relevance of the distinction drawn here will be clear if we think of the means through which alternatives are themselves introduced. Suppose that

---

6. J. M. Buchanan and G. Tullock, *The Calculus of Consent: Logical Foundations of Constitutional Democracy* (Ann Arbor: University of Michigan Press, 1962).

Table 1. Two-set classification by majority dominance
(six units, three persons)

I *Majority nondominated*	II *Majority dominated*
6 0 0	4 1 1
0 6 0	1 4 1
0 0 6	1 1 4
5 1 0	3 2 1
5 0 1	3 1 2
1 5 0	2 3 1
0 5 1	1 3 2
1 0 5	2 2 2
0 1 5	2 1 3
0 3 3	1 2 3
3 0 3	
3 3 0	
4 2 0	
4 0 2	
2 4 0	
0 4 2	
2 0 4	
0 2 4	

the status quo is described by the payoff imputation $(5, 0, 1)$ in Column I, with members of the ruling coalition, AC, dividing the units of available value between themselves in the ratio indicated. Suppose, now, that Person B considers the prospect for organizing a new majority with C. What will B rationally propose as the alternative collectively determined distribution? It seems evident that B will select one alternative from the set $(0, 4, 2)$, $(0, 2, 4)$, $(0, 1, 5)$, $(0, 3, 3)$, all of which strongly dominate the initial position for the new majority, BC. It would be irrational for B, or for C, either of whom, or both, might be the entrepreneur, to propose any of the payoff imputations in Column II, even one of those that dominate $(5, 0, 1)$ for the BC majority, for example $(1, 3, 2)$, because each of these is dominated in payoffs for BC by one of the imputations in the nondominated set listed in Column I.

The familiar majoritarian cycle will be limited to the alternatives listed in Column I, which is the majority nondominated set, as defined earlier. Any of these positions may, analogously to the Paretian logic, be dominated for an alternative majority by positions that lie outside the Column I set. But the alternative majority, itself, will never propose any of the Column II imputations, since each one of these is dominated for the majority in authority by one or more imputations in Column I.

The example illustrates the point made earlier. All imputations are Pareto optimal, but only the subsets listed in Column I are "majority optimal." Note that the analysis here does not challenge the standard voting theory result to the effect that pairwise comparisons between separate alternatives under majority voting will generate cycles over the whole of the space. This standard result is, however, based on the unexamined presumption that the alternatives to be compared are presented exogenously to those who make up majority coalitions. The classification that is suggested here, that between the nondominated and dominated sets of alternatives for majority coalitions in being, arises when we recognize that the alternatives to be placed before the group for majority vote are endogenous to the process itself.[7]

6. A Public-Goods Example

Another application of the classification scheme introduced in this paper involves the sharing of genuinely public goods along separate dimensions of adjustment by a number of persons (greater than 2), with pairwise majority voting over the relevant set of multidimensional alternatives.

Consider the familiar three-person (A, B, C), two-public-goods (X, Y) model in the geometry of Figure 1. The separate bliss points for the three persons are shown as a, b and c. For expositional simplicity only, think of the indifference contours around these points as concentric circles.

The Pareto optimal set of positions includes all positions within the area defined by the three contract loci, including all positions along the loci themselves. The set of majority nondominated positions, as defined earlier, includes only those positions that lie along the loci.

Suppose that a position on one of the loci, say, 1, is the status quo, with A and C in the existing majority coalition. Suppose that B now senses the opportunity to form a new coalition with A by proposing some shift away from position 1. Note that any point in the shaded ogive, whether inside or outside the area enclosed by the contract loci, dominates 1 for members of the AB coalition, the new majority. But why would B (or A) propose any position

7. Buchanan, "Foundational Concerns."

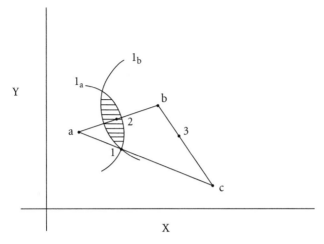

Figure 1. Three-person, two-public-goods model

other than one that lies on the locus *ab*? One or more such positions will always yield higher (or equally high if a weak-ordering relationship is used) payoffs to both members of the majority that has assumed decision authority, higher than payoff in any position in the ogive but not on the locus.

The cycle that will be generated as majority coalitions change will involve shifts among such positions as 1, 2 and 3, all of which will lie along the loci, and fall neither inside nor outside the area enclosed by the three loci.

7. Assessment and Evaluation

The classification scheme that is presented in this paper is a straightforward extension of the familiar Paretian construction applied to the majoritarian decision setting. For purposes of expositional simplicity, the analysis is limited to a pure distributional model in Section 5 and a pure public-goods model in Section 6. Work in progress combines publicness and privateness (partitionability) and generates analogous results.[8]

The possible contribution of the exercise emerges from the perspective that is offered on the workings of majoritarian democracy. The dominant concentration of emphasis and inquiry in both public choice and social choice theory has been on the properties of majority voting that generate cycles and thereby prevent the attainment of political equilibrium. This con-

---

8. Buchanan, "Rule Feasibility."

centration has distracted attention away from an examination of the behavior of members of majority coalitions, whether those in being or in prospect. The analysis here employs utility-maximizing logic to suggest only that majority coalitions will attempt to maximize payoffs to their members. This result is hardly surprising. By comparison, however, orthodox public choice theory has worked with a nonrestricted domain of individual preference orderings along with a set of exogenously defined social states. The orthodox approach has failed to recognize that the use of majority rule, in itself, along with the preference orderings, greatly restricts the size of the set of alternatives that qualify for possible selection.

At least to this extent, orthodox public choice theory could be said to have remained trapped in a paradigm analogous to the search for *the public interest*, something that is presumed to exist out there waiting to be discovered. The processes of democracy become means of selecting among "states of the world" that exist independent of the preferences that act to bring such states into being.

Public choice theory has often been criticized because it allegedly models behavior as if persons act so as to maximize utilities. In choosing among alternative choice options, as presented in the voting booth, public choice theory does, indeed, invoke the economists' utility-maximizing calculus. But public choice theory has not, surprisingly, been consistent in its own methodology. If persons may be usefully modeled as utility maximizers when they choose among collective alternatives, they should also be so modeled when they invent the very alternatives among which choices are to be made. A model driven by utility maximization should not embody behavior that involves the eschewing of the differential advantages offered by definition of alternatives that is a necessary component of majoritarian politics.[9]

Collective outcomes that embody generality in treatment among all members in a polity will not emerge from the workings of nonconstrained majoritarian democracy. Members of majority coalitions will be treated advantageously by comparison with the treatment accorded to persons in minorities. This elementary conclusion stems directly from the logic of majority voting itself.

---

9. Note that the theory of agenda control, which has been a part of public choice orthodoxy, assumes the prior existence of the choice alternatives. It does not extend to the endogenous creation of the alternatives by the coalition in authority.

PART FIVE

Rent Seeking

Rent Seeking under External Diseconomies

The papers in part II of this book were the first efforts to extend economic analysis to allow for rent-seeking or profit-seeking behavior in the *creation* of monopoly positions, whether this behavior takes place within a dynamic model of market interaction or within a political-governmental decision structure. Several important principles have emerged from this discussion, despite the early stage of development of what remains essentially a new extension of economic theory. First of all, as Tullock demonstrates, the orthodox measure of the welfare costs of monopoly, which is concentrated on estimates of value of the familiar Harberger welfare triangles, tends to be far too low. Second, as Krueger shows convincingly, any arbitrary restrictions on market freedom created through governmental auspices will attract investment in rent seeking, setting off a process that will tend to dissipate the potential rents available ex ante to those investors who succeed in securing the scarce permits.

My purpose in this paper is to develop a further application, one that has not, to my knowledge, been made. I shall demonstrate that when profit- or rent-seeking behavior is fully incorporated into familiar situations where external diseconomies exist, serious questions are raised concerning the efficacy of the efficiency-generating policy steps almost universally recommended by economists. A second but equally important aspect of the analysis demonstrates that, quite apart from the questions that might be raised about the net welfare effects of policy actions, the prospects for securing

From *Toward a Theory of the Rent-Seeking Society*, ed. James M. Buchanan, Robert D. Tollison, and Gordon Tullock (College Station: Texas A&M University Press, 1980), 183–94. Reprinted by permission of the publisher.

agreement among politically decisive members of the community depend critically on the precise manner in which efficiency-producing institutional reforms are proposed. These public-choice implications suggest the policy efficacy of narrowing the range of policy options that should be seriously discussed.

External Diseconomies with Nonspecialized Resources

Consider a situation where there exist genuine Pareto-relevant external diseconomies. Further, we explicitly define this to be a setting where the absence of private ownership rights is acknowledged to be the underlying structural or institutional defect. We have a "tragedy of the commons," where separate decision-takers, persons or firms, utilize a commonly available, unowned and, hence, unpriced resource. Examples can be the familiar ones—pollution of a stream, traffic on a freeway, despoliation of a public beach. The familiar welfare results emerge: independent action produces an overutilization of the common facility. Efficiency criteria dictate that usage be restricted, and, in this case, the assignment of private ownership rights can be predicted to accomplish the results required by standard efficiency criteria.

In the common-usage setting, the average product of resources employed in utilizing the facility will be equated to the marginal product (in value terms) of resources employed elsewhere in the economy. The initial situation may be depicted in figure 10.1. The assignment of ownership rights will cause owners to reduce the application of resources to the facility; the previously existing externalities will be internalized.[1] Usage will be cut back to the point where the marginal product from resources applied to the facility is equal to the marginal product of resources applied elsewhere in the economy. The owners will be able to secure the marginal product of the facility itself, measured by the triangle R in figure 10.1, by reducing application of resources to the facility. This is (with linear functions) equivalent to the triangle G in the construction, which measures the social wastage under the common-usage

---

1. The classic paper on this is F. H. Knight, "Some Fallacies in the Interpretation of Social Cost," *Quarterly Journal of Economics* 38 (1924): 582–606.

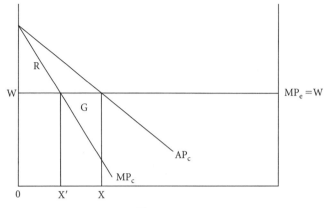

Figure 10.1

situation. The potential value of the facility, measured by its potential marginal product when efficiently utilized, is "destroyed" by the overusage.

In this initial model, we assume that resources applied to the facility are not specialized. Hence, resource owners who shift to other employments neither gain nor lose by the institutional change toward private ownership. The net wealth of the community increases by the marginal product of the optimally used facility, and this increase in social product accrues exclusively to those who secure the ownership rights.

To this point, the analysis has not jumped outside the bounds of elementary textbook discussion. Let us now apply the theory of rent seeking. Suppose that the external diseconomies are recognized to exist in the initial situation, and further suppose that it is generally predicted that the government will, in fact, step in and create private ownership rights as a means of ensuring efficient facility usage. This prediction on the part of rent- or profit-seeking entrepreneurs will prompt investment in efforts to secure the scarcity rents that ownership rights will offer. Such investment will vary in form, depending on accompanying predictions concerning the manner in which rights are to be created. We may examine several possible cases.

If the scarce ownership rights are to be auctioned off, prospective purchasers need do little more than estimate the discounted value of the facility. The successful bid will be approximately equal to this value, as viewed ex ante, and the proceeds of the auction sale of ownership rights may be shared among members of the general public. In this case, the wealth increment generated by the change in institutional structure is channeled from the new owners of the rights to the members of the community at large.

Suppose, however, that ownership rights are not to be auctioned off, but are instead to be "assigned" by politicians-bureaucrats to "deserving" citizens. Let us suppose further that these politicians-bureaucrats are totally "incorruptible," and furthermore that they are totally immune to influence of any sort. In this case, the wealth generated by the institutional shift to private ownership accrues exclusively to those who are differentially favored in the allocation. This is the model that accords most closely with the textbook discussion, where the manner of assignment is not discussed and where rent-seeking behavior in anticipation of favorable treatment is implicitly assumed not to take place.

Suppose now, however, that the politicians-bureaucrats are totally corruptible, and that explicit bribes in money are widely observed. In this third case, those who have the power to assign property rights can secure the full value of the facility. The net wealth increase that is due to the efficient use of the facility through time is fully captured by the politicians-bureaucrats.

Note that the differences between the three models of assignment discussed to this point are purely distributional. These differences involve the sharing of the present-value equivalents of the net gains that the efficient use of the facility will generate for the community. In each case, the presumption is that the facility will henceforward be operated efficiently and that overall there will be a clear "social gain" in making the initial institutional shift from common to private ownership. In none of the cases examined is there social waste involved in rent-seeking activity.

Let us now, however, introduce a rent-seeking model with quite different results. Suppose that politicians-bureaucrats are totally incorruptible in money, but that they are subject to influence by indirect means of persuasion, familiar in pressure-group or lobbying discussion. Prospective bidders for ownership rights will be prompted to invest in methods of persuasion, in influence, in lobbying of all forms. To the extent that entry into such activity is not itself restricted, the expected returns from such investment may be predicted to approximate the rate of return on investment in the economy generally. But if such rent-seeking activity is not directly beneficial to the politicians-bureaucrats whose behavior is the target of the efforts, there may be no net wealth increase in the community. Rent seeking may fully dissipate the "social gains" anticipated from the institutional shift. In such a case, there may be no efficiency-related argument for trying to make the institutional shift to ensure that the facility will be operated efficiently. To be sure, efficient operation will characterize the facility after the change, but the efficiency gains will have been fully offset by the "inefficient" rent-seeking efforts of prospective owners. In the net, the community will be no better off with than without the institutional change from common usage to private ownership.

This is, of course, a limiting case, and the complete dissipation of efficiency gains through rent seeking may occur only in particular circumstances. Some net increments to wealth might be expected to accrue to successful bidders for the new ownership rights, some to the politicians-bureaucrats who make the assignments, and possibly some gains would be expected to spill over to the public generally in most settings. But the argument does indicate that the promised gains implicit in the familiar welfare-economics applications may be much less significant than they are often made to appear. When this is recognized and when we acknowledge further that the existence of genuine external diseconomies cannot be observed readily, the whole "internalization of externalities" analysis must be treated with considerable skepticism.

External Diseconomies with Specialized Resources

This general result may be strengthened and extended when we modify the example in only one way. We now assume that the persons or firms who are initially applying resource bundles to the common-usage facility must suffer some reduction in direct resource return from a shift to alternative employments. This situation may arise for any one of several reasons. The facility may be large relative to the total area of the economy within which resources are applied. Resources may have become specialized for usage on the common facility. The costs of shift themselves may be significant. All these may be depicted generally in figure 10.2, which differs from figure 10.1 only by the downward slope of the marginal product curve for the economy external to the facility.

The necessary conditions for attaining efficient usage remain unchanged. Resource employment on the common facility should be reduced from $0X$ to $0X'$, where the values of marginal product for like units of resources are

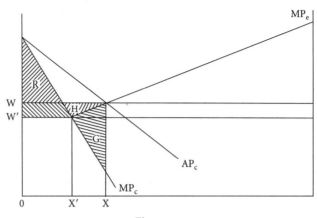

Figure 10.2

equalized as between the usage of the facility and other employments. Private ownership will, as before, effectively internalize the external diseconomy in usage that previously existed. The difference between this and the model depicted in figure 10.1 lies in the impact of internalization through ownership on those persons and firms who are initially applying resources to the common-usage facility. The equalization of marginal product required by efficiency criteria here involves a reduction in the marginal products of the resource units that can be shifted. The direct payments per unit of mobile resource that would be generated by a competitive process will be less after the institutional change than before.

One way of stating this is to say that the resource owners applying mobile units of resource to the common-usage facility before the assignment of ownership secure some share of the marginal product of the facility itself, and that this share will accrue to the new owner of the facility after the institutional change that assigns private ownership rights. This may be shown readily in terms of the geometry of figure 10.2. The marginal product of the facility under private ownership arrangements is shown by the shaded triangle, R, in figure 10.2. In market equilibrium, all of this product would be earned by the assigned owners of the facility. The "social wastage" generated by the usage of the facility as if it were a free good is shown by the shaded triangle, G, which is smaller than $R (G < R)$. That is to say, a shift to efficient operation through the restriction of usage resulting from the assignment of private ownership rights will generate scarcity rents to owners in excess of the "social wastage." The difference is owing to the fact that some share of the facility's marginal product is secured by those who apply mobile resource units in facility usage before the ownership assignment. All owners of mobile resources will find their direct resource returns reduced, from W to W' in figure 10.2. Most of this reduction in resource returns to owners of mobile resources will be offset by increases in payments to rent recipients in other sectors of the economy. The sum of these offsetting increases is not, however, sufficient to offset fully the decline in net "wages" to the owners of mobile resource units. The difference is shown in figure 10.2 by the small shaded triangle, H, which must be subtracted from the scarcity rentals on the facility to secure a measure of the net "social gains."

Let us now apply the several rent-seeking cases introduced in the first section to this setting. Consider first the case where private ownership rights are simply auctioned off among bidders. The successful bids will sum to approximately the marginal product of the facility that has been commonly used before the change, that is, to R, in discounted value terms. The general public may in this way secure an increment to net wealth. The sum of the successful bids will, however, exceed the net efficiency gains (in discounted value) that the efficient operation of the facility guarantees. The net wealth of owners of mobile resource units (call this "labor" for simplicity in analysis) will be reduced, whether such resource units be employed on the particular facility under efficient operation or elsewhere in the economy. The net wealth of rent recipients elsewhere in the economy will be increased because of the increase in the supply of complementary resource inputs.

If the politicians-bureaucrats are totally incorruptible and are known to be immune to any influence, our second case considered above, the institutional change to private ownership will increase the wealth of the successful applicants straightforwardly. The subsequent reallocation of mobile resources will also increase the net wealth of rent recipients elsewhere in the economy. Offsetting these increases will be some reduction in the net wealth of all owners of mobile resources. In the net, however, the total gains will be larger than the total losses.

If the politicians-bureaucrats are totally corruptible, our third case, the only change is that the members of this decision-making group, rather than those who are successful in securing the new ownership rights, will acquire the value of the marginal product of the facility under efficient operation.

As in the first section, the differences between these first three cases considered are exclusively distributional; these differences involve only the sharing of the net increment to wealth that the efficient operation of the facility will guarantee, along with the sharing of the gains and losses that the subsequent resource reallocation will generate.

Let us now examine, however, the rent-dissipation case, in which prospective facility owners are prompted to invest resources in indirect efforts to influence political decision makers. In the limiting case, all the potential scarcity rents will be dissipated as before, but note here that there will arise a *net efficiency loss* for the community as a whole as a result of the shift from common usage to private ownership, despite the fact that such arrangements are guaranteed to produce an efficient operation of the facility through time. The net loss arises here because the returns to the owners of mobile resources are reduced in the process of shifting to an efficient usage of the facility, while at the same time the full marginal product of the facility itself is competed away in wholly wasteful rent seeking.

As we move away from the limiting case in which all potential scarcity rents are dissipated and as we allow for some differential rents to be secured by successful seekers of ownership rights, by politicians-bureaucrats through explicit payments or through the enjoyment of perquisites, and by the public generally, these conclusions about net efficiency losses to the community must be modified. However, these residual rents must remain equal to or higher than the difference between the initial "social wastage" and the marginal product of the facility under efficient operation if a "social gain" to the community is to be generated by the shift to private ownership. This finding once again suggests that the possible external diseconomies must be reckoned to be considerably more serious than the orthodox analysis might indicate before any restriction of common-usage arrangements can be justified.

Public-Choice Implications

To this point, the analysis has been confined to the rent-seeking activity of prospective private owners as this might possibly affect the net welfare gains or welfare costs of institutional attempts to internalize external diseconomies. I have deliberately refrained from introducing the obvious questions raised concerning the effects of rent-seeking behavior, and the predictability of this behavior, on the acceptability of institutional rearrangements to members of the community, to the voting constituency, and through this to the potential decision makers. These public-choice questions may be easily answered in the separate cases discussed in both the first two sections.

In the basic model described in the first section, where nonspecialized resources are applied to the common usage of the facility, there is no net transfer of wealth between rent recipients and the owners of mobile resources. By construction here, the scarcity rentals made possible by the internalization of the externality are the only rental prospects anywhere in the economy. Owners of mobile resource units will, therefore, remain indifferent as to the proposals that will either allocate the net increments to wealth to the successful applicants for ownership rights, as new owners, or to the politicians-bureaucrats themselves (envy considerations aside). These owners of mobile resource units will also tend to look indifferently on the rent-dissipating activity under the free-entry, indirect-influencing case. By dramatic contrast, the owners of mobile resources, as members of the voting-taxpaying-beneficiary public, should positively support the assignment of ownership rights through the auctioning process, since this can ensure that the net efficiency gains are neither dissipated by unproductive rent seeking nor distributed exclusively to others in the community. To the extent that citizens make the required connection between governmental receipt of the bid monies and the return of these monies in the form of tax reduction, public expenditure increases, or direct transfers, we should predict that the auction method of assigning new ownership rights would tend to dominate alternative schemes in some political sense when we recognize that mobile resource owners make up a larger voting group than those who might secure rents.

The second basic model is more interesting in terms of its public-choice implications. As I have shown, any restriction on common usage by newly assigned owners will reduce the directly imputed payments to the owners of the mobile resources. Insofar as this effect is recognized in advance, owners of mobile resources, who would have been indifferent in the first model, will tend to oppose any and all arrangements predicted to generate some shift of resources away from the common-usage facility unless, of course, appropriate compensations are included. To the extent that the incremental rents promised by the efficient usage of the facility attract rent-seeking investment that tends to be dissipated in wasteful influence-affecting activity, the scope for possible compensations to those adversely affected will be reduced. If the scarcity rents are not "used up" in rent seeking, compensations are conceptually possible; the institutional shift to private ownership is, potentially, Pareto-superior to the common-usage status quo ante. The compensations required here would, however, be quite complex; transfers would have to be made between rent recipients, generally, and owners of mobile resource units, generally, and not just those directly involved in the reallocation away from the facility itself.

The public-choice aspects of the institutional adjustment both in this model and in the setting of the second section suggest that the auction method of assigning ownership rights may dominate other methods, in terms of both welfare gains and political acceptability. The auction method tends to ensure, first of all, that rent-seeking investment be directed productively in the bids made for the scarcity rights, rather than wastefully in attempts to influence decision makers. Second, the method ensures that there are no opportunities for political corruption, either directly or indirectly, through the perquisites of lobbying activity. Third, and perhaps most important, the auction method tends to make possible a *distribution* of these social gains among members of the public in such a way as to generate widespread political support.

Somewhat interestingly, those economists who have been most closely associated with the proposals for auctioning off scarce rights in the usage of inherently crowdable facilities have not, to my knowledge, stressed the advantages that this analysis emphasizes. Ronald Coase, John Dales, and others who have advocated the auction method have done so largely, if not exclusively, on allocative efficiency grounds, as means of ensuring that those best able to utilize scarce facilities effectively secure access to these facilities. This orthodox efficiency-based argument is relevant, especially in situations where resale of assigned rights is either prohibited by law or strongly discouraged. The more important efficiency argument may, however, be that analyzed in this paper, that of ensuring that gains will not be dissipated in rent seeking and that these gains will be distributed in such a way as to benefit the public generally, not just the successful rent seekers.[2]

We do observe the assignment of ownership rights through auctioning, the most familiar example being perhaps the assignments of rights to drill for offshore oil and gas. We do not, however, observe the auction method in use in many circumstances where it might seem to be applicable. We do not observe auctioning in the assignment of rights to use radio spectrums, in the assignment of rights to pollute, in the assignment of airline routes, in the assignment of franchises to bus and trucking companies, in the assignment of local and regional utility franchises. In all these examples and many others we observe direct political-bureaucratic regulation through the assignment of franchises, permits, and licenses.[3] The analysis of this paper suggests that these noncontract or nonauction methods of regulation are institutionally more viable than the auction alternative. Simple public-choice analysis suggests that the political support for such noncontract or nonauction methods is likely to arise directly from those who are successful in the assignment process, along with those who occupy decision-making positions in the political-bureaucratic structure. The fact that these groups do seem to support direct

---

2. The argument in favor of the auctioning method must be tempered when we recognize that the target for rent-seeking activity may be shifted "upward" to the level of the politician-bureaucrat who has the power to dispose of the auction receipts, the second stage discussed in chapter 1.

3. This listing is not to be taken to imply that all regulated activities are necessarily inefficient in a totally unregulated setting. Regulation may, of course, be initially justified on common-usage arguments similar to those assumed in the analysis of this paper. Or comparable regulation may be justified on "natural monopoly" arguments. However, many industries may be subjected to regulation on wholly specious arguments unrelated to the efficiency properties of the unregulated setting. Much of the argument developed in this paper may be applied, however, regardless of the initial causes for regulation. The auctioning of bids to franchises may be compared with more direct regulation independent of whether the restricted licenses of franchises are warranted in the first place. Interestingly, the common-usage facility has been discussed in the literature independent of the discussion of natural monopoly. Yet these clearly reduce to the same thing. For a recent treatment of some of the historical development of ideas on natural monopoly, especially as applied to the contracting of franchises, see Mark Crain and Robert Ekelund, "Chadwick and Demsetz on Competition and Regulation," *Journal of Law and Economics* 19 (April 1976): 149–62.

regulation suggests empirically that the scarcity rents are not fully dissipated.[4] The acquiescence of the public in the distributional results of direct regulation, as opposed to the alternative distribution that might be available under the contract or auction alternative, suggests empirically that the differential effects are probably not fully recognized.

4. The basis for the support of direct regulation by those who are regulated is analyzed in James M. Buchanan and Gordon Tullock, "Polluters' Profits and Political Response: Direct Controls versus Taxes," *American Economic Review* 65 (March 1975): 139–47.

Rent Seeking, Noncompensated Transfers, and Laws of Succession

[Men] will spend years in degrading subserviency to obtain a
niche in a will; and the niche, when at last obtained and enjoyed,
is but a sorry payment for all that has been endured.

—Anthony Trollope, *Doctor Thorne*
(Oxford University Press, 1980), p. 246

I. Introduction

My purpose in this paper is to analyze inefficiencies that may emerge from
the noncompensated transfer of valued rights between persons. This source
of inefficiency has not, to my knowledge, been fully incorporated either in
the economic theory of property rights or in orthodox tax analysis. My discussion is based on the elementary fact that all noncompensated transfers are
rents to the recipients. Implications for the emergence of rent-seeking behavior follow straightforwardly. The now-familiar propositions to the effect
that rent seeking may dissipate economic value can be applied to a variety of

From *Journal of Law and Economics* 26 (April 1983): 71–85. Reprinted by permission of
the publisher.
    I am indebted to my colleagues Geoffrey Brennan, Dwight Lee, and John Pettengill
and to William Landes for helpful comments. The paper is also strictly "Tullockian" in
character, although Gordon Tullock was not in Blacksburg during its writing. Indeed, a
junior colleague, on hearing the argument orally, said that Tullock must have made its
central point. That he did not do so indicates that Tullock may, indeed, have a "blind
spot" when he discusses inheritance.

transfer settings, only a few of which are explored in this paper.[1] To the extent that the efficiency criterion is the relevant norm, direct implications may be drawn for policy with respect to the laws or rules for succession.

In a broad and very general sense, the resource-wasting struggles for access to noncompensated transfers of value (and power) have long been recognized. For example, quasi-economic arguments have been made for hereditary succession, and tragically wasteful conflict for highly valued prizes has long been the stuff of classic fiction. Nonetheless, a more explicit analysis that takes rent-seeking behavior as its central organizing element seems to be warranted.

In Section II, I discuss the meaning of noncompensated transfers. Section III analyzes the model in which the power to transfer is totally unrestricted. Section IV discusses rules or laws of succession that restrict the choice options of potential donors. In Section V, I explore briefly the elements of what might be required for a transfer policy that combines the norms of economic efficiency and intergenerational equity. Section VI discusses the problem of succession in attenuated-rights settings. A few conclusions are offered in Section VII. In an Appendix to the paper, I use a highly simplified construction to demonstrate conceptually how an efficient transfer restriction might be determined.

II. Compensated and Noncompensated Transfers

The rentlike attribute of noncompensated transfers cannot be questioned, but the significance of such transfers of value among persons may be subject to challenge. A strictly "economic" approach to interpersonal and particularly intrafamily relationships might suggest that many of the transfers of valued assets or claims, which do not seem to be explicitly compensated, may represent only one side of a complex exchange in which a reciprocal transfer

---

1. The seminal papers are those by Gordon Tullock, "The Welfare Costs of Tariffs, Monopolies, and Theft," *Western Economic Journal* 5 (1967): 224; Anne O. Krueger, "The Political Economy of the Rent-Seeking Society," *American Economic Review* 64 (1974): 291; and Richard A. Posner, "The Social Costs of Monopoly and Regulation," *Journal of Political Economy* 83 (1975): 807. These papers are reprinted, along with others, in the volume edited by James Buchanan, Robert Tollison, and Gordon Tullock, *Toward a Theory of the Rent-Seeking Society* (1980).

of value has been or is expected to be made. Transfers that take the form of gifts or bequests are, on their face, noncompensated. Some part of such transfers may, nonetheless, represent payment by the apparent donor for reciprocal services that have been or are to be rendered by the designated donee. A person may will his estate to an identified legatee in exchange for services that the legatee agrees to perform prior to the death of the legator.

To the extent that gifts and bequests are literally payments for equal values received in exchange, no matter how complex the process of exchange may be, there is no net transfer of value among persons involved and there is no incentive for the emergence of rent-seeking behavior. Hence, for purposes of the analysis in this paper, fully compensated transfers of value can be neglected. It should be noted, however, that noncompensated elements may remain even in those cases where prospective donees make some reciprocal transfers of value to the donor. If the "terms of trade" offered to prospective donees are favorable, rent seeking will emerge among prospective entrants as in those settings where no part of the transfer is offset by a reciprocal flow of services. The analysis, as such, applies only to noncompensated transfers or that portion of total transfers that is noncompensated. The distinction between compensated and noncompensated transfers must, of course, be made in any attempts to formulate a legal-political policy for restricting interpersonal transfers of value.

Noncompensated transfers that become rents to potential recipients will motivate rent-seeking behavior, but there is no necessary linkage between such behavior, in itself, and inefficiency in resource use. In the familiar rent-seeking examples, the payment of direct money bribes to those who hold decisive powers of control over access to artificially scarce rental opportunities (for example, import quotas) may reflect minimal resource wastage, at least by comparison with a situation where direct bribes are not possible while the rental opportunities remain. In all such cases, however, those persons who control access to the opportunities are, in a sense, ensuring that the transfers of value will, in fact, be directly compensated. Rent seeking becomes wasteful only in those situations where those who control access to rents do not or cannot ensure direct compensation. In the familiar examples, rent seeking becomes wasteful because standards of moral-legal behavior make direct bribes inappropriate. In the cases to be analyzed here, direct compensation, in effect, would negate the transfer of value away from the person who controls access. The objective sought for may be that of accomplishing a net transfer of value. Hence, a prospective donor will explicitly eschew relationships that convert noncompensated into compensated transfers. In so doing, the donor ensures that the rent seeking that emerges will represent allocative inefficiency.

III. Unrestricted Powers of Transfer

Consider first a setting in which a single individual is sole owner of a nonhuman asset that commands a value in the market. This asset may be marketed costlessly and instantaneously at any time. Further, assume that income from the asset can be costlessly converted into additions to the capital stock and vice versa. There are no restrictions on consuming or "eating up" either the income from the asset or the capital value itself. There are no restrictions on the owner's power and authority to transfer title of the asset to other persons. There are no taxes on such transfers, whether by gift or bequest.

In this model, there is no incentive for the owner of the asset to depart from present-value maximization as a norm for managing the flow of income from the asset and the capital value of the asset itself. Regardless of the owner's rate of time preference, sustained maximization of the remainder value of the asset is dictated by simple precepts of rationality. Moreover, since there are no restrictions, either direct or indirect, on the transfer of value to other persons, the owner of the asset accumulates (or decumulates) value in accordance with nondistorted maximization of his own utility. The ultimate amount and direction of the capital value that is transferred to others will depend on the arguments within the owner's utility function. The trade-offs among these arguments that he confronts are not distorted in any way by elements exogenous to the potential transfers.

There is no attenuation of ownership rights in this setting. The orthodox theory of property rights, or of welfare economics for that matter, suggests that the efficiency norm will be fully satisfied under these conditions. The potential donor will make capital accumulation (decumulation) decisions in the knowledge that an additional dollar projected for transfer to another person will involve an opportunity cost of precisely one dollar in current consumption. This orthodox analysis, however, has overlooked (at least to my knowledge) a possibly important source of inefficiency. The implications of the fact that transfers (gifts or bequests) are net rents to the persons who receive them has not been incorporated in the standard analytics. Because receipt of such values are rents, we should predict the emergence of rationally motivated rent-seeking behavior in all settings where there remains any uncertainty about the identity of the potential recipients. If, as in the model described here, the initial owner of the capital asset or value retains unrestricted freedom to select the potential recipient of the transfer or transfers, rent-seeking competition will arise among all those persons who place a positive value on the prospect of being among the recipient group. A substantial portion of the investment of effort, time, and resources in this rent-seeking activity will be socially wasteful.

The magnitude of net resource waste involved is not easy to estimate, either conceptually or empirically. Early contributors to the analysis of rent seeking, and notably Gordon Tullock[2] and Richard Posner,[3] implicitly or explicitly suggested that rent-seeking investment would be extended to the point where all net rents are dissipated. More recent developments in the theory, again by Gordon Tullock,[4] suggest that total investment in rent seeking may exceed, be equal to, or fall short of the value of the net rents to be transferred. The magnitude here depends critically on the precise characteristics of the institutional setting within which the transfers are made and on the procedures within the rent-seeking interaction itself.

An example may be helpful. Suppose that it is widely known that a potential donor plans to make a gift of $1 million at a specified date, say, January 1984, to a "deserving" person. It is assumed that his choice of this amount will not be affected by any activity of the potential rent seekers. How much rent seeking will take place?

The answer will depend on the setting. Assume that the "players" in the game can be identified in advance. They may be, for example, the ten direct lineal descendants (sons and daughters) of the man who promises to make the gift of $1 million to one of them on the date specified. Rent seeking in-

---

2. Tullock, "The Welfare Costs of Tariffs," note 1.

3. Posner, "The Social Costs of Monopoly," note 1.

4. Gordon Tullock, "Efficient Rent Seeking," in *Toward a Theory of the Rent-Seeking Society*.

volves the equivalent in this model to the purchase of chances to win in a lottery with an open-ended number of tickets. It is as if the ten bidders are offered tickets at $1.00 each, with the option that each may purchase as many tickets as desired, tickets which, once purchased, are put into the urn making the chances for winning directly proportional to the number of tickets purchased.[5]

Many other variants of the transfer "game" might be developed, either in terms of abstracted models with explicit numerical payoffs and outlays or in terms of more general formulations. In the setting where individual powers to transfer are unrestricted, the above simplification may not seem adequately descriptive. The set of potential entrants may not be defined. The man who promises the $1 million may have ten direct heirs, who may expect to occupy a favored place among potential donees, but he remains free to make the gift, in whole or in part, to persons other than his own children. Differentially valued prospects for qualifying as a potential donee and for success in the final transfer process will be predicted to motivate differentially valued investments in rent seeking.

It becomes intuitively clear that the ratio between the predicted total resource investment in rent seeking and the size of the expected transfer will be determined by the particular characteristics of the institutional setting. The two children of the wealthy recluse who has no close relatives and no friends would be predicted to invest less, relative to the size of the expected transfer, than would the many children and other relatives and friends of the gregarious wealthy *padrone* of the whole community. In the first case, total rent-seeking effort may dissipate a relatively small proportion of the transfer value; in the second case, rent seeking may more than dissipate the expected total value of the transfer ultimately made.

For purposes of my general argument, the ratio between total rent-seeking investment and the value of the interpersonal transfer is irrelevant. (See App. for a simplified analysis that shows how this ratio is important in particular

5. Variations of this precise game are analyzed in some detail by Gordon Tullock in his paper "Efficient Rent Seeking." In the particular example here, where there is a potential prize of $1 million and ten potential recipients, each member of the group will tend to invest roughly $90,000, for a total outlay of $900,000 in pursuit of the single prize of $1 million.

problems.) Once the probable emergence of wasteful rent seeking is acknowledged in all settings of unrestricted transfer power, the efficiency basis for the argument against any and all restrictions on the transfer power vanishes. The central proposition of the orthodox argument must, of course, be accepted. Any restriction on the donor's freedom of disposition over his asset values will introduce distortions in his choice, and these distortions will reduce the value of the donor's surplus that he expects to secure from transfer activity. But missing from this traditional argument is any recognition of the possibly offsetting reductions in rent seeking that restriction on the transfer power may induce.

Critics will have noted what may seem to be several qualifications of the analysis to this point. I have implicitly assumed that the potential legator or donor is either not interested in or informed about the rent-seeking activity that his own expected behavior in giving or bequeathing may stimulate. Whether or not such an assumption is appropriate depends, in part, on the ultimate motivation for making interpersonal transfers. If bequests emerge more or less as residual by-products of life-cycle uncertainties and unavoidable transactions costs of estate planning, and particularly if the maintenance of control over valued assets yields utility directly, potential legators may be unconcerned about rent seeking.

If, on the other hand, transfers are motivated by donor interests in the prospective utilities of identified recipients, any wasteful rent seeking on the part of those whose utilities are relevant will be undesirable to the prospective donor. Efforts will be exerted to arrange transfers in such a way as to minimize such rent-seeking activities. The prospective donor will not, however, be concerned about rent seeking on the part of persons whom he has not internally identified as being among those whose utilities matter to him. At the same time, for reasons to be noted, the prospective donor may seek to avoid advance identification of those whom he has targeted as potential recipients. In this setting, rent seeking may be widely observed even if utility interdependence remains a primary motivation for transfer activity.

Rent seeking will tend to be eliminated only in those settings where utility interdependence is strong, where there is a well-identified group of potential recipients, and where the prospective donor can readily monitor the behavior of the potential recipients. This interaction is essentially that which is analyzed by Gary Becker.[6] Rent seeking, on the part of a potential legatee, will not emerge because he will know, in advance, that any effort to increase his own distributional share will be self-defeating. The potential legator retains ultimate allocative power; his distributive choice is unaffected by rent seeking. Such activity becomes totally unproductive to any prospective donee. The informational as well as the interdependence requirements for ensuring such results seem strong indeed.

A second qualification involves the possibility that rent-seeking activity on the part of potential recipients of transfers may, in itself, yield value or utility to the person who proposes to make the ultimate transfer, even if, as we have assumed here, the donor does not enter into either the explicit or an implicit exchange with his potential donees. That is to say, even if the transfer itself is uncompensated, rent-seeking behavior may increase the utility of the donor. For example, whether or not it may be so intended by the rent seekers, their activity may yield valued information to the donor. To the extent that it does so, this increase offsets some part of the resource waste that rent seeking involves. However, it must also be recognized that rent seeking, as he observes it, may actually reduce the utility of the donor, hence adding to the loss of value that rent seeking embodies.

A third qualification to the argument involves the "relative wastefulness" of the rent-seeking activity that any prospective transfer of value generates. To the extent that such activity takes a form that may yield unanticipated utility gains to participants, notably in subsequent periods, the "social waste" is reduced. When the problems analyzed here are considered in a context of institutional and family history, and when it is acknowledged that at least some adjustments have been made to minimize the overt and apparent inefficiencies, the question of the direction or channels through which rent seeking has been allowed to accrue would surely warrant further examination.

A potential donor can effectively close off rent seeking by making unannounced and unanticipated gifts. Totally unanticipated transfers are, of course, equivalent to lump-sum payments that cannot, by definition, induce behavioral changes that will modify the expected value of the individual transfers. In such event, the prospective donor would also attempt to re-

6. Gary Becker, "Altruism in the Family and Selfishness in the Marketplace." *Economica* 48 (1981): 1.

main secretive about the amount of total value to be transferred to others. In actuality, concealment is difficult to achieve, even if desired, and, in addition, it would be hard for a donor to succeed in making a totally unanticipated gift to a person whose utility level really matters for his own utility.[7]

IV. Succession within Rigidly Defined Rules: Restrictions on Powers of Transfer

Rent seeking will tend to be eliminated where the donors' *discretion* over selection of the beneficiary is absent, even if the donor is allowed to carry out transfers. So long as there exist well-defined and widely known enforceable rules or laws that determine the identity of the potential recipients, independent of the choice of the donor, there is no profit to be gained from engaging in rent seeking.[8]

Such a rule as primogeniture comes to mind as perhaps the most obvious example. If the firstborn is designated by law as the necessary legatee of any capital transfer by a potential legator with offspring (and if there is a comparable well-defined equivalent for potential donors without direct offspring), there would be no purpose to be served by others than the firstborn making efforts to change the direction of the intergenerational transfers.

Primogeniture is, of course, only one among many possible sets of rules for succession that might serve the same efficiency-enhancing objective. The rule for equal division among direct heirs would work equally well, provided that the rule is well defined and known in advance by everyone who might be potentially concerned. It is the *predictability* of the rules for succession rather than any intrinsic content of the rules themselves that is relevant for the elimination of rent-seeking behavior.

There may, however, be serious difficulties in the implementation of the

---

7. To the extent that an implicit exchange is present, in which the prospective donee modifies his or her behavior in order to increase the utility of the prospective donor, there is an incentive for the transfer of value to be announced but not made.

8. Gordon Tullock comes close to recognizing the point here in his discussion of bias in selectivity processes as a means of reducing rent seeking. See note 4, above. It is somewhat surprising, therefore, that in his earlier paper on inheritance Tullock seems to have altogether missed the point. Gordon Tullock, "Inheritance Justified," *Journal of Law and Economics* 14 (1971): 465

predictability norm, even if the efficiency criterion is dominant in any re-form proposals. A set of rules or laws of succession that seems definitive on its face may be subject to varying legal interpretation which will, of course, guarantee investment in litigation. Such investment reflects socially wasteful rent seeking, even if it is now directed toward a different object from that which occurs when discretionary power remains with the potential donor of transfers. With nominally explicit rules or laws for succession, rent seeking is redirected from efforts to modify donor choices to efforts to influence the judicial interpretation of the rules. Adjudication in the courts becomes the institutionalized form. Observed experiences in modern legal struc-tures when persons die intestate, where there presumably exist quite explicit laws for succession, suggest that this source of inefficiency may be large.[9]

Donor Precommitment through Wills and Testaments. The relationship be-tween pretransfer rent-seeking behavior and predictability or the absence thereof in the rules for succession suggests that even in the absence of overt legal restrictions on the transfer powers rent seeking may be eliminated by precommitment behavior of the potential donor. The wealthy person who observes the rent seeking among his potential heirs may seek to eliminate this activity, once and for all, by precommitting himself through the making of an irrevocable will, provided that this action is sufficiently publicized and provided that potential heirs believe that the assignment of succession is indeed irrevocable. Irrevocability is the essential requirement here. If it is known that wills, once made, can be amended at the behest of the makers, there may be minimal effects on rent seeking produced by resort to the in-struments of wills and testaments.[10]

---

9. Frank H. Easterbrook has discussed the relative importance of what I have here called rent seeking in the whole process of litigation. He suggests that since litigating par-ties' interests are primarily in what he calls the stakes-dividing function of litigation there may be inefficient overinvestment in litigation. See Frank H. Easterbrook, "Insider Trad-ing, Secret Agents, Evidentiary Privileges, and the Production of Information," *Supreme Court Review* 309 (1981), see especially 358–60.

10. Noncompensated transfers may or may not emerge from nonreciprocal promises. In their analysis of the latter, Goetz and Scott introduce a possible source of inefficiency that arises from behavioral adjustments made by prospective donees in expectations of transfers that are not finally made. Legally enforceable precommitments to transfer would serve to eliminate this source of inefficiency as well as the rent-seeking source stressed

Even with effective precommitment, however, rent-seeking behavior of the second sort may still be predicted to emerge. Efforts will continue to be made, and perhaps on an accelerated scale, to modify the legal interpretations of the assignments of assets made through wills, no matter how specific the apparent terms of the documents might appear to be.[11]

V. Toward a Policy for Interpersonal Transfers

The analysis suggests directions for institutional reform if the objective is that of increasing efficiency in resource use. If we ignore posttransfer litigation, there are two major sources of allocative distortion, one within the pretransfer choice of the potential donor, the other within the pretransfer choice of the potential donees. The efficiency objective would be the minimization of the loss of value generated by the two sources combined. As noted, the imposition of restrictions on the powers to transfer may substantially eliminate incentives for potential donees to engage in wasteful rent seeking, but it does so at the expense of introducing necessary distortions in the choice calculus of the potential donor. Minimal violation of the efficiency norm, considering the two separate sources of waste, would seem to exist when the rules of succession restricting the transfer power correspond with or map reasonably well with the set of transfer results that might emerge from unrestricted exercise of such power. If a person would, under unrestricted transfer power, plan to divide his patrimony equally among his direct heirs, an explicit law of succession requiring him to do precisely this would minimally affect his choice between current consumption and capital accumulation (decumulation). Any rigid set of rules for succession, sufficiently rigid to affect the level of rent seeking, will in some individual cases seriously distort the capital accumulation (decumulation) choices of prospective donors. The person who is totally alienated from his children would, under such rules as primogeniture or equal division, have a strong incentive to consume all of his capital value before any transfer is made. At best, the cor-

---

here. See Charles J. Goetz and Robert E. Scott, "Enforcing Promises: An Examination of the Basis of Contract," *Yale Law Journal* 99 (1980): 1261.

11. There are important normative implications to be drawn from the analysis relating to the comparative tax treatment of gifts and bequests. Geoffrey Brennan has a paper in process on this aspect of the issue.

respondence or mapping that might be indicated for an economically efficient transfer policy would reflect some average or representative person's desired plan for transfers. Differing societies or even the same society at differing stages of its history may embody differing preferred patterns of transfer for their average or representative donors.

Economic efficiency rarely occupies a position as the exclusive or even overriding norm or objective for policy reform. Competing norms intrude, and particularly in the case of transfer arrangements. Norms of intergenerational justice or equity may be as significant as or even more significant than those of efficiency. I shall not discuss such norms in detail in this paper, but it will perhaps be useful to evaluate briefly the transfer institutions identified above against the entitlement norm and against nonentitlement norms generally.

Consider, first, Robert Nozick's entitlement theory of justice, which holds that persons possess assets justly if these have been justly acquired.[12] Transfers by gift or bequest qualify as just acquisitions. They do so because persons who hold assets justly *voluntarily* transfer ownership rights to others of their own choosing. It seems evident, however, that this argument for justice in holdings or entitlements could not readily be extended to apply to assets received through an *involuntary* transfer implemented as a result of a strict rule or law of succession. It would seem to follow, therefore, that any restrictions on the powers to transfer that might be dictated by a recognition that the rent-seeking incentives would be inconsistent with Nozick's entitlement theory of justice.

Most nonentitlement norms for justice are consistent with restrictions on the powers to transfer but would be inconsistent with those rules of succession (such as primogeniture or equal division) that reflect overt discrimination in favor of genetically identified potential beneficiaries. Exclusive concentration on the furtherance of these norms for intergenerational equity, in total disregard for those of efficiency, might lend support to a policy that would prohibit altogether interpersonal transfers. Incorporation of the rent-seeking analysis into the evaluation of alternative arrangements lends at least limited efficiency-based support to those who advance the nonentitlement norms, in that the efficiency costs of imposing restrictions on transfer pow-

12. Robert Nozick, *Anarchy, State and Utopia* (1974).

ers are demonstrated to be less than might otherwise have been assumed. But there are perhaps relatively few persons who would argue exclusively in terms of intergenerational norms of justice to the total neglect of efficiency considerations.

The norm for economic efficiency and the norm for intergenerational equity might be appropriately combined or balanced by a set of arrangements that would allow potential donors to retain powers of transfer in a quantitatively limited sense. The amount of value transferred might be restricted, in total and/or per person terms. Such institutional arrangements would distort to some extent the donor's choices concerning capital accumulation (decumulation), but often less so than in the case of specifically directed transfers. The arrangements suggested would also stimulate investment in rent seeking by potential donors, but again less investment than would be forthcoming under quantitatively and directionally restricted powers of transfer. These arrangements, while not fulfilling the norm for intergenerational equity to the extent desired by many persons, would at least mitigate the gross and apparent injustices in holdings that would emerge from either totally unrestricted transfers or from strict rules of succession that embody overt discrimination.

VI. Rent Seeking in Attenuated-Rights Settings

In the preceding parts of this paper I have explicitly confined the discussion to settings in which potential donors of transfer values retain full ownership rights over all domains of possible usage other than noncompensated transfers to other persons. Owners of valued assets have been presumed to be able to sell such assets freely to others in the economy and/or to convert values readily into direct consumption of any goods or services that may be desired. In these nonattenuated rights settings, rent seeking emerges among potential beneficiaries of noncompensated transfers.

The motivation for rent seeking may, however, be even greater in those institutional settings where the initial "ownership" rights are attenuated in other ways than those involving the transfer authority. With nonattenuated rights, the owner of an asset might, in response to a restriction on the transfer power, convert value into direct consumption. In doing so, he can ensure that a lower value is available for transfer than otherwise. Suppose, however, that the nominal owner of an asset or enterprise cannot convert the capital value into current consumption. He does not have the option of "eating up" his capital. Rent seekers will, in this case, operate with an expectation that becomes almost literally like the fixed-prize lottery. In our earlier example, we referred to the person who planned to bequeath $1 million, but the setting was such that rent seekers would know that the donor could, at any time, modify the total to be bequeathed, even to the extent of eliminating all bequests. Contrast this setting with that now examined; the current owner of the capital value enjoys the income from the asset, but he is required to transmit the capital value intact in the form of bequest. It seems evident that the amount of rent seeking in the second case will exceed that in the first.

As a further constraint on the initial owner's rights, suppose that he is not allowed to bequeath the asset at all, even though he must maintain its capital value. He cannot designate his heir or successor. In this model, unless there are strict rules for succession, rent seeking will perhaps be at its maximum. This model approaches the classically familiar case of succession in nonhereditary dictatorships. There are, of course, notorious examples in which the values inherent in political authority have been transformed into Swiss bank accounts, in which cases the dictator can indeed designate his legatees. To the extent that such indirect exercise of "ownership" rights is not possible, rent-seeking activity takes on maximal proportions.

VII. Conclusion

The dictator example should not, however, be allowed to distract attention from the ubiquity of this setting. To the extent that positions in the upper echelons of modern bureaucracies carry with them elements of reward that are understood to embody rents, behavior that has been discussed at some length in the orthodox rent-seeking analysis will emerge. The orthodox analysis has, however, implied, at least implicitly, that rent seeking generates social waste only in settings where *artificial* scarcities are created, for the most part by political agency.[13] The creation and dispensation of access to such ar-

---

13. I can directly cite my own confusion here. In the concluding paper in *Toward a Theory of the Rent-Seeking Society*, I stated: "Rent seeking, as such, is totally without allocative value, although, of course, *the initial institutional creation of an opportunity for*

tificially created rents will, indeed, bring forth inefficient rent-seeking behavior. What I have suggested in this paper is that rent seeking emerges as wasteful activity in any uncompensated transfer of value, and notably with respect to gifts and bequests among persons.

The rents involved in uncompensated transfers are not themselves "artificial" in the usual meaning of this term. The value embodied in the gift or bequest that a person plans to make may represent accumulation from a stream of returns that have been earned solely in competitive markets; there need be not one whit of monopoly rent or profit involved. To the set of potential recipients, however, any such value becomes precisely analogous to a rental opportunity that has been artificially created. The frugal rich man whose fortune must be transferred by gifts or bequests stands before his potential heirs in precisely the same relationship as Queen Elizabeth before her courtiers when she announced the possible assignment of a playing-card monopoly.

As I noted in my introductory essay to the volume *Toward a Theory of the Rent-Seeking Society*, rent seeking and profit seeking are behaviorally equivalent. The latter is socially efficient because it facilitates the flow of resources to their highest valued uses. Profit seeking (and loss avoidance), *as a process*, creates value in itself. By contrast, rent seeking is socially inefficient because the process in itself creates no value while utilizing scarce resources. The analysis of this paper suggests that any value that is to be transferred without compensation exists independent of the investment in attempts to redirect its disposition. No value can be created by such attempts. In terms of the efficiency norm, therefore, the identification of the succession in the ownership of valued assets is totally irrelevant.

Finally, a point about significance. I should not claim that this paper "discovers" a source of inefficiency that is quantitatively important in the aggregate transfers of value among persons. The rent-seeking ratio may be relatively small in many of the institutional settings within which transfers take place, although further empirical and institutional analysis would be required to make serious estimates. I consider this paper more as a "tidying

---

rent seeking ensures a net destruction of economic value" (p. 359, italics added). This statement is ambiguous in its implication that wasteful rent seeking emerges only when value is initially destroyed by the creation of monopoly rents.

up" of the analysis of transfers than as a new motivation for ultimate policy reform. The theory of rent seeking remains novel; it is therefore not at all surprising that its range of applications has not been exhausted.

Appendix

My purpose in this Appendix is limited to the demonstration that in the presence of rent seeking quantitative restrictions on the unlimited rights or powers to make uncompensated transfers can increase rather than decrease allocative efficiency. Through a highly simplified abstract example I shall compare the losses stemming from reductions in donor's surplus and those embodied in rent seeking. The example suggests that the efficient or optimal degree of quantitative restriction depends directly on the elasticity of demand for making transfers and on the size of the rent-seeking ratio.

Consider Figure 1, which is drawn in unit squares of value for expositional clarity. The donor's demand for making transfers is shown by D, drawn with a negative slope of unity. If there are no restrictions, 4 units of value will be transferred to recipients. There will be a donor's surplus of 8 units generated in the transfer process. In the presumed absence of rent seeking, the donor's cost of 4 units of value will just be matched by the recipient's gain of 4 units. Under these conditions it is clear that any restriction on the transfer power

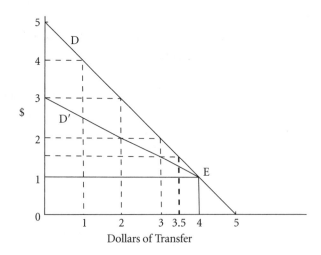

Figure 1

will reduce efficiency. If these restrictions take the form of quantitative limits on amounts transferred, the welfare losses can be measured by the familiar welfare triangles.

Assume now that the rent-seeking ratio is ½. This ratio measures the relationship between total outlay on rent seeking and the net value of the transfer made. In this setting, if there are no quantitative restrictions on the power to transfer, there will be a net value of only 6 units generated. There will be a resource investment of 2 units in the attempts to qualify as recipients of the 4 units of value transferred. By comparison, consider a restriction that allows the donor to transfer a maximum of only 3 units. In this case, donor's surplus is reduced by ½ unit, but rent seeking is also reduced by ½. There are still 6 units of value generated as before; the restriction does not generate allocative inefficiency.

The "optimal" or "efficient" degree of restriction is at 3½ units. Note that, in this setting, the donor's surplus is reduced by only ⅛ unit below that which is enjoyed without restriction. But rent seeking is reduced by ¼ unit. There is a net efficiency gain of ⅛ unit of value in moving from totally unrestricted transfers to the quantitative restrictions that allow gifts or bequests of only 3½ units to be made.

If the quantitative restrictions should take the form of a tax on transfers (and if we can make the *highly questionable assumption* that access to governmental revenues does not itself set off further rent seeking), note that the optimal restriction under the simplified conditions specified is a tax of 50 percent of net transfer, or a tax of 33.3 percent of gross transfer, inclusive of tax.

The optimal degree of restriction clearly depends on the size of the rent-seeking ratio. If this ratio falls to ¼, the optimal degree of restriction is reduced. In terms of tax rates, under the assumptions noted, the rate that will generate the efficient restriction becomes 25 percent of net transfer, or 20 percent of transfer value gross of tax.

As the construction of Figure 1 indicates, the efficient degree of restriction will also depend on the elasticity of demand for making transfers. If we examine demand curves of differing slopes, it is relatively easy to see that there is a direct relationship between demand elasticity and restrictiveness. With demand curve, D', for example, the optimal restrictiveness is to limit transfers to 2½ units of value rather than 3½ units as in the earlier case. Note, however, that the tax rate required to produce this result is the same in both cases, 50 percent of net transfer value, or 33.3 percent of gross value, if the rent-seeking ratio is ½.

In somewhat more formal terms, the necessary condition for a maximally efficient level of transfers is given by

$$\frac{\delta U_d}{\delta t} = \frac{\delta R}{\delta t},$$

where the left-hand side defines the change in donor's surplus (converted into a numeraire) as transfer values increase and the right-hand side defines the change in rent seeking (valued in the numeraire) as transfers (t) increase. Unrestricted transfer power will produce a solution where $\delta U_d/\delta t = 0$, which will be optimal only if, also, $\delta R/\delta t = 0$.

The Incumbency Dilemma and Rent Extraction by Legislators

James M. Buchanan and Roger D. Congleton

Abstract: An incumbent is able to shirk or otherwise obtain rents based on his tenure of office because more-senior representatives are better able to advance their legislative agendas than are more-junior members. The realization of incumbent rents implies that an electoral prisoners' dilemma occurs at the level of voters across electoral districts. Pivotal voters in each district would benefit if all incumbents were replaced by challengers with similar legislative programs because the cost of incumbent rents can be avoided, but each benefits if his representative has more seniority than those from other districts.

1. Introduction

In November 1991, voters in the state of Washington defeated a proposed constitutional change that would have imposed term limits on congressional representatives, including those currently incumbent. This result emerged despite the pre-election polls that suggested dominance of public support for the change. The outcome was attributed to a successful incumbent strategy that emphasized the differential disadvantages that might be experienced by statewide constituencies which impose term limits independent of action by other states' constituencies. Our purpose in this paper is to model the in-

From *Public Choice* 79 (April 1994): 47–60. Reprinted by permission of the publisher, Kluwer Academic Publishers.

cumbency dilemma that the Washington result seems to describe, to examine some of the implications of the dilemma, and to suggest one possible mitigating factor that may act to reduce its impact.

2. Legislation as a Distributive Game

It is useful to model the legislative process as a distributive game. Each member of the legislature is a political agent for a defined set of constituents, and there are no intersections as among the separate sets. Each legislator purports to secure the maximal net gains for his or her constituents relative to the gains secured by other members of the legislature. Note that this purported objective function for the legislator, whether successful challenger or incumbent, remains the same whether or not the overall "game of politics" is positive, zero, or negative sum. Even if political action is limited to the financing of "efficient" levels of pure public goods in the Samuelsonian sense, there remains the distributive game involved in the assignment of the tax shares as among the separate constituencies or "districts." And, at the other extreme, if legislation involves nothing other than pure transfers, the distributive game separates the net gainers from the net losers.

It is necessary for clarity to abstract from many of the descriptive complexities of legislative representation. We assume that all voters in the inclusive polity are identical, both those within each set of constituents and those among the separate sets. Further, for expositional clarity only, we assume that the distributive game to be analyzed takes the form of legislative selection among special benefit projects to be financed by general taxation.[1] Each project yields benefits shared equally by all constituents in a single legislative district, but yields no benefits to anyone outside the district's limits. And each project is financed by a general tax levied uniformly on all members of the polity. (This property of the model could be reversed with no change in results. That is, a general-benefit, differential-tax model would be equally applicable analytically. Or, pure transfers may be modelled, in which some constituencies make direct transfers to others.)

---

1. See G. Tullock, "Some Problems of Majority Voting," *Journal of Political Economy* 67 (1959): 571–79.

3. The Incumbency Dilemma

It is necessary to model the behavior of the legislator, both in an initial term in office and as an incumbent in later terms. Assume, as an analytical starting point, that all members of the assembly are newly elected. Assume, further, that each member is equally capable for the task in hand and that there are no parties that become vehicles for coalition construction. In this setting, we can presume that the expected value of each district's legislative agent's action is equal. The expected net value (expected benefits minus costs) for each district will be some positive, zero, or negative sum, equal across all districts. There are no differentially advantaged districts during this initial term. Assume, now, however, that incumbency gives any legislative agent a differential advantage. Then consider a second legislative term during which there are both incumbents and newly elected members of the assembly. The expected values of benefits will vary as among the districts, in accordance with the breakdown between newly elected legislators and incumbents.

There are now differential advantages for districts that are represented by incumbents, and this is acknowledged by everyone. The voters in the disadvantaged districts will seek to "catch up" by returning legislators to office. If we ignore possible seniority advantages and simply consider the differential as between incumbents and non-incumbents, electoral equilibrium will be re-established in which incumbency advantages cancel out. All districts will be represented by incumbents, and the expected value of legislative agents will, again, be equated over all districts. Despite the equality in expected values across all districts represented by incumbents, there remains a differential between the expected value of incumbency and non-incumbency. If some district should install a challenger, that district would experience significant reduction in expected value from the political process. It would face a lower prospect for securing special benefit projects, but would share in the tax payments for special benefits projects located in other districts. This potential differential value between incumbency and non-incumbency provides the opportunity for incumbent legislators to secure rents that increase the costs of all special benefit projects. Incumbents have a "cushion" that may be exploited to their own advantage. In this setting, voters in all constituencies will find it advantageous to adopt generalized constitutional constraints, such as term limits.[2] But voters in a single constituency may find themselves "locked in" to the game to such an extent that unilateral action may be disadvantageous.

4. Example

Essential features of the incumbency dilemma may be analyzed in the following model. Suppose there are only two districts with large electorates, equal in size, and a two-member, unicameral legislature. The only political-legislative choice is the location in each electoral period of a single localized-benefit project that is financed by a general tax imposed uniformly on all citizens across the two-district polity. (The process through which the choice is made is of no concern here. The absence of a majority in a two-member legislature is irrelevant for our purposes.) Incumbency is modelled as changing the probability of securing the location of a project within a district.

Terms are defined as follows:

B   expected project benefits per person in a single district, equal across all constituents in the district.

C   cost per person of special benefit project, equal across all constituents in the whole polity.

p_i probability of incumbent success.

p_c probability of elected challenger success.

For an initial Period I, both districts elect new legislators, who are equally capable. The per person expected values in Period I are as follows:

2. D. R. Lee, *Fiscal Pollution and the Case for Congressional Term Limits*, Contemporary Issues Series 51, Center for the Study of American Business (St. Louis: Washington University, 1992), develops a general argument that has some parallels with our analysis. W. R. Reed and D. E. Schansberg, "An Analysis of the Impact of Congressional Term Limits" (Department of Economics, Texas A&M University, 1991, mimeographed), examine the economic effects of term limits. After completing a final draft, we discovered a forthcoming paper by A. R. Dick and L. R. Lott, Jr., "Reconciling Voters' Behavior with Legislature Term Limits," *Journal of Public Economics* (1992, forthcoming), that analyzes incumbency and term limits in a PD model similar to our own. Their interest-group structure is more complex than our direct constituency-agent structure, and their treatment does not include potential rent extraction by incumbent legislators.

Period I	District 1	District 2
Benefits	.5B	.5B
Costs	.5C	.5C
Net	(.5B − .5C)	(.5B − .5C)

The inclusive political game is positive sum if the expected benefit-cost ratio (B/C) exceeds unity.

Assume now that for a second electoral period, District 1 returns the incumbent while District 2 elects a challenger. The probability of legislative success shifts from .5 for each legislator to a p_i/p_c ratio in favor of the incumbent, where $p_i/p_c > 1$, and ($p_i + p_c = 1$). The results are as follows:

Period II	District 1	District 2
Benefits	p_iB	p_cB
Costs	.5C	.5C
Net	(p_iB − .5C)	(p_cB − .5C)

In this situation, the inclusive game is positive sum for the voter in District 1 if the benefit-cost ratio exceeds $.5/p_i$. But for the voter in District 2, special benefit projects must be expected to yield ($.5/p_c$) times aggregate cost for the political game to reach the positive-sum range. (Since $p_c < 1/2$, the benefit-cost ratio must always exceed unity to make the game worthwhile.) There is a differential incumbency advantage as measured by ($p_i − p_c$)B.

Presumably, the *representative* voter in District 2 will recognize this disparity in expected values, and for the next period (Period III) will also elect the incumbent. If we ignore seniority, the results are once again equivalent to those in Period I. There is no positive "social" advantage to incumbency in this model.[3]

To this point, we have assumed implicitly that the incumbency rents,

---

3. There may be generalizable benefits from legislative incumbency in models of politics that do not make the distribution of gains and losses central. Such models are not easy to construct, and even the generalized benefits that might exist would seem relatively small.

which seem to arise only in Period II, are exclusively enjoyed by voting constituents. This assumption is not sustainable once the incumbent in either district recognizes the uniqueness of the incumbency position. A share of the incumbency rent will be claimed by the legislators themselves, and this claim will amount to constituents' cost increases for special benefit projects. Incumbents will demand, and be able to receive, direct constituency payments (perhaps in the form of contributions) over and beyond the generalized tax costs.[4] These payments will modify the results:

Period IV	District 1	District 2
Benefits	.5B	.5B
Costs	$.5C + R_1$	$.5C + R_2$
Net	$.5B - (.5C + R_1)$	$.5B - (.5C + R_2)$

where R_1 and R_2 measure payments made directly or indirectly by constituents to incumbent legislators.

Note the maximal rent extraction by an incumbent from the constituents of a district is defined by $(.5 - p_c)B$, which is the difference between the expected net benefit under generalized incumbency $(.5B - .5C)$ and the expected net benefit when a single district returns a challenger $(p_cB - .5C)$. The setting that confronts the *representative* voters of the two districts is that of the classical prisoners' dilemma, which may be put in standard form in Figure 1.

Row and column dominance are present if R_1 and R_2 are less than $(p_i - .5)B$, which is, of course, equal to $(.5 - p_c)B$, since $p_i + p_c = 1$. As long as incumbents do not fully exploit potential rents, the *representative* voter in each district will find it advantageous to return the incumbent, and to do so regardless of the action taken in the other district. If, however, R_1 and R_2 are both positive, the *representative* voters in both districts could benefit from a binding agreement upon joint action that would involve the selection of challengers in both districts simultaneously. The gain for each *representative*

---

4. The model suggests a somewhat different perspective on rent-seeking from that which has been implicit in some of the rent-seeking discussion. In the model here, it is the incumbent legislators who initiate and demand a share of the rents, and who effectively force constituents to pay up. (Senator Cranston approached Charles Keating.)

| | | Representative voter in District 2 | |
		Elects challenger	*Elects incumbent*
Representative voter in District 1	Elects Challenger	$(.5B - .5C)$ $(.5B - .5C)$	$(p_cB - .5C)$ $[p_iB - (.5C + R_2)]$
	Elects Incumbent	$[p_iB - (.5C + R_1)]$ $(p_cB - .5C)$	$[.5B - (.5C + R_1)]$ $[.5B - (.5C + R_2)]$

Figure 1

voter from this change would be measured by the size of the incumbency rents extracted by the legislative incumbents, R_1 and R_2, or, in the limiting case, $(.5 - p_c)B$. If incumbency rent extraction exceeds $(.5 - p_c)B$, the dilemma of course disappears and a single district will find it advantageous to elect a challenger. Maximal aggregate rent in the example here is $(1 - 2p_c)B$, which is positive if there is any incumbency advantage, and which is inversely related to the value of p_c.

Note that the aggregate benefit-cost ratio is irrelevant in this distributive game. The incumbency dilemma remains whether the special benefit projects yield strongly positive "social" value or cost far more than they are worth to members of the inclusive polity. In the limiting case where incumbents extract maximal rents, a benefit-cost ratio of $.5/p_c$ must be present in order to insure that the inclusive game be positive sum for constituents in any district. We should, of course, expect that pressures for constitutional change would increase as special benefit projects yield lower net returns due to observed rent extraction, and such changes may incorporate devices, such as term limits, designed specifically to reduce incumbency.

5. Incumbency Advantage under Ideological Challenge

The model of politics introduced to this point has been based on the implicit assumption that challengers seek legislative office exclusively to engage in the ongoing distributive game. There is no difference in the objective functions of challengers and incumbents; each seeks to secure special benefit projects for district constituents. Incumbency advantage takes the form of an en-hanced probability of success in this effort.

Suppose now, however, that a challenger appears who seeks to reduce, generally, the size and scope of collective-political activity, and who makes a commitment to oppose all special benefit projects, regardless of location, and to base this opposition on principle rather than interest. As before, sup-pose that if elected the challenger, as legislator, can succeed with some prob-ability of success, p_c, with $p_c < p_i$. In this setting, however, success is mea-sured by killing special benefit projects. Constituents of the newly elected ideological legislator will expect a return of $(-.5p_iC)$. This expected value may be compared with that which might be promised by a distributive chal-lenger $(p_cB - .5C)$. Setting these to be equal,

$$p_cB - .5C = .5p_iC. \tag{1}$$

By the algebra, and using the unit summation of the two probabilities, we get

$$B/C = 1/2. \tag{2}$$

If the benefit falls below one-half of the aggregate costs, an ideological chal-lenger can offer constituents-voters an argument from economic interest that will be stronger than any distributive challenger. But, of course, the in-cumbency advantage remains so long as the benefit-cost ratio exceeds $p_c/2p_i$. (For numerical illustration, in the two-district legislature, if an elected chal-lenger is only one-third as successful as the incumbent, benefits would only have to cover more than one-sixth of total costs to insure incumbent elec-toral success.)

The exercise suggests that there are limits to the gross exploitation of the legislative process described in the distributive game model, limits repre-sented by the potential entry of ideological challengers. These limits may, however, be very wide. Exploitation can take two forms: Benefit-cost ratios may fall well below plausible utilitarian bounds, and incumbents may de-mand, and succeed in collecting, rents from incumbency itself.

6. Size of Legislature, Incumbency Rents, and Ideological Challenge

We have analyzed the simplest possible legislative setting, the two-member body. It is necessary to examine, at least in general terms, the effects of legislative size on the operation of the incumbency dilemma. The analysis is made difficult by the loss of symmetry between incumbent and the non-incumbent that is present in the two-member model. As the size of the legislature increases beyond two, we must specify the ratio between incumbent members and newcomers. It seems best here to commence with a setting where all members are incumbents, and then to examine the effects when a single district elects a newcomer.

It is also necessary to specify how the probabilities change as legislative size changes. It seems likely that in almost all cases the legislative prospects for success on the part of a single newcomer to the legislature would fall relative to the prospects for an incumbent as legislative size increases. But, in an extreme case, we can maintain constancy in the p_i/p_c ratio although, of course, both p_i and p_c must fall as the size of the legislature increases. If we maintain constancy in the p_i/p_c ratio, legislative size can be shown to be positively related to overall incumbency rents, although the rents of individual incumbents diminish.

Consider the case where the odds that any single incumbent gets the local project in any period, relative to the odds of a newcomer, are fixed with $p_i/p_c = K$. Suppose initially that there are N districts and N incumbents. Consider the situation of a single community that might elect a challenger and thereby generate a new legislature with $(N - 1)$ incumbents and a single challenger (freshman) in the decision body of interest. Columns 1 and 2 of the following table represent the expected benefits and costs that result from a successful challenge of an incumbent for District 1 and 2 with no rents extracted. Column 3 represents the *status quo ante*.

	District 1	District 2	All incumbents
Benefits	$p_i B$	$p_c B$	B/N
Costs	C/N	C/N	C/N
Net	$p_i B - C/N$	$p_c B - C/N$	$(B - C)/N$

The maximum rent for an all incumbent legislature is again a matter of the expected cost of replacing an incumbent with a challenger. Each incumbent can receive at most a rent equal to the difference between the lower cell of column 1 and column 3, $R = (1/N - p_c)B$. The maximum aggregate rents for all incumbents in an all incumbent legislature is N times this amount, or

NR. The assumed constancy of the favorable odds of incumbency allows the probabilities of challenger success to be written in terms of the constant odds, K, and the size of the legislature.[5]

$$p_c = 1/[K(N - 1) + 1] \qquad (3)$$

Consequently, the maximum incumbency rents are also determined by the size of the legislature as well as the value of the local project to be awarded:

$$R = (1/N - 1/[K(N - 1) + 1])B, \qquad (4)$$

which clearly falls as the number of either incumbents or challengers increases.[6] Any single district becomes less and less likely to receive the local project. However, total legislative rents increase as the size of the legislature increases:

$$NR = (1 - N/[K(N - 1) + 1])B$$

or

$$NR = 1 - 1/[K(N - 1)/N + 1/N]B. \qquad (5)$$

In the limit as N increases, total incumbent rents approach $1 - 1/K$.[7]

The algebraic examples suggest that aggregate incumbency rents increase as the size of the legislature increases, even if the success of a single newcomer relative to that of any single incumbent remains constant over changes in legislative size. In the example where the ratio between the prospects for success of any single incumbent relative to that for a single newcomer is constant at

5. Recall that $p_i/p_c = K$, and $(N - 1)p_i + p_c = 1$, which implies that $(N - 1)_i Kp_c + p_c = 1$. It follows directly that $p_c = 1/[K(N - 1) + 1]$, and, since $p_i = Kp_c$, that $p_i = K/[K(N - 1) + 1]$.

6. The derivative of equation 4 with respect to N is $[-1/N^2 + 1/(KN - K + 1)^2]B$. Recall that the probability of a challenger succeeding is below that of an incumbent, consequently $KN - K + 1 > N$, and $[-1/N^2 + 1/(KN - K + 1)^2]B < 0$.

7. In the general case, the upper bound of legislative rents is $N_i R = N_i(p_i(N_i, 0) - p_c(N_i, N_c))B$, where N_i is the number of incumbents and N_c is the number of freshmen. The derivative of total legislative rents with respect to N_i equals $(p_i - p_c)B + N_i(\delta p_i/\delta N_i - \delta p_c/\delta N_i)B$, which is unambiguously greater than zero for $\delta p_i/\delta N_i \geq \delta p_c/\delta N_i$. This condition is met whenever an additional incumbent reduces the success rate for freshmen by at least as much as it does for incumbents.

a value of 3, the aggregate value of incumbency rents approaches a maximum of .6666, or two-thirds of the benefits as legislative size expands. As a generalization, in the limit, incumbent legislators can extract a maximum of $1 - 1/K$ of the value of benefits from the projects that are financed from general taxation. This suggests that for legislatures of more or less standard sizes (from, say, 25 through 500) and with the probability of incumbency success constant at three times that of newcomer success spending projects would need to yield benefits at least three times aggregate costs in order for voting constituents to secure positive gains in the inclusive game of distributive politics.

Incumbents will not, of course, extract maximal rents; risk averseness will cause them to limit their efforts to collect funds from constituents. The simple examples suggest, however, that, even with severe incumbency self-restraint, constituents are likely to lose rather than gain from the inclusive political game.[8]

The size of the legislature may also affect the prospects for successful ideological challenge, discussed above in the simplified two-member legislative setting. Because of the relative powerlessness of any single challenging ideologue in a large legislature, the benefit-cost relationships for projects would have to fall to extremely low levels before effective challenge might arise. Again, however, the relationship between benefit-cost ratios and rent extraction should be noted. In a ten-member legislature, with constant ratio of probabilities at three, an ideological electoral challenger can offer a more effective appeal than a distributive challenger if project benefits yield less than one-third its costs. But such a challenge could not offer effective argument against an incumbent, who takes out no rents, until and unless the benefit-cost ratio falls below one-tenth. If incumbents extract maximal rents, the decisive benefit-cost ratio becomes one-third. At benefit-cost reactions above one-third, distributive challengers have the best of the argument against the ideologues. As ratios fall below one-third, the ideological challengers dominate those who seek to join the same game.

---

8. It bears noting that, as legislative size increases, the benefit of having an incumbent tends to diminish, although it remains positive. An increase in legislative size may thus lead to an increase in turnover with a consequent reduction of incumbent rents.

7. Legislative Seniority and Rent Extraction

To this point in the analysis, we have classified all legislators into two categories, incumbents and successful challengers (newcomers), but we have assumed homogeneity among incumbents. This assumption is clearly not descriptive, even for our limited purposes, because it neglects the relationship between the length of legislative service and probabilities of success in the ongoing distributive game. Among incumbents, seniority cannot be left out of account. A legislator who has been returned to office for many terms is clearly a better "player," as measured by the probability of getting special benefit projects for his district, than the legislator who is only a second- or third-term incumbent.

The general effects from the introduction of seniority are clear. As a legislator becomes more experienced, the success rate increases and the differential in expected value creates the potential for the extraction of more rents. The senior member of a legislature can be replaced only by a newcomer; there is no prospect of substituting a three-term incumbent for a sixteen-term incumbent, who is observed to be extracting high rents from his constituents.

We can use basically the same example analyzed earlier. But, now, consider a legislature of fixed size N, that may include three rather than two types of members. There are senior incumbents, junior incumbents, and, possibly, newcomers. The probabilities of success are known to be ranked as follows: $p_{si} > p_{ji} > p_c$. We assume that, within each group, members are homogeneous.

An all-incumbency equilibrium will tend to emerge, but expected values will not be equated over all districts in this model because some incumbents are, by historical construction, senior to others and hence, by definition, more likely to succeed in the distributive game. The all-incumbency equilibrium will contain both senior and junior incumbents.

We want to examine the prospects that may face a single challenger who might seek office, against either a senior or a junior incumbent. In the all-incumbent setting,

$$p_{si}(N_s) + p_{ji}(N - S) = 1, \tag{6}$$

where S is the number of senior incumbents.[9] The incumbency rent that is available either for constituents or for extraction by incumbent legislators is, in both the senior and the junior incumbent cases, determined by the difference in probabilities and by the benefits of the projects. As before, the maximal rent is $(p_{si} - p_c)B$ for senior incumbents and $(p_{ji} - p_c)B$ for junior incumbents.

Maximal rent extraction, over all legislators, is given by,

$$[(p_{si} - p_c)B][S - 1] + [(p_{ji} - p_c)B][N - S - 1]. \qquad (7)$$

Under plausible assumptions about the ratios between probabilities over varying legislative sizes, it seems clear that the higher the number of senior incumbents relative to junior incumbents, the larger is the potential for rent extraction.

8. Limitations of the Representative Voter as a Model of Electoral Choice

The above analysis is perhaps more pessimistic than may be warranted. We have deliberately emphasized the word *representative* voter each time it was used earlier. We want now to suggest that the modelling of the incumbency dilemma as if it is a game among *representative* voters of separate districts may be behaviorally incorrect. In the institutional reality of modern politics there exists no person who confronts the choice options that the general analysis, or the illustrative example, suggests. No individual "acts for" the whole constituency, as such, and it is wrong to assume that an individual, any individual, who does exercise the voting franchise in majoritarian processes of agent selection finds himself or herself in the choice setting posed. Strictly speaking, the model, as presented, directly applies only for a *one-voter* district, and its implications hold, approximately, only for *very* small constituencies. If we incorporate, realistically, the effects of large-district constituencies, the processes of making collective decisions become relevant. There

---

9. Because any probability of newcomer success, p_c, is less than p_{ji}, the election of a newcomer must increase both p_{si} and p_{ji}. These new probabilities are not, however, relevant to the analysis here.

is only a *very weak incumbency* dilemma facing a single voter in a district with a large number of constituents whose representatives are selected by majority or plurality rule.

The usual voting model is less useful in analyzing voter incentives in large elections because it embodies the presumption that the individual, as voter, chooses between an incumbent and a challenger in an election of a legislative representative. The individual voter in a large electorate does not choose among the ultimate options listed on the ballot. The individual voter chooses between (1) *voting* for the incumbent and (2) *voting* for the challenger, and (3) *not voting*, which is a totally different thing. There is no direct relationship between the individual's act of voting and the collective outcome that emerges.

The argument here is familiar and is based on the relatively small influence that any voter exerts in the determination of an electoral outcome, an argument discussed widely in public choice theory in rational abstention and rational ignorance models. In an earlier paper, Geoffrey Brennan and James Buchanan extended the logic to apply to what they called "expressive voting."[10] Buchanan and Brennan argue that, strictly speaking, the measurable economic interest of individual voters will tend to be swamped in influence by ideological or expressive preferences if the latter exist.

If incumbents extract rents to the limit, the constituent voter will, of course, be indifferent to the choices that are faced in the electoral booth. Let us suppose, however, that incumbents rationally leave constituents with some epsilon value differential over the expected net benefit from the election of a challenger. This value differential does *not* measure the difference in the value of the choice options faced by the voter. The latter value is only a small fraction of the epsilon value. In a voting constituency of 200,000 (a quasi-realistic estimate for the electorate in a single congressional district), the difference in the value of a vote for the incumbent and a vote for the challenger will be only some .001775 times the difference in the expected value of benefits between the two electoral outcomes. Even if the incumbent extracts no rents at all, this latter value is .0643B in the ten-district legislature, which reduces to .000115B as the value of voting for the incumbent.

---

10. G. Brennan and J. M. Buchanan, "Voter Choice," *American Behavioral Scientist* 28 (1984): 185–201.

If we suppose that B (expected value of project benefits per voter) is $1000, the value of voting for the incumbent is $.115. This size of B would imply that a special benefit project worth 200 million dollars, over and above incumbency rents extracted, is located in one district each period. The numerical illustration is sufficient to suggest that expressive preferences, not directly tied to economic interest, may assume dominant importance in the actual behavior of persons in the electoral process. In the example, a voter need only "feel" that the choice among votes is worth more than $.11 in order to disregard the incumbency advantage, as such, even if no rents are extracted from constituents by legislators. If these expressive considerations embody such characteristics as the physiognomy of candidates, no general bias can be predicted between incumbents and challengers.

Expressive elements in voting behavior may, however, exhibit directional bias. A directional bias against incumbents seems likely to emerge, however, when, as, and if incumbents are observed to collect the rents that their positions make possible, and when, as, and if the benefit-cost ratios of special benefit projects become small. In both of these settings or in combination, expressive voting may become the means through which the individual constituent can act in furtherance of the "general interest" without overly felt sacrifice of his own economic interest. Expressive voting acts to allow the individual person to step behind the veil of insignificance (Hartmut Kliemt's term), and, in this manner, to escape from the incumbency dilemma. Viewed in this perspective, the dilemma may be more apparent than real.

Speaker Thomas Foley may have doubly succeeded in his November 1991 efforts in the state of Washington. He apparently convinced voters in Washington that each of them did indeed "represent" the state in an ongoing game with voters from other states. Further, he convinced voters that their generalized opposition to incumbency, on principle, was "irrational" when reckoned in terms of their own economic interests. Many voters were led to abandon their initial private calculus of choice that dictated *expressive* support *for* term limits.

9. Conclusion

In suggesting that expressive voting may offer a limited means of escaping from the incumbency analogue to the prisoners' dilemma, our argument may seem to run counter to the conventional wisdom. In received analysis, an increase in the size of the interacting group of players (number of "prisoners") tends to reduce, and possibly in dramatic fashion, the prospects that individuals will choose cooperating rather than defecting strategies. By comparison, the argument in Section 8 suggests that increase in the number of voters in a constituency may increase rather than reduce "cooperation," here defined as removing incumbents from elected office. The apparent contradiction disappears, however, when it is recognized that the increase in the number of voters in a district operates differently from an increase in the numbers of districts, that is, in the size of the legislature. The incumbency dilemma appears in the distributive game among the districts, and not at all among voters within a district.

Although the 1992 electoral results are encouraging, we do not want to suggest that the potential for expressive voting, motivated both by principled opposition to rent-gouging and/or flagrant waste through overextension of projects, provides a sufficient avenue of escape from the incumbency dilemma that may describe modern American politics. Our efforts in this paper should be interpreted only as offering some offset to the despair that may seem to arise from a simultaneous recognition of the presence of the incumbency dilemma and the nearly insuperable difficulties of accomplishing basic constitutional change that would limit the range and scope of the legislative distributive game.

The Coase Theorem and the
Theory of the State

Things were really quite simple in the post-Pigovian world of microeconomic policy, a world characterized by possible divergencies between private and social marginal cost (or product). The classically nefarious factory might be observed to spew its smoke on the neighboring housewife's laundry, and in so doing impose costs that were not reckoned in its presumed strict profit-maximizing calculus. The remedy seemed straightforward. The "government" should impose a corrective tax on the factory owner, related directly to the smoke-generating output (or, if required, a particular input) and measured by the marginal external or spillover cost. Through this device the firm would be forced to make its decisions on the basis of a "socially correct" comparison of costs and revenues. Its profit-maximizing objective should then lead it to results that would be "socially optimal."

Things have not seemed nearly so simple since R. H. Coase presented his analysis of social cost.[1] Coase's central insight lay in his recognition that there are two sides to any potential economic interdependence, two parties to any potential exchange, and that this insures at least some pressure toward fully voluntary and freely negotiated agreements. Moreover, such agreements tend to insure the attainment of efficiency without the necessity of governmental intervention beyond the initial definition of rights and the enforcement of contracts. Applied to the example in hand, if the damage to the

From *Natural Resources Journal* 13 (October 1973): 579–94. Reprinted by permission of the publisher.

I am indebted to my colleagues Winston Bush, Dennis Mueller, and Gordon Tullock for helpful suggestions.

1. Coase, "The Problem of Social Cost," *Journal of Law and Economics* 3 (1960): 1–44.

housewife's laundry exceeds in value the benefits that the firm derives from allowing its stacks to smoke, a range of mutual gain exists, and utility- and profit-maximizing behavior on the part of the two parties involved will result in at least some reduction in the observed level of smoke damage, a reduction that can be taken to be efficient in terms of total product value. No governmental remedy may be called for at all, and indeed Coase argued that attempted correction by government might create inefficiency. Such intervention might forestall or distort the negotiations between the affected parties. As a further aspect of his analysis, Coase advanced the theorem on allocational neutrality that now bears his name. This states that under idealized conditions when transactions costs are absent and where income-effect feedbacks are not relevant, the allocational results of voluntarily negotiated agreements will be invariant over differing assignments of property rights among the parties to the interaction.

Much of the discussion since 1960 has involved the limitations of this theorem in the presence of positive transactions costs. In this setting, differing assignments of rights may affect allocative outcomes. Furthermore, the transactions costs barrier to voluntarily negotiated agreements that can be classified as tolerably efficient may be all but prohibitive in some situations, notably those that may require simultaneous agreement among many parties. The generalized transactions costs rubric may be used to array alternative institutional structures, with the implied objective being that of minimizing these costs.

My purpose in this paper is not to elaborate these extensions and/or limitations of the Coase analysis, many of which have become familiar even if an exhaustive taxonomy of cases has not been completed. My purpose is almost the opposite. I want to extend the Coase analysis, within his assumptions of zero transactions costs and insignificant income-effect feedbacks, to differing institutional settings than those that have normally been implicitly assumed in the discussions of the neutrality theorem. This approach leads to the question, Why did Coase suggest that the Pigovian prescriptions might produce inefficient results? Or, to put this somewhat differently, Why does the theorem of allocational neutrality stop short at certain ill-defined institutional limits? Why can it not be extended to encompass all possible institutional variations, variations that may be broadly interpreted as differences in the assignments of property rights? What is there in the implied Pigovian institutional framework that might inhibit the voluntary negotiations among parties, always assuming zero transactions costs? If the neutrality theorem holds, why should the political economist be overly concerned about institutional reform, as such?

There is a paradox of sorts here between the theorem of allocational neutrality, interpreted in its most general sense, and Coase's basic policy position. One implication of the theorem, so interpreted, would be that the thrust of classical political economy may have been misdirected. Adam Smith's central message points toward institutional reform and reconstruction as means of guaranteeing overall efficiency in resource usage, and, as noted, we can always interpret institutions as embodying specific property rights. Governmental authorities were to be stripped of their traditionally established rights to interfere in the workings of the market economy; or, stated conversely, individual traders were to be granted rights to negotiate on their own terms. The central theorem of classical economics might be summarized as the demonstration of the differences in allocational results under divergent institutional structures. I do not think that Coase would disagree with my statements here, and I think that he shares with me an admiration for Adam Smith and that Coase, too, places Smith's emphasis on institutional-structural reform above the modern policy emphasis on detailed and particularistic manipulation of observed results.

The apparent paradox may be resolved when we take account of the theory of the state or of government that is, perhaps surprisingly, shared by Adam Smith, Pigou, and Coase. My argument proceeds in several steps. First, it is necessary to distinguish carefully between property rights and liability rules. Secondly, I shall demonstrate that governmental or collective action, if conceived in the Wicksellian framework or model, does not modify the applicability of the neutrality theorem. Thirdly, I shall show that government, conceived in a non-Wicksellian model, need not modify the applicability of the theorem, but that in such case property rights are explicitly changed with the introduction of governmental action. Finally, I shall suggest that the theory of government decision-making implicit in both classical and neoclassical economics, and carried over in Coase's analysis, offers the source of the seemingly paradoxical limits on the neutrality theorem.

Property Rules and Liability Rules

In his basic paper, Coase did not make a careful distinction between the assignment of rights to particular individuals and the rules determining the liability of particular individuals for damage that their behavior might impose on others. His example, the now-familiar one of the interaction between the rancher and the farmer, was discussed in terms of alternative rules for bearing liability for damages. Either the rancher, whose cattle strayed onto the neighboring croplands, was liable for damages that the farmer might suffer, or he was not liable. If both cattle and grain were marketed competitively, the neutrality theorem showed that the same allocative outcome would be generated, regardless of which set of liability rules should be in existence. In the former case, the rancher, knowing in advance that he would be liable for damages caused by his straying animals, would include these payments as an anticipated cost in making his size-of-herd decisions. In the latter case, the farmer, knowing that he can collect no damages from the rancher (and that he must respect the property rights of the rancher to cattle), will find it advantageous to initiate payments to the latter in exchange for agreements limiting the size of herd, if indeed the value of crop damage at the margin exceeds the value of the additional grazing to the rancher.

Coase overlooked the fact that the institutional structure was significantly different in the two cases. In the second case, the shift toward an efficient outcome takes place through an ordinary market or exchange process, in which none other than the two parties need get involved. In the first case, however, as presented by Coase, there must be third-party interference by a "judge" to assess charges for damage that has been done. In the context of his discussions, this institutional difference does not matter, since the third party can, presumably, measure and assess damages with complete accuracy. The difference is nonetheless important in the more general setting. Consistency should have dictated that the first case be presented, not as one where the rancher was liable *ex post* for damages caused by his straying animals, but as one where the farmer held enforceable property rights in his croplands, rights that were inviolate except on his own agreement. In this framework, the rancher would have had to negotiate an agreement with the farmer in advance of any actual straying of cattle. This converts the institutional setting on this side into one that is parallel to the converse case. No third party, no judge, is required to intervene and to assess damages *ex post.*

We may define this setting as one in which property rules are established and enforced, as opposed to liability rules.[2] This setting calls direct attention to the motivation that both parties have to exploit the potentially realizable surplus by moving from the initial inefficient position. This setting also allows for an extension of the neutrality-efficiency theorem beyond those strictly objectifiable circumstances suggested to be present in the Coase example. If the precise degree of damage caused by external imposition is ambiguous, the third party must necessarily exercise his own best judgment in making a settlement. By contrast, if property rules are defined, with the necessity of prior agreement on the part of the potentially damaged party, the latter's own subjective assessment of potential damage becomes controlling in determining the range over which final outcomes may settle. This assessment is, of course, a better measure of actual value lost than the estimate made by any third party.

Wicksellian Unanimity

For my purposes in this paper, the specification that parties to an interaction are defined by property rather than liability rules facilitates relating the Coase theorem on allocational neutrality to the underlying conception or theory of government or of the State. In the simplest possible model, we may conceive of a polity that is limited in membership to the parties directly involved in the potential interaction. The interacting group can be made coincident in membership with the political unit. On this basis, we can in-

---

2. This terminology is adopted from the discussion by Calabresi and Melamed, whose paper clarifies the distinction between these two. As they state, a property rule "is the form of entitlement which gives rise to the least amount of state intervention." See Calabresi and Melamed, "Property Rules, Liability Rules, and Inalienability: One View of the Cathedral," *Harvard Law Review* 85 (1972): 1089–146; see also Demsetz, "Some Aspects of Property Rights," *Journal of Law and Economics* 9 (1966): 64–65.

In a paper to be published, I have also called attention to the distinction between these two institutional arrangements, noting in particular the necessary resort to third-party action under liability rules. See Buchanan, "The Institutional Structure of Externality," *Public Choice* (forthcoming).

terpret the "trades" among the parties as being analogous to collective or governmental decisions reached under the operation of a Wicksellian rule of unanimity.[3] Consider either the earlier factory-housewife example, or Coase's familiar rancher-farmer one. In either illustration, we can think of the two-party group as comprising the all-inclusive membership in the political community, in which case agreement between the two parties on any matter is equivalent to unanimous accord. Resort to third-party adjudication is impossible for the simple reason that no third party exists.

From this context, it becomes easier to conceive "the State" merely as the instrumental means or device through which individuals attempt to carry out activities aimed at securing jointly desired objectives. This is, of course, the traditional framework for all theories of social-contract origins of government. In this setting, all activities of the public sector are explained in exchange terms, even if it is recognized that the exchange process is significantly more complex than that which makes up the central subject matter of orthodox economic theory. There is at least no conceptual or logical necessity to think of "the State" as an entity that exists separate from and apart from citizens.

If we remain within the strict contractarian conception of collective action, where all decisions require unanimous consent by all members of the political community, and if we retain the assumption that transactions costs are absent, the Coase theorem on allocational neutrality may be applied beyond those limits within which it has normally been discussed. In this model, collective or governmental decision-making remains equivalent to freely negotiated voluntary exchange. Hence, there is little or no cause for concern about "governmental intervention" as such, because any action that might properly be classified as "governmental" would not emerge unless all parties agree on the contractual terms.

Differences in the assignment of rights might, as in the standard simple exchange cases, generate differences in distributional outcomes, but the con-

3. Collective decision-making under a rule of unanimity is associated with the name of Knut Wicksell in modern public-finance-theory analysis because he proposed institutional reforms that embodied unanimity in the reaching of tax and expenditure decisions. See K. Wicksell, *Finanztheoretische Untersuchungen* (1896). The central portion of this work appears in English translation as "A New Principle of Just Taxation," in *Classics in the Theory of Public Finance*, ed. R. Musgrave and A. Peacock (1959), 72–118.

tractual process would lead to allocational results that are both efficient and invariant. Consider a classic example that introduces what we may appropriately call collective or public goods, David Hume's villagers whose utility would be increased by drainage of a meadow. The neutrality theorem, applied to this example, demonstrates that an efficient and unchanged allocational result will emerge from freely negotiated contract whether the postulated initial position should be one in which individuals own separate plots of land through which the swampy stream flows or whether the whole meadow is defined as communal property, accessible to all parties. With an effective unanimity rule, and with zero transactions costs, the complex exchange that is required for efficiency would be worked out under any initial structure of individual rights. The sharing of the gross gains-from-trade among separate persons would, of course, be influenced by the particular property assignment in being. If the sharing of such gains modifies individual demands for the common good, at the margin, that is, if income effects are present, differing assignments can produce slight differences in allocational results, but, under the assumptions here, those results produced will continue to be efficient.

Simple Majority Voting

When the unanimity requirement for collective decisions is abandoned, governmental action no longer represents a complex equivalent of a voluntary exchange process.[4] If decisions that are to be binding over the inclusive group can be made by a subset of this group, there is no guarantee that a particular individual holds against the imposition of net harm or damage. Once his own contractual agreement to the terms of governmental or collective action is dropped as a requirement, an individual can no longer be certain that he will share in the gross gains that governmental action will, presumably, generate. From this it seems to follow that collective action,

4. It is possible to use the analogue to voluntary exchange at the level of constitutional, as opposed to day-to-day choice. That is to say, we might analyze the selection of a political constitution, the rules for the reaching of collective decisions, under a postulated unanimity rule. It is then possible to derive a logical basis for nonunanimity rules from unanimous agreement at the constitutional level. This is the approach taken in J. Buchanan and G. Tullock, *The Calculus of Consent* (1962).

motivated by improvement in the positions of members of a decisive coalition smaller than the totality of community membership, need not produce results that are efficient, even with zero transactions costs.[5] Any nonunanimity voting rule, for example, that of simple majority voting, would seem to produce results that may be, in the net, inefficient.

The neutrality theorem is, however, more powerful than might be suggested by cursory attention to this example. Efficient outcomes will tend to emerge from the contractual process, even under less-than-unanimity voting rules for collective action, if the modified structure of property rights consequent on the departure from unanimity is acknowledged, and if individuals are allowed freely to negotiate trades in these rights. Economists have not fully incorporated the property-rights structure of less-than-unanimity voting rules into their orthodoxy, and they tend to stop short of the extension of the neutrality theorem herein suggested.

Consider a situation in which individuals hold well-defined rights, which are acknowledged by all parties, and which are known to be enforceable without costs. If no collective action is undertaken, individuals trade such rights among themselves in simple exchanges, insuring mutuality of gain. If collective action is undertaken, but only on the agreement of all parties, mutuality of gain (or, at the limit, absence of loss) is insured. If this requirement is dropped, and individuals may be subjected to damage or harm through collective action, the value of their initial holdings is necessarily changed, again on the assumption of zero transactions costs. Individuals no longer hold claims that are inviolate against imposed reductions in value. A new and ambiguous set of rights is brought into being by the authorization of governmental action taken without the approval of all parties. Any potentially decisive decision-making coalition, a simple majority of voters in our example here, possesses rights to the nominal holdings of the minority. These rights are, in this instance, ambiguous because they emerge only upon the identification of the majority coalition that is to be decisive with respect to the issue under consideration for collective action. Once identified, however,

---

5. With zero transactions costs, any departure from unanimity voting rules for collective action would hardly be acceptable at the constitutional level. But this modification is introduced here for purposes of developing the exposition of the argument, not for descriptive relevance.

members of the effective majority hold potentially marketable rights. These may be exchanged, directly or indirectly, and the contractual process will again insure that the efficient allocative outcome will be achieved, and that this will be invariant, given the appropriate assumptions about transactions costs and income effects.

We may illustrate this in a highly simplified three-person example. Consider a community that includes three men: A, B, and C. Collective decisions are to be made by simple majority voting. Initial holdings of units of an all-purpose and numberable consumption good are, let us say, 100 for A, 60 for B, and 30 for C. In this environment, let us suppose that a governmental project is proposed, one that promises to yield benefits of 30 units, distributed equally among the three persons. The gross costs of this project are, however, 40 units; clearly, the proposal is inefficient. Despite this, if B and C can succeed in organizing themselves into a majority coalition, and if they can impose the full tax costs of the proposal on A, they can make net gains. In this case, the results would appear as follows:

Person	Benefits	Costs	Net
A	10	40	− 30
B	10	0	10
C	10	0	10

Once B and C are identified as the decisive members of the coalition, however, individual A can negotiate trades, or side payments, that will be mutually beneficial to all parties, and which will keep this inefficient outcome from being achieved. Individual A can, for example, offer either B or C a net gain of 15 units to join a different majority coalition that will disapprove the project. Or, if both B and C hold firm, they can exact from A a payment of 10 units for their agreement to withhold the project. The side payments, which must be allowed to take place under our assumption of zero transactions costs, will insure that all inefficient projects are forestalled, and, similarly, that all efficient projects will be carried out.[6]

6. It is often erroneously argued that individuals with the superior economic power, A in our example, can exercise more influence in the formation of dominant coalitions than

The values to individuals of the "property rights in franchise" embodied in a majority-voting regime depend critically on the constitutional limits within which majorities are allowed to take collective-political action. These values will also depend on the technological possibilities for potential coalition gains within the given set of constitutional constraints defined. Detailed exploration of these interesting and mostly unresolved issues would not be suitable in this paper. For present purposes, the points to be recognized are, firstly, that any departure from unanimity in collective decision processes modifies the structure of rights from that which is defined exclusively by private-sector claims and obligations, and, secondly, that even with this modified set of rights, the theorem on allocational neutrality remains valid within the required, and highly restricted, assumptions concerning transactions costs and income effects.[7]

Administrative Authority

In traditional economic-policy discussions, the arguments for and/or against governmental intervention in the private sector rarely take place under explicitly defined models for collective decision-making. For the most part, those who propose "corrections" to the outcomes of voluntary exchange processes, like those who oppose them, are content to treat governmental decisions as exogenous to the valuations of the persons in the economy itself.

---

individuals with inferior economic power, C in our example. If, however, C fully recognizes the exploitation potential available in the situation described, he can offer B precisely the same terms as those offered by A. In the basic arithmetic here, there is no more likelihood that the net gains from not undertaking the project, 10 units, will be shared by A rather than by B or C. In effect, the von Neumann–Morgenstern solution set of imputations to the simple majority game becomes:

$$(5,5,0) \qquad (5,0,5) \qquad (0,5,5).$$

For an elaboration of this analysis, see Buchanan and Tullock *supra* note 4, at chs. 11 and 12.

7. In another paper, I have developed somewhat more fully some of the possible implications of the modified rights structure that majority voting rules embody. See Buchanan, "The Political Economy of the Welfare State," Center for the Study of Public Choice Research Paper No. 808231-1-8 (June 1972). This paper was prepared for the Conference on Capitalism and Freedom, in honor of Milton Friedman, in Charlottesville, Virginia, October 1972; it will be published in the volume of conference proceedings.

If, however, these arguments are interpreted consistently within any collective decision-making framework, the structure that can most readily be inferred is neither that of unanimity nor simple majority voting. The model of government that accords most closely with economic policy discussions is one in which authority to take collective action is vested in an administrator, a bureaucrat, an expert, who chooses for the community, presumably on the basis of his own version of the "public interest," or, in technical economist's jargon, some "social welfare function."

It is useful, therefore, to extend our analysis of the theorem on allocational neutrality to this administrative-decision model of public choice. Probably because the model is essentially implicitly rather than explicitly postulated, little or no attention has been paid to the alternative means through which the single decision-maker for the collectivity may be selected. Nor need this concern us here. Strictly speaking, the conclusions developed below follow whether the decision-maker be divinely ordained, democratically elected, arbitrarily appointed, selected in competitive examination, or hereditarily determined.[8] I want to examine a model in which a single person has been empowered to make decisions for a whole community. This defines a specific structure of rights, an assignment, and the problem is to determine the allocative results that will emerge in comparison with those predicted under alternative structures. The first point to be noted is the same as that made with respect to simple majority voting. The delegation of decision-making power to the single person modifies the set of rights in existence, even prior to the onset of any imposed governmental action. The designated chooser for the community holds potentially valued claims that were nonexistent before he is constitutionally authorized to act.

Consider again Hume's drainage of the village meadow. Instead of operating through a rule of unanimity, we now assume that the village has empowered a single person to act on behalf of all persons in the group and, furthermore, it is acknowledged that his decisions will be enforced. Formally, it does not matter whether the decision-maker is chosen from within or from outside the group. For expositional simplicity, however, we shall assume that

---

8. The method of selection may affect the motivation of the decision-maker and, in this way, modify the likelihood that the behavioral hypotheses implicit in the orthodox conceptions will be corroborated.

he is selected from outside the village. We now assume that a drainage project, lumpy in nature, will yield symmetrically distributed benefits to villagers valued at 1000 units of the numeraire commodity. The project will cost a total of 800 units, and the taxing institution requires symmetrical sharing. The project is clearly Pareto-efficient, and, as indicated earlier, under an operating rule of unanimity, the project will be undertaken, given our zero transactions costs assumption, and including all free-rider behavior under the transactions costs rubric. The question becomes: Would this project necessarily be selected by the single decision-maker, the alternative structure of property rights under consideration?

It is illegitimate to assume that the single administrator knows the preferences of the citizens, or, even should these be estimated with accuracy, that he would necessarily embody individual values dollar-for-dollar in his own choice calculus. The administrator or bureaucrat will select the project if the costs that he bears are less than the benefits that he, personally, secures. But these costs and benefits are not, and cannot possibly be, those of the community of citizens. Apparently, there is nothing in this model to insure correspondence between the bureaucrat's choices and those results that are to be classified as efficient by orthodox economists' criteria. This suggests that the theorem of allocational neutrality breaks down.

If, however, we move beyond this naive model of administrative behavior, the applicability of the neutrality theorem may be restored. By acting in accordance with his own subjective evaluation, the bureaucrat may be failing to maximize the value of the property right that has been assigned to him constitutionally. To show this, let us assume that, naively, the decision-taker decides against the project noted. In this decision, he deprives the citizenry of benefits valued at 1000 units and, at the same time, avoids the imposition of tax costs of 800 units on the community. In a setting with zero transactions costs, where large numbers can readily reach contractual agreements, the citizenry, as an inclusive group of taxpayers-beneficiaries, would be willing to offer side payments up to a total of 200 units to secure a change from negative to positive action on the project.[9] If the decision-maker, the admin-

---

9. In the numerical example, the potentially capturable rent seems to be 200 units because of the assumptions that both benefits and costs of the drainage project are shared

istrator or bureaucrat, uses these side payments, either indicatively or actually, to determine his final choice, the drainage project will be carried out. The theorem of allocational neutrality is apparently validated in this more sophisticated model for bureaucratic behavior. So long as the decision-maker acts to maximize the potential rent on the property right delegated to him, the right to make the final decision for the whole community, the allocative result will be identical to that forthcoming under alternative rights structures, with, of course, the transactions costs, income-effect assumptions postulated. As in all property-assignment shifts, the distributional results may be quite different under differing assignments. If the bureaucrat maximizes the potential rent on his right to choose for the group, and, furthermore, if he collects this in the form of a personal side payment, there is an income transfer from members of the original group to the "outsider" selected as decision-taker.[10]

Objection may be raised to rent-maximizing as the appropriate norm for bureaucratic behavior, even if we neglect ethical considerations (these will be introduced in Section V). To postulate that the designated decision-maker maximizes the potential side payments that he can receive from taxpayers-beneficiaries, as a group, implies that the decision-maker, himself, is indifferent as among the choice alternatives, that he places no personal evaluation on the differences among those opportunities available to him. If, in fact, the bureaucrat or administrator is external to the affected group of persons in the community, this assumption may seem plausibly realistic. If, however, he is chosen from within the community itself, his own evaluation must be

---

symmetrically among all of the villagers. If these assumptions are relaxed, the decision-maker can collect a larger sum in rent. His potential gain will, in all cases, be the sum of the *larger* of the *positive* or the *negative* differences between benefits and costs, the sum being taken over all members of the community.

10. This modifies the standard economist's treatment of the distinction between allocational and distributional results. The latter may, for certain purposes, be neglected if the zero-sum aspects are confined to a stable group of "members." If, however, a new rights assignment, such as that discussed, generates distributional transfers outside the original group, the effects, for this group, are negative-sum. Applied to the realistic setting in which transactions costs are present, this suggests that a community may, under certain conditions, find it advantageous to put up with allocative inefficiency rather than to secure its removal at the expense of distributional transfers to delegated decision-takers.

taken into account. Whether the decision-taker is selected from within or without the original group of members, his own evaluation can be, and must be, included in any correct assessment of costs and benefits.

We may return to the numerical illustration introduced above. Suppose that the gross benefits of the proposed drainage project, to all persons other than the decision-taker, amount to 1000 units of a numeraire good (we may call these "dollars"), and that the gross costs, to all persons other than the decision-taker, amount to 800. Suppose, however, that the decision-maker, himself, places a monetary value of, say, 400 dollars on the "natural beauty" of the swampy and undrained meadow. Even should he be required to pay no part of the tax costs of the project, this 400 units of value necessarily becomes a component in the total opportunity cost of the drainage scheme. Under these conditions, the bureaucrat will refuse the proffered side payment of 200 units. The project will not be undertaken.

Does this result suggest that the theorem of allocational neutrality breaks down? The question of whether the decision-taker is selected from within or without the initial membership of the group becomes critical at this point. If the selection is internal, the project is inefficient under the conditions suggested, and it will not be undertaken under any rights assignment. This is because the person's negative evaluation would be an input in any internal contractual negotiations that might produce an allocative outcome. In this case, the neutrality theorem remains valid. Suppose, however, that the bureaucrat is not in the initial group of members. In such case, his own personal evaluation of the project alternatives will not enter and will not affect allocative outcomes when the assignment of rights is limited to initial members. This decision-maker's evaluation will, however, enter as a determinant when he is assigned the rights to choose for the group. The neutrality theorem would not hold valid under these conditions unless the decision-maker should be, in fact, wholly indifferent as among the choice alternatives.

This result should not be at all surprising. The theorem on allocational neutrality, even under its restricted set of required assumptions, should hardly be expected to extend to rights assignments that embody differing memberships in the group. For fixed memberships, the theorem remains fully valid. Even when the decision-maker is selected from outside, the theorem suggests that any change in rights assignments, once the additional member is included, among this new membership will produce identical allocational results.

The Theory of the State

It is possible to interpret both the policy implications of Coase's theorem on allocational neutrality and Pigovian corrective policy prescriptions in terms of the underlying conceptions, models, or theories of government. As the analysis above has suggested, under certain conceptions of governmental process, neither Coase nor the Pigovians should have been greatly concerned about institutional change as a means of generating allocative efficiency. If distributional considerations are neglected, and if decision-makers for the community are chosen from within the group, the structure of rights will modify allocative outcomes only because of differentials in levels of transactions costs, provided that the decision-takers are motivated by economic self-interest. The policy thrust of Coase's discussion is, however, to the effect that governmental or collective intrusion into the negotiation processes of the market economy tends to retard rather than to advance movement toward allocative efficiency. Conversely, the policy thrust of the whole Pigovian tradition is that governmental or collective intrusion into the market economy tends to be corrective of distortions and leads toward rather than away from those results that might satisfy agreed-on efficiency criteria.

The Pigovian model of the state may be examined first. The decision-taker, the person or group empowered to impose the corrective taxes and subsidies, is presumed to act in accordance with rules laid down for him by the welfare economist. His task is that of measuring social costs and social benefits from alternative courses of action, a task that he is presumed able to carry out effectively. On the basis of such measurements, the decision-taker is to follow the rules laid down, quite independent of the personal opportunity costs that he may face in refusing side payment offers. The Pigovian policy-maker must be an economic eunuch. The idealized allocative results are, of course, identical with those that would emerge under a regime where the decision-maker is wholly "corrupt" in the sense of strict maximization of the potential side payments or rents on his rights to make decisions. If he is expected to behave as a rent-maximizer, however, there would be no need for elaborated and detailed instruction in the form of rules or norms, as derived from the theorems of welfare economics. Within this Pigovian conception, the decision-maker for the group does not and/or should not maximize the rental value of the rights of decision that he is granted. This may be treated either as a positive prediction about bureaucratic behavior or as a normative proposition for bureaucratic behavior.

In the Coase conception,[11] an interpretation that is similar in certain respects seems to follow. If, in fact, governmental decision-makers act as strict rent-maximizers, the neutrality theorem suggests that there should be little or no concern about allocative results, per se. The evidence of such concern must, therefore, indicate some denial of the rent-maximizing behavioral hypothesis. Again, this may be taken as positive prediction or normative statement. The governmental decision-maker, the bureaucrat, empowered to act on behalf of the group, either does not maximize rents on the rights that he commands or he should not do so on moral-ethical grounds. In either case, the Coase concern for allocational efficiency returns since the negotiating pressure toward optimality is removed once the decision-making power is shifted from the market to the public sector.

It is perhaps surprising to find common elements in the basic conceptions of political process held by the proponents of essentially opposing policy positions. But in both the Pigovian framework and in that imputed here to Coase, the governmental decision-maker, either singly or as a member of a choosing group, is and/or should be "incorruptible." In this respect, the two conceptions of governmental process seem identical, despite the sharp differences in information possibilities attributed to the governmental authority in the two models. In the Pigovian tradition, the bureaucrat is both informed and incorruptible; in the Coase framework, he is ignorant and incorruptible.

Agreement on this "incorruptibility" characteristic of governmental decision-makers, and indeed the introduction of the term "corruptible" in this familiar usage, suggests that there exist widely shared ethical presuppositions concerning the inalienability of the delegated rights to make collective

---

11. For an explicit statement of the Coase-Chicago position, see Demsetz, "The Exchange and Enforcement of Property Rights," 7 *Journal of Law and Economics* (1964): 21–22.

choices. That is to say, some shift away from the unanimity rule for collective decisions may be accepted as necessary, with the accompanying acknowledgment that new and previously nonexistent "rights of decision" are brought into being, rights that have economic value that is potentially capturable by the subset of the citizenry empowered to take decisions on behalf of all. Such rights may, however, be considered to be inalienable; that is, the holder is not entitled to sell them or to exploit his possession of them through collection of personal rewards, either directly or indirectly.[12] It would be inappropriate in this paper to examine in detail the validity of such ethical presuppositions, although this opens up many interesting and highly controversial topics for analysis.[13]

The existence of such presuppositions can scarcely be denied. The pejorative content of such terms as "vote-trading," "logrolling," "political favoritism," "spoils system," "pork barrel legislation"—these attest to the pervasiveness of negative attitudes toward even minor attempts on the part of possessors of political decision-making rights to increase rental returns. If these attitudes are sufficiently widespread, prohibitions against bureaucratic and political rent-maximization may extend beyond the mere promulgation

12. In the paper previously cited, Calabresi and Melamed discuss the inalienability of rights at some length, and particularly they draw attention to several examples where inalienability is accepted. See Calabresi and Melamed, note 2, above.

The precise location of "inalienability" in the situation discussed may be questioned. In delegating decision-making authority to an agent, citizens may not be considered to be transferring the economic value inherent in the "right to choose." In this framework, it is the rights of the citizenry which are "inalienable" in some fundamental sense, and the agent could scarcely transfer a "right" which he does not possess. In my discussion, I have equated the empirically observed delegation of decision-making authority with an effective transfer of a valuable "right" which is then supposed to be "inalienable."

13. The ethical bases for such widely shared attitudes may be challenged when the economic analysis is carefully developed. In the case of marketing rights to make decisions for the community, the relative undesirability of the distributional results provide a sufficient reason for inalienability. Conceptually, the decision-maker can capture *all* of the potential surplus from constitutionally authorized action. In this limit, those who presumably make the constitutional delegation of authority, the citizenry, find themselves with zero net gains from collective action. So long as the delegation of decision rights along with inalienability is predicted to generate positive net gains, the citizenry's economic position is enhanced. The possible inefficiency in the standard allocative sense is more than offset by the distributional gains.

of ethical norms for behavior. The rewards and punishments that are consciously built into the governmental structure may be specifically aimed at making such rent-maximization unprofitable for any person empowered to take decisions on behalf of the whole group. The designated bureaucrat who is assigned authority over one specific aspect of public policy may not be morally or ethically inhibited from accepting side payments. But he may face harsh legal penalties should he accede to monetary temptations. To the extent that these constitutionally determined constraints insure that the economic self-interests of governmental decision-makers dictate behavior unresponsive to proffered side payments (direct or indirect) it may be argued, almost tautologically, that any outcomes chosen for the community by the "incorruptibles" must be, by definition, classified as "efficient." This would produce the paradoxical conclusion that the conditions for efficiency depend critically on the institutional structure and that, even with unchanged personal evaluations, solutions which are deemed efficient under one set of institutions may be inefficient under another.

The avoidance of this paradox becomes possible if we are content to define as allocationally efficient only that set of possible outcomes that could emerge from the contractual negotiation process among persons in the community, on the assumption that no rights are inalienable. In this case, the introduction of inalienability in the rights of governmental decision-takers clearly makes the theorem of allocational neutrality invalid. Under the highly restricted assumptions of zero transactions costs, any activity will be efficiently organized in the absence of governmental intervention, and, absent income effect feedbacks, the allocational outcome will be invariant over differing assignments of private and alienable rights. Under such conditions as these, it is the inalienability of rights that the shift to the public sector introduces which removes the guarantee that outcomes will be efficient, not the shift to governmental decision-taking per se. If we avoid the apparent paradox in this manner, however, the implication is left that the constitutional shift of activities to the public sector is an almost necessary source of inefficiency. When other considerations are accounted for, however, this implication need not follow. When transactions costs are recognized, and especially when distributional implications are considered, efficiency "in the large" may dictate the governmental organization of activities along with the inalienability of the rights delegated necessarily to bureaucratic decision-makers. There is no final escape from the requirement that each particular institutional change proposed must be examined on its own merits, on some case-by-case procedure, with the interdependence among separate organizational decisions firmly in mind.

Consumerism and Public Utility Regulation

I. Introduction

In this paper I shall develop an analytical model of public utility regulation that has not, to my knowledge, found its way into the textbook treatments by economists. This "theory" embodies the emergence of consumer interests and the possible influence that these interests may exert on politicians and regulatory bureaucrats. For purposes of identification, we may call this the Henry Howell–Ralph Nader model of public utility regulation. I shall make no attempt to test the model against observations. Those who are insiders in the industries regulated along with those outsiders who are more competent in empirical testing can make the applications that seem appropriate. In advancing this consumerism model, I am suggesting only that it may be of some influence. I am not suggesting that it is, or will become, the dominant explanation of regulatory behavior.

I shall present the argument with the aid of old-fashioned, indeed elementary, tools of economic theory. The innovation in the paper, if one exists, consists in using these familiar tools within the public choice or political context. Before presenting the central arguments of the paper, I shall sketch out, very briefly, my own version of the history of public utility regulation, as this has developed in the conceptions of economists over nearly a century. Early on, there arose a thrust for governmental regulation of "natural mo-

From *Telecommunications, Regulation, and Public Choice*, ed. Charles F. Phillips, Jr. (Lexington, Va.: Washington and Lee University Press, 1975), 1–22. Reprinted by permission.

I am indebted to my colleagues Robert Spann, N. Tideman, and Gordon Tullock, for helpful discussions.

nopoly," of industries "affected with the public interest," of "public utilities." Much of the early discussion amounted to justification of governmental action, followed by attempts at identification of those areas of the economy to be subjected to regulation and control. Although not represented as such, these were the halcyon days for socialist dreams. Little or no concern was expressed, or felt, for the possible failures of government to fulfill the reformists' promises.

Regulation became legitimate, and regulatory agencies, at all levels of government, were established with legally defined responsibilities. At this point, economists shifted their attention to actual problems of control. "Public utility regulation" courses showed up in the curricula of economics departments, and textbooks in "public utilities" were published. The issues centered around valuation. How should assets be valued for regulatory purposes? We are familiar with the continuing controversies over replacement cost and original cost of assets.

In the 1930's and 1940's, theoretical welfare economics occupied center stage, with its carefully defined norms for "efficiency," including its emphasis on "marginal-cost pricing." Principles for ideal operation were laid down; prices should be made equal to marginal costs, even if this involved general taxation to subsidize the increasing returns facilities. Little thought was given to the need to define marginal cost in a sense that could be externally monitored by a regulator. Proposals for two-part or multipart pricing arose as partial offsets to the more naive and extreme versions of marginal-cost pricing principles. And, for the most part, regulatory agencies continued on their assigned way, oblivious to the theoretical discussions of idealized norms among the welfare economists.

In the years following World War II, two new strands of argument appeared. Examination of rate-of-return constraints which were almost universally employed as the regulatory instruments led to the now-familiar thesis that these constraints provided incentives for inefficient combinations of inputs. The Averch-Johnson work, along with that of others, showed how regulated firms were offered profit-maximizing incentives for an inefficient deepening of capital.[1] The second major development represented, for the first time, an examination of the regulatory process itself, both empirically

1. H. Averch and L. L. Johnson, "Behavior of the Firm Under Regulatory Constraint," *American Economic Review* 52 (December 1962): 1052–69.

and analytically. Through the work of George Stigler and his colleagues, regulation was shown to have had little or no effect, and further work has gone on to suggest that the objective function for the regulatory agency tends to incorporate protection of the industry that is regulated, as opposed to furtherance of "the public interest," more generally defined.[2]

Note that little or no recognition has been given to the possible domination of consumers' interests in the regulatory process. Yet it seems clear that consumers' interests have taken on more political representation during the decades of the 1960's and 1970's, with the publicity accorded consumerism in all of its guises. It would indeed seem surprising if the regulatory process has remained wholly immune from this change in political climate. The "theory" that I shall develop in this paper incorporates the possible political dominance of these interests. The results suggest that if regulation is aimed at maximizing consumers' interests exclusively, inefficiency may be produced.

II. The Simple Analytics of Regulated Monopoly: Increasing Costs

Much of the early discussion of regulated monopoly was based on the presumption that increasing returns (decreasing average costs) characterize the operation at equilibrium levels of output. In the model that is central to this paper, I make the opposing presumption, that decreasing returns (increasing average costs) are characteristic of the regulated firm, at least with respect to certain output parameters.[3] Note that this presumption does not eliminate

2. G. Stigler and Claire Friedland, "What Can Regulators Regulate? The Case of Electricity," *Journal of Law and Economics* 5 (October 1962): 1–16, reprinted in *Utility Regulation*, ed. W. G. Shepherd and T. G. Gies (New York: Random House, 1966), 187–211; G. Stigler, "The Theory of Economic Regulation," *Bell Journal of Economics and Management Science* 2 (Spring 1971): 3–21; G. Stigler, "The Process of Economic Regulation," *The Antitrust Bulletin* 17 (Spring 1972): 207–35. For a comprehensive review of the literature, with all references, see L. De Alessi, "Government Ownership and Regulation: The Evidence from the Electric Power Industry," *Public Choice* 19 (Fall 1974): 1–42.

3. The assumption of increasing average costs does not, of course, suggest that the grounds for regulation are absent. Total demand may be insufficient to allow the efficient operation of the number of firms required for effective competition, or even for more than a single enterprise. Casual evidence suggests that many regulated monopolies do, in fact, operate in increasing cost ranges for certain parameters, for example, telephone switching operations.

the conflict between the marginal-cost and the average-cost pricing norms, although it does generate somewhat different financing problems. (The disposing of surplus funds is more tractable than the covering of deficits.) The presumption of increasing long-run average costs does, however, allow for the exertion of *monopsony* power, something which is irrelevant under decreasing costs. The central feature of the consumer-oriented model involves the manipulation of the regulatory agency as the instrument for the exercise of this monopsony power, the analysis of which has not, to my knowledge, been fully treated in the literature.

Consider Figure 1. The long-run average-cost curve for the regulated firm is shown by AC; the related marginal-cost curve is shown by MC. (The precise reasons for the increase in average costs with increases in output are analytically important when we come to assess the welfare implications. These reasons will be discussed at a later point, but I shall neglect these at this stage of the argument.) The market demand curve for the firm's output is shown by D.

If consumers are to be in equilibrium, the solution must lie on D. If the

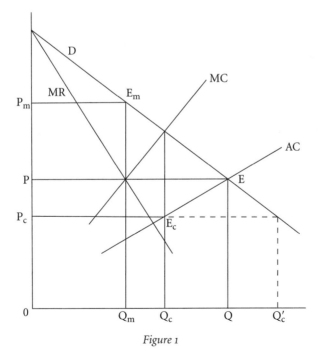

Figure 1

regulated firm is to be constrained to make a reasonable or normal return on its capital investment, the solution must lie on AC. The solution shown at E, and *only* this solution, meets both of these requirements. Let us refer to this as the *practical* objective for regulation. At E, the firm makes a reasonable and allowable return on its investment, while all demanders, as quantity adjustors, are satisfied at the allowable rate or price, shown by P. Output of the firm is Q.

We may first compare this regulated solution with that which would emerge if the firm should occupy a monopoly position without regulation, or if the regulatory agency has been wholly "captured" by producer interests. To show this, we draw the curve, MR, marginal revenue, related to D, and find the firm's profit-maximizing position by equating this to marginal cost. Output would be Q_m, and price would be P_m. These alternative solutions are, of course, familiar to anyone who has had a course in economics.

Consider, however, a third possible solution to this simple example, and one that is somewhat less familiar. Suppose that the regulatory agency seeks to maximize the interests of the consumers of the firm's product and that discrimination in rates among separate classes of consumers is not possible. It would hold the firm to the constrained rate of return or price shown by P_c, and the firm would produce at output Q_c.[4] Note the following relationships between the three nondiscriminatory solutions:

$$P_m > P > P_c,$$
$$Q > Q_c > Q_m.$$

In the absence of discrimination, producers' rents or profits are maximized under the monopoly solution; consumers' rents are maximized under the monopsony solution.

---

4. This definition of the ideal solution under nondiscriminatory monopsony requires the assumption that these potential demands which remain unsatisfied at the monopsony price, P_c, are those demands which reflect lower marginal evaluations than those which are satisfied. That is to say, the consumers' surplus under P_c is measured by the demand curve. If this assumption is not made, for example, if demands at P_c were to be met at random from all who desire to purchase at this price, the area under D would not measure consumers' surplus. In this case, the nondiscriminatory monopsony solution will be less than Q_c, and price less than P_c.

There are significant differences in what we might call the market characteristics of the three solutions. As noted, only in the practical regulator's solution, shown at E, are both sides of the market in full equilibrium adjustment. Under the monopoly solution, consumers or demanders are kept on their demand curves. They are able to purchase desired quantities of the product or service at the prices or rates established by the profit-maximizing monopolist. But investors are forced out of equilibrium in this solution. To the extent that entry is possible, more funds will seek outlet in the area of production covered by the monopolized industry umbrella. Differentially attractive profit opportunities will be apparent. Under monopsony pricing, by contrast with this, investment remains in adjustment, at least within the confines of the regulators. Since the monopoly firm is now constrained to remain on its average-cost curve, no more than a normal or reasonable rate of return is being earned. There is no incentive for investment to flow toward this industry, save in the case where regulation might be circumvented in some manner. On the other hand, this monopsony solution requires that consumers be shifted off their demand curves, that they be placed in disequilibria. The output which is supplied by the regulated firm under this solution, at the price or rate that is approved by the agency, will not be sufficient to meet all demands. Overt shortages and nonprice rationing will necessarily emerge.

The tendency for unregulated monopoly to reduce output and to raise price is, of course, familiar. And indeed it was in putative recognition of this result that the argument for regulation was initially made in many cases. The tendency for unrestricted monopsony to reduce output and to reduce price has not been so fully recognized. This asymmetry presumably stems in part from the common socialist presupposition that regulation will always be aimed toward the correctly defined social objective and, furthermore, that this regulation will be fully effective in attaining whatever objective is chosen.

Consider, however, the problem that is faced by the politically sensitive regulatory agency, or by the bureaucratic personnel who must make decisions on behalf of this agency. These persons confront two opposing interests: those of the regulated firm, which seeks to attain monopoly profits, and those of consumers of the product, who seek to attain maximum consumers' rents.[5] There is no necessary representation of the "public interest" or the "social welfare" in the day-to-day workings of the forces that bear on the regulatory agency. Ma Bell and Ralph Nader stand at the ends of the spectrum, with interests that are opposed with respect to pricing or rate-of-return norms. Neither Ma Bell nor Ralph Nader will seek to secure the norm which we have defined as that appropriate for the practical regulator.

We may make some inferences about the location of the actual regulatory situation by observing behavior. If consumer interests have, indeed, captured the agency, which forces the firm to operate at price P_c with output Q_c in Figure 1, representatives of the producing firm will offer to expand rates of output in exchange for allowed rate or price increases. Some shift from E_c toward E will be desired by the producing interests. Behavior on the part of consumers may tend to corroborate this hypothesis about location of an existing situation. If consumers are observed to be unsatisfied by the output produced by the firm, if nonprice rationing is observed, either in waiting time for installations, in service delays, or in reduced qualities of service (e.g., brownouts), in the absence of selling and service effort on the part of the producing firm's employees and staff—all of these would suggest that the situation may be that approximated by E_c in Figure 1. Behavior of potential investors outside the regulatory network may also be observed in partial confirmation. Despite the fact that allowable prices or rates of return do nothing more than insure normal profits for the regulated firm, consumers' net evaluation of the service exceeds these levels. Potential entrants who think that regulation may be circumvented and that, at least for some elements of the product bundle, they will be allowed to price at market clearing levels will seek to chip away at the regulatory package, to expand, where possible, the area of free market operation. This combination of behavioral observations would suggest that the regulatory agency has responded to consumer interests and has successfully managed to squeeze producers.

Different behavior would be observed if producer interests dominate the regulatory agency, if the solution is at or close to that shown at E_m. As a

---

5. My colleague Robert Spann has developed an interesting model for the regulatory-legal process which incorporates the struggle between these opposing interests. See R. Spann, "Regulatory Capture" (Center for Study of Public Choice, Virginia Polytechnic Institute and State University, May 1974, typescript).

group, consumers would be roughly satisfied with the quantity and quality of services offered to them at the established prices; there would be no non-price rationing. There would be few, if any, service and installation delays. The personnel and the staff of the regulated firm would tend to be highly re-sponsive to demands made by consumers. There would be no observable de-terioration in quality of service. The behavior of potential investors would tend to corroborate the monopoly-solution hypothesis if attempts were made to enter product lines that are still under regulation. Profits would be prom-ised even under the nominally regulated umbrella, and investors would try to secure some of these opportunities.[6]

Careful empirical work could be helpful in testing these alternative hy-potheses, along with that which postulates the achievement of the practical regulator's solution at E. In the latter position, none of the behavioral char-acteristics listed above would be observed. Demanders would be satisfied with the services made available at the regulated price or rate; nonprice ra-tioning would not be observed in any of its forms. And there would be few attempts made by potential outside investors to secure profit opportunities within the industry, either within or without the confines of the regulated rate structure. If the existing position should be approximated by E, however, note that the conflicting pressures by producers and consumers would be unidirectional in the output dimension. Producers would seek increased al-lowable rates or prices which would insure a shift back along the demand curve with lowered quantities of output. Consumers' groups would seek lowered prices and rates, even at the predicted expense of reduced output, in effect shifts back along the average-cost curve. Because of this unidirection-ality of pressures in the quantity dimension, bias toward any expansion of output beyond the position defined by E in Figure 1 seems highly unlikely.

III. Inflationary Growth, Regulatory Lag, and the Bias Toward the Monopsony Solution

To this point, the analysis has been exclusively in terms of static models; implicitly, we have assumed that demand and cost conditions remain un-

---

6. To the extent that discrimination is observed, these behavioral implications could be tested against each class of consumers.

changed through time. When we introduce time into the analysis, predictable dominance of the monopsony bias emerges, given the direction of the external changes that may be observed.

Assume that at time T_0 the regulatory agency has successfully achieved what we have labeled its practical objective; it has reached a position defined by E in Figure 1, where both demanders and suppliers are in equilibrium. Superimpose on this position overall growth in the economy, either real growth or monetary growth reflected by general inflation. Defined in monetary units, both demand curves and cost curves will shift upward. To maintain the regulatory result, allowable rates or prices, designated in monetary units, would have to be adjusted upward continuously. But the process of regulation is itself time-consuming, and it is surely plausible to introduce some regulatory lag between the underlying change in economic conditions and the final adjustments in regulatory instruments. Over the period of this lag, prices or rates will be below the level required to return the system back to the situation that prevailed prior to the change in underlying conditions. Producers, owners, and managers of the regulated firms will, of course, seek to secure such adjustments. They will bring pressure to bear on the regulatory agency to increase allowable rates or prices.

Consumer group representatives will, however, be quite likely to oppose, and strenuously, any change in regulated prices, even in the face of the underlying economic pressures for increases. They may do so despite the fact that they fully recognize that maintenance of the old price or rate structure will insure disequilibrium in demand or consumption and, at the same time, may cause the producing firm to reduce its rate of output as it tries to get back on its average-cost curve. In effect, the maintenance of the old prices or rates in the face of underlying monetary growth becomes the means through which consumers' interests may successfully force the regulatory agency to move toward the monopsony solution. This result becomes more likely as the monetary growth continues through a succession of periods.[7]

The analysis itself is, of course, symmetrical. If the economy should ex-

---

7. As sketched out in these two paragraphs, we assume that the initial position is that shown by E in Figure 1 rather than the monopoly solution at E_m. If we make the assumption that, before the onset of the inflation, the monopoly solution prevails, regulatory lag will still have the effects indicated. Inflation must bias the regulatory process toward consumer rather than producer interests, regardless of the initial position.

perience a decline in real output or monetary deflation or both, with the result that both demand and cost curves shift downward, there is a bias toward the monopoly solution. In this case, regulatory lag will insure that prices or rates remain above those required to restore the *status quo ante* in real terms, a situation that the regulated firms will try to preserve and that consumer groups will try to prevent. But while the analysis, as such, is symmetrical, historical experience seems to be unidirectional. In the world of inflationary growth that we observe, the bias toward monopsony seems clear.

The results summarized above may be demonstrated geometrically with the aid of Figure 2, which is a variant on Figure 1, although readers who accept these results need not bother with the geometrical discussion. As noted, we assume that the initial position is at E. Inflationary growth occurs in the economy, pushing all incomes and nonregulated prices upward. Defined in money units, demand and cost curves shift upward, as shown by the displacements in Figure 2. At the old price P, both demanders and producers are in disequilibrium. The regulated firm will find it necessary to reduce output to Q′ in order to maintain an allowed rate of return on investment, in

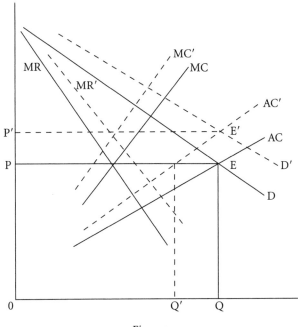

Figure 2

order to cover average costs, defined to include this normal rate. The consumers' lobby recognize this effect. But note that, at the output Q' along with the old price P, consumers, as a group, are in a much better position than they would be in the new market equilibrium position E', with price at P'. Ideally, of course, consumers might be best off at the more restricted monopsony solution, but, failing the achievement of this limit, they can secure gains, relative to full market adjustment, by remaining at the Q'P solution.

IV. Inflationary Growth, Regulatory Lag, and Possible Monopsony Expropriation of Asset Values

In the preceding section, I have discussed the inflation-induced bias toward the monopsony solution on the implicit presumption that the regulatory agency retains sufficient "protective" strength to insure that regulated firms secure a normal rate of return. The monopsony solution within this framework acts only to determine the rate of output along a given average cost schedule. Regulation does not, in this model, force the regulated firm off its own cost schedule.

In a more comprehensive model of possible consumer dominance, however, it is necessary to go beyond these restrictive limits. As noted, consumers, as a group, will press toward the monopsony solution, even if this forces demanders out of equilibrium and necessitates some form of nonprice rationing. Recognizing this, however, pressures may arise to force producers to meet all demands for its services or product at or near the monopsony price. In terms of Figure 1, price might be controlled at P_c, but the consumer-captured agency may, in the limit, try to force the regulated firm to meet all demands at this price, or to produce an output Q'_c.

The firm cannot, of course, long meet such requirements since it will find it impossible to raise sufficient capital for expanded investment, and it will also find that internal sources will be insufficient to finance replacement. If these results should be instantaneous, there need be little or no concern about this possible degree of monopsony expropriation of the regulated firm's assets. By the nature of capital investment, however, these effects take place through calendar time, and it may indeed be possible to force some such solution on the regulated firm so long as it is allowed to cover its average variable costs. Through quite lengthy adjustment periods, the regulatory agency may be able to "mine" the capital values of the regulated firm in the limit to expropriate fully these values to the benefit of short-term consumers of the firm's product or service.

Under stable conditions, this may not represent a danger. But under conditions of continuous and rapid inflation, this result may be much more likely, and for several reasons. If consumer groups are successful in freezing nominal prices of regulated firms during periods of inflation while forcing these firms to meet all demands, the expropriation of capital may occur without overt appearance of this taking place. Questions may be raised, however, concerning the genuine interests of consumers in such a result. Even if they succeed in fully capturing the regulatory agency, will consumers, as a group, find it to their interest to expropriate the capital value of the investment in regulated firms? Will not the maintenance of a viable industry in, say, twenty years in the future be of sufficient value to consumers to insure against the expropriation suggested as possible here? Whether or not this will or will not be the case depends partly on the rate of discount. There is no *a priori* reason to expect that fully rational consumer interests might not, under certain conditions, dictate the expropriation of the capital values of regulated firms.

This result would not emerge if future consumers' interests could somehow be counted alongside of those in the current consuming group. When we consider the political or public choice instruments through which consumer interests may possibly be expressed, however, the effective representation of future consumers' interests seems highly unlikely. Politicians who succeed in arousing general public attention concerning regulation, exemplified by Henry Howell in Virginia, are motivated by the prospect of securing political support in the here-and-now. Ralph Nader, who is a professional in consumerism, seeks to find his financial support from among those who are currently consumers, not from those in future years.

V. Efficiency Criteria for Regulated Firms

To this point, I have deliberately avoided discussion of the "ideal output" for the regulated monopoly firm, with "ideal" being defined in terms of the satisfaction of the necessary conditions for overall economic efficiency. While it seems clear that expropriation of asset values would not be part of an effi-

cient policy package, there is no necessary implication that the standard monopsony solution might not be preferred, on pure efficiency grounds, to that
which I have called the practical regulatory objective. The latter was defined
as that solution at which price is equated to average cost, including normal
return on investment, but no statement was made to the effect that this solution meets the norms of theoretical welfare economics. Entrance into this
sometimes murky domain cannot longer be postponed.

Return to the case of the regulated firm operating under increasing average costs in a period of stable economic conditions. Simplistic application of
the marginal-cost pricing norm would suggest that the ideal output is that
shown at Q_c in Figure 1, that which would result from monopsony direction
of the regulatory agency so long as expropriation of capital values does not
take place. This would suggest that the emergent pressures from consumers'
interest groups are, in the net, efficiency-promoting, despite the possible disequilibria that are generated. Note particularly that this monopsony solution
requires that demanders rather than suppliers be shifted out of equilibrium
adjustment, that price be set at P_c, with quantity Q_c, that the marginal evaluations of consumers exceed the allowed price.

In another version of the marginal-cost pricing norm, output Q_c would
be produced while consumers are charged P_{mc}, shown in Figure 3. In this
case, suppliers are shifted off their average-cost curves; excessive profits are
made in the industry and investment will seek to enter. The difference between these two pricing rules, both of which will generate ideal output, involves the identification of the rent recipients. In the one case, rents are
captured by consumers, the only result that consumer dominance of the
regulatory agency would countenance. In the other case, rents are captured
by the producers, a result that would, of course, be accepted by the firm, even
if it is less desirable than the monopoly profit-maximizing solution.

Under what conditions is the monopsony output, Q_c in Figure 1 or Figure
3, equivalent to that output which is socially optimal or efficient? Leaving
aside all second-best considerations, the answer to this question requires that
we examine the reasons for the increase in average costs as output increases.
If the expansion in output of the industry embodies the utilization of resources that are increasingly less specialized to the industry, average costs will
rise with output because of the increasing prices that inputs will command.
If the increase in average costs arises solely from this type of consideration,

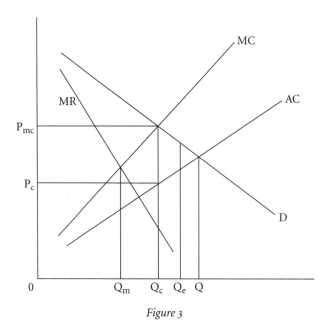

Figure 3

the efficient output is that defined by Q in Figures 1 and 3, not that defined by Q_c. *Social* marginal cost is, in this case, different from the marginal cost faced by the firm itself, since the latter will include transfer rents. In this model, the monopsony solution will clearly be nonoptimal.

On the other hand, if the regulated firm's average costs rise with output due to general scale factors, if it simply becomes more costly, in per unit terms, to produce larger and larger inputs, even at constant input prices, the marginal cost faced by the firm will be the same as marginal cost to society as a whole. If the increase in average costs arises solely from this source, the output which the nonexpropriating monopsonist control would dictate is socially optimal.[8]

---

8. The distinction between these two cost-increasing elements, along with the implications of these differences for efficiency in resource allocation, occupied the minds of leading neoclassical economists during the decades prior to World War II, and produced the most interesting controversy in economic theory over the interwar period. For a general summary discussion, see Howard Ellis and William Fellner, "External Economies and Diseconomies," *American Economic Review* 33 (September 1943): 493–511, reprinted in *Readings in Price Theory*, ed. G. Stigler and K. Boulding (Homewood: Richard D. Irwin,

In the real world, the increases in average costs that may be observed for a regulated firm probably involve a mix as between these two sources, which we may call pecuniary and technological. This would suggest that the omniscient regulatory agency, motivated solely by the true "public interest," and immune from constituency pressures, might aim for an ideally efficient output that would fall somewhere between that which I have called the practical regulators' objective and that which would result from the nonexpropriating monopsonist domination of the regulatory process, something like that shown as Q_e in Figure 3.[9] Almost surely, full adherence to the output level optimally preferred by the monopsonist would represent undue restrictiveness. By the same token, however, expansion of output of the maximum range required to keep both sides of the market in full adjustment would probably represent a socially inefficient level of production.[10]

VI. Conclusions

The analysis of this paper employs the elementary tools of price theory to show that in the political environment in which regulation must operate, the pressures generated by potential consumer interests may be symmetrical with those more familiar pressures from the owners and managers of regulated firms. Difficulties in monitoring producer performance, including difficulties in measuring genuine opportunity costs, may suggest a bias toward producer-benefiting regulatory adjustments. This may seem especially relevant when the reward-punishment structure for the regulatory bureaucrat is

---

1962), 242–63; and for a treatment specifically applicable to public utility pricing, see Dean A. Worcester, "Optimal Pricing Policy for Public Utilities as Optimal Taxation: Electric Power and Water," *Philippine Economic Journal* 7 (1969): 145–65.

9. If output Q_e is optimal (or any output less than Q), there still remains the question concerning disposition of rents. If demand price is set so as to allocate Q_e among demanders, producers will secure above-normal profits. If supply price is set so as to just insure the supply Q_e, consumers who secure allocations will receive rents, and those who are left out of the market secure nothing. The problems introduced when either side of the market is thrown out of equilibrium increase the attractiveness of what I have called the practical regulator's objective.

10. The final result of the neoclassical debate for competitive industries, as opposed to regulated firms, was agreement on the point that pecuniary elements tended to predominate, and, hence, that the output generated under competition, where prices equal average costs, would tend to be socially efficient.

incorporated into the analysis. This bias may, however, be offset at least in part by the larger number of consumers, who, when organized into and represented by pressure groups, possess significantly more political potential.

The critical factor in assessing the importance of consumer interests is organizational. Independently, the single consumer of the regulated firm's product or service has little or no incentive to engage in pressure-group or lobbying activity. And any attempt at organizing large groups will face continuing problems of securing cooperation and maintaining cohesion. To the extent that these basic organizational problems may be overcome, by an upsurge of "consumerism" as an intellectual-social fad or fashion, by governmentally sponsored "public interest" movements, by governmentally funded consumer advocates, by the success of political entrepreneurs who sense the vote potential of consumers, the monopsony pressures may become more significant in the regulatory climate of the late 1970's and 1980's.

Inflation, which has reluctantly but increasingly become accepted as a fact of American economic life, introduces a bias of its own toward the monopsony solution. Regulatory lag is a necessary part of the process, and the freezing of prices and rates during inflationary periods shifts any situation toward that desired by consumers.

At a minimum, regulatory agency bureaucrats, elected politicians, and consulting economists should recognize that the interests of consumers are not necessarily equivalent to those of the community at large. Regulatory agencies which come to respond exclusively to the demands of consumer interest groups may produce results that are, relatively, more efficient than those agencies which respond exclusively to the demands of the regulated firms. In both a conceptual and an actual sense, however, we should expect the regulatory agencies to produce results better than either of these constituency-dominated outcomes.

Appendix

Regulated Monopoly: Decreasing Costs

For completeness, it will be useful to examine the regulated firm that operates in the range of decreasing average costs. We impose the requirement that the demand curve cut the average-cost curve from above; this insures

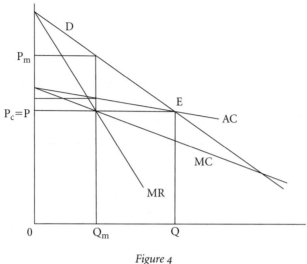

Figure 4

that the orthodox monopoly solution satisfies conditions for a maximum rather than a minimum.

Consider Figure 4, with the curves labeled as before. This model differs sharply from the increasing-cost case in that, here, the straightforward monopsony solution and the practical objective for the regulator become identical. The monopsony interests of consumers cannot be furthered by any restriction of output below that which will allow both producers and demanders to attain full adjustment equilibrium, the solution shown at E in Figure 4. Since average costs fall throughout the range of output, there is no producers' surplus which the monopsonist purchaser, or the agency representing this purchaser, can exploit. The monopsonist's criterion becomes the maximization of consumers' surplus, straightforwardly considered. The identity of solution as between the monopsonist and the practical regulator here partially explains the lack of attention to the monopsony solution in the increasing-cost case.

If the consumer-dominated agency goes beyond the simple monopsony solution, however, and seeks to expropriate the capital values of the regulated firm, there is nothing in the decreasing-costs situation to prevent this from occurring. The firm may, as in the increasing-cost case, be forced to operate below long-run average costs so long as variable outlays are covered.

In Defense of Advertising Cartels

Monopoly, Competition, and Allocative Efficiency

If a monopoly is able to discriminate perfectly among its customers and over various quantities to each separate customer, profit-maximization criteria will cause it to produce an output that meets the conditions for Pareto optimality, or efficiency, in resource use. Considered in isolation, the monopoly will in these circumstances employ just the proper amount of resources relative to the rest of the economy. There will be no monopoly-induced restriction of product. Monopoly of this nature generates no allocative distortions. The perfectly discriminating monopolist may, of course, be able to secure a share of real income that violates distributional objectives, but economists have found it analytically useful to separate the distributional issues from the allocative ones.

Monopoly creates allocative distortions only when it is unable to discriminate perfectly. If it cannot, for reasons of product characteristics or of institutional rules, squeeze out the surplus benefits secured by customers over all ranges of output, profit-maximization criteria will dictate overt restriction of output for the purpose of increasing product price. Considered in isolation, the monopoly will under these circumstances employ too few resources relative to the rest of the economy; its output will remain below efficient levels. Overall efficiency criteria would dictate a relative expansion in the monopolist's output.

Institutions have been deliberately invented or have been allowed naturally to emerge that are designed to insure against such monopoly restrictions. If the single monopoly is replaced by a sufficient number of separate

From *Pubblicita e Televizione* (Rome: RAI, 1969), 84–93. Reprinted by permission.

sellers, no single producer-seller acting independently has an incentive to restrict output. Even though the ability to discriminate is absent, the independent behavior of the separate sellers will remove the allocative distortions of monopoly. When the critically required number of sellers is attained, economists refer to the industrial structure as "competitive." This structure tends to produce overall efficiency in resource allocation, provided that each industry is treated in isolation and, also, provided that other possibly complicating requirements can be neglected.

In an effectively working competitive structure, no single seller finds it advantageous to restrict output in order to achieve a higher selling price. Profit-maximization criteria dictate that output decisions be made independent of price-effect considerations. For the group of sellers in an industry, treated as a whole, however, no such results apply. If collusion among all these sellers could be implemented, *all* sellers in an industry would find it advantageous to join in an agreement to restrict output. Pressures for such cartelization will always be present, and public policy norms suggest that institutional rules be established which prevent such agreements from being realized. Allocative efficiency alone demands that cartel agreements among separate firms on pricing, output, and market-sharing be prohibited, and, if such agreements should arise, that they be non-enforceable.

Allocative Efficiency and Selling Activity

The summary analysis above implicitly assumes that potential customers are fully informed about the product of either the monopoly or the competitive firms. No attention is paid in the textbook-like summary to the potential productivity of investment in selling the product, in making potential customers aware of a product's existence, aware of the "true" benefits that they might receive from its purchase. This represents a gap in traditional economic analysis that has never been satisfactorily closed. The question may be put as follows: In order to satisfy the necessary conditions for efficiency, how many resources should be devoted to selling a product?

The answer must be sought in the same way as that advanced for the more familiar allocation problem. The institutional or organizational structure that produces results must be examined, not the results as such. Lacking omniscient insight into the preference functions of individuals, the economist must try to define efficiency criteria in terms of the efficacy of institutional structures in meeting individuals' desires, whatever these might be.

When the question is approached in this fashion, the answer turns out to be identical with that provided for the similar question with respect to output. Some repetition is suggested. Considered in isolation, if a monopoly is able to discriminate perfectly among its customers and over various quantities to each separate customer, profit-maximization criteria will cause it to invest resources in selling that will meet the conditions for Pareto optimality, or efficiency. Under such circumstances, an efficient allocation of resources to marketing the product, in all forms, will be insured, along with the accompanying efficient allocation of resources to producing the product so marketed.

This elementary allocative principle provides a benchmark from which further analysis can proceed. Again the summary analysis of the first section can be followed. Considered in isolation, if a monopoly is unable to discriminate perfectly, profit-maximization criteria will cause resource allocation to selling-marketing activity to fall below optimal, or efficient, levels. The reason is basically the same as that which explains why output is restricted. If the monopoly is unable to secure the full effects of its marketing investment, measured by the increased customer evaluation of its product, it will necessarily make less investment than it would where such full exploitation is possible. This conclusion applies even when the monopoly succeeds in reducing output below efficient levels; for whatever output he markets, the non-discriminating monopolist will invest relatively too few resources in marketing because of his inability to capture the full effects of his investment.

If the monopoly is replaced by a sufficient number of sellers, the incentive to reduce output is removed for each single seller. The allocative distortions stemming from monopolistic output restriction disappear. But what about resource allocation to marketing and selling the product?

Competition and Advertising

In the elementary textbook setting of perfect competition, information is also perfect. All potential customers know all that there is to know about products. No single firm has an incentive to invest resources in overt selling efforts. This provides the basis for the conclusion that in genuine competition *no* advertising would be observed.

Even without perfect information, this structure of industry may be approached when the product is highly standardized, as, for example, with certain basic agricultural goods. In industries like this, no single producer-seller has much incentive either to restrict his own output for price-influencing reasons or to engage in overt marketing activity. Each seller is both a price-taker and a market-taker; no seller is either a price-maker or a demand-maker.

In such a situation it would, nonetheless, be to the interest of *all* sellers to enter into enforceable cartel agreements, both to restrict output *and* to contribute toward investment in marketing, in advertising. To this point, the pricing and selling aspects of competitive industry are behaviorally identical. Sharp differences emerge, however, when other, non-selling, members of the community are included. As noted earlier, the competitive industrial structure tends to produce allocative efficiency, and hence the community should try to prevent monopolistic or cartel behavior which restricts output or increases selling price. The behavior will benefit the selling firms in an industry, but it will harm the economy considered as a whole. Allocative distortions will emerge. Therefore, output-restricting, price-fixing activity can be deemed socially undesirable, quite apart from distributional considerations.

The behavior of firms in selling activity cannot be similarly condemned. The potential cartelization of a competitive industry in order to promote the industry's product, apart from other cartel objectives, will not be inefficient. Selling firms in the industry will secure benefits, and other members of the community will not be harmed, at least in any direct sense comparable to that generated by output-restricting behavior. If each industry is treated in isolation, any agreement by selling firms to engage cooperatively in advertising the whole industry's product marks a shift toward rather than away from the satisfaction of the overall conditions of efficiency in the use of the economy's resources.

Competitive Monopoly and Monopolistic Competition

The analysis becomes much more complex with industrial structures that fall between the poles of effective competition among many sellers on the one hand and a single monopolist on the other. The general indeterminacy of the predictive models for such structures is familiar to all economists. The predictions about resource investment in demand-increasing activity are no exception to this pattern.

The first point to be noted is that in any in-between industrial structure each seller has *some* elements of monopoly. In the technical jargon of economics, each seller confronts a downsloping demand curve for his output. Hence, each seller is, within limits, both a potential price-maker and a potential market-maker for his own product. Profit-maximization will lead each seller to invest resources in advertising, in selling activity generally.

If we analyze the situation of each seller *in isolation,* the conclusions reached earlier with respect to the monopolist are valid. Unless he is able to discriminate perfectly, the single seller will underinvest in marketing because he cannot fully exploit the incremental consumer evaluation that his activity creates. At this point, however, the model becomes absurd because it is patently obvious that *a single seller cannot be treated in isolation* from other sellers in the same broad industrial category. With the earlier models of either competitive or monopolized industries, the treatment of one industry in isolation from another is legitimate, within limits, despite the general interdependence of the whole economy. But within a single industry composed of separate quasi-competitive, quasi-monopolistic selling units, the treatment of each unit's behavior in isolation is not acceptable. Any results obtained from such partial analysis must be jettisoned. The effects of one seller's behavior on the circumstances of his competitors in the industry must be explicitly taken into account.

Overinvestment in Advertising

The interdependence among the separate firms in an industry with respect to demand-increasing or selling activity must be specifically examined. Acting independently, a firm will carry its own investment in such activity to the point where expected returns are equated with those stemming from other activities within its control, including the extension of production. Investment in marketing is productive to the firm because it increases potential purchasers' knowledge about, awareness of, and valuation of its product. The demand curve faced by the firm is shifted outwards as a result of its selling efforts.

What effect does this sort of activity by a single firm have on the position of other firms in the same industrial category? As one firm increases the demand for its own product, potential demand for its rivals' products may be reduced. To the extent that this takes place, the increased valuation placed on the one firm's product represents decreased valuation on others' products. To this extent, therefore, advertising activity is analogous to engaging in a zero-sum game. While it continues to be rational for each firm, taken separately, to engage in the activity, it becomes advantageous for *each* firm in the whole industry to join in an enforceable cartel agreement to restrict such activity. And, in this case, there are no offsetting damages to the rest of the community, at least in any direct sense. It follows, therefore, that the proposal for allowing cartel agreements remains desirable for these in-between industrial structures, even though the agreements now might take the form of restrictions on investment. The contrast between the advertising-selling cartel and the output-restricting cartel should again be stressed. With the former, there is no community interest in forcing sellers to remain in the "prisoners' dilemma" situation they confront under independent behavior. With the latter, there is an important community interest, based strictly on efficiency criteria, in keeping selling firms as close as is possible to the competitive "prisoners' dilemma."

The Advertising Cartel

The analysis suggests that in all cases firms in specified industrial categories should be allowed to join enforceable cartel agreements with respect to marketing activity generally, and to advertising standards and outlay in particular. This conclusion is based on the recognition that allocative gains are to be expected from industry-wide promotion campaigns in fully competitive industries and that no allocative gains result from excessively competitive selling activity in oligopolistic industries. Further, the specific policy device embodies the corollary acknowledgement that there exists no means through which a detached observer, or expert, can determine when, in fact, demand-increasing activity is either too small or too large. Observed agreement among the separate units of an industry provides the only criterion for judgment here. Cartel agreements may lead either to an increase or a reduction in marketing effort. In the highly competitive structure, where there are many firms producing highly standardized goods, a cartel would tend to result in an expansion in marketing investment. In the industry that is characterized by many separate firms each selling a differentiated, brand-named, product, cartels may result in modifications in the form of marketing activity, with a reduction of emphasis on brands and an expansion of emphasis on product category. In the industry with only a few major producers, advertising outlay would probably be substantially reduced by cartel arrangements.

In no cases would cartel agreements be predicted to reduce advertising-selling activity to zero. At the absolute limit, a cartel agreement would reduce selling activity to the level which a monopolist would find advantageous. If, however, cartels are not allowed to function with respect to output or price, the industry output will be higher than it would be under a monopoly. Hence, total outlay on advertising should normally be expected to be somewhat in excess of that which would be present under an industrial structure characterized by the non-discriminating monopolist.

The advantage of the cartel agreement, as the institutional device for encouraging efficient resource investment in demand-increasing effort, whether this be in an expansionary or a contractionary direction, lies in the reliance that is placed on the decisions made by participants in the industry itself. Investment that is advantageous to the industry as a whole will tend to be approved; mutually cancelling efforts will tend to be eliminated. The achievement of efficient results, within tolerable limits, is attained without the necessity of calling upon the advice of "expert" outsiders, the bureaucrats or the politicians, in determining when demand-increasing investment is too small or too large. The result is attained *institutionally*, and there is no requirement that efficiency be defined independent of the choice-making of individual units in the economy.

Problems in Cartel Operation, I: Output Restriction, Market Sharing, and Price Fixing

There are several important difficulties presented by the proposal to allow and to encourage the formation of advertising-marketing cartels. The first of these may be dealt with briefly. If the separate selling firms in an industry are allowed and encouraged to enter into enforceable cartel agreements for the purpose of setting industry-wide standards and levels of advertising and marketing investment, the task of preventing these same firms from entering similarly organized cartel arrangements for output restriction, market sharing, and price fixing is made more difficult. In addition, even if firms are prevented from participating in explicit cartel agreements of these types, the same objectives may be secured indirectly through the specification of marketing-advertising standards. The problems involved in limiting cartel agreements must be acknowledged, but these are common to trade association generally, and they are not peculiar to the specific proposal advanced here. In partial response, it could be argued that if regulatory agencies could redirect some of their efforts at controlling advertising, they would be able to release resources into a more effective policing against those forms of cartel agreements that violate allocative norms.

Problems in Cartel Operation, II:
Internal Decision-Making Rules

The cartel proposal is based in the recognition of the dilemma that *each* firm (either in the many-firm, homogeneous-product industry or in a few-firm, differentiated-product industry) finds itself in with respect to its own investment in demand-increasing activity. It is potentially advantageous for each firm to enter into a cartel agreement as compared with its position in the absence of such agreement. However, as once again the analogue with the familiar "prisoners' dilemma" makes evident, a single firm will consider itself to be still better off if it can secure a result where *all other firms* reach agreement while it remains free to act as it pleases. This applies whether or not the cartel results in a higher or lower overall marketing investment in the industry. To the single grapefruit farmer in California, his most advantageous position is attained when all other grapefruit farmers join in and contribute to a cooperative advertising-promotion scheme while he remains outside, contributing nothing. To the single detergent-producing firm, its most advantageous position is one in which all other detergent producers agree to restrict advertising while it remains free to invest resources at will in this sort of activity.

This problem, which is identical to that discussed under the name "free rider problem" in public-goods theory, prevents any wholly voluntaristic solution to the organizational-constitutional aspects of cartel formation. Despite the acknowledged gains to *all* potential participants, cartel agreements of the sort discussed here cannot necessarily be predicted to emerge, even in the presence of governmental encouragement. And, if such agreements should emerge, they cannot be predicted to be stable. By necessity, therefore, something more than a passive role for public policy is suggested at this point. Firms must be placed in a situation where they can consider only two options: The absence of any industry-wide cartel agreement, or the presence of such an agreement which includes *all* units in the industry. Governmental sanctions against partial agreements may be applied, but the necessity that all firms must participate if a cartel is to be organized raises difficult issues of decision making.

When is a cartel agreement to be enforced for an industry? Ideally, of course, since all units in an industry must participate, there should be an expressed willingness to join on the part of each firm. A unanimity rule, even at the organizational stage, is scarcely workable, however, since a single recalcitrant firm could prevent any agreement being made. To forestall this possibility, some departure from the rule of unanimity must be accepted, despite the obvious costs in equity and in efficiency. There is no need for the effective decision rule to be reduced to one of simple majority, and there are probably strong reasons for making the final rule for decision much more inclusive than this. One such rule might be as follows: When three-fourths of the units in an industry agree to join in an industry-wide cartel with respect to demand-increasing activity, the cartel shall be formed and its rules enforced for *all* firms in the industry, including those who do not initially agree. This qualified majority rule (which might equally have been suggested as one requiring the agreement of two-thirds, five-sixths, or seven-eighths) insures against the undue obstruction of the "anti-group" deviant while tending to advance genuine group interests.

The decision-rule problems discussed to this point will arise even if an industry contains firms that are identical in size and other relevant economic characteristics. When the presence of firms of differing size and differing economic characteristics is allowed, additional decision-rule complexities appear. How is a voting unit to be defined? Systems of voting weights must be introduced, systems that reasonably reflect the relative economic interests of the group's separate units. The determination of these weights, along with the determination of the voting rule itself, can hardly be expected to be settled voluntaristically. The government must assume a positive role here, and these "constitutional" elements of the potential cartel arrangements imposed from the outside. Governmental decisions should, of course, be based upon and informed by a full knowledge of the industry. The aim must be that of providing a quasi-legal framework within which internal agreements can be made and enforced, hence reducing to a minimum the range for arbitrary governmental action.

Problems in Cartel Operation, III: New Entry

To this point, discussion has been based on the "as if" assumption that each industry is composed of an existing set of separate selling-producing units. This is severely at odds with real-world industrial structures, and the analysis must be extended to allow for the entry and egress of firms from an industry. In the preceding section, stress was placed on the necessity of including all firms in the potential cartel agreement on the expansion of limiting demand-increasing effort. Strictly interpreted, this would imply that one condition for entry into an industry would be membership in the cartel along with adherence to its standards.

Such a condition would place the newcomer at a severe competitive disadvantage in all in-between industrial structures. It is precisely the new firm that must create its own demand, and if a cartel agreement limiting advertising should be applied alike to existing and to new firms, a genuine barrier to entry would be insured. Entry of new firms in response to potential profit prospects is, however, recognized to be one of the most effective means of promoting allocative efficiency in a changing economy. Any institution that inhibits entry must be subjected to critical scrutiny.

It seems evident that the cartel rules cannot be applied to the new entrant in an industry, even when it is recognized that each new entrant must secure some of its own demand at the expense of the demand of existing firms. The allocative gains promised by the ease of entry probably outweigh this potentially wasteful demand-shifting. But the whole thing can be turned over. The very fact that new entrants can be explicitly exempted from cartel participation may be used as a device for enhancing entry. The productivity of demand-increasing investment by a new entrant will be higher in the face of an existing cartel agreement among existing firms than it would be in the absence of such an agreement. The exemption cannot, of course, be permanent. And once again, a positive role for governmental policy is suggested.

For each industry, a specific length of exemption period can be imposed, with this depending on particular characteristics of the industry.

When and if existing firms recognize that potential entrants are to be exempted from the cartel rules, they will be somewhat less willing to organize cartels in the first place, and, once organized, they will be less willing to impose restrictive rules. This trade-off must be acknowledged, and in industries where entry is relatively easy, no cartel agreements may emerge. It is precisely in such industries, however, where the length of the exemption period should be short, and, in the limit, non-existent. A policy of uniform exemption periods over all industries would clearly be grossly inefficient. There is no escaping the necessity for a careful weighing of the trade-off prospects on an industry-by-industry basis and the imposition of varying exemption periods.

Problems in Cartel Operation, IV: Interindustry Interaction

Strictly considered, the analysis and policy suggestions advanced above are valid only if the separate industrial categories are rather sharply distinct one from the other. Only under such circumstances is it legitimate to consider a single industry in isolation from other parts of the total economy. Economists are familiar with the dangers of overly facile use of partial analysis to reach general conclusions. In a very real sense, all parts of a national economy are interdependent. For some purposes, these chains of interdependence may be neglected, but they can never be wholly forgotten. All industries are in competition for the expenditures of consumers. Additional purchasing power allocated by the consumer to one product category reflects a reduction in purchasing power allocated to other product categories. To an extent, therefore, any demand-increasing activity, even that carried out by the monopolist or by the industry-wide cartel, may be "wasteful" in the same sense that was shown to be relevant for the separate firms in a single industry. In the general setting of the whole economy, the benchmark for allocation initially introduced, the selling effort of the perfectly discriminating monopolist, is not fully acceptable.

What new benchmark or standard can be introduced in its stead? There is no proper answer to this question. It is important to see why this is true.

A preliminary reaction might suggest that because the total income that is available to the consumers in the economy must be spent on goods and services any investment of resources aimed at shifting demand around among the many separate products and services must, in the net, be wasteful. Such an inference would be wholly incorrect because it fails to take into account the elementary fact that income in a market economy is measured in terms of the *values* that individuals place on goods and services, expressed by their behavior as buyers and sellers in the marketplace. Once this point is accepted, it becomes clear that there exists no uniquely determinate or fixed level of income that may be produced by the resources and the skills available in an economy, even if varying rates of resource use are neglected. Any activity that increases buyers' evaluation of goods is productive of real income, just as much so as an activity that increases the physical supply of goods. It seems reasonably certain that real income would be lower in an economy where marketing investment is severely and arbitrarily curtailed than it would be in an economy where such investment is allowed to take place.

Nonetheless, excessive demand-increasing effort is a possibility, even if controlled by industry-wide cartel agreements. If industry classifications are such that closely related products, good substitutes for each other in the choice patterns of consumers, are separately organized, an argument can be made for extending the scope of cartel arrangements. In defining the appropriate industrial groupings for purposes of encouraging and facilitating cartel agreements on advertising and sales promotion, account must be taken of inter-product substitutability. If care is taken in making these classifications, the cartel device remains probably the most effective means of insuring that total investment in demand-increasing activity will come tolerably close to that which meets overall efficiency criteria.

Conclusions

This essay is entitled "In Defense of Advertising Cartels." This title was deliberately chosen for the purpose of emphasizing the categorical distinction between the effects of cartel agreements on output and price and those on marketing. The purpose is not one of advocating a specific and detailed policy program with respect to advertising and sales promotion. The analysis along with the policy suggestions is designed to provide an approach to the whole set of issues that emerge in this highly controversial sector of the modern economy. With respect to the advertising and marketing methods that are currently observed in Western economies, the analysis is intended to provide neither an apology nor a defense. These institutions probably embody both efficient and inefficient elements; they serve to increase real income at the same time that they generate waste. They cannot be, and should not be, either praised or condemned in blanket terms. It would indeed be surprising if any existing set of institutions should exhibit either full efficiency or complete waste.

The problem is, as always, that of isolating the efficiency-increasing aspects of modern advertising and marketing from the efficiency-reducing aspects. My emphasis here has been on the impossibility of "expert" discrimination; any bureaucratic set of rules must be largely arbitrary. The approach suggested involves using the choices of participants who are directly engaged to produce the necessary discrimination between efficient and wasteful effort. This seems preferable to using the choices of the politicians. In order that this approach can be implemented, the institutions within which choices are made must be reconstituted so that tolerably efficient outcomes can be predicted to more or less automatically emerge. The suggested modification of the industrial structure to allow for governmental encouragement of industry-wide cartel agreements on marketing methods, standards, and investment typifies one outcome of the approach that is recommended. More careful and critical examination may reveal that the specific institutional change proposed is undesirable. In the process of such an inquiry, however, still other and perhaps more workable institutional rearrangements might suggest themselves.

Reform in the Rent-Seeking Society

Rent seeking involves social waste. Resources that could otherwise be devoted to value-producing activity are engaged in competitive effort that determines nothing other than the *distributive* results. Rent seeking, as such, is totally without allocative value, although, of course, the initial institutional creation of an opportunity for rent seeking ensures a net destruction of economic value. The distributive results are, nonetheless, important when we come to examine the political prospects for the institutional-legal changes that might be required to reduce the scope for rent seeking in modern society.

The community, the aggregate of persons in the defined political unit, loses value in two respects. First, there is the destruction of value when the initial decision is somehow made to create artificial scarcity and thereby to make possible rents over and above competitively determined rates of return to resource use. In the diagrams of basic price theory, this loss is measured by the familiar welfare triangles. Second, as the analyses contained in this volume have demonstrated, there is the loss reflected in the competitive struggles for the capture of the net rents made possible by the artificial scarcity. The appropriate measure for this second loss of value is less certain. Several contributors to this volume argue that this loss is measured approximately by the rents themselves, an argument based on the supposition that the rate of return on efforts to secure rents will itself be adjusted to rate of return elsewhere in the economy. As Tullock's paper on efficient rent seeking suggests, however, this equalization of rates of return between rent seeking

From *Toward a Theory of the Rent-Seeking Society*, ed. James M. Buchanan, Robert D. Tollison, and Gordon Tullock (College Station: Texas A&M University Press, 1980), 359–67. Reprinted by permission of the publisher.

and other economic investment does not necessarily emerge in some institutional settings.

In this concluding essay, my concern is not with the measure of the opportunity losses that the creation and the maintenance of rent-seeking institutions impose on the community. For my purposes, it is sufficient that these losses be acknowledged to exist and that they are or may be significant. My concern is with the prospect for community or collective action aimed at reforming the institutional structure so as to reduce or eliminate the opportunities for rent-seeking behavior. I shall demonstrate that the required shift from a set of inefficiency-generating to a set of efficiency-generating institutions may be particularly difficult to accomplish in a rent-seeking environment, relative to other settings that may generate comparable inefficiency.

Elementary Principles of Welfare Economics

It is helpful to commence with a brief review of some elementary principles of welfare economics. If an existing situation is shown to be "inefficient," by the standard meaning of this term, there must exist a means of moving from such a situation to one that is "efficient," with gains to at least one person in the community and without loss to anyone. To implement such a change, it may be necessary that the net gainers compensate the net losers, particularly if the potential losers must agree to any change before it is made effective. If we interpret the working of democratic process to require consensus on deliberately organized collective decisions involving major institutional change, the prospects for accomplishing efficiency-improving changes depend critically on the prospects for organizing the required compensations for the net losers.

If there are no net losers from a prospective change, if everyone is a net gainer, it seems evident that the prospects for collective agreement on a change aimed at eliminating an institutional barrier to efficiency should be relatively high. Even here, however, we should note that collective agreement may be required. Individuals acting independently cannot implement the changes needed, and within unchanged institutional structures, rational individual behavior may continue to be that which generates overall results that may be judged to be inefficient.

One way of classifying or describing this setting of interaction is to say that the net gains and losses are symmetrical over the different persons or players.

The Classic Prisoners' Dilemma as a Fully Symmetrical Payoff Structure

A familiar example is provided in the classic prisoners' dilemma, where the two persons involved are assumed to be identical in payoffs, whether these be positive or negative in the construction as presented. The structure of the game is such that both persons are led to behave in such a manner as to produce a "solution," where the payoffs to each person are lower than the payoff that could be secured from a joint and binding agreement to behave differently, hence to generate a different joint outcome. Figure 22.1 illustrates the familiar game here. Cell IV is, of course, the solution if the players are forced to play the game. Cell I is the efficient solution, on the assumption that A and B are the only members of the relevant community. Hence, a joint and

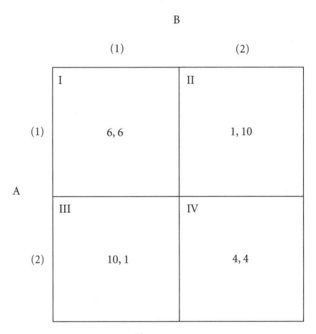

Figure 22.1

binding agreement between *A* and *B* that involves each person in strategy (1) should be easy to secure.

A Prisoners' Dilemma with Nonsymmetrical Payoffs

Although less attention seems to have been devoted to it, most interactions that exhibit characteristics described by the prisoners' dilemma involve non-symmetrical rather than symmetrical payoff structures. Players are not identical with respect to anticipated payoffs, whether these be negative or positive in absolute value. This absence of symmetry in payoffs is not relevant for my purposes here, except to the extent that it modifies the relative ranking of the individual payoffs in the differing cells of the matrix. In the illustration of figure 22.1, for example, both persons receive higher payoffs in cell I than in cell IV. So long as this relationship within individual orderings holds, there can exist some differentials between the absolute value of individual payoffs without modifying the structure.

Consider figure 22.2, however, where the asymmetry introduced violates this condition. Note that the payoff for *A* is now lower in cell I than in cell IV, the "solution," despite the fact that the combined payoffs are higher in cell I than they are in cell IV. That is to say, cell I remains the "efficient" outcome in the standard sense. Note that row and column dominance still exists, ensuring that the solution under simple strategy is still cell IV.

When we examine the prospect for getting agreement on a proposed commitment to a behavioral change, a significant difference emerges between this game and that depicted in figure 22.1. Until and unless individual *B* makes a side payment or compensation to individual *A*, outside of and beyond the activity represented in the game itself, individual *A* will not agree to any change from the cell IV outcome, nor will he agree to modify the rules establishing the game. Gains-from-trade between the two players will continue to exist, but the exploitation of these gains requires side payments. No such side payments are required in the game of figure 22.1; agreement can be limited to the parameters defined by the activities that take place within the game. Agreement clearly seems more readily attainable in a game like that shown in figure 22.1 than in that shown in figure 22.2.

B

(1)   (2)

	(1)	(2)
(1)	I 5, 7	II −1, 8
A		
(2)	III 8, −1	IV 8, 0

Figure 22.2

Application to Rent Seeking

Rent-seeking "games" are of the nonsymmetrical, second type. There are "winners" as well as "losers," and the problem of getting consensus on institutional change to eliminate such games is relatively much greater than in other "games" that economists play at discussing. It is necessary, however, to distinguish carefully between symmetry and nonsymmetry in the ex ante and the ex post sense. Games that are symmetrical in the ex ante sense of expected payoffs may be nonsymmetrical in the ex post sense of realized payoffs. Consider the game depicted in figure 22.3; the payoffs in cell IV are (8, 0 or 0, 8), with the players having only a probabilistic expectation as to which one of these results will emerge. Note that in this formulation the game becomes symmetrical ex ante. Expected payoffs are identical as between the two players.

Suppose, however, that once the initial round has been played the payoff structure is fixed. Ex post, the structure is nonsymmetrical, and this structure

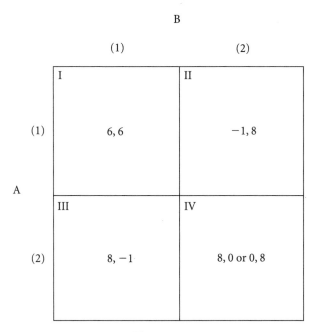

Figure 22.3

is assumed to be anticipated for the continuing sequence of rounds subsequent to the initial one. The cell IV solution will continue to emerge; the relative "loser," *B* in the example if the payoff emerges as (8, 0), cannot do better by changing his behavior within the game itself. But, when consideration for a rules change occurs, when the prospect for eliminating the game arises, the game depicted becomes analogous in all respects to that depicted in figure 22.2. Gains-from-trade exist, but the exploitation of these will require side payments outside behavior in the game itself.

With rent seeking, however, it may be particularly difficult to get agreement on such side payments. Individual *B*, the "loser," may be extremely reluctant to acknowledge the "entitlement" that individual *A* seems to have secured in the nonsymmetrical game. The loser, *B*, may be able to observe that he has himself "invested" the same resources as *A*, the winner. The latter has merely been lucky in getting the relatively higher payoff, but does luck establish moral claim?

This reluctance on the part of losers in rent seeking to make the side payments or compensations that may be required becomes more intense if they think that the winners rigged the game from the outset, that is, if they think that the payoff structure was nonsymmetrical even in the ex ante sense.

Piecemeal versus Generalized Agreement

The simple exercises here serve to demonstrate a point that has long been familiar in the theory of economic policy. Attempts to eliminate efficiency-reducing institutional barriers to trade, which include all rent-seeking opportunities, are likely to founder if they are approached piecemeal, or one at a time. Those persons and groups who have established what they consider to be entitlements in the positive gains that have been artificially created will not agree to change, and those persons and groups who suffer losses will not willingly pay off what they consider to be immoral gainers. This moral barrier to agreement does not depend on the existence of positive transactions costs or on the relative disparity in the sizes of the members on the two sides of the potential transaction, an argument often adduced in this connection. Even if transactions costs are zero, the difficulty remains.

As more and more efficiency-reducing institutions come to be established, however, as more and more opportunities for rent-seeking behavior are opened up, resolution may become easier rather than harder. General agreement on major constitutional change may prove easier to attain than piecemeal agreement on changes made separately. Constitutional rather than legislative change may be possible. Whereas no single set of winners will acquiesce in relinquishing their own gains without full compensation, many groups may, simultaneously, agree to a generalized elimination of all rent-seeking opportunities, since, by so doing, each group gains more than it loses in net.

In order for such a "constitutional revolution" to become possible, however, it is necessary that the evolution of rent seeking take the form of different groups of winners in each new establishment of artificial scarcity. If the *same* group in the community become winners in each and every extension of rent seeking, losers may cease to play. They may reduce investment in rent seeking, but, at the same time, they may reject the increasingly disparate distributional outcomes. At some point, the search for agreement upon change

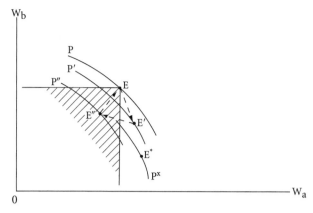

Figure 22.4

will also cease, and prospects for "nonconstitutional revolution" emerge to replace those for its more orderly counterpart.

These points are familiar, but it may be useful to illustrate them geometrically with a construction introduced by Robert Tollison.[1] Consider figure 22.4, where the wealth positions of two persons, A and B, are measured along the abscissa and ordinate respectively. P depicts the possibility frontier, and E is the fully efficient initial position. Assume that the introduction of what we may call symmetrical inefficiency pushes the position inward to any point within the shaded area. In such cases, as noted, agreement to return to E should be relatively easy to secure.

Suppose, however, that rent-seeking institutions emerge, and that the two-person group shifts to a position like that shown at E', on a new and lower frontier, P'. Note that in this shift individual A's position has been improved, but that of B has been damaged. Gains-from-trade exist at E', but to exploit these, B must first acknowledge A's net entitlement.

Suppose, now, that at a second stage in the evolution of rent seeking, individual B succeeds in winning a new and different game, shifting the frontier inward to P'', and to the position E''. Note that, at E'', an agreement can

1. Robert D. Tollison, "The Prospect for Liberal Democracy: Comments," in *Fiscal Responsibility in Constitutional Democracy*, ed. James M. Buchanan and Richard E. Wagner (Boston: Martinus Nijhoff Social Science Division, 1978), 177–80.

be reached to shift back to E, with gains to both parties and *without* the necessity of side payments or compensations outside the activities that are depicted in the game itself. The "constitutional revolution" is depicted by the shift from E'' back to E.

In a less hopeful scenario, however, suppose that the second stage in the evolution of rent seeking shifts the group from E' to, say, E^*, with individual A securing still further improvement in his own position at the expense of individual B. At E^*, exploitation of the gains-from-trade required to shift back toward the frontier becomes more rather than less difficult to implement than at E'. The distributional disparities all but overwhelm the importance of the allocative gains. The stage is thereby set for "nonconstitutional revolution."

Reform in the rent-seeking society depends critically on the history of its evolution, as well as upon the ability of political and intellectual leaders to think in terms of, and be persuasive about, general constitutional changes in the whole structure of social and economic institutions. The classic American syndromes, incrementalism and pragmatism, must be nonstarters in this search.

PART SIX

Regulation

The Politicization of Market Failure

James M. Buchanan and Viktor J. Vanberg

Furthermore, there is no reason to suppose that the . . . regulations, made by a fallible administration subject to political pressures . . . , will necessarily always be those which increase the efficiency with which the economic system operates. . . . But equally there is no reason, why, on occasion, such governmental administrative regulation should not lead to an improvement in economic efficiency. This would seem particularly likely when, as is normally the case with the smoke nuisance, a large number of people are involved and in which therefore the costs of handling the problem through the market or the firm may be high.

—R. H. Coase, 1975, "The Problem of Social Cost"

1. Introduction

Much of the externality literature has concentrated on the issue of whether or not what is diagnosed as "market failure" requires politically orchestrated correction and, if so, what the appropriate political measures *should* be. Far less often the question has been asked of what kind of "corrections" the political process can actually be expected to generate if a politicization of market failure occurs. Our purpose in this paper is to address just this question, though in the confines of a highly stylized and simplified model of both, of the externality generating economic process and of the political decision-

From *Public Choice* 57 (May 1988): 101–13. Reprinted by permission of the publisher, Kluwer Academic Publishers.

Paper presented at Public Choice Society Meetings, 27–29 March 1987, Tucson, Arizona.

making process. In the context of our analysis we will find it useful to differentiate between two cases which the standard interpretation of the external effects notion tends to lump together. While the "external" is normally understood as meaning *external* to the contracting parties, we will make an explicit distinction between what we call "internal" and "external" externalities. As *internal externalities* we classify those effects that are *external* to a given contractual relation but *internal* to the group of contracting parties. As *external externalities* we classify those that are external to both, to the respective transaction and to the group of contractors.

2. Private and Political Responses to Externalities

To "correct" for a negative externality is normally understood as making those parties who decide on the externality-causing activity to account for the negative impact on third parties as a *cost* in their decision making. In Pigovian terms, correction means that the decision makers take the full *social costs* of their choice into account. Such "correction" can, in principle, result from *private* as well as from *political* responses to externalities. The general principles of private correction have been lucidly analyzed in Coase's seminal "The Problem of Social Cost." As Coase pointed out, in the absence of transaction costs the damage done to a third, nonconsenting, party will in any case show up as an opportunity cost in an economic actor's calculation, whether he can be held liable in the existing legal system or not. The difference is only in the particular form these opportunity costs take. If he is liable it will be in the form of damages he is to pay; if he is not liable it will be in the form of foregone payments which the third harmed parties would be willing to make in order to induce him to restrict or altogether to abstain from the externality-causing activity.[1] Whether the one or the other applies is obviously of distributional significance, but the Pigovian problem—the "divergence between private and social costs"—would not exist under Coasian bargaining, as long as transaction costs are negligible. Another type of

1. H. Demsetz ("When Does the Rule of Liability Matter?" in *The Economics of Legal Relationships*, ed. H. G. Manne [St. Paul: West Publishing Company, 1975], 168–83): "[The] Coase theorem . . . is based on the proposition that an implicit cost (the foregone payment from the farmer) is just as much a cost as is an explicit cost (the liability damage) . . ." (174).

private response to externalities, which may actually be considered a specific variant of the bargaining solution, would be a merger between an externality-creating and an externality-receiving unit (the farmer and the rancher in Coase's familiar and classic example). Such a merger will fully correct for any pre-merger allocative distortions. It internalizes the prior externality by insuring that the same decision maker secures the possible benefits of carrying out the damaging activity and the possible spillover costs that the activity involves.[2] Utility- or profit-maximizing strategy dictates that the activity in question be adjusted so as to maximize net rent on the combined unit of operation.

Private responses to externalities, such as the bargaining or the merger solution, operate via some reassignment or rearrangement of rights within a given legal structure or, more generally, within a given framework of socially sanctioned rules and laws. In other words, private corrections are a matter of *in period* adjustments among market participants—of trades made within a defined institutional context. In contrast to such private responses, *political* corrections work via some change in the "rules of the game"; they imply some alteration in the rule structure itself.[3] Politicization, as such, amounts to an abrogation of existing prior legal "rights" concerning the activity in question. Political corrections are about *redefining* the rights which the market participants hold, not about *trading* defined rights. Where transaction costs render private bargaining or merger solutions non-viable,[4] political

---

2. It should be noted that "the same decision maker" may be a collective decision-making unit and that in those cases the structure of the decision-making process may have an impact on how the possible benefits and the possible spillover costs will be balanced against each other. We ignore this problem in the present, private-merger context; it will be of particular concern, however, in our later analysis of the political response to externalities.

3. On the distinction between private, *in period*, and political, *constitutional*, responses to externalities, see V. Vanberg, "Individual Choice and Institutional Constraints: The Normative Element in Classical and Contractarian Liberalism," *Analyse & Kritik* 8 (1986): 113–49, especially 123ff.

4. E. J. Mishan ("The Postwar Literature on Externalities: An Interpretative Essay," *Journal of Economic Literature* 9 [1971]: 1–28): "In the absence of government intervention, whatever the legal position, the unfavored party has a clear interest in trying to bribe the other party to modify the 'uncorrected' output. Successful mutual agreement between the parties, however, presupposes that the maximum possible amount of the shared gains, G, in moving to an optimal position, exceeds their combined transaction costs T. . . . Fail-

responses become particularly relevant, though it should be noticed that independent of transaction costs barriers, negatively affected parties, for distributional reasons, may always have an incentive to take recourse to the political process.

Transaction costs typically increase significantly as we move beyond small-number to large-number interactions, and, as a consequence, neither a merger nor a set of Coase-like bargained solutions may be predicted to occur.[5] This is often assumed to be relevant for many environmental issues such as air and water pollution, the classic example being the factory whose smoke dirties the laundries of the neighborhood housewives. If a viable private response to externalities in large-number interactions requires collective organization, the high organization costs may render politicization, that is, recourse to the existing organization *government,* the cheaper alternative.

There are basically three forms that political responses to externalities can take: The legal structure can be redefined so as to make the externality-creating party fully liable for the damage it causes; the externality-causing activities can be made subject to some kind of direct regulation; and, finally, a tax can be imposed on the externality-creating activity.

The first alternative, though certainly a suitable instrument for distributional corrections, will not necessarily bring about a Pigovian allocational improvement. Given the inherently reciprocal nature of the externality problem,[6] a shift in the liability rules may, if transaction costs matter, simply result in a shift from an excessive supply to an under-supply of the externality-

---

ure to reach mutual agreement, on the other hand, can be regarded as *prima facie* evidence that $(G - T) < 0$" (17).

5. For some necessary qualifications of the "large-number argument," see J. M. Buchanan, "The Institutional Structure of Externality," *Public Choice* 14 (1973): 69–82, where the argument is made that not the large-number feature, as such, but "the presence of a 'publicness interaction' among 'consumers' or bearers of a potential external diseconomy is critical for the predicted failure of voluntary contractual arrangements."

6. R. H. Coase ("The Problem of Social Cost," in *The Economics of Legal Relationships,* ed. H. G. Manne [St. Paul: West Publishing Company, 1975], 127–67): "The question is commonly thought of as one in which A inflicts harm on B and what has to be decided is: how should we restrain A? But this is wrong. We are dealing with a problem of a reciprocal nature. To avoid the harm to B would inflict harm on A. The real question that has to be decided is: should A be allowed to harm B or should B be allowed to harm A?" (127f.).

creating activity.[7] An allocational net-improvement could result, though, if the transaction costs barriers are "non-symmetrical" in the sense that it is less costly to achieve a private bargaining solution under the new legal arrangement than under the old one.

Debates on political corrections of externalities mostly concentrate on the *direct regulation* and *taxation* alternatives,[8] and it is those methods, particularly the latter, on which our analysis will concentrate. Different from the standard treatment in welfare economics, our interest is not in examining the "efficient regulations" or "efficient Pigovian taxes" that could be recommended for political implementation. Instead of assuming, as much of welfare economics implicitly seems to do, that there is some idealized efficiency-seeking despot to whom such policy recommendations can be suggested, our purpose in this paper is to address the question that the welfare economists overlook, namely, can politicization of external diseconomies be expected to insure correction? Or, more specifically: Under what conditions could we predict that the political process would generate results that correspond, even if roughly, to those produced by genuine internalization of the external diseconomy? Using a simple majority-voting model we shall analyze the outcomes on externality-correcting decisions that can be expected to result under different compositions of the voting population, compositions in terms of subgroups that are benefiting from and/or being harmed by an externality-creating activity.

3. Majoritarian Voting and Direct Regulation

According to the standard interpretation of the notion of "external effects," the word *external* means *external to the group* of those who take part in the

---

7. Buchanan ("The Institutional Structure of Externality"): "[T]he assignment of rights to the . . . 'producer' of the external effect biases the outcomes in favor of an excessive supply of the diseconomy whereas the reversal of this assignment biases the results toward an undersupply of the diseconomy" (75f.).

8. As R. Cornes and T. Sandler (*The Theory of Externalities, Public Goods, and Club Goods* [Cambridge: Cambridge University Press, 1986]) argue with regard to "policy intervention to deal with externalities": "The most celebrated form of intervention—suggested by Pigou and clarified, extended, and criticized by countless others—consists of a system of taxes and subsidies designed to distort individuals' choices toward an optimal outcome. An alternative to such manipulation of the price system involves the enforcement of quantitative constraints such as a set of environmental standards that must be maintained" (48).

decision to engage in the relevant activity. The implicit presumption is that the beneficiaries and the sufferers of the externality-creating activity are necessarily *different* sets of persons or firms. This presumption may be misleading in the case of externalities which are considered to occur in the context of transactions involving two or more parties, the case to which Pigou actually referred in his exposition of the issue.[9] In analyzing such cases it seems to be more fruitful and appropriate to interpret the "external" as meaning external to the respective *transactions or contracts* rather than external to the transacting or contracting *parties*. Externalities in this sense may be *external* as well as *internal* to the parties to the transaction, two cases that, for reasons of terminological convenience, we propose to label "external externalities" and "internal externalities."

Distinguishing between these two types of externalities by no means rules out that external effects may be both *internal* and *external*, in the sense defined. What is assumed is that these two types of effects can be usefully distinguished, not that all externalities can be exclusively classified into one or the other of the two categories. To make this distinction is particularly useful for our purpose of analyzing expected patterns of political responses to externalities. As an example for our following analysis, imagine a competitive industry which operates in a polity P and, in producing a good X, creates some environmental spillover damage. Members of the polity may or may not benefit from the externality-creating industry by consuming or not consuming good X. And they may or may not suffer from the spillover damage, dependent on where they reside within the community. All members are assumed to fall into one of the four categories that result from combining the two classifications, as indicated in the matrix below.[10]

9. In dealing with the divergences between social and private net products, Pigou referred to a situation where "one person A, in the course of rendering some service, for which payment is made, to a second person B, incidentally also renders services or disservices to other persons (not producers of like services) of such a sort that payment cannot be exacted from the benefited parties or compensation enforced on behalf of the injured parties" (A. C. Pigou in *The Economics of Welfare*, quoted here from Coase [1975: 149]).

10. The distinction between the categories S(b,c) and S(c) corresponds, of course, to the before-mentioned distinction between *internal* and *external* externalities.—Incidentally, Mishan (1971: 18) uses the notion of an "internal externality" in a sense similar to ours when he argues: "[E]nvironmental spillovers . . . pose a problem not so much as between firms or industries, but as between, on the one hand, the producers

	beneficiary-consumer	non-beneficiary
sufferer	S(b,c)	S(c)
non-sufferer	S(b)	S(i)

If the beneficiaries and the sufferers of an externality-creating transaction are strictly different (non-intersecting) sets of persons—S(b) and S(c) in the matrix—any proposed politicization of the interaction places members of the two groups in directly opposing positions. Those who benefit from carrying out the activity will oppose any restriction or control, while those who suffer the spillover damages will support any restriction or control. If all persons in the relevant political community belong to one or the other of these two mutually exclusive sets, the simple majoritarian result will, of course, depend on the relative sizes of the two groups of constituents. Note that no member of either group prefers a solution that allows *some* restriction on the activity as opposed to no restriction or total prohibition. The person who is the beneficiary will clearly prefer that no restriction be placed on his freedom of action. The person who suffers spillover damage will equally prefer that the activity be altogether banned. In this two-group model of politics, a political solution that is analogous to that produced by merger or Coasian bargaining in the small-number setting seems beyond the range of the possible.

If, on the other hand, all members in the polity would fall into category S(b,c), that is, if they all consume good X and all suffer from the spillover damage, and if they all benefit and suffer to the same extent, then politicization would produce a solution analogous to a merger solution.[11] Each

---

and/or the users of spillover-creating goods and, on the other, the public at large. The implications . . . are not diminished by the observation that, in important instances, the users of the spillover-creating goods and the affected public are all but indistinguishable—this being but a special case of external diseconomies *internal* to the activity in question" (emphasis added).

11. In fact, as Coase (1975) has pointed out, politicization is in some sense analogous to a "super-merger": "The government is, in a sense, a super firm (but of a very spe-

voter would balance the costs in terms of reduced consumption of good X against the benefits in terms of reduced spillover damages. And since, under our simplifying assumptions, all voters are affected in the same way, they will choose the efficient level of activity unanimously. Note that the same result cannot be achieved under private adjustment, since by individually and separately reducing his own consumption of good X a person in the polity cannot control the level of spillover damage.

If we modify the assumptions of our first scenario where all persons in the polity are classified into the two mutually exclusive sets of beneficiaries, S(b), and sufferers, S(c), and allow for some persons to be both beneficiaries and sufferers, S(b,c), we may demonstrate that at least under certain conditions majoritarian solutions will produce results that are broadly analogous to those of merger-like internalization. Consider an extremely abstract and unrealistic model. There are equal numbers of pure beneficiaries and pure sufferers of an external diseconomy. There is one person, however, who is both a beneficiary and a sufferer. Further, all beneficiaries are equal in the benefits secured from carrying out the activity, and all sufferers are similarly identical in the costs that they endure, both in total and over the range of action. The person who is both a beneficiary and a sufferer is equivalent, in benefits enjoyed and damages suffered, to persons in both of these separate sets.

In this highly simplified model, simple majority voting will guarantee that the efficient level of the activity will be selected from among the set of all possible alternatives that may be presented for a vote. This model is, by construction, equivalent to the merger in the two-person setting. The single person who is both beneficiary and sufferer effectively internalizes the externality, and since all preferences are single-peaked, he becomes the median voter whose preferences determine the majoritarian outcome.

We may relax the extremely restrictive assumption to some degree without affecting this result. Suppose that, instead of postulating that there are precisely equal numbers of pure beneficiaries, S(b), and pure sufferers of the diseconomy, S(c), we allow the sizes of these groups to differ, while also allowing the size of the group that both enjoys benefits and suffers costs,

cial kind) since it is able to influence the use of factors of production by administrative decision" (143).

S(b,c), to be extended. Suppose that the polity is subdivided into the three subsets S(b), S(c), and S(b,c), and assume, as before, that all members of S(b) are identical, all members of S(c) are identical, and all members of S(b,c) are identical with members of the other groups on each side of the interaction. In this case, so long as

$$S(b,c) > [S(b) - S(c)],\tag{1}$$

the simple majoritarian result will be ideally efficient. Note that (1) may be satisfied even if S(b,c) is quite small relative to the sizes of the two pure groups.

The efficient result emerges, of course, because of the single-peakedness of preferences and because of the assumed equality among all beneficiaries and sufferers. The single-peakedness feature of the model seems quite robust in ordinary diseconomy settings, but the assumption of equality among benefit and cost streams must, of course, be relaxed. We need not concern ourselves with the differences among the pure beneficiaries and the pure sufferers. Presumably, each of the pure beneficiaries will prefer that the activity be unrestricted, regardless of the level of benefits secured; similarly, each of the sufferers will prefer that the activity be totally curtailed, regardless of the level of costs endured. Idealized efficiency need not emerge from simple majority process, however, once we allow for the prospect that the median-preference member of the S(b,c) group may not enjoy benefits or suffer damages that are equivalent to the mean values for benefits and damages over the inclusive group. We need not carry out a detailed analysis of the many possible subcases here. So long as (1) is satisfied, the majoritarian result will always be located *between* the extreme solutions preferred by the pure beneficiaries on the one hand and the pure sufferers of the diseconomy on the other. That is to say, *some* restriction will be placed on the activity that embodies the diseconomy, but this politically determined restriction will fall short of total prohibition. So long as (1) is satisfied, members of S(b,c) determine the majoritarian outcome, and these members, by virtue of their simultaneous enjoyment of benefits and sufferance of costs, are motivated to "merge" the two sides of the interaction in their decision calculus. Any failure to achieve idealized efficiency stems from a bias of the median-voter's preference away from that preference that would incorporate mean values for benefits and costs.

To this point in the discussion, we have assumed that the alternatives presented for political (majoritarian) consideration are defined exclusively by levels of the externality-generating activity. That is to say, the alternatives are:

R(0)   no restriction on the activity;
R(1), . . . , R(m − 1)   restrictions ranging from minimal, R(1), to maximal, R(m − 1);
R(m)   total prohibition of the activity.

We may remain within this model and introduce the fourth category of members of the inclusive polity, S(i), persons who are neither beneficiaries of the activity nor sufferers of the damage. So long as we retain the assumption that members of this set vote strictly in terms of their own interests, they will not directly participate in the electoral process, or, if they do participate, they will reflect no bias in the distribution of votes over the set of political alternatives. The addition of this fourth set of persons will not affect the results.[12]

4. Majoritarian Voting and Taxation

Pigovian welfare economists proposed that externality-creating activities be controlled indirectly by the imposition of corrective taxes (or subsidies for external economies) rather than directly by explicit political determination of activity levels.[13] They apparently failed to recognize that authorization of taxation for control opens an additional constitutional dimension for political action, with consequences that may be quite different from those predicted to emerge under conditions where politicization is limited to direct control.

As the simple analysis in Section 3 showed, neither beneficiaries nor suf-

12. This conclusion depends critically, however, on the presumption that persons vote their interests. If we introduce expressive voting into the model, this result no longer holds. On the issue of expressive voting, see G. Brennan and J. M. Buchanan, "Voter Choice: Evaluating Political Alternatives," *American Behavioral Scientist* 29 (1984): 185–201.

13. A third alternative to direct regulation and to imposing a general tax is the auctioning of licenses to pollute. On the auctioning alternative which we will not separately discuss in this paper, see, e.g., J. E. Meade, *The Theory of Economic Externalities* (Leiden: A. W. Sijthoff, 1973), 65.

ferers will prefer any non-extreme solutions. The levy of an ideally corrective tax will not, therefore, be preferred by either pure beneficiaries or pure sufferers *if the disposition of the tax revenues is disregarded.*[14] If, however, the return of tax proceeds is taken into account in voters' considerations of interest, this result need not hold. Beneficiaries of the activity, upon whom any tax is levied, will not, of course, prefer any attempted tax-induced restriction, even upon guaranteed return of all tax revenues.[15] Sufferers of spillover damages may, however, prefer taxation to direct restriction, even if the latter may allow for total prohibition of the externality-generating activity, so long as they share in the tax revenues. That is to say, pure sufferers need not prefer the levy of prohibitive taxes on the activity. They may be able, through the utilization of taxation, to secure a rent over and beyond the benefits involved in a reduction in the extent of spillover damages suffered.

If *all* persons in the polity belong in category S(b,c), if they all are equally damaged by and equally benefit (as consumer-buyers of good X) from the externality-generating activity, and if the revenues from the per unit tax are equally shared among all persons, then politicization will obviously insure full correction, whatever the particular political decision rule is. It will be in each and every person's interest to impose the idealized Pigovian tax.

Compare this with a setting in which there are only two groups in the polity, S(b) and S(c), pure beneficiaries and pure sufferers. Assume that S(c) > S(b) and that the tax proceeds are equally shared among all persons in the dominant majority coalition. The tax chosen by members of S(c), here

14. It should be noted that the issue that will concern us here—namely: Whether an "ideally corrective" tax will be chosen under political decision making—is different from the issue of whether an ideally corrective tax is, in the absence of an appropriate transfer scheme, equivalent to a Coasian bargaining solution. On the latter issue, see Coase (1975: 161): "Modern economists tend to think exclusively in terms of taxes and in a very precise way. The tax should be equal to the damage done and should therefore vary with the amount of the harmful effect. As it is not proposed that the proceeds of the tax should be paid to those suffering the damage, this solution is not the same as that which would force a business to pay compensation to those damaged by its actions, although economists generally do not seem to have noticed this and tend to treat the two solutions as being identical." Also see J. M. Buchanan and W. C. Stubblebine, "Externality," *Economica* 29 (1962): 371–84.

15. This aspect is more fully discussed in J. M. Buchanan, "Market Failure and Political Failure," in *Individual Liberty and Democratic Decision-Making*, ed. P. Koslowski (Tübingen: J. C. B. Mohr [Paul Siebeck], 1987), 41–52.

assumed equally affected, will be that rate which maximizes the difference between revenues from the tax and the costs incurred by spillover damages from the activity. This rate will (in all cases where the coalition cannot act as a discriminating monopolist) be such as to induce a level of activity *lower* than the efficient level, although at a level that is higher than the zero level that the same coalition would choose under the direct control instrument. Taxation allows members of this coalition to share in the rents that beneficiaries receive from the activity.

The rent-maximizing rate of tax, and associated level of activity, becomes analytically equivalent to the total prohibition of the activity in the direct control model. This solution emerges when members of the damaged group of voters hold an absolute majority. The solution that emerges when those who benefit from imposing the diseconomy are in the majority remains as before; there will be no tax levied and the activity will remain unrestricted.

We now introduce the third set of voters, S(b,c), those persons who are both beneficiaries and sufferers of the externality. If these voters are in the determining position, that is, if condition (1) above holds, the solution will be similar to that traced out in the direct control model. Because a person in the S(b,c) group will be both a taxpayer (as a beneficiary-consumer) and a recipient of transfers (as a member of the dominant coalition), the distributional effects will be offsetting. The person in this group will, therefore, be motivated by the basic efficiency trade-off between benefits and costs that he faces. If the mean values of benefits and costs characterize the median voter, the majority-voting process will generate the ideally efficient outcome. If the median-voter's position does not embody these mean values, there will, of course, be some departure from idealized efficiency. But the solution will be bounded, as before, by the two extreme limits.

In the direct control model of Section 3 the introduction of a fourth constituency group, S(i), persons who neither benefit from carrying out the externality-generating activity nor suffer damages from it, does not modify the majoritarian results so long as individuals strictly vote their own economic interests. This conclusion is dramatically changed as we allow the added taxing dimension. A person who is uninterested in the externality, *per se*, has a distributional interest in any tax revenues collected via the fisc.[16] A

16. For a similar argument, see G. Tullock, *Private Wants, Public Means* (New York and London: Basic Books, 1970), 77.

member of S(i) will prefer a unit tax levied at the rate that will maximize total revenues so long as he anticipates being able to secure any positive share in the return of revenues collected. The preferred tax rate for a member of S(i) will be below that preferred by a member of S(c), and the induced level of activity will be above that generated by the preferences of the latter. The relationship between the preferred tax rate of a member of S(i) and a member of S(b,c) is more complex, since the strict revenue-maximizing rate may lie above or below the rate dictated by personal efficiency considerations as optimal for a member of S(b,c).

If we array rates of the unit tax along the abscissa, as in Figure 1 and Figure 2, we may depict the ordinal preferences of members of each of the four sets [S(b), S(c), S(b,c), S(i)]. These rates of tax range from zero, shown by T(0), to T(p), that rate which insures total prohibition of the externality-generating activity. The preference ordering over the tax alternatives will exhibit single-peakedness for each of the four representative persons. Hence, a stable majority voting solution is assured, regardless of the relative numbers of persons in each group.

Note that the possible outcomes are necessarily bounded by the tax rates T(0) and T(c), the latter being that rate of tax that will maximize the rent to those who are pure sufferers of the spillover damage. T(c) is less than T(p) because of the potential distributional gains secured from the return of tax

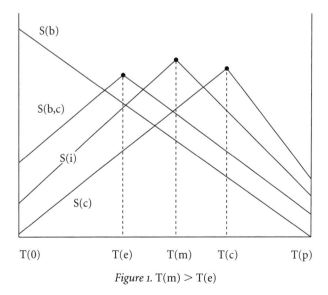

Figure 1. T(m) > T(e)

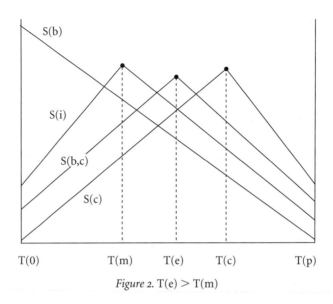

Figure 2. T(e) > T(m)

revenues. If neither the pure beneficiaries, members of S(b), nor the pure sufferers, members of S(c), are in an absolute majority, the bounds or boundaries
of possible majoritarian outcomes shrink to T(e) and T(m). The first, T(e),
is that unit tax preferred by the member of S(b,c), the person who effectively
"internalizes" the external effect within his own decision calculus. This preferred rate approximates, within the qualifications noted earlier, that rate
which might be dictated by the orthodox efficiency criterion of the welfare
economist. T(m) is that rate of tax preferred by the member of S(i), who is
not directly affected by the externality, but who retains a potential interest in
securing positive transfers from the distribution of the tax revenues. Note
that the only difference between Figures 1 and 2 is in the relationship between
T(e) and T(m).

    If T(e) is less than T(m), as in Figure 1, and if beneficiaries and internal-
izers of the externality make up an absolute majority, the solution will settle
at T(e). If the sufferers and unaffected make up an absolute majority, the solutions will settle at T(m). If T(m) is less than T(e), as in Figure 2, and if
beneficiaries and unaffected make up the majority, the result will be at T(m),
the revenue-maximizing tax rate. If sufferers and internalizers make up the
majority in this case, the result will be T(e).

5. Implications: Politicization and Efficiency

In our above analysis we have assumed that voters strictly vote their interests as defined by our classification into the four sets $S(b)$, $S(c)$, $S(b,c)$, and $S(i)$. As one recognizes that, in large-number settings, persons vote behind a "veil of insignificance,"[17] not considering their vote as being decisive for the overall outcome, it is well conceivable that voting takes on a more expressive than a strictly interest-oriented character.[18] To the extent that such expressive voting actually occurs, the outcomes generated would, of course, depart from those which we predicted in the context of our simplified model of majoritarian voting. But there seems to be no reason to assume that expressive voting would systematically tend to generate outcomes that are closer to an efficient solution than the outcomes of directly interest-oriented voting. If expressive voting can be assumed to reflect political fashions then, in the present climate, politicization would almost surely embody a bias toward excessive restriction.

The overall conclusion from our analysis is the negative one that politicization of market failure is unlikely to generate the ideally corrective measures which the welfare economist recommends. Only under very specific assumptions about the composition of the polity does the politically chosen solution approximate the efficient solution. Certainly, our model extremely simplifies the political-decision-making process. But this does not imply that the problems diagnosed would necessarily be less severe under more realistic assumptions. Serious predictions about political corrections of market failure cannot be made without analysis of the actual working properties of the political process. The predicted results under politicization will depend on the political decision rule and on the relative sizes of the various sets of differentially interested persons in the polity.

17. H. Kliemt, "The Veil of Insignificance," *European Journal of Political Economy* 2/3 (1987): 333–44.
18. See Brennan and Buchanan (1984).

A Public Choice Approach to
Public Utility Pricing[1]

In orthodox discussions of economic policy, economists tend to assume that they are providing advice to a benevolent despot who will, costlessly and willingly, implement those measures which analysis suggests to be efficient. This often unrecognized assumption about the political order may not exert relevant feedback effects on the policy analysis itself in many cases. In fact, some such assumption may be necessary to achieve an appropriate division of labor between economists and other social scientists. In certain important areas of policy, however, the model of political decision-making that is assumed may influence the analysis itself. If this is not understood, economists may be frustrated by their entrapment in a theory of policy that explains little about the behavior of the effective decision-makers. The replacement of the benevolent-despot model by the more plausible, even if still simplified, model that assumes individuals make their own collective decisions may be highly productive in particular applications.

This paper is one such application. The traditional and much-discussed problem of pricing and investment for decreasing-cost enterprises is examined in a model based on the assumption that individuals make collective as well as private decisions. As the analysis demonstrates, this change in the underlying decision-making model produces relatively sharp contrasts with orthodox analyses at specific points. In a fully closed behavioral model, the analysis shows that when the necessary equality between marginal cost, mar-

From *Public Choice* 5 (Fall 1968): 1–17. Reprinted by permission of the publisher, Kluwer Academic Publishers.

1. The analysis contained in this paper was first presented in seminars at Purdue University and Northwestern University during the fall of 1967.

ginal price, and marginal evaluation is satisfied, *average price must equal average cost.* The policy conflict between average-cost pricing and marginal-cost pricing for increasing-returns facilities does not exist. Somewhat less dramatically the analyses may be interpreted as a defense of the multi-part tariff or club principle of pricing for decreasing-cost facilities.

I

If the necessary marginal conditions for Pareto optimality are fully satisfied, the marginal cost of supplying-producing a unit of product must be equal to the buyer's marginal evaluation of a unit. If the consumer or purchaser is allowed to adjust independent of price offers, this equality is behaviorally generated when *marginal* price is made equal to marginal cost. It is essential to insert the modifying adjective "marginal" before "price." Marginal price need not equal average price, and in a general sense this equality *cannot* be realized when average costs fall throughout the relevant output range. This is the standard characteristic of a facility that embodies the controversial, and thereby interesting, pricing-investment problem.

    This summarizes the argument of the paper, but it will be useful to illustrate the argument geometrically in the familiar textbook diagram that economists have accepted, taught, and reproduced. In Figure 1, average-cost pricing, interpreted in the traditional sense, would require a price of P_a, with an output of Q_a. By apparent contrast, marginal-cost pricing, as a rule, would require a price of P_m, with an output of Q_m. The alleged conflict reduces to one between the profitability criterion, every facility standing on its own bottom, and the general welfare criterion, resources optimally allocated to the facility in question, provided that the required total conditions are also met.

    Initially, I suggest that we forget the paradigmatic model depicted in Figure 1. Consider a simpler example, a one-man Crusoe economy where the isolated individual is confronted with the possibility of producing one good at increasing returns. We assume that all of his other activities are in equilibrium adjustment and that no "profit" opportunities are available among these alternatives. Under these conditions, we ask: Will the isolated individual produce the decreasing-cost good, and, if he does so, how much will he produce?

    The obvious response is that the individual will produce the good if the

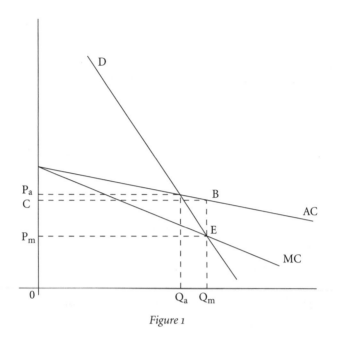

Figure 1

necessary total conditions are met and that if produced the output will be extended to the point where the necessary marginal conditions are satisfied. The isolated individual will behave optimally. It remains useful, nonetheless, to look at the simple geometry of the individual's behavior here. Figure 2 depicts the individual's tastes for the good in question in relation to some numeraire good, one that we assume to be fully divisible over quantity units and one that is itself produced at constant costs. The "public utility" good is measured along the abscissa; the numeraire or "private" good is measured along the ordinate. The transformation function is shown as TT′, and the equilibrium position is shown at E. In this position, the individual is giving up an amount, TY, of the numeraire good in exchange for an amount, 0X, of the decreasing-cost good. He attains a higher utility level by producing-consuming this good than by remaining at T. At equilibrium, he is paying a marginal price, defined by the slope of the transformation curve, equal to marginal cost, defined also by this slope. This is brought into equality with his own marginal evaluation of the good, defined by the slope of the appropriate indifference curve. It should be noted, however, that, at E, the individ-

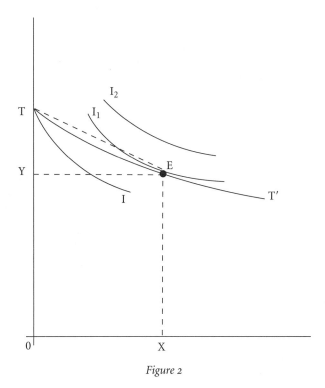

Figure 2

ual is paying an average price that is higher than marginal price. Average price is measured by the ratio, TY/YE, in Figure 2.

Figure 3 incorporates a straightforward translation of the data depicted in Figure 2 into the more familiar Marshallian coordinate dimensions. The ordinate now measures price and cost per unit, defined in the numeraire. The marginal-cost curve, MC, is derived by taking the absolute values for the slope of the transformation curve, TT′, over all quantities. The average-cost curve, AC, is derived by taking the appropriate ratio between total cost and output at all levels. This latter curve, that for average cost, can also be interpreted as representing the "price-offer" curve that the isolated individual confronts. This traces, conceptually, the set of prices and associated quantities that the individual faces as he tries to make a decision. He can, for example, "purchase" X_0 units at a P_0 price per unit. The third basic curve in Figure 3, that for marginal evaluation, ME, is derived by taking the slopes of

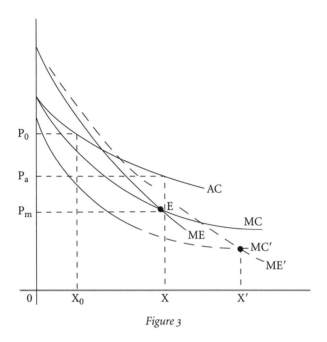

Figure 3

successive indifference curves as these cut the transformation curve, TT', in Figure 2. Equilibrium is again shown at E, where marginal evaluation equals marginal cost. At this point, all of the necessary conditions for optimality are fully satisfied. Note especially that there is no conflict between average-cost and marginal-cost "pricing" here. The individual, at E, pays an average price, P_a, which is equal to average cost, and a marginal price, P_m, which is equal to marginal cost. In the average-price sense, he is, of course, off his "demand curve." In such a model as this, however, the very notion of a "demand curve" drawn in the orthodox manner is highly questionable.[2]

As drawn in Figures 2 and 3, the total conditions are satisfied, along with the marginal conditions. The limiting case would be that in which the transformation possibilities exhaust the total valuation placed on the public-utility good by the individual. This is the perfectly discriminating monopolist example of standard theory. Geometrically, in our one-person case, this would

---

2. Economists' proclivity to think always in terms of positions on the demand curve, as normally derived, may have been one of the factors that has inhibited critical recognition of the simple points made in this argument.

require that the TT′ curve in Figure 2 lie along but just below an indifference contour over some positive range. The individual would secure no net surplus over inframarginal ranges, and, in the limit, he would remain indifferent as between a resource commitment to this activity and a noncommitment.

Little more needs to be added to the formal structure of the argument, but the theory of public-utility pricing has been conducted along quite different lines. Some departure from the simplified model may, therefore, be necessary to convince the adherents to orthodoxy. For present purposes, we remain in a one-person model, but let us allow the individual to split himself into two quite separate and distinct capacities or roles. This may be done by supposing that he has, somewhere in a past life, heard about Hotelling, Lerner, and the marginal-cost pricing rule. Having done so, the individual decides, if he produces the good at all, he must offer it to himself, as a consumer, at a price that is equal to marginal cost and that this price must be uniform over the whole quantity range. That is, marginal price must be equal to average price.

He will recognize, however, that under these restrictions the "revenues" collected from his payments as a direct consumer will not cover the outlays that he must make as a producer. It becomes necessary, therefore, to analyze his behavior, not only as a consumer, but also as a taxpayer-purchaser of the facility. Initially, let us assume that he adopts a policy of complete passivity in this role. He decides that he will make consumer decisions on the basis of marginal-cost pricing rules but that he will simply make up any losses that might be incurred through residual "taxation." He sets prices at marginal cost. Hence, as a consumer he confronts a price-offer curve or schedule now shown by the MC curve of Figure 3. Faced with this, and limiting himself to his consumer's role, he reaches an equilibrium position, of sorts, where the appropriately derived marginal evaluation curve, ME′, cuts the new curve for marginal price, MC′. The actual marginal-cost curve becomes, in this construction, the curve of average cost to the consumer. Equilibrium is attained at E′, with an output of the facility set at X′.

This output is clearly excessive. It is nonoptimal because at the margin the individual's evaluation falls below his anticipated outlay. Through the attempt to price at marginal cost, in a confused effort to follow the standard welfare norms, the individual has so modified his conditions of choice that he is trapped into an excessive production-consumption of the public-utility good.

II

Serious objection may, however, be raised to the one-man model at this point. The many-person model differs from the single-person model precisely in those respects that generate the apparent contradiction in results. Individual consumers-purchasers, when acting in the large-number setting, do not act as if their own purchases exert an influence on price. They accept price as a parameter for their own behavior. When this point is recognized, the conflict between average-cost and marginal-cost pricing seems to be restored.

This objection is partially justified, but the explanatory potential of the one-man model may be retained provided that we introduce the appropriately restrictive assumptions about the individual's behavior. Let us continue to assume, now, that the individual bifurcates himself into two capacities or roles, those of consumer-buyer-user on the one hand and taxpayer-producer on the other. As before, let us assume that price at all outputs is set equal to marginal cost. However, in a significant departure from the model examined above, we now assume that the individual, in his role as consumer-buyer, acts as if price is parametric. By this assumption, we convert the behavior of the individual, as consumer-buyer, into a pattern that is directly analogous to the behavior of the consumer-buyer in a large-number market setting.

In this modified model, the consuming-buying behavior of the individual can be represented by an orthodox demand curve (which is not a marginal-evaluation curve). Equilibrium will be established where this curve cuts the orthodox marginal-cost curve. The construction of Figure 1 illustrates this standard analysis. Total revenues that are generated by this combination of pricing policy and individual response will not cover total outlays that are anticipated at any level of output. In the model discussed immediately above, we assumed that the individual in his second role as a taxpayer-producer of the facility reacts passively and finances any deficit that might emerge. It should be obvious that this assumption cannot be maintained in any remotely realistic model for behavior. By necessity, the choice behavior of the individual in his role as taxpayer-producer must be explicitly examined. Under what conditions will he choose to invest the required resources in the facility, given the postulated response behavior as a consumer-buyer?

We may begin by examining the individual's choice behavior as a taxpayer-producer in a reasonably straightforward cost-benefit calculus. What are the tax-costs, considered *ex ante*, that the facility or enterprise embodies over varying output ranges? What are the "public" benefits? Tax-costs may be identified without difficulty. These are simply the total outlays anticipated minus the total revenues that will be collected at the planned pricing scheme. In the geometry of Figure 1, the total tax-cost at output Q_m would be the rectangle P_mEBC. It becomes relatively simple to derive a curve for total tax-costs over all possible outputs, given the production function and the predicted direct buyer response pattern. From this we may derive schedules or curves for both average tax-costs and marginal tax-costs; these are depicted in Figure 4. The curve, MTC, represents marginal tax-cost. Note that by construction marginal tax-cost becomes zero at the output where the individual attains consumer-buyer equilibrium. Total tax-cost is minimized at this output, given the preference and production schedules. The individual's marginal evaluation of the facility over differing output ranges must also be derived before we can determine whether he will, as a taxpayer-producer, attain equilibrium at the *same* output. This requires that we measure the difference between the value that the individual places on successive units of consumption and the direct user prices that he must pay under the marginal-cost pricing rule. Geometrically, the curve for taxpayer-producer marginal evaluation is measured by the difference between the appropriately drawn curve for direct user marginal evaluation and the supply curve that the individual confronts (horizontal at price P_m).[3] This subtraction process yields a curve which is the marginal evaluation for the individual as taxpayer-purchaser of the facility as a "public" enterprise. This is shown as ME_t in Figure 4. Note that again by construction this curve also reaches the abscissa at the same output which defines consumer-buyer equilibrium.

Marginal tax-price (-cost) equals marginal taxpayer evaluation of the facility which produces output X; marginal user price (set at marginal cost) equals marginal user evaluation at this same output. The necessary marginal

---

3. The two marginal evaluation curves must be kept distinct, one for the individual as direct user-consumer and the other for the individual as taxpayer-producer-purchaser. The marginal evaluation curve for the individual as direct user is not drawn in Figure 4. However, if income effects are neglected, the orthodox demand curve of Figure 1 becomes this marginal evaluation curve.

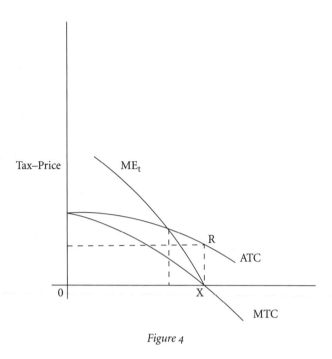

Figure 4

conditions for Pareto optimality are met, and there seems to be no conflict between the individual's behavior as a direct consumer-user and his behavior as a taxpayer-purchaser.

Nothing has yet been said about the total conditions, however, and the analysis remains incomplete until the investment decision is examined. We have postulated that, as a consumer-buyer-user, the individual acts as if his own rate of purchase of the good has no influence on price. We have also assumed that price is set at the uniquely determined level where marginal user demand equals anticipated marginal outlay (cost). But what about the companion calculus of the individual in his role as taxpayer-producer-purchaser of the facility? If we adopt the *same* convention for this aspect of his behavior, the marginal tax-price will always be set at the unique level where marginal taxpayer demand equals marginal tax-cost, which is zero. But with a direct user price of P_m (Figure 1 or Figure 3) and a tax-price of zero (Figure 4), total outlays cannot be covered. The enterprise cannot possibly be viable on these assumptions.

The escape route from this genuine dilemma seems obvious. We cannot adopt the *same* assumptions about individual behavior in the two roles. As a direct consumer-buyer, we may continue to assume strict price-taking reaction on the part of the individual. As a taxpayer-producer-purchaser, however, the individual must be allowed the possibility of acting differently, that is, not as a "price taker." In this latter capacity, the individual must be assumed to realize that, because of the nature of the production function, any decision on his part to purchase-produce a larger output of the facility will reduce average costs on all inframarginal units. In other words, the tax-price offer curve confronting the individual as taxpayer-purchaser must be that shown by ATC in Figure 4. Faced with such an offer curve, the individual adjusts his "purchases" to the point where marginal tax-price equals marginal taxpayer evaluation. He reaches full behavioral equilibrium at X, where marginal tax-price is zero, but where average tax-price is XR. This average tax-price is by construction equal to P_mP_a (Figure 3).

In this more complex model for individual behavior in the one-person setting, the simplistic conclusion reached at the outset is restored. Even though we have allowed the isolated individual to behave, in his role as a direct consumer, in precisely the manner of the single consumer among many buyers in a large-number market setting, his pattern of rational response as a taxpayer-purchaser of the decreasing-cost facility insures that both the required marginal and total conditions for optimality will be satisfied. This means, of course, that he will extend the output of the facility to the point where marginal cost equals marginal evaluation, but that he will pay an average price equal to average cost. There is no conflict between average-cost and marginal-cost criteria. If, by mistake, the individual should extend the output of the facility only to the point where direct-user payments equal total anticipated outlays, the point shown by Q_a in Figure 1, his marginal taxpayer evaluation of the facility would clearly exceed marginal taxpayer cost. The individual would stand willing, in his role as a taxpayer-purchaser, to contribute something toward the expansion of output beyond this limit.

III

To this point the one-man model for behavior has been consistently employed, even if the various assumptions about behavior may have appeared somewhat extreme. This model is helpful in forcing concentration on *dual* capacity or role that the single individual must play when his behavior as a direct consumer is postulated to be inconsistent with the characteristics of the production function. This model may also be a helpful stage toward analysis of the more complex collective decision process which all decreasing-cost facilities must introduce. Given the institutions of the market, when there are many buyers, no single person considers the influence that his own rate of purchase exerts on price. He adjusts to prices parametrically; he behaves as a price taker. If all consumers do this, however, they *must* behave differently when they take up their roles as voters-taxpayers considering the problem of public or collective investment in the facility. In this latter role, rational behavior dictates that they behave precisely as the individual in the isolated situation was shown to behave. Given the appropriate institutions for making collective decisions, they will tend to approve investment in the facility so long as the total conditions are met.

These results seem evident on their face, but some of the problems involved in aggregation are interesting in themselves. When we move beyond the one-person model, it becomes necessary to specify the characteristics of the collective organization and its rules for reaching decisions. Initially, we may assume that *all* persons in the collectivity are consumers-users of the good that is produced by the decreasing-cost facility or enterprise that we are examining. For absolute simplicity in analysis, we assume first that all persons are identical and that there are only two.

The marginal evaluation that each person places on the facility, as a "public facility," is measured by the difference between marginal consumer evaluation and user price, as noted in the one-person model. To distinguish the two evaluations here, we refer to *marginal taxpayer evaluation* and *marginal consumer evaluation*. The former is, in the limiting case where there are not interpersonal or intertemporal consumption externalities, simply Marshallian consumer's surplus. To get at the total taxpayer evaluation for the facility, we need to add the separate individual curves *horizontally*, as we do with an ordinary derivation of a market demand curve. Note that, initially, we do not add curves vertically, as with a genuine public good. The curve for aggregate taxpayer evaluation intersects the marginal taxpayer cost curve at the output which is generated by direct-user pricing at marginal cost. To this point the two-person model remains identical to the single-person model. As such, however, the construction tells us nothing, either in an explanatory or a representational sense, concerning the allocation or pricing of the facility, as a "public" enterprise. At the margin, aggregate marginal taxpayer evaluation equals zero, which is equal to marginal taxpayer cost; the necessary marginal conditions are met. As noted in the single-person models, however, some measure of taxpayer evaluation over inframarginal ranges of facility output must be made in order that some of the surplus be captured for the financing of public investment.

Individuals must "vote for" investment in the facility, with variations in capacity reflecting the alternatives of collective choice. As a "voter," the single person knows that the collectivity faces a *public* production possibility indicated by the curves for average and marginal tax-costs, ATC and MTC in Figure 5. The question becomes one of comparing an individual share in this cost with an individual marginal evaluation. There may be, of course, a sub-infinity of possible sharing arrangements, all of which satisfy the necessary marginal requirements. Since we have assumed the two persons are identical,

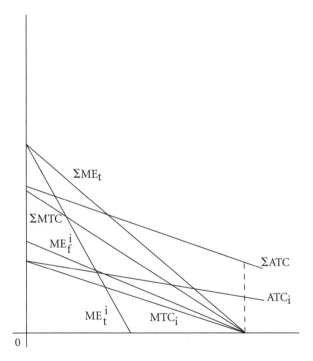

Figure 5

let us further assume prior agreement on equal sharing of collective costs. This allows us to draw curves for individual average and marginal tax-cost, ATC_i and MTC_i in Figure 5.

The difficulty arises in deriving curves or schedules for individualized marginal evaluation. As we have assumed throughout the analysis, the good is fully divisible among separate users. The aggregate curve for marginal tax-payer evaluation was derived by the *horizontal* not by the *vertical* summation of the individual curves. But these latter, derived from individual evaluations of discrete units of output, cannot be used to represent evaluations for output capacities of the facility. What evaluation will an individual, as a potential taxpayer-voter-beneficiary, place on, say, a facility that has the capacity of supplying two units per period. Clearly, this evaluation will depend on his anticipations about the *sharing* of this output among users. With some appropriate sharing rule, the model can be converted into one that is fully analogous to a public-goods model. If the individual thinks that he will secure one-half of the output of the facility in each period, which he knows will be priced to him as a direct user at marginal cost, he will value the two-unit facility equally with *one unit* of user output. In the two-man setting, therefore, an individual's marginal taxpayer evaluation of a unit increase in the capacity of the facility, considered strictly as a collective enterprise that will follow marginal-cost pricing rules, will be one-half his evaluation of a one-unit increase in the quantity of the good that will be made available to him directly as a user, at marginal-cost prices. Geometrically, therefore, we can derive curves for individual marginal "voter-taxpayer" (ME_f^i) by taking one-half the slopes of the marginal taxpayer evaluation curves drawn as in the one-man model. One such curve is shown as ME_f^i in Figure 5. By this device, we have effectively converted the fully divisible good into a purely public good for purposes of examining the collective division process. Note that we can now generate the aggregate taxpayer evaluation curve, ΣME_t in Figure 5, either by adding the conventional output-unit evaluation curves (ME_t^i) horizontally or by adding the derived "facility" marginal evaluation curves (ME_f^i) vertically.

The geometry here is really more complex than the point requires. It is evident that there exists no scheme whereby the individual member of the collectivity, as taxpayer-voter, can react to a uniform tax-price and, at the same time, reach behavioral equilibrium that is consistent with his behavior as a direct user. As a taxpayer-voter, the individual must be confronted with either a tax-price offer that embodies a reduction in unit charges as a larger facility is selected or a tax-price offer that embodies an all-or-none choice in which both quantity and charges are fixed. In either case, as the geometry makes clear, the test for the satisfaction of the total conditions being met is the observed unanimity among all members of the group.

The model becomes considerably more complex, of course, when individual differences are introduced. For now, we assume that all members of the community remain direct users. Here under the same construction, individual marginal taxpayer evaluation curves would differ, and agreement among all members of the collectivity could be reached only if separate persons should be confronted with differing price-offer conditions, either declining over facility size or all-or-none offers at the fixed-size facility. The problem here becomes one that is similar to, but somewhat more complex than that faced in any public-goods decision process. Voluntarily, individuals will not, of course, contribute to the cost-sharing for the nonuser financing of the facility, and collectively, there is no direct means of ascertaining individualized evaluations which are required to determine the efficient set of differential price-offers. With nondecreasing-cost public goods, however, tax-prices may be uniform over quantity, but not necessarily so. In the case under consideration here, tax-prices must, by the nature of the problem posed, decline over facility size. The voting alternatives become, therefore, necessarily somewhat more complex than those which represent the essentials of the public-goods problem generally speaking.[4]

Let us now introduce the further complication that some members of the collective group are not demanders-users of the decreasing-cost facility. At marginal-cost prices, these persons demand none of the good. It seems self-evident that, in any collective-decision process, and neglecting possible consumption externalities, this group will unanimously oppose any proposal that will embody their own support of tax charges to finance the facility. The argument strongly supports the financing of decreasing-cost facilities by the imposition of multi-part tariffs levied directly on users, and on users only.

---

4. Samuelson apparently disagrees. In his comment on my interpretation of his own basic contribution to the theory of public goods, Samuelson appears to suggest that decreasing-cost phenomena are an inherent aspect of "publicness." See P. A. Samuelson, "Pitfalls in the Analysis of Public Goods," *Journal of Law and Economics* 10 (October 1967), 199–204.

The convenient fiction of the lump-sum tax that has been used by economists who ignore the collective-decision process had best be discarded as fiction. This is perhaps best indicated by asking the simple question: Who would vote to impose a lump-sum tax on himself? Conceptually at least, there always exists some scheme for sharing the costs of the facility, over and above those financed by marginal-cost user prices, among direct users, so long as the facility is efficient in the overall sense. No such scheme could possibly exist for sharing costs among nonusers in the absence of consumption externalities.

Practically, therefore, the analysis here lends support to the early arguments by Coase and others that multi-part tariffs provide the best means of financing decreasing-cost facilities.[5] The objections raised by apparent purists to multi-part pricing are clearly invalid in the general setting developed here. The analysis provides a general approach that also allows for the introduction of any degree of "publicness" or "indivisibility" to be introduced without difficulty. There is no necessity that the marginal taxpayer evaluation add up to the same as the Marshallian consumer surplus. Indeed this is the exception or the extreme rather than the rule.[6]

Finally, the methodological relevance of the analysis deserves stress. Problems of economic efficiency should always be examined within the framework of models that hold some potential applicability for the making of real-world decisions. The one-man models presented initially here are absurd simplifications, and the two-person models later introduced may seem little improvement. But in my view, even such models as these are considerably more meaningful than the Hotelling-like models which assume the presence of some benevolent despot whose shining will guides us all to bliss.

5. See R. H. Coase, "The Marginal Cost Controversy," *Economica* 13 (August 1946), 169–82.

6. In this connection, see B. Weisbrod, "Collective-Consumption Services of Individual-Consumption Goods," *Quarterly Journal of Economics* 78 (August 1964), 471–77, and Millard F. Long, "Collective-Consumption Services of Individual-Consumption Goods: Comment," *Quarterly Journal of Economics* 81 (May 1967), 351–52.

Cartels, Coalitions, and Constitutional Politics

James M. Buchanan and Dwight R. Lee

While every industry desires political protection against the rigors of competition, no industry would see advantage in having that protection generalized to the entire economy. The ideal from the perspective of a given industry is to receive protections for itself, while the remainder of the economy remains competitive. Such a privileged outcome is not possible, of course, in a broadly democratic regime, and the industry that obtains protections for itself does so by joining into a coalition, explicit or otherwise, which obtains protections for everyone in the coalition. A simple model is developed in which an equilibrium coalition emerges. While it is obviously better for an industry to be inside, rather than outside, such an existing coalition, it is shown that even those who are members of a protected coalition may be better off under a constitutional regime that prevents any industry from receiving protections against competition.

Introduction

In broad outline, the welfare properties of a competitive economic order have been understood by economists since Adam Smith. Restrictions on vol-

From *Constitutional Political Economy* 2, no. 2 (1991): 139–61. Reprinted by permission of the publisher, Kluwer Academic Publishers.

We thank Ronald Heiner and Robert Tollison for helpful comments on earlier versions of this paper. The standard disclaimer applies. Much of the work on this paper was

untary exchange—on entry into and exit from markets, on terms of trade voluntarily negotiated—lower economic value in the aggregate. Resources are prevented from moving toward their most highly valued uses. Under either a utilitarian or an individualist-contractarian evaluative standard, politically imposed constraints on exchange cannot pass muster. Exceptions to this general normative principle require justification by proof either of market failure or of adverse distributional consequences.

Despite the generalized normative argument from welfare economists, however, politically imposed restrictions on markets seem pervasive. The efficiency norm seems to carry little political clout. In a preliminary attempt to explain the politics that we observe, public choice theory appears to be successful. The interaction among special interest groups, as these operate within the institutions of democratic governance, generate analytically predictable patterns of intervention. But public choice theory does not explain the limits to politically imposed controls over markets. If politics is everywhere dominated by organized special interests, why do we not observe even more politicized markets than we do, in fact, see?

Our purpose in this paper is to demonstrate that the gains from politically generated restrictions on markets, even to organized producing interests, are more apparent than real. The analysis demonstrates that under plausibly realistic assumptions concerning coalition sizes, excess burdens, organizational costs, and rent-seeking outlay, a genuine utility-maximizing calculus may dictate support for *constitutional* prohibition of all market restrictions, by *all* members of the polity, including those producer interests that might be considered to be the potentially identifiable beneficiaries of cartelization. Careful consideration of the inclusive "welfare politics" of a competitive order may suggest that generalized free exchange, if examined strictly as a constitutional alternative, is much more viable than public choice models of interest group interaction in ordinary politics may indicate.

Organized producer interests may seek politicized protection in any of several forms: price floors or ceilings, restrictive licensing, prohibitions or

done while Dwight Lee was the John M. Olin visiting scholar at the Center for the Study of American Business, Washington University.

limits on entry and exit, direct production controls, monopoly franchise, cartel enforcements, tariffs, and quotas. We shall limit analysis here to cartelization of potentially competitive industries within a domestic economy, although the analysis could readily be extended to other forms.

Section I sets out the general outlines of the analytical argument. Section II introduces the specific model. Sections III and IV extend the analysis upon recognition that costs are involved in coalition formation. Section III concentrates on organizational and enforcement costs in a stylized setting of direct democracy. Section IV drops the direct democracy restriction and examines the effects of introducing politicians who have their own economic interests to pursue. Section V develops the differentiation between inclusion and exclusion from politically protected markets and demonstrates how this differentiation motivates competitive rent seeking among prospective entrants into the included set. Section VI suggests that expected profits or rents from market restrictions may be more than dissipated in the competitive rent-seeking "game," and Section VII analyzes the effects of this prospect for constitutional reform. Section VIII relaxes the severe assumptions of the model and generalizes the conclusions.

I. Producers-Sellers as Consumers-Buyers

The central proposition of the argument may be stated succinctly. Those persons who expect to secure rents from market restrictions in their roles as producers must also reckon on the losses suffered in their roles as consumers of other products than that which they produce and sell. And, when it is necessary to accept restrictions on other markets in order to secure the anticipated benefits from restrictions on a single market, promised gains in rents will be reduced, and, under many conditions, eliminated or turned into net losses.

This proposition is evident if we impose generalization as a condition. Suppose that in order to secure cartel-generated rents (profits) from a single industry, producers-suppliers in that industry must accept cartelization of *all* the remaining industries in the economy. In this setting, the role of any person as a general consumer dominates his role as a specialized producer; no one would voluntarily choose the generalized regime that requires cartel-like restrictions on the output of all industries. This model presents the familiar efficiency argument for the competitive order in terms of the Kantian generalization principle.

The opposing end of the policy spectrum is described as that in which only *one* of the many potentially competitive industries in the economy is cartelized. In this case, the potential for producer-seller rents clearly dominates any consumer-buyer interests for those who occupy the producer-seller roles in the single-favored industry. On the other hand, even if consumers, as such, remain wholly unorganized and hence politically ineffective, producers-sellers in all other industries than the differentially favored one will strictly oppose the formation of the one-industry cartel, presuming only that these groups act in their own economic interest.

To secure political support for government enforcement of cartel restrictions of industry output, an organized producer group representing an industry must reckon on (1) the formation of a coalition of similar groups, representing producers in other industries, who seek comparable cartel restrictions, or (2) direct investment rent seeking to secure the support of legislators, or (3) some combination of (1) and (2). If we limit attention, initially, to (1), the size of the minimally effective coalition of cartels will, of course, depend on the voting rules under which the constituted legislative assembly operates. In any setting within which politics is described to be broadly democratic, some minimal-sized coalition of producer interest groups, each one of which seeks own-industry cartelization, could be expected to form. The politically feasible regime of cartelization would, therefore, fall somewhere along the spectrum between generalized cartelization over all industries and the single-industry cartel.[1]

There are several questions to be addressed. Where, along this coalition-of-cartels spectrum, can an equilibrium, of sorts, be located, and what are the critical institutional factors that determine this location? What is the profit-maximizing degree of output restriction for the single industry that is at the same time a member of a coalition of similarly protected output-

---

1. For one of the few papers that analyze the effects of a coalition of producer groups on policy outcomes, see Robert H. Bates and William P. Rogerson, "Agriculture in Development: A Coalition Analysis," *Public Choice* 35 (1980): 512–27, especially 513.

restricting industries? How does this profit-maximizing degree of output restriction vary with coalition size? At what point, and under what conditions, will a producer interest group, representing a single industry, find it profitable to support *constitutional* proposals to eliminate all cartels?

II. A Simplified Model

It is necessary to use a highly stylized model of an economy in order to introduce formal analysis. We can ignore many considerations that do not seem relevant to the central questions at issue. We shall in Section VIII examine the effects of relaxing the several restrictive assumptions of the model.

The economy is totally specialized in production and totally non-specialized in consumption. All persons are producers-suppliers; there are no pure consumers. Each person supplies inputs for only one industry; each person consumes products of all industries. There are equal numbers of persons employed in each of the industries, at least initially, and each person consumes an equal share of the products of each industry.

There are N industries in the closed economy, each one of which faces an identical demand curve for its product, although each product is different from others. Initially, each industry is organized competitively, with many separate producing firms. The inverse demand function for each industry is given by $P(Q)$, where Q is the product quantity denominated in some normalized unit. Assume that the constant $\overline{MC}$ represents both average and marginal costs of production in each industry when the economy is both fully employed and fully competitive.

We propose to examine the situation when $n(n < N)$ of the industries in the economy successfully secure support for government enforcement of profit-maximizing cartel restrictions on output for each of the n-included industries, with each industry member of the coalition of cartels being identically treated. We allow the output restrictions within the n-industry coalition to affect the consumer's surplus generated in the $N - n$ remaining industries that are competitive. This effect results from a reduction in the constant marginal cost in the $N - n$ competitive industries as resources flow to them from the cartelized industries. We ignore any change in consumer demand for the output of the $N - n$ competitive industries that might result from the price changes that the output restrictions in the *n* industries generate.[2]

Persons who are producers-suppliers in each industry in the *n*-industry coalition expect to secure net benefits from own-industry output restriction, through the induced price increase, but expect to suffer loss as consumers of products of the other $n - 1$ industries that are in the coalition and which also reduce output rates, and hence, increase prices. This loss is to some extent offset by the lower costs, and prices resulting from the shift in resources to the competitive sector. The total value of benefits expected to be received by all members of a single industry in the coalition of cartels can be expressed as:[3]

$$[P(Q)Q - \overline{MC}Q] + \frac{n}{N}[\int_{0}^{Q} P(\tau)d\tau - P(Q)Q]$$
$$+ \frac{(N - n)}{N} [\int_{0}^{Q^*(nQ)} P(\tau)d\tau - MC(nQ)Q^*(nQ)]. \qquad (1)$$

In (1), Q is, as noted, the output of each of the *n* industries in the coalition. The competitive output in each of the $N - n$ industries outside the coalition is given by Q^*, which is a negative function of coalition output, nQ. *The marginal cost of each competitive industry is the same increasing function of nQ* for all levels of nQ up to the point where each industry in the coalition is producing the competitive output, at which point the marginal cost of each competitive industry is $\overline{MC}$. It is assumed that the return to factors of production in the coalition industries is maintained at a level consistent with a marginal cost of $\overline{MC}$.

The first of the three terms in (1) measures net profits to an industry from cartel output restriction on its own production. The second term measures the total consumer surplus to an industry in the coalition from the products supplied by itself and other industries in the coalition of cartels. The third term measures the total surplus to an industry in the coalition from the products supplied and sold by the $N - n$ industries outside the coalition.

---

2. We also ignore any change in the political influence of an industry in the coalition if employees in that industry move into a competitive industry as the coalition industry reduces output.

3. The weights used in expression (1) assume that the number of people associated with each industry remains approximately equal.

Given any size, n, of the coalition, the choice variable is Q, the rate of industry output (which we assume to be uniform for each industry in the coalition). The coalition will choose Q, given any n, so as to maximize (1). Maximization must satisfy the condition:

$$MR - \overline{MC} + \frac{N}{n}[P - MR] + \frac{N - n}{N}[nQ^{*\prime}(P - MC)$$

$$- nQ^*MC'] = 0, \tag{2}$$

where MR represents the marginal revenue of each coalition industry, and the prime represents a derivative.

Examination of (2) reveals familiar results. Recognizing that $P = MC$ in all competitive industries, condition (2) becomes

$$MR = \overline{MC} - \frac{n}{N}(P - MR) + \frac{(N - n)n}{N}Q^*MC'. \tag{3}$$

In the limit, as n goes to N the third term on the right vanishes, $n/N = 1$, and (3) becomes the competitive solution $P = \overline{MC}$. When there is no differential gain possible to participants in any industry, the best for each is the competitive solution for all. At the other limit, when $n = 1$, (3) becomes

$$MR = \overline{MC} - \frac{1}{N}(P - MR) + \frac{(N - 1)}{N}Q^*MC'. \tag{4}$$

Condition (4) indicates that the sole monopolist will not necessarily find the standard $MR = \overline{MC}$ solution the maximizing one. The second term on the right represents the marginal consumers' surplus accruing to the monopoly industry from expanding its own output. Therefore this term is deducted from the marginal cost of production. On the other hand, the third term on the right represents the marginal loss to members of the monopolized industry from expanding output because of the higher costs which result in the competitive sector. Both of these terms can be expected to be small, and since they exert offsetting influences the standard monopoly condition $MR = \overline{MC}$ remains a good approximation of the solution in this case. A reasonable assumption then is that the single monopolists can ignore all but profit considerations when deciding on the optimal output. The connection between n and Q is clear. The larger the size of the coalition of cartels, the smaller the maximizing reduction in output below competitive levels in each of the industries included in the coalition.[4]

It is evident that the total gains (measured in [1]) to each industry included in the coalition of cartels is a decreasing function of n. The single-industry monopoly, $n = 1$, is obviously the most preferred situation, and profit per included industry falls continuously as n increases, due both to the moderated reduction in output within the industry and to loss of surplus as more industries shift from the competitive to the cartelized sector of the economy. If, as an abstract exercise, (1) is maximized over all positive integer values for n, then the maximizing $n = 1$. But, as noted earlier, n is not a choice variable in any direct sense. The gain to an industry expressed in (1) is derived on the presumption that the coalition of cartels is politically effective, for any n.

The central proposition of our analysis, however, depends on the relationship between political effectiveness and the costs of coalition formation, both in terms of size and other outlay. Representatives for any industry will have incentives to incur such costs, both to secure the expected gains from coalition membership, measured in (1), and to avoid the shortfall in net benefits imposed on those industries that are excluded from membership.[5] The net benefits position for any excluded industry will also be a function of coalition size.

---

4. The expression (3) provides a precise formulation of Olson's observation that "the incentives facing an encompassing special interest organization are dramatically different from those facing an organization that represents only a narrow segment of society. . . . Clearly, the encompassing organization, if it has rational leadership, will care about the excess burden arising from distributional policies favorable to its members and will out of sheer self-interest strive to make the excess burden as small as possible." See page 48 of Mancur Olson (*The Rise and Decline of Nations* [New Haven: Yale University Press, 1982]). Similarly, Downs observes that "if [an individual] receives many benefits from 'special interest' projects, he can expect his taxes to be swelled by the cost of similar projects benefiting other minorities, which the government must undertake to 'buy off' the people who paid for his gains. Thus, he might be better off if all minority benefits were eliminated and taxes lowered for everyone." See page 557 of Anthony Downs ("Why the Government Budget Is Too Small in a Democracy," *World Politics* 12 [July 1960]: 541–63). Also, in another related argument, Allan Meltzer and Scott Richard see the political demand of low-income groups for wealth transfers limited by the recognition that beyond a certain point these transfers impose a more-than-offsetting loss on the recipients by reducing the general productivity of the economy. See Meltzer and Richard, "A Rational Theory of the Size of Government," *Journal of Political Economy* 89 (October 1981): 914–27.

5. The value to an industry not included in the cartelized coalition is measured by the summation of the second and third terms in (1), given any n. If $0 < n < N$, this value

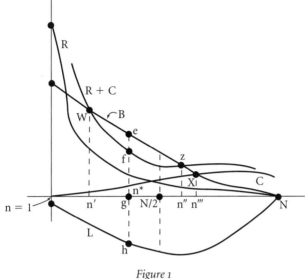

Figure 1

Before explicitly introducing the political parameters, it will be useful to present the relationships of the model geometrically, which is done in *Figure 1*. Along the abscissa, we measure coalition size, n, from 1 to N. The ordinate measures expected industry gains and opportunity losses relative to the fully competitive solution. As noted, the benefit per cartelized industry is greatest when $n = 1$ and declines until $n = N$ when it equals the fully competitive level. The benefit per industry in the coalition, as a function of n, is shown by B in *Figure 1*.

For an industry that is excluded from the coalition of cartels, and hence remains competitively organized with no output restriction, there are opportunity losses throughout the range of values for n. These losses are shown by L in *Figure 1*. At $n = 1$, L lies close to the abscissa, since, with the exception of one industry, the economy is fully competitive. Up to a point as n increases so

---

always is below that which could be attained by a single industry in the fully competitive solution. Hence, relative to this benchmark, cartelization imposes an opportunity loss on any non-coalition industry. Against an absolute value of zero in the numeraire, however, the presence of consumers' surplus insures that the last two terms add to a positive value throughout the range of n.

do the opportunity losses from exclusion, and L decreases in n. However, at some point L begins to increase in n, since the opportunity losses vanish when $n = N$ and all industries are competitive. Because of the dead weight loss associated with any output restriction below competitive levels, the general relationship between B (the distance of B above the abscissa) and L (the distance of L below the abscissa) is given by $Bn < L(N - n)$ for all positive $n < N$.

III. Politicization: Direct Democracy and Coalition Costs

We now proceed to examine the political environment within which we might expect output restricting coalitions among separately cartelized industries to emerge. In order to simplify exposition, we shall initially assume that political decisions are made through some form of direct democracy. By direct democracy we mean only that the representatives of each industry, as a body politic, make decisions directly and without the necessary intervention of professional politicians or bureaucrats. With our assumptions of approximately equal membership in each industry, we can think of one person acting for each producer-supplier group.

As noted, each industry would prefer to secure political enforcement of its own cartel, with all other industries remaining competitive. But clearly this single-industry ideal is politically impossible; each industry that seeks cartelization must reckon on forming a coalition with other industries. At best, a single industry can hope to become a member of a politically effective coalition of several industries, each one of which enjoys political support for its own cartel.

There are three distinct costs that each prospective coalition member must expect to bear: organizational costs, external policing costs, and internal policing costs. The first of these costs involves the familiar difficulties of getting any collective action undertaken, including the free-rider temptations for any prospective member to shirk on agreed-on contributions to common effort. The second of these costs, which we have called external policing costs, involves the enforcement of agreed-on norms for output restrictions among the separate industries in the coalition. Each single industry will continue to prefer monopoly restrictions on its own rate of output, while at the same time preferring that other members of the coalition restrict output only to that uniform level agreed on to be optimal for the whole set of cartelized industries. Member industries will expect to bear the major share of this external policing burden, including the reduction in the value of gains, expressed in (1), as some industries successfully violate the agreed-on output restriction targets. This cost will clearly increase as n increases. The third type of costs that must be expected involves the familiar difficulties of keeping separate firms in line within the cartel for each industry. Each firm, under the protective umbrella of the cartel restriction, will seek to expand its own rate of output. These costs counter those of external policing, at least in direction, as these costs will decrease as n increases since the desired output reduction for each firm decreases.

The anticipated costs of organizing an effective coalition in the direct democracy setting will be some aggregate of these three sorts of costs. It is difficult to establish, with any precision, on any *a priori* argument, the shape of the per industry relationship between such coalition formation costs and the size of coalition. Quite generally, it seems reasonable that these costs will be relatively small when $n = 1$ (since only the internal policing cost is relevant), increase for a while as n increases, and become relatively small again when $n = N$ (since an all-inclusive coalition calls for no restrictions, and only the external policing cost is relevant). Within these general restrictions we impose, somewhat arbitrarily, the curve C in *Figure 1*, where the value of C is referenced with respect to a zero value along the abscissa.

Nonetheless, we can derive interesting implications from the construction. Since the B curve falls continuously as n moves toward N, and touches the abscissa at N, the C curve must intersect B, almost independent of the shape of the C curve. As drawn, this intersection is at X. At this point, the expected gains from coalition membership (the gains in excess of those realized under full competition) are fully offset by the expected costs of organizing and enforcing the effective coalition. There are no net gains to prospective coalition member industries beyond those expected under the fully competitive solution. But it does not follow from this that at X an industry within the coalition will choose, unilaterally, to withdraw and organize itself competitively. Even if it does no better at X than it would do in the fully competitive solution, it still does better than the industry that remains outside the coalition, which suffers opportunity losses measured by the distance between the horizontal axis and the L curve below X. On the other hand, at X, or to the right of X, each industry within the coalition would favor a constitutional change that would prohibit any cartelization in the economy. And, of course, all industries outside the coalition would also favor such a proposed constitutional change, even more strongly.

To this point in this section, we have not specified the effective decision rule for the direct democracy model introduced. If the effective decision rule allows decisions to be made with n less than n''', say, at $N/2$, then industries that successfully join in the coalition will secure net gains in relation to the fully competitive solution, and these industries will not support constitutional change that would prohibit all cartels.

IV. Politicization: Representative Democracy and Rent-Seeking Costs

We can move the analysis toward institutional reality by recognizing that political decisions are not made by direct democracy, and that no model of direct democracy can be sufficiently explanatory, even at the stylized level of treatment here and even if we resort to "as if" decision-rule constructions. The activity of persons in roles of political agency cannot be ignored. Decisions for the polity, including those made to support and enforce industrial cartels, are made by persons who occupy specialized professional roles as politicians. These persons may be responsible to constituencies, and they may be subject to rejection at periodically scheduled elections. They do not, however, "represent" the particular constituencies directly, and they may, under the appropriate incentives, act in their own interest contrary to the interests of constituents. In addition, the basis of constituency representation need not correspond to the distribution of persons who are producers-suppliers among industries.[6]

The introduction of political agents dramatically changes the setting faced by representatives of industries that may seek political support for the formation and enforcement of cartels. Given any decision rules in the legislative assembly (for example, simple majority voting), there will exist some level of

---

6. For example, the bases for political representation in a legislature may be spatial, but the pattern of industrial production-supply may involve no particular spatial concentration of particular industries.

lobbying effort, some level of rent-seeking investment, that will secure the enactment of the sought-for legislation, quite independent of the size of the coalition of industries. For our purpose, we need not distinguish among direct bribes, campaign contributions, non-pecuniary inducements, and lobbying activity of the "persuasive" variety.[7]

The rent-seeking investment that would be required for a single industry to be successful in securing isolated differential legislative support would presumably much exceed any value that the single industry might expect to gain from cartelization (in this case, from the monopoly solution). We can depict the general relationship between the required amount of rent-seeking outlay and the size *(n) of the coalition of cartels in Figure 1* by the curve *R*. This function will decrease as *n* increases, and for two separate reasons. First, as noted, the amount of outlay required to secure favorable legislative action, given any decision rule, has fixed-cost characteristics. As additional industries join the coalition, the costs of "persuading" the required number of legislators can be shared, thereby reducing the cost per member industry. Secondly, as coalition size (*n*) increases, the size of the political constituency included within the persons who are producers-suppliers for the industries in the coalition increases, thereby introducing a direct-democracy-like correspondence for the political agents, and hence tending to reduce the total rent-seeking outlay required for success. We can expect that *R* will lie below the rectangular hyperbola in the familiar fixed-cost diagram.

The summation of the two curves *C* and *R* in *Figure 1* traces the relationship between the expected cost, per successful industry member of the coalition of cartels, and the size of the coalition, *n*.[8] As drawn in *Figure 1*, note that *W* and *Z* are break-even points for industry members of the coalition of cartels. The size of the coalition must be larger than *n'* in order to make expected gains from membership larger than those expected under fully com-

---

7. The distinction between direct money transfers and resource-using efforts to persuade is relevant for any measure of the aggregate welfare costs, but our interest is in costs to prospective members of the coalition, in which case the distinction is irrelevant.

8. Section VI, below, addresses the question concerning the identification of membership and also the possible costs for non-members, over and beyond opportunity losses in surplus. Also, notice that we are assuming that the move to representative democracy, and the opportunity to influence politicians through rent seeking, does not alter the relationship between coalition costs and *n* discussed in Section IV. For the purposes of our analysis, this is an innocuous assumption.

petitive conditions. And the size of the coalition must, at the same time, be less than n''. As depicted in the diagram, the optimal coalition size, for a successful member of the coalition, is at n^*, where the net gains from membership, over and beyond those that might be expected under the competitive solution, are measured by *ef*.

It is essential, however, to distinguish between the net gains expected by comparison with those expected under the fully competitive solution and the net gains by comparison with those expected by an industry that remains outside the coalition of cartels. As depicted in *Figure 1*, an industry that makes no attempt to secure cartelization will, at coalition size n^*, suffer net opportunity loss in the amount measured by *gh*. The differential between the position of an industry within the coalition and an industry outside the coalition is, therefore, *ef* + *gh*.

V. Competitive Rent Seeking and the Identification of Coalition Members

To this point in the analysis we have assumed, arbitrarily, that the potential members of the coalition of cartels are readily identifiable separately from those industries that remain outside the cartelized umbrella, an assumption that is clearly untenable, given our model of equally situated industries in the whole economy. We shall, for now, retain the assumption that each industry will face the same incentives to seek entry into the coalition of cartels.

One plausible behavioral proposition here would involve each industry in the economy, and not only those who are ultimately successful, undertaking both organizational and rent-seeking investment. In this case, the differential in gains between politically successful and the unsuccessful is larger than the amount indicated above. In terms of the construction in *Figure 1*, the unsuccessful attempted entrant into the coalition loses (*fg* + *gh*) by comparison to the fully competitive benchmark and the full amount *eh* by comparison with the successful entrant into the coalition of size n^*. This "solution" presumes that the successful entrants contribute only marginally more than unsuccessful non-entrants.

The optimal-sized coalition, n^*, per successful member, is not, however, an equilibrium in any behaviorally meaningful sense. The differential gains between the two sets of identically situated industries remain large, and the existence of these differential rents insures that incentives for further rent-seeking investment remain. In particular, those industries which are excluded from membership in the politically protected coalition of cartels will seek to invest more in efforts to secure inclusion in the politically favored set of industries.

At this point, it is necessary to specify the structure of the rent-seeking game more carefully. In the analysis above, we derived the relationship between rent-seeking investment, per member of the successful coalition, that was *minimally* necessary to secure political support and n, the size of the coalition. This relationship was plotted as the curve R in *Figure 1*. However, because those industries which are unsuccessful will also seek entry into the politically favored set of industries, there is no force at work to keep rent-seeking outlay at these minimal levels. Industries competing for favored treatment by the political agents will obviously be willing to invest more, per industry, than the amount indicated by R over some relevant ranges of n. But how much more?

To get an answer to this question, we need to specify some of the political parameters. If the political agents act monolithically, they will as a unit seek to squeeze the maximal rent from their authority to grant favors through cartel enforcement. These agents would, in this setting, extract all net rents from groups of producers-suppliers, and, further, they would adjust the size of the favored coalition so as to maximize the aggregate rents that all industries would be willing to pay. This monolithic model for political agency would, presumably, involve severe restriction on the number of industries that are cartelized, with large sums being extracted from each such industry, along with additional sums from other industries seeking entry.[9]

It does not seem useful, for our purposes, to elaborate the analysis of the monolithic model. We now assume, more realistically, that authority is lodged in a multi-party legislative assembly that operates in accordance with some constitutionally set decision rule, for example, simple majority. Rent seeking by industrial groups seeking cartel enforcement takes the form of in-

---

9. The ideal coalition size from the perspective of such monolithic political agents can be determined by multiplying (1) by n, subtracting nC (where C is a function of n as discussed in Section IV), and setting the derivative with respect to n equal to zero.

vestment, both pecuniary and non-pecuniary, in securing the support of individual members of this assembly, each of whom acts independently.

Assume that there are M members of the legislature, and that the basis for
constituency representation does not precisely correspond to the distribution of persons as producers-suppliers among industries in the economy. As
before, there are N industries, with it possible for N to be greater than, equal
to, or less than M. Assume now that a provisional coalition of $N/4$ industries
invests sufficiently in rent seeking to secure the support of the $(M/2 + 1)$
members of the legislature which operates under simple majority rule. This
"solution" is highly unstable because there are $3N/4$ industries that are excluded from political protection, and there are $(M/2 - 1)$ members of the
legislature who receive no rents. Each excluded industry will have incentives
to invest in efforts to get into the protected set, and each legislator that does
not receive rents will have incentives to encourage the establishment of differing coalitions.

There will be a natural tendency for additional members of the legislature
to be included as rent recipients, even from those industries that are in the
initially successful coalition. Further, there will be a comparable tendency to
extend political support to a larger number of industries, even by that particular majority in the legislature that initially forms. The dynamics of the model
here guarantee that the size of the coalition of cartels will increase toward N,
the all-inclusive coalition, and that the size of the rent-recipient set of legislators will expand toward M, the all-inclusive membership. Any position short
of the extreme values, in either of these dimensions, will leave room for further rent seeking. In one sense, the all-inclusive coalition of industries, N, and
the all-inclusive set of legislative rent recipients, M, are the "equilibrium" values toward which the system may converge. But even these values, if attained,
are unstable in the stylized model because, as noted earlier, neither the industries nor the political agents will be able to secure above-competitive
rents in this solution. There will remain opportunities for new legislation
again restricting the size of the coalition of cartels, hence guaranteeing net
rents for both sets of possible participants.[10] It seems evident that there exists
no stable equilibrium under the conditions of the model presented here.

10. The stylized model discussed here has similarities with the log-rolling analysis developed in public choice theory. For an early treatment, see Gordon Tullock, "Some Prob-

VI. Over-Dissipation of Rents

Our primary concern in this paper is not, however, with defining an equilibrium or with proving that any equilibrium exists. Our central argument aims to show that the principle of free exchange, when considered *constitutionally*, is more viable than simple models of interest-group politics may indicate. The analysis of Section V, above, was designed, in part, to suggest that the prospects for retention of positive profits (rents) after incurring organizational enforcement and rent-seeking costs may be non-existent, even for an industry that succeeds in getting politicized protection for cartelization over some transitional period.

As indicated in Section IV, even when we totally ignore competitive rent seeking (investment in efforts to secure inclusion in the cartelized sector), there is only a restricted range of coalition sizes within which successful industry members can expect net gains by comparison with the benchmark of the fully competitive economy (the range $n'n''$ in *Figure 1*). If we now introduce competitive rent seeking (not shown in *Figure 1*), and also recognize the dynamic pressures toward increases in the size of the coalition of cartels, the tenuous expectation of *any* net gains to *any* industry becomes apparent.

As we noted in the preliminary analysis of the direct democracy model earlier, the absence of expected net gains, even for the successful industry member of the coalition of cartels, will not deter investment in efforts to secure politicized support for market restrictions. Even if the expected gains to the politically successful industries are negative relative to the benchmark value defined by operation in a fully competitive economy, the opportunity losses remain significantly lower than those that might be expected from any industry that is excluded from the cartelized sector. There will remain value

---

lems of Majority Voting," *Journal of Political Economy* 67 (December 1959): 571–79. The tendency toward inclusion of all members of the legislature has been the subject of analysis by both economists and political scientists. See Randall G. Holcombe, "Non-Optimal Unanimous Agreement," *Public Choice* 48 (1986): 229–44; Kenneth A. Shepsle and Barry R. Weingast, "Political Preferences for the Pork Barrel: A Generalization," *American Journal of Political Science* 25 (February 1981): 96–112; and Morris P. Fiorina, "Legislative Facilitation of Government Growth: Universalism and Reciprocity Practices in Majority Rule Institutions," Washington University, Center for Study of American Business, Working Paper no. 48, October 1979.

differentials between the positions of the included and excluded industries, and these differentials will continue to motivate investment that aims at "buying" inclusion.

If even the politically successful industries, those that secure governmental-legal enforcement for cartel restrictions, expect opportunity losses rather than gains by comparison with the fully competitive benchmark, the profits (rents) that differentially accrue from the output restrictions of the cartels are more than dissipated by the industries' outlay on organization, enforcement, and rent-seeking costs. This result, at first glance, seems to counter those that were derived in the early versions of the theory of rent seeking. In the early treatments of rent seeking the existence of an opportunity for differential rent was predicted to motivate investment in efforts to secure this opportunity in some amount roughly equivalent to the promised rent itself, thereby insuring more or less full dissipation or exhaustion, but not over-dissipation or super-exhaustion.[11]

The setting for the stylized model analyzed here guarantees that the familiar result does not hold. The non-viability of any over-dissipation of expected rents depends critically on the presumed ability of potential participants to exit or "walk away from" the "game" with no net opportunity loss. In our model, this avenue of costless exit is not possible for any industry. By refusing to enter into the efforts to secure political protection, the single industry must reckon on having to suffer very substantial opportunity losses by comparison to its position in a fully competitive economy and differentially higher losses than those that might be generated by full participation in the political "game" of cartel formation.[12]

VII. Over-Dissipation and Constitutional Politics

The prospect that even the politically successful industries, those that form effective cartels, may suffer opportunity losses is a relevant consideration for potential constitutional change. We know, from the welfare economics of the

---

11. See Gordon Tullock, "The Welfare Costs of Tariffs, Monopolies, and Theft," *Western Economic Journal* 5 (June 1967): 224–32; and Richard A. Posner, "The Social Cost of Monopoly and Regulation," *Journal of Political Economy* 83 (August 1975): 807–27.

12. This part of our analysis has been influenced by the work of Ron Heiner, who has worked out the formal theory of over-dissipation or super-exhaustion of rents. See Ron Heiner, "Super Exhaustive Rent Seeking," Mimeograph, Brigham Young University, 1987.

competitive model, that any cartel-induced restriction of output generates a net loss in economic value for the economy. The cartel-formation "game" is a negative sum. In the standard treatment, however, those who are the net losers are not able, politically, to withstand the efforts of the concentrated and organized net gainers. And, in this standard scenario, any proposal for effective constitutional reform guaranteeing competition over all markets would be strictly opposed by the net gainers from cartelization.

Our analysis suggests, by contrast, that there may exist no net gainers from "play" in the cartel formation "game." The overall, inclusive "game" remains negative sum in the aggregate, but in our extension-emendation, the "game" generates negative-sum consequences for *all* players. This result suggests that while no successful player (industry) will be motivated to undertake unilateral action to oppose the game, and while costless exit from the "game" itself is not possible for any individual player, *all* players should stand willing to support constitutional prohibitions on all politically enforced cartels.

In this, as in many other applications, constitutional politics trumps interest-group politics. It does so because constitutional politics places individuals in positions where they must choose among alternative institutional arrangements that are necessarily generalized over the whole membership of the polity. In our stylized model, it comes to be in the economic interest of the representatives for each and every industry to support constitutional rules that prevent government from creating cartels. The special interest model of democratic politics relies for its predictive content on the presence of expectations of special or discriminatory favorable treatment. Such expectations cannot arise in a constitutionally protected market order.

The analysis also suggests how the much discussed inconsistency and/or alleged hypocrisy in the attitudes of business leaders toward market competition may be resolved. Businessmen are often charged with inconsistency because they tend to support competition in all markets other than their own. Such a stance reflects the working of straightforward self-interest in any setting where groups expect discriminatory political treatment. But business leaders may recognize, even as they engage in political activity aimed at securing their own protection against competition, that their own economic interest would be best served by constitutional guarantees of competition over all markets.

The professional politicians, as our model also suggests, would tend to oppose any and all constitutional changes that would threaten to reduce or to eliminate the rents that they might otherwise secure through the exercise of their authority to dispense political favors in the form of output restriction allowed to some industrial groups. We presume here that, in a setting where all producers-suppliers could be brought to support the constitutional politics of a market order, the effective blocking power of the relatively small number of politicians could be overwhelmed. But we should never predict that pressures for genuine constitutional change would arise out of the established political leadership in a highly politicized economy. The constitutional politics of free exchange can only emerge in a revolt against special interest politicians.

VIII. Constitutional Politics with Complex Interdependence

As we stated at the start of Section II, we imposed a severe set of assumptions on the analytical model for the purpose of tractability. It is now necessary to re-examine these assumptions to determine whether or not, and how, they might seriously undermine or modify our central results.

We can first summarize those assumptions the relaxation of which tends to strengthen our results or, at the least, to leave these results largely unaffected. The assumption of total specialization in production and total generalization in consumption does not seem critical. Either the introduction of a set of pure consumers or a set of highly concentrated consumers in the model would strengthen rather than weaken the results. Relaxing the assumption that the industries remain of equal size, population-wise, as the cartelized industries restrict output would increase the necessity for those industries to rely on rent seeking for their political influence and therefore strengthen our conclusion. Industrial categories are always somewhat arbitrary, and we could produce equal-sized groups by definitional classification if required. Relaxation of the assumption that there is no interdependence on the demand side can strengthen our conclusion. If cartel-induced restrictions in output and price increases reduce outlay on cartelized products, more funds will be expended on competitively produced goods, reducing the advantage the politically dominant coalition received from cartelization and indirectly generating increased support for constitutional reform of the type discussed.

By contrast with these non-critical simplifying assumptions of the model, the assumption that the separate industry groups face identical demand functions for their separate products requires more careful examination. Relaxation of this assumption will introduce much more complexity in the model, and some of the results will surely be modified. Consider a coalition of cartels made up of two sets of equal-sized industries; the industries in each set differ only in the elasticity of demand that they face. It is, first of all, evident that the industries in the high-elasticity demand set will suffer higher losses, as consumers, from the output restrictions of the industries in the low-elasticity demand set than the converse. The industries facing the relatively less elastic demand function will, also conversely, gain more in rents from comparable restrictions on their own output. Examination of the analysis in Section II reveals that there is no solution to the maximizing problem, defined in (3), that is common over both sets of industries. If each industry in the coalition must impose the same degree of output restriction, those industries in the set facing the relatively less elastic demand will maximize rents at a larger degree of quantity restriction than will those industries in the other set.[13]

This conflict in the joint-maximization problem suggests that concerted or integrated output restricting behavior over the industries in the coalition that face differing demand conditions may be impossible and that, once in place, each separate industrial cartel may act independently, one from another. Each industry's cartel will, under this condition, act "as if" it is the only industry that restricts output in the economy; it will attempt to set the monopoly output and maximize producers' rents without regard to consumers' rents. This independent-behavior setting for the operation of units in the effective coalition of cartels substantially strengthens our results in one critical respect but tends to weaken these results in another. In the determination of *Figure 1*, the curve *B* that measures benefits per coalition member will no longer remain positive throughout the range of values for *N*, suggesting that even without any outlay on organization, enforcement, or rent seeking some industries in the coalition of cartels may achieve positions yielding less in value than they would receive in the fully competitive setting, although here, as before, these industry members of the coalition will still be differentially better off than excluded industries.

13. The value of the second term in (3) is different for the two sets of coalition members.

On the other hand, differentiation among the demand conditions that face the separate industries tends to weaken the claim that the negative-sum outcome is generalizable over the whole set of included industries. Those industries that face the relatively more inelastic demands for their products at the fully competitive solution will have more incentive to seek cartelization, and these industries will also expect to gain more by remaining in the coalition of cartels as additional members are added.[14]

We should predict, therefore, that such industries will seek, and secure, political enforcement in advance of other industries, and, more importantly for our purposes, that a small set of such industries might continue to enjoy net opportunity gains by comparison with the fully competitive benchmark well after many other industries in the coalition of cartels discover that the game of cartel formation is negative sum. There remains the prospect that the first set of situationally favored industries in the coalition might be compensated for accepting the constitutional change, but if the set is sufficiently small the interests of these industries might simply be overwhelmed in the exigencies of realistic constitutional politics.

More or less the same conclusions would hold with respect to specialized inputs to particular industries, which we have assumed non-existent in the formal model. To the extent that such specialized resources exist, the differential gains expected from cartelization are larger, and likewise the incentive to oppose any constitutional proposal to prohibit all cartels.

Even with some relaxation of the critical assumptions of our model, the analysis remains far removed from institutional reality. We should claim, nonetheless, that our argument in this paper effectively contributes to and advances the "state of play" in the intersection between welfare economics and public choice. The argument builds on the central public choice insight that political outcomes emerge from the interaction of persons and groups that

14. The analysis here is analogous to Gary Becker's extension of a similar model to excise taxation. Becker argues that faced with a given revenue to be raised governments responsive to interest-group pressures will tend to levy taxes on those groups which produce goods with the less elastic demands, because they will suffer lower excess burdens than other groups with relatively more elastic demands. By the same logic, the first of these groups will have more to gain from cartelization and will, therefore, tend to invest more in efforts to secure political protection for cartel formation. See Gary Becker, "A Theory of Competition Among Pressure Groups for Political Influence," *Quarterly Journal of Economics* 98 (August 1983): 373–400.

seek to further their own interests. At the same time, the argument serves to re-establish the relevance of the welfare economists' efficiency norm, as it offers a basis, first for analysis itself and secondly for constitutional change.

The principle of non-discriminatory political treatment in economic policy, if applied and extended, can be as important for our economic well-being as the principle of non-discriminatory treatment in more personal relationships is, has been, and can be, for social interaction. Both norms are essential components in a well-functioning liberal order.

Politics and Meddlesome
Preferences

Each of us has a preferred pattern of behavior for others, whether they be members of our family, our neighbors, our professional peers, or our fellow citizens. I prefer that my neighbors control their children's noise-making and disposal of their tricycles; I prefer that these neighbors refrain from rock music altogether, and if such "music" is to be played that the decibel level be kept low. I prefer that their backyard parties be arranged when I am out of town. I also prefer that my neighbors plant and maintain shrubs that flower in May for my own as well as their enjoyment.

I do not, however, exert much effort to enforce my own preferences on my neighbors' behavior. I trust largely to their own sense of fair play, common decency, and mutual respect. I do this because I know that my neighbors, also, have their own preferences about my behavior. They prefer that I control the barking of my dogs, and if dogs must bark, that this be allowed only in normal hours. The neighbors also prefer that I refrain from operating my chain saw or power mower early on Sunday mornings.

There is an implicit recognition by all parties here that, although each may have preferences over the others' behavior, any attempt to *impose* one person's preferences on the behavior of another must be predicted to set off reciprocal attempts to have one's own behavior constrained in a like fashion. An attitude of "live and let live," or mutual tolerance and mutual respect, may be better for all of us, despite the occasional deviance from ordinary standards of common decency.

From *Smoking and Society: Toward a More Balanced Assessment*, ed. Robert D. Tollison (Lexington, Mass.: D. C. Heath, 1986), 335–42. Reprinted by permission of the publisher.

Such an attitude would seem to be that of anyone who claimed to hold to democratic and individualistic values, in which each person's preferences are held to count equally with those of others. By contrast, the genuine elitist, who somehow thinks that his or her own preferences are "superior to," "better than," or "more correct" than those of others, will, of course, try to control the behavior of everyone else, while holding fast to his or her own liberty to do as he or she pleases.

Private Spaces

I commenced this chapter with reference to my own personal relationships with my neighbors. Each person could fill in his or her own bill of particulars that would be descriptive of his or her own set of "social interdependencies." The general point to be emphasized is that such social interdependencies are necessary elements of life in civil society and that such interdependencies cannot be eliminated even in the most idealized allocation and assignment of "individual rights" among separate persons. A somewhat different way of putting this point is to say that there are no self-evident "natural boundaries" that define the "private spaces" within which individuals may be allowed to behave as they wish without affecting the utility or satisfaction of other persons, whether negatively or positively. Robinson Crusoe on the island before Friday arrives is useful as an expository device precisely because such a setting of total social isolation can *never* be experienced by an individual in a society.

To say that social interdependencies must always be present is not to argue that the assignment of property rights to persons cannot be of great value in reducing the potential for conflict among persons. As Thomas Hobbes recognized, the definition of what is "mine and thine," combined with the coercive power of the state to enforce the boundary lines so drawn, allows individuals to get on with producing their own goods rather than fighting over goods that belong to no one. The point is that no matter how carefully drawn and detailed is the assignment of rights, there must remain some potential for conflict. The fact that my preferences extend to your behavior over activities that are well within your defined rights, and vice versa, insures that my satisfaction is influenced by the way that you behave and that your satisfaction is also affected by my behavior.

The extent, range, scope, intensity, and importance of the social interdependencies among persons depend on the characteristics of the setting. The hermit in the forest may approach the Crusoe extreme. The frontiersman who ventures to the trading post only once a year remains largely independent, behaviorally and socially. By contrast, the suburbanite who lives in the townhouse must affect and be affected by the behavior of neighbors, fellow commuters, fellow consumers in the shops, those from whom he or she purchases goods and services, fellow workers, and numerous other separate interacting groups. So long as his or her allowable activities are well defined and enforced, the suburbanite coexists with others in the urbanized society without undue potential for overt conflict, retaining his or her preferences over the behavior of other persons in many of the roles that he or she confronts. But the suburbanite also proceeds to behave within his or her own well-defined and legally protected sphere of behavior on the presupposition that this sphere will be respected by others, that the set of rights he or she possesses will not be subject to invasion, either by other persons or by the collectivity as a unit. Civil order is described by each person "doing his own thing" within the limits of his assigned "private space," even when each person recognizes that some elements in his or her behavior will affect the satisfaction of other persons, and that, reciprocally, the behavior of others, again within their own "private spaces," will influence his or her own well-being.

The Emergence of Potential Conflict

A potential for conflict may emerge from any one of several sources. The social juxtaposition of persons from totally divergent cultures may destroy the behavioral reciprocity that normally characterizes stable civil order. (For example, the alleged behavior of Asian political refugees in eating dogs created major social tensions in long-established communities.) The explicit violation of established patterns of behavior for the sheer purpose of attracting attention may create antagonisms that were not previously recognized. (For example, the flaunting of manners, hairstyle, and dress in the 1960s, primarily by the young, opened up the generational conflict that remained present in the 1980s.) An increase in moral fervor accompanied by conversion to life-styles that are dictated by a "new religion" may make tolerance for contrasting life-styles more difficult to accept.

My concern here is not with these, or other, possible sources of potential conflict among persons, families, and communities in the areas of social interdependencies. From the fact that we do have preferences about the behavior patterns of others, there is always a latent potential for conflict. And, as with other preferences, the attempted expression of these will depend on the relative prices required for their satisfaction. I shall suggest later that the relative prices of satisfying our preferences over the behavior of others are dramatically reduced, in an apparent sense, by the overt *politicization* of social interdependency. Before exploring this process more fully, it will be useful to examine nonpolitical means of adjusting to potential conflicts in areas of social interdependence.

Conflict Resolution Through Voluntary Adjustment

Because each of us has preferences over the behavior of others in many separate social interdependencies, there remains always a potential for conflict. There is no guarantee that tolerable levels of mutual adjustment in behavior will be acceptable to all parties in an interaction. It may well be necessary to initiate or to undertake actions aimed at a voluntary resolution of the potential conflict. I may feel intensely negative toward the life-style of my neighbor, a life-style that does not allow me to invoke the laws of nuisance. If my preferences about his or her behavior patterns are so important to me as to suggest initiation of action on my part, there are several avenues open. I may make some effort to bribe or compensate my neighbor to modify his or her behavior in ways more pleasing to me. (To economists, this would be the avenue suggested by the Coase theorem. To noneconomists, this would perhaps seem one of the least plausible approaches to the problem.[1]) Or I may

---

1. See R. H. Coase, "The Problem of Social Cost," *Journal of Law and Economics* 3 (October 1960), 1–44. Briefly stated, the Coase theorem is that efficient outcomes of interactions will emerge so long as persons are free to enter into voluntary contractual agreement. In the example, if I place a higher negative value on silence than the positive value

take actions that will reduce the spillover harms that the behavior exerts on me: I may install sound barriers, for example, to keep out the sound of rock music. As an ultimate step, I may consider shifting my location to a new set of neighbors, and, indeed, this potential for residential, locational, occupational, professional, purchasing, selling mobility is one of the most attractive features of the American society by comparison with those of other more rigid structures. The mere existence of effective alternatives, even if I never choose to exercise the exit option, insures that there are relevant thresholds of spillover effects that cannot readily be crossed. These thresholds are important for each of us, and their existence surely helps make life in society tolerable.

The point to be emphasized about each and every one of these voluntary adjustments to potential conflict among interacting persons and groups is that the satisfaction of preferences over others' behavior within their legal rights is *costly*. That is to say, if my neighbor does not act in accordance with my preferences, I can either compensate him or her, build protection against the damage, or move. Each of these activities involves cost to me, and this cost will insure that my interest in my neighbor's behavior is important enough to make the outlay worthwhile. There is a great difference between being merely irritated at the behavior patterns of my slovenly neighbor and actually paying him or her to "clean up his act." My "meddlesome preferences," to use Amartya Sen's expression, can be satisfied only at a positive opportunity cost.[2]

Conflict Resolution Through Politics

There is no such rough matching of costs and benefits when the resolution of conflicts in social interdependence is approached through political mechanisms. If my neighbor's behavior irritates me, but not sufficiently to make it worthwhile to seek voluntary resolution, I may still be quite pleased if the

---

that my neighbor places on rock music, I can successfully bribe him or her. Perhaps only to economists would this explicit approach to mutual adjustment seem plausibly meaningful. Indirect exchanges, in behavioral rather than monetary dimensions, would be normal in many settings.

2. See Amartya K. Sen, "The Impossibility of a Paretian Liberal," *Journal of Political Economy* 78 (1970), 152–57.

town council will pass a regulation outlawing the behavior in question. It will cost me little or nothing to vote for the prospective councilman who will promise to outlaw leaf burning on the lawn; I may gain perhaps a few cents' worth of utility on one or two autumn afternoons by imposing, through politics, my preferences on the actions of my neighbor. The costly steps that might be required in the absence of political institutions seem to be avoided. It seems that I can impose my own preferences on others at relatively low prices.

The cost saving here is only apparent, however. If I can resort to politics to impose my own preferences on the behavior of others, even if these preferences are not highly valued intrinsically, then it would seem that other persons, in working democratic process, can do the same to me. I may find that the political process is double-edged. If it can be used to my advantage in imposing my personal preferences over the behavior of other persons, it can be used to my disadvantage in imposing the preferences of others on my own behavior. I may gain a few pennies' worth of utility by the regulation against leaf burning, but find that possessing a handgun in my house is politically prohibited. And it may happen that I very strongly value the liberty to possess a handgun. The political process, which is allegedly open equally to all citizens, is evenhanded here. It generates a few pennies' worth of utility to me in restricting my neighbor's leaf burning; it generates a few pennies' worth of utility to my neighbor by outlawing the possession of handguns. But, in so doing, it imposes many dollars' worth of loss on me through preventing my possession of a handgun, and imposes many dollars' worth of damage on my neighbor who highly values the liberty of burning his or her own autumn leaves.[3]

The Partitioning of Political Issues

The central thrust of my argument should be clear. The majoritarian institutions of modern democratic politics are exceedingly dangerous weapons to call upon in any attempts to reduce conflicts in areas of social interdepen-

3. For a more technical discussion of the potential externalities of political process, see my paper "Politics, Policy, and the Pigovian Margins," *Economica* 29 (February 1962), 17–28.

dence. They are dangerous precisely because the institutions are democratic and open to all citizens on equal terms: what is sauce for the goose is sauce for the gander. Unless the person who calls upon politics can insure that he or she retains some monopoly of political power, his or her own preferences are as likely to be imposed upon as imposed.

This danger inherent in democratic institutions tends to be overlooked because political decisions are partitioned so that each potential conflict is handled separately and one at a time. The interdependencies among the separated political decisions tend to be obscured and overlooked, with the result that it is quite possible that *all* persons will be placed in positions less desired than those which would be present in the total absence of politicization.

This central point may be illustrated by concrete examples, all of which have been at least partially politicized at one level of government or another in recent years in the United States or in other Western countries. Consider the following politically orchestrated regulations:

1. Prohibition on private leaf burning.
2. Prohibition of the possession of handguns.
3. Prohibition of the sale or use of alcoholic beverages.
4. Prohibition of smoking in public places or places of business.
5. Prohibition on driving or riding in an automobile without fastening seat belts.
6. Prohibition on driving or riding on a motorcycle without wearing crash helmets.

The listing here could be expanded greatly if we should add activities that some persons or groups have advanced as candidates for politicization. The six activities listed are, however, sufficient for my purposes here, and these are all familiar examples.

It seems quite possible that at least in some political jurisdictions a majority of voters might be found to support each and every one of the six activities listed. As noted earlier, however, the critical weakness in ordinary majoritarian procedures is that the intensities of preference are not taken into account. A bare majority of voters may support the prohibition on handgun possession, but a small minority may value highly the liberty to own handguns. The same result may hold for each of these activities. Yet, because the issues can be isolated and considered one at a time for political action, all of the regulations listed might secure majority support. But the handgun owners may find their loss of liberty much more valuable than the very mild feelings of benefits they secure from having the other activities prohibited. The same thing may hold for those who value intensely the liberty of drinking or smoking. The political process may well work so as to make each and every person in the relevant community worse off with enactment and enforcement of all of the prohibitions listed than he or she would be if none of the prohibitions were enacted.

There is a message in my argument here. Let those who would use the political process to impose their preferences on the behavior of others be wary of the threat to their own liberties, as described in the possible components of their own behavior that may also be subjected to control and regulation. The apparent costlessness of restricting the liberties of others through politics is deceptive. The liberties of some cannot readily be restricted without limiting the liberties of all.

The "Scientistic" Mentality

Critics of my argument here can charge that I have discussed the dangers of using the political process to impose one set of private and personal preferences over the behavior of others as if these preferences were mere whims, analogous to my dislike of the hairstyles of the youth of the 1960s. These critics might suggest, with respect to the set of activities listed above, and others, that the sumptuary prohibitions or regulations need not reflect purely private preferences. These prohibitions and regulations, existing or proposed, may be based on "scientific grounds." These critics might allege that leaf burning releases dangerous elements in the atmosphere; that handguns kill people; that alcohol is addictive and a causal factor in disease; that smoking is dangerous to health; and that seat belts and crash helmets save lives.

These arguments are highly deceiving in that they attempt to introduce, under the varying guises of "science," an objective value standard, one that "should" be imposed on all persons. Strictly interpreted, of course, almost any activity each of us undertakes is, in some way or another, a possible risk to our health. Once this is recognized, the question is one of drawing lines, and there is no well-defined set of activities that fall into one category or the other.

Towards a Sumptuary Constitution

We have been caught up in a wave of politicization for several decades. As a result, the set of activities that have been subjected to governmental-bureaucratic prohibition, regulation, and control has been expanded dramatically. Once politics was discovered as the apparent low-cost means of imposing preferences on behavior, a Pandora's box was opened that shows no signs of closing itself.

In these as in other aspects of the relationship between the citizens and the government, the dangers of excessive politicization cannot be avoided merely by a change in the makeup of political parties or by a change of politicians. In democracy, politicians respond to the electorates, and electoral majorities may, in a piecemeal fashion, close off one liberty after another. Prediction of such a prospect suggests that genuine reform can come only by *constitutional* rules that will prevent ordinary democratic majorities, in the electorates or in legislative assemblies, from entering too readily into the sumptuary areas of activities. Until and unless we recognize that politics, too, must operate within constitutional limits, each of our liberties, whether valued highly or slightly, is up for grabs.

Polluters' Profits and
Political Response
Direct Controls versus Taxes

James M. Buchanan and Gordon Tullock

Economists of divergent political persuasions agree on the superior efficacy of penalty taxes as instruments for controlling significant external diseconomies which involve the interaction of many parties. However, political leaders and bureaucratic administrators, charged with doing something about these problems, appear to favor direct controls. Our purpose in this paper is to present a positive theory of externality control that explains the observed frequency of direct regulation as opposed to penalty taxes or charges. In the public-choice theory of policy,[1] the interests of those who are subjected to the control instruments must be taken into account as well as the interests of those affected by the external diseconomies. As we develop this theory of policy, we shall also emphasize an elementary efficiency basis for preferring taxes and charges which heretofore has been neglected by economists.

From *American Economic Review* 65 (March 1975): 139–47. Reprinted by permission of the publisher.

We wish to thank the National Science Foundation for research support. Needless to say, the opinions expressed are our own.

1. Charles J. Goetz imposes a public-choice framework on externality control, but his analysis is limited to the determination of quality under the penalty-tax alternative ("Political Equilibrium vs. Economic Efficiency in Effluent Pricing," in *Economic Decision Making for Environmental Control*, ed. J. Richard Conner and Edna Loehman [Gainesville, 1973]).

I

Consider a competitive industry in long-run equilibrium, one that is composed of a large number of n identical producing firms. There are no productive inputs specific to this industry, which itself is sufficiently small relative to the economy to insure that the long-run supply curve is horizontal. Expansions and contractions in demand for the product invoke changes in the number of firms, each one of which returns to the same least-cost position after adjustment. Assume that, from this initial position, knowledge is discovered which indicates that the industry's product creates an undesirable environmental side effect. This external diseconomy is directly related to output, and we assume there is no technology available that will allow alternative means of producing the private good without the accompanying public bad. We further assume that the external damage function is linear with respect to industry output; the same quantity of public bad per unit of private good is generated regardless of quantity.[2] We assume that this damage can be measured and monitored with accuracy.

This setting has been deliberately idealized for the application of a penalty tax or surcharge. By assessing a tax (which can be computed with accuracy) per unit of output on all firms in the industry, the government can insure that profit-maximizing decisions lead to a new and lower industry output that is Pareto optimal. In the short run, firms will undergo losses. In the long run, firms will leave the industry and a new equilibrium will be reached when remaining firms are again making normal returns on investment. The price of the product to consumers will have gone up by the full amount of the penalty tax.

No one could dispute the efficacy of the tax in attaining the efficient solution, but we should note that in this setting, the same result would seem to be equally well insured by direct regulation. Policy makers with knowledge of individual demand functions, the production functions for firms and for the industry, and external damage functions could readily compute and

2. This assumption simplifies the means of imposing a corrective tax. For some of the complexities, see Otto A. Davis and Andrew Whinston, "Externalities, Welfare, and the Theory of Games," *Journal of Political Economy* 70 (June 1962): 241–62, and Stanislaw Wellisz, "On External Diseconomies and the Government-Assisted Invisible Hand," *Economica* 31 (November 1964): 345–62.

specify the Pareto-efficient quantity of industry output.[3] Since all firms are identical in the extreme model considered here, the policy makers could simply assign to each firm a determinate share in the targeted industry output. This would then require that each firm reduce its own rate of output by X percent, that indicated by the difference between its initial equilibrium output and that output which is allocated under the socially efficient industry regulation.[4]

Few of the standard arguments for the penalty tax apply in this setting. These arguments have been concentrated on the difficulties in defining an efficient industry output in addition to measuring external damages and on the difficulty in securing data about firm and industry production and cost functions. With accurately measured damage, an appropriate tax will insure an efficient solution without requiring that this solution itself be independently computed. Or, under a target or standards approach, a total quantity may be computed, and a tax may be chosen as the device to achieve this in the absence of knowledge about the production functions of firms.[5]

In the full information model, none of these arguments is applicable. There is, however, an important economic basis for favoring the penalty tax over the direct control instrument, one that has been neglected by economists. The penalty tax remains the preferred instrument on strict efficiency grounds, but, perhaps more significantly, it will also facilitate the enforcement of results once they are computed.[6] Under the appropriately chosen penalty tax, firms attain equilibrium only at the efficient quantity of industry output. Each firm that remains in the industry after the imposition of the tax attains long-run adjustment at the lowest point on its average cost curve only

3. See Allen V. Kneese and Blair T. Bower, *Managing Water Quality: Economics, Technology, Institutions* (Baltimore, 1968), 135.

4. No problems are created by dropping the assumption that firms are identical so long as we retain the assumption that production functions are known to the regulator.

5. This is the approach taken by William J. Baumol, who proposes that a target level of output be selected and a tax used to insure the attainment of the target in an efficient manner ("On Taxation and the Control of Externalities," *American Economic Review* 62 [June 1972]: 307–22).

6. See George A. Hay, "Import Controls on Foreign Oil: Tariff or Quota?" *American Economic Review* 61 (September 1971): 688–91. His discussion of the comparison of import quotas and tariffs on oil raises several issues that are closely related to those treated in this paper.

after a sufficient number of firms have left the industry. At this equilibrium, there is no incentive for any firm to modify its rate of output in the short run by varying the rate of use of plant or to vary output in the long run by changing firm size. There is no incentive for resources to enter in or to exit from the industry. So long as the tax is collected, there is relatively little policing required.

This orthodox price theory paradigm enables the differences between the penalty-tax instrument and direct regulation to be seen clearly. Suppose that instead of levying the ideal penalty tax the fully informed policy makers choose to direct all firms in the initial competitive equilibrium to reduce output to the assigned levels required to attain the targeted efficiency goal for the industry. No tax is levied. Consider Figure 1, which depicts the situation for the individual firm. The initial competitive equilibrium is attained when each firm produces an output, q_i. Under regulation it is directed to produce only q_0, but no tax is levied. At output q_0, with an unchanged number of firms, price is above marginal cost (for example price is at P'). Therefore, the firm is not in short-run equilibrium and would, if it could, expand output within the confines of its existing plant. More importantly, although each firm will be producing the output quota

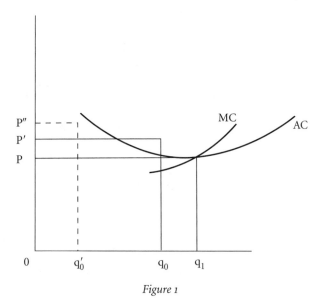

Figure 1

assigned to it at a somewhat higher cost than required for efficiency reasons, there may still be an incentive for resources to enter the industry. The administrator faces a policing task that is dimensionally different from that under the tax. He must insure that individual firms do not violate the quotas assigned, and he must somehow prevent new entrants. To the extent that the administrator fails in either of these tasks, the results aimed for will not be obtained. Output quotas will be exceeded, and the targeted level of industry production overreached.

If the administrator assigns enforceable quotas to existing firms and successfully prevents entrants, the targeted industry results may be attained, but there may remain efficiency loss since the industry output will be produced at higher average cost than necessary if firms face U-shaped long-run average cost curves. Ideally, regulation may have to be accompanied by the assignment of full production quotas to a selected number of the initial firms in the industry. This policy will keep these favored firms in marginal adjustment with no incentives for in-firm adjustments that might defeat the purpose of the regulation. But even more than under general quota assignment there will be strong incentives for firms to enter the industry and to secure at least some share of the rents that the restriction of industry output generates. If the response to this pressure should be that of reassigning quota shares within the unchanging and targeted industry output so as to allow all potential entrants some share, while keeping all firms, actual and potential, on an equal quota basis, the final result may be equivalent to the familiar cartel equilibrium. No firm will be earning more than normal returns, but the industry will be characterized by too many firms, each of which produces its assigned output inefficiently.

II

When we examine the behavioral adjustments to the policy instruments in the manner sketched out above, a theory of policy emerges. Regulation is less desirable on efficiency grounds even in the presence of full information, but this instrument will be preferred by those whose behavior is to be subjected to either one or the other of the two policy instruments. Consider the position of the single firm in the fully competitive industry, depicted in Figure 1. Under the imposition of the tax, short-run losses are necessarily incurred, and the firm reattains normal returns only after a sufficient number of its competitors have shifted resources to other industries. The tax reduces the present value of the firm's potential earnings stream, whether the particular firm remains in the industry after adjustment or withdraws its investment and shifts to alternative employment. In terms of their own private interests, owners of firms in the industry along with employees will oppose the tax. By contrast, under regulation, firms may well secure pecuniary gains from the imposition of direct controls that reduce total industry output. To the extent that the restriction is achieved by the assignment of production quotas to existing firms, net profits may be present even for the short term and are more likely to arise after adjustments in plant. In effect, regulation in this sense is the directional equivalent of cartel formation provided that the individual firm's assigned quota falls within the limited range over which average cost falls below price. Such a range must, of course, exist, but regulatory constraints may possibly be severe enough to shift firms into positions where short-term, and even possibly long-term, losses are present, despite increased output price. Such a result is depicted by a restriction to q_0' in Figure 1, with price at P''.

Despite the motivation which each firm has to violate assigned quotas under regulation, it remains in the interest of firms to seek regulatory policy that will enforce the quotas. If existing firms foresee the difficulty of restricting entry, and if they predict that governmental policy makers will be required to accommodate all entrants, the incentive to support restriction by regulation remains even if its force is somewhat lower. In final cartel equilibrium, all the firms will be making no more than normal returns. But during the adjustment to this equilibrium, above-normal returns may well be available to all firms that hold production quotas. Even if severe restriction forces short-term losses on firms, these losses will be less than those under the tax. Rents over this period may well be positive, and even if negative, they will be less negative than those suffered under the tax alternative. Therefore, producing firms will always oppose any imposition of a penalty tax. However, they may well favor direct regulation restricting industry output, even if no consideration at all is given to the imposition of a tax. And, when faced with an either/or choice, they will always prefer regulation to the tax.

III

There is a difference between the two idealized solutions that has not yet been discussed, and when this is recognized, the basis of a positive hypothesis about policy choice may appear to vanish. Allocationally, direct regulation can produce results equivalent to the penalty tax, providing that we neglect enforcement cost differentials. *Distributionally*, however, the results differ. The imposition of tax means that government collects revenues (save in the case where tax rates are prohibitive) and these must be spent. Those who anticipate benefits from the utilization of tax revenues, whether from the provision of publicly supplied goods or from the reduction in other tax levies, should prefer the tax alternative, and they should make this preference known in the political process. To the extent that the beneficiaries include all or substantially all members of the community, the penalty tax should carry the day. Politicians, in responding to citizenry pressures, should heed the larger number of beneficiaries and not the disgruntled members of one particular industry. This political choice setting is, however, the familiar one in which a small, concentrated, identifiable, and intensely interested pressure group may exert more influence on political choice making than the much larger majority of persons, each of whom might expect to secure benefits in the second order of smalls.

There is an additional reason for predicting this result with respect to an innovatory policy of externality control. The penalty tax amounts to a legislated change in property rights, and as such it will be viewed as confiscatory by owners and employees in the affected industry. Legislative bodies, even if they operate formally on majoritarian principles, may be reluctant to impose what seems to be punitive taxation. When, therefore, the regulation alternative to the penalty tax is known to exist, and when representatives of the affected industry are observed strongly to prefer this alternative, the temptation placed on the legislator to choose the direct control policy may be overwhelming, even if he is an economic theorist and a good one. Widely accepted ethical norms may support this stance; imposed destruction of property values may suggest the justice of compensation.[7]

7. For a comprehensive discussion of just compensation, see Frank I. Michelman,

If policy alternatives should be conceived in a genuine Wicksellian frame-work, the political economist might still expect that the superior penalty tax should command support. If the economist ties his recommendation for the penalty tax to an accompanying return of tax revenues to those in the indus-try who suffer potential capital losses, he might be more successful than he has been in proposing unilateral or one-sided application of policy norms. If revenues are used to subsidize those in the industry subjected to capital losses from the tax, and if these subsidies are unrelated to rates of output, a two-sided tax subsidy arrangement can remove the industry source of op-position while still insuring efficient results. In this respect, however, econo-mists themselves have failed to pass muster. Relatively few modern econo-mists who have engaged in policy advocacy have been willing to accept the Wicksellian methodological framework which does, of course, require that some putative legitimacy be assigned to rights existent in the status quo.[8]

IV

To this point we have developed a theory of policy for product-generated ex-ternal diseconomies, the setting which potentially counterposes the interest of members of a single producing industry against substantially all persons in the community. External diseconomies may, however, arise in consumption rather than in production, and these may be general. For purposes of analysis, we may assume that all persons find themselves in a situation of reciprocal external diseconomies. Traffic congestion may be a familiar case in point.

The question is one of determining whether or not persons in this sort of interaction, acting through the political processes of the community, will im-pose on *themselves* either a penalty tax or direct regulation. We retain the full information assumption introduced in the production externality model. For simplicity here, consider a two-person (A, B) model in which each per-son consumes the same quantity of good or carries out the same quantity of activity in the precontrol equilibrium, but in which demand elasticities

---

"Property, Utility, and Fairness: Comments on the Ethical Foundations of 'Just Compen-sation' Law," *Harvard Law Review* 80 (April 1967): 1165–1257.

8. For a specific discussion of the Wicksellian approach, see James M. Buchanan, "Positive Economics, Welfare Economics, and Political Economy," *Journal of Law and Economics* 2 (October 1959): 124–38.

differ. Figure 2 depicts the initial equilibrium at *E* with each person consuming quantity *Q*. The existence of the reciprocal external diseconomy is
discovered. The community may impose an accurately measured penalty
tax in the amount *T*, in which case *A* will reduce consumption to Q_a and *B*
will reduce consumption to Q_b. Total consumption is reduced from 2*Q* to
$(Q_a + Q_b)$, but both *A* and *B* remain in equilibrium. At the new price *P'*,
which includes tax, neither person desires to consume more or less than the
indicated quantities. The government collects tax revenues in the amount
[2(*PP'JH*) + *HJLK*]. Alternatively, the community may simply assign a restricted quantity quota to each person. If the government possesses full information about demand functions, it can reduce *A*'s quota to Q_a, and *B*'s
quota to Q_b, securing results that are allocatively identical to those secured
by the tax. However, under the quota, both *A* and *B* will find themselves out
of equilibrium; both will, if allowed quantity adjustment, prefer to expand
their rate of consumption.

It will be useful to examine the ideal tax against the quota scheme outlined above, which we may call the idealized quota scheme. If individuals expect no returns at all from tax revenues in the form of cash subsidies, public
goods benefits, or reductions in other taxes, both *A* and *B* will clearly prefer

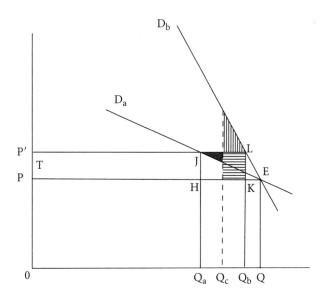

Figure 2

the direct regulation. The loss in consumers' surplus under this alternative is small relative to that which would be lost under the penalty tax. Each person willingly trades off marginal quantity adjustment for the more favorable inframarginal terms offered under direct regulation, given our assumptions that both instruments achieve the same overall externality control objective.

Under extreme fiscal illusion, individuals may ignore benefits from tax revenues, but consistent methodological precept requires that we allow persons to recognize the benefit side of the fiscal account, at least to some degree. Let us allow all revenues under the penalty tax to be returned in equal shares to all taxpayers. Under this arrangement, each person expects to get back one-half of the amount measured as indicated above for Figure 2. Simplifying, each expects to get back the amount *PP'JH*, which he personally pays in, plus one-half of the amount measured by the rectangle *JHKL*, all of which is paid in by *B*. From an examination of Figure 2, it is clear that individual *A* will favor the penalty tax under these assumptions. The situation for individual *B* is different; he will prefer direct regulation. He will secure a differential gain measured by the horizontally shaded area in Figure 2, which is equal to the differential loss that individual *A* will suffer under this alternative. The policy result, insofar as it is influenced by the two parties, is a standoff under this idealized tax and idealized quota system comparison.

For constitutional and other reasons, control institutions operating within a democratic order could scarcely embody disproportionate quota assignments. A more plausible regulation alternative would assign quotas proportionate to initial rates of consumption, designed to reduce overall consumption to the level indicated by target criteria. The comparison of this alternative with the ideal tax arrangement is facilitated by the construction of Figure 2 where the initial rates of consumption are equal. In this new scheme, each person is assigned a quota Q_c, which he is allowed to purchase at the initial price *P*. We want to compare this arrangement with the ideal tax, again under the assumption that revenues are fully returned in equal per head subsidies. As in the first scheme, both persons are in disequilibrium at quantity Q_c and price *P*. The difference between this model and the idealized quota scheme lies in the fact that at Q_c, the marginal evaluations differ as between the two persons. There are unexploited gains-from-trade, even under the determined overall quantity restriction.

It will be mutually advantageous for the two persons to exchange quotas and money, but, at this point, we assume that such exchanges do not take place, either because they are prohibited or because transactions costs are too high. Individual *A* will continue to favor the tax alternative, but his differential gains will be smaller than under the idealized quota scheme. In the model now considered, *A*'s differential gains under the ideal tax are measured by the blacked-in triangle in Figure 2. Individual *B* may or may not favor the quota, as in the earlier model. His choice as between the two alternatives, the ideal tax on the one hand and the restriction to Q_c at price *P* on the other, will depend on the comparative sizes of the two areas shown as horizontally and vertically shaded in Figure 2. As drawn, he will tend to favor the quota scheme, but it is clearly possible that the triangular area could exceed the rectangular one if *B*'s demand curve is sufficiently steep in slope. In any case, the choice alternatives for both persons are less different in the net than those represented by the ideal tax and the idealized quota.

While holding all of the remaining assumptions of the model, we now drop the assumption that no exchange of quotas takes place between *A* and *B*. To facilitate the geometrical illustration, Figure 3 essentially blows up the relevant part of Figure 2. With each party initially assigned a consumption

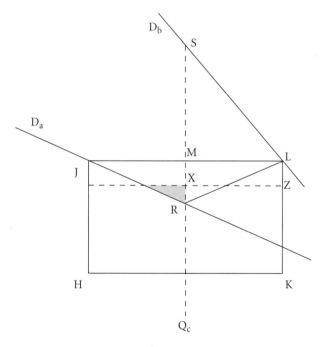

Figure 3

quota of Q_c, individual A will be willing to sell units to individual B for any price above his marginal evaluation. Hence, the lowest possible supply price schedule that individual B confronts is that shown by the line RL in Figure 3. The maximum price that individual B is willing to pay for additional units of quota is his marginal evaluation, shown by SL. The gains-from-trade are measured by the triangular area RLS. The distribution of these gains will, of course, be settled in the strict two-man setting by relative bargaining skills, but let us assume that individual B, the buyer, wants to purchase consumption quota units from A, but also to do so in such a way that individual A will come to prefer this system over the tax. To accomplish this, he must insure that A gets a share of the net gains at least equal to the area RML on Figure 3. Individual B, the buyer, retains gains of MSL under this division of the spoils. But in this arrangement, both persons are indifferent as between the policy alternatives. The system is on the Pareto frontier, and the quota scheme plus the exchange process produces allocative and distributive results identical to those generated under the ideal tax. This becomes the analogue of the Coase theorem in the context that we are examining.[9]

V

These somewhat inconclusive results may seem to provide anything but a positive theory of policy akin to that presented with respect to production externalities. The comparisons are, however, a necessary stage in developing such a theory. Recall that we have made these comparisons under the most favorable possible assumption concerning anticipated return of revenues under the penalty tax. In the real world, individuals will not anticipate that these will be returned dollar-for-dollar, and they will tend to place at least some discount on the value of benefits that they expect.

Let us say that each person expects an aggregate benefit value of only 80 cents on the dollar from tax revenues collected under the penalty tax. Consider what this single change does to the results of the last comparison made,

---

9. See Ronald H. Coase, "The Problem of Social Cost," *Journal of Law and Economics* 3 (October 1960): 1–44. For a related extension of the Coase theorem, see James M. Buchanan, "The Coase Theorem and the Theory of the State," *Natural Resources Journal* 13 (October 1973): 579–94.

that which involves proportionate quota assignments along with a free market in quotas. In this case, individual B, the buyer, can offer individual A, the seller, more than the amount required to make him prefer the quota alternative, while himself continuing to secure differential benefit under this alternative. Individual A's differential gains from the ideal penalty tax are reduced to the shaded area in Figure 3. By paying individual A the amount measured by RML, he has improved A's position relative to the penalty tax. And, in the process, he has retained for himself a differential gain measured by the area $MXZL$. Both persons in full knowledge of the alternatives will prefer the quota system, and political leaders will presumably respond by opting for regulation.

The same reasoning can readily be extended to apply to any quota system. In the idealized quota assignment first considered, we demonstrated that one person would favor the penalty tax and the other the quota. Individual A, who favors the penalty tax, loses no consumer's surplus, and he does expect to secure an income transfer through the return of tax revenues. When we modify the assumptions concerning expectations of the value of returned revenues or benefits, however, this conclusion need not hold. Individual A will, of course, expect to get back in benefits some part of the tax revenues paid in by B that is in excess of that contributed by A himself. If, however, individual A applies the same discount factor to all revenues collected, the deadweight loss may more than offset the income transfer effect. Examination of Figure 2 indicates that under the 80 percent assumption, one-fifth of the area measured by $PP'JH$ will represent deadweight loss to A from the revenues that he pays in. This deadweight loss may well be larger than the measure of the income transfer that he expects, which amounts to 80 percent of the horizontally shaded area in Figure 2. Once we introduce any plausible discount factor into the expectation of individuals concerning the return of tax revenues, it is relatively easy to demonstrate situations under which both persons may be led by private self-interest to favor the direct regulation alternative.

VI

We have developed a positive theory of externality control policy for both the production and consumption interactions under highly abstract and simplified models which allow us to isolate influences on policy formation which have been neglected. Decisions on the alternative policy instruments in democratic governments are surely influenced by the preferences of those who are subjected to them. The public-choice approach, which concentrates attention on the individual's choice as between policy instruments, allows us to construct hypotheses that explain the prevalence of direct regulation.[10] For economists who continue to support the penalty-tax alternative, the analysis suggests that they had best become good Wicksellians and begin to search out and invent institutional arrangements that will make the penalty tax acceptable to those who are primarily affected.

10. Much of the analysis developed in this paper can be applied more or less directly to policy alternatives proposed in the energy crisis of late 1973 and early 1974. For such application, see James M. Buchanan and Nicolaus Tideman, "Gasoline Rationing and Market Pricing: Public Choice in Political Democracy," Research Paper no. 808231-1-12, Center for Study of Public Choice, Virginia Polytechnic Institute and State University, January 1974.

PART SEVEN

Public Choice and Public Expenditures

Easy Budgets and Tight Money

Despite the old saying, taking candy from the baby is more difficult than not, and governments, even more than ordinary mortals, are delighted by smiles and fearful of screams. As between monetary policy and fiscal policy there is, as the Radcliffe Committee put it, "always a choice," but the alternatives may not be equally pleasant to the chooser. The factors influencing such a choice are worthy of more attention than has been given them, by the Committee and by others, especially when governments are recognized for what they are and must be in any real world.

I propose to discuss here the choice among *instruments* of stabilization policy. I want to leave out of account, so far as possible, discussion of the choice among *objectives* for economic policy. There is also a "line of least resistance" in the choice of objectives for policy. I shall not discuss this problem, however, for three reasons: First, the political pressures impinging on choices among objectives have been more widely recognized than those similarly impinging on choice among instruments. Secondly, governments do not explicitly choose objectives; they choose instruments. Finally, and more importantly, only by unscrambling these two parts of stabilization policy can we make sense out of either of them.

For my purpose, we may assume that a particular objective or set of objectives has been selected. There remains the choice among instruments, and, broadly speaking, there are two instruments of stabilization policy, *fiscal* and *monetary*. There is little direct connection between the choice between these two means of implementing policy and the objective to be pursued. Fiscal policy may be utilized primarily to achieve a surplus in the international bal-

From *Lloyds Bank Review* 64 (April 1962): 17–30. Published by consent of *Lloyds TSB Economic Bulletin.*

ance of payments, or monetary policy may be used to promote full employment and rapid economic growth. In the most likely case, a mix of instruments will be used, more or less successfully, to achieve a mix of objectives. I shall assume, without arguing the point here, that either of these two instruments, properly employed, can be equally successful in achieving the objectives selected.

There is a "theory" of choice here, but practice seems at odds with it. Many economists argue, for example, that fiscal policy should be relied on as the primary instrument of stabilization. And the Treasury, in its evidence given to the Radcliffe Committee, paid lip service to this predominance of fiscal policy as the primary stabilizing device in the modern economy. As the Committee noted, in its review of the experience, however, easy budgets have been presented against the backstop of a "flexible monetary policy" which can, if need be, be relied on to keep inflationary pressures in check.

The clearest statement of the practice, as opposed to the theory, was made by Professor Frank Paish, who, in *The Statist* for November 10th, 1961, said:

> It is important that the measures taken to control the economy should be symmetrical. In recent years the measures to expand demand have taken the form mainly of tax reductions, while the main burden of restricting demand has been placed on monetary policy and higher interest rates. A continuation of this policy could raise interest rates without limit.

This observed asymmetry in the practical application of fiscal policy and monetary policy over the different phases of the cycle merits attention. Most reasonably well-informed persons will recognize this asymmetry as being broadly characteristic of the policy experience of Great Britain and the United States, as well as other Western countries, in the years since the second world war, and especially during the decade of the 1950's. It has come to be more or less accepted that the budget provides the major weapons for stimulating spending (public and private), while monetary policy comes into its own only in periods of threatened or actual inflation. Only very recently, as reflected in the statement by Professor Paish, or in an October speech by Lord Cromer, has concern come to be expressed about the fundamental disproportion that such a policy structure must involve.

Few will quarrel with the facts of the matter. But few go beyond these to the interesting questions. Why has the asymmetry in the choice of instruments come about? Could this have been predicted to occur? Can it be expected to continue? I shall try to show that some elementary considerations for political realities will, in fact, suggest that the observed facts could readily have been predicted. If this is accepted, however, I shall show that the implications for the theory or principle of public debt are highly damaging to the ideas of "modern" economists.

Familiar explanations for the emphasis on fiscal policy in expanding demand and on monetary policy in restricting it may be found. For one thing, such a policy combination might seem to be just the ticket after a reading of almost any of the standard textbooks in elementary economics. These books, all written within the framework of the so-called Keynesian theory, will usually refer to that deceptively simple analogy "you can't push on a string." This analogy has probably had more influence on ordinary thinking than any of the more complicated, because more qualified, analytical models. In any case, the impact on thought is that monetary policy is of quite limited usefulness in stimulating demand, since people are not necessarily induced to spend by the mere availability of funds. Hence, so the argument goes, fiscal policy, the deliberate use of the budget for stabilization purposes, must become the primary anti-recession weapon. And, since some symmetry seems better than none, cyclical "balance" between fiscal and monetary measures is secured by employing the latter to restrict demand when needed. This crudely simple policy model is widely accepted today, by economists and informed politicians alike, despite the ratchet effect on the interest rate noted by Paish, the implications for budgetary balance, and the demonstrated effectiveness of monetary policy in stimulating as well as restricting demand.

The Bias of Fiscal Policy

A second explanation is considerably more sophisticated, but still familiar. If political reality is recognized at all (and it seldom is by academic scribblers), surely it suggests the strong bias of fiscal policy towards the creation of budget deficits rather than budget surpluses. Governments, that is to say, politicians, faced with any sort of responsive citizenry, or electorate, are surely cognizant of two powerful and ever-present forces. Constant pressure is exerted upon them to reduce (not to increase) the level of taxes, and, at the same time, to expand (not to reduce) both the range and the extent of the

various public services. As the Plowden Committee quite properly noted, the
third pressure for budgetary economy, so strong in former times, no longer
exists as an effective counterforce comparable in strength to the other two.

Both of the dominant pressure groups, the tax reducers and the expenditure expanders, direct their fire at the politicians, who must, other things
equal, respond (otherwise, they will not remain politicians for long). These
pressures assume especial importance in an economy where tax rates are
already prohibitively high in the view of many people, and where ever-expanding public spending programmes have been firmly "built in" to the
structure of expectations. Governments will, quite predictably, seize on any
opportunity or excuse for deficit creation offered to them by the economists,
as is the case during modern recessions. Deficit financing enables both of
these groups to be satisfied simultaneously: the politicians' dream world
come true.

The situation during booms is exactly the reverse. To carry out effective
stabilization measures through the budget then requires that both of these
pressure groups be countered. Tax rates must be maintained or increased,
and public spending programmes curtailed or at any rate not expanded. The
experience in Great Britain during recent months suggests that the latter is
especially difficult, even when an explicit curtailment objective is announced
in advance. And, if the Chancellor presents a "tough" budget in April, this
will be the exception that proves the rule. Can anyone express serious surprise that budget surpluses have so rarely occurred, except by accident, since
fiscal policy has "matured," so to speak, while budget deficits have been the
order of the day?

The Independence of the Monetary Authorities

The suggested bias in fiscal policy is, however, only one-half of the story. It
may be that fiscal policy will tend to be used only to expand demand but as
yet nothing has been said to indicate that there is an offsetting bias in the use
of monetary policy. Is monetary policy biased towards restriction?

There is an argument that attempts an answer here, although, as I shall
indicate, I do not think it need be accepted. It is sometimes advanced, however, that because of the nature of the institutions, monetary policy instruments can be, and are, relatively divorced from current "political" pressures.

The monetary authorities are presumed to remain considerably more free than their Treasury counterparts from day-to-day, week-to week influences of public opinion which, in this argument, are inherently "evil." Because of this relative freedom, these authorities can safely take "unpopular" steps that the politicians dare not take. The comparative isolation places the task of restricting demand on these authorities almost by default. Being the wise and good men they are, they must pick up the dirty linen left over by the one-sidedness of fiscal policy and, to a degree, redress the balance.

This argument is a persuasive one, especially in a superficial sense, and especially in application to the United States, where the Federal Reserve Board is, to a large but undetermined and unpredictable extent, independent of Treasury authority and control. It is less persuasive in a British context, where the central bank is, officially, within the public sector. Thus the Radcliffe Report points out that Bank of England witnesses sometimes drew a distinction between the activities of the Bank as agent of the Treasury and "the affairs of the Bank" in which it is supposed to have a wider measure of autonomy. "During this decade," the Committee comments, "this distinction has had no practical force, and we therefore do not propose to complicate our description of the Bank's activities by further reference to it."

A Simpler Explanation

Elements of both the explanations sketched above are, no doubt, helpful in understanding the policy asymmetry with which we are concerned. We can, however, explain the asymmetry more simply. And, as I recall, one principle of scientific method, attributed usually to William of Occam, tells us that we should always choose the simplest explanation of phenomena when alternative explanations are possible.

We do not need to assume that the monetary authorities have relatively greater autonomy, nor to posit the existence of a bias in fiscal policy in its crudest form. It is possible to explain our asymmetry between the use of fiscal policy and monetary policy over the course of the cycle on the assumption that these instruments are, to the same degree, influenced by "politics." This is a less restricted approach which is, at the same time, somewhat more realistic for the institutions of democratic societies when these are considered generally and over long periods.

I assume only that governments will, when faced with a choice between these two policy instruments, tend to choose the one that creates the lesser disturbance and that generates the less violent reaction on the part of the citizenry. This is all that is required to show that during recessions governments will implement stabilization objectives through fiscal policy measures instead of monetary policy measures and that, conversely, during periods of threatened or actual inflation, they will resort primarily to monetary methods of control. I do not, of course, suggest that governments will always act in this way, or that the asymmetry is an inevitable result of democratic decision-making. I shall show only that, in the present state of thinking about fiscal-monetary institutions, this behaviour on the part of governments seems predictable, and, as noted, the limited facts available to us do support this prediction.

Note also that governments may or may not be successful in achieving the stabilization that they aim to achieve. Success or failure in this respect is not relevant to the discussion here, which attempts only to explain governments' choices between the *instruments* of policy.

An "Ideal Type" Fiscal Policy

Before proceeding, it will be useful to reduce each of the broad policy alternatives to one simple variant, to one stylized model, or "ideal type," so to speak. For fiscal policy, I propose to mean the deliberate unbalancing of the cash budget of the national government (with budget defined in an over-all or inclusive sense) to promote stabilization purposes, whether these be defined in terms of employment, growth, price-levels, or balances of payments. In unbalancing the budget, I assume that changes will be made in the rate of taxation, rather than in the rate of government spending. Finally, I assume that a budget deficit, when created, is financed wholly by the issue of *new currency*, or, in its modern institutional context, by "borrowing" from the central bank. Conversely, I shall assume that a budgetary surplus, when and if created, is disposed of by some effective neutralization of the excess revenues collected: for example, by building up government's cash balance or by retiring national debt held by the central bank.

This idealization of fiscal policy allows us to discuss a whole set of related instruments in terms of a single simple policy action. It eliminates confusion by ruling out of account the operation of the automatic fiscal stabilizers. Perhaps more importantly, it removes the complexities that arise when budget deficits are financed by the issue of genuine public debt rather than new currency.

An "Ideal Type" Monetary Policy

More objections may be raised to my idealization of monetary policy. I shall use this term to refer to the purchase and sale of government securities in the open market by the central bank and/or the monetary authorities, with the objective, of course, of furthering economic stabilization. In other words, the open-market weapon becomes the model here for analysing any and all types of monetary action. When deflation or unemployment threatens, corrective monetary policy consists in the purchase of government securities (bonds) from the public with newly created funds: that is, commercial bank reserves. When inflation threatens, corrective monetary policy consists in the sale of government securities in the open market, thereby reducing the cash reserves of the banking system. In the first instance, the public ends up with more cash and fewer government securities, quite apart from any secondary effects stemming from the operation of the deposit multiplier. In the second instance, the public ends up with more bonds and less cash. Monetary policy in this "ideal type" amounts to a modification in the asset structure of individuals and firms, with central bank purchases adding to over-all liquidity during periods of recession and sales subtracting from over-all liquidity during periods of inflation.

Note that in this model of monetary policy interest rate changes, in themselves, are *not* considered the instruments of monetary policy. Interest rates change only as a result of changes in the demand for and the supply of bonds. This is, I think, a legitimate model, and all monetary policy can be reduced to what might be called an "open-market equivalent." Interest rates, as prices, cannot be changed arbitrarily without some changes in the underlying demand-supply conditions, unless excess demand or excess supply is to be produced. If this is allowed to happen, problems of credit rationing or surplus credit arise. It seems preferable, and more realistic, to remain in an equilibrium model, which is, of course, present when the authorities take action to initiate or to follow up Bank Rate changes by accompanying open-market action which may include an exchange of long-term and short-term national debt.

Considerable authoritative support for this model is to be found in the testimony of the Chief Cashier of the Bank of England before the Radcliffe Committee. He suggested that changes in Bank Rate are made effective only because, through open-market action, the discount houses are forced to borrow at that rate. Many modern discussions of monetary policy (including those of the Radcliffe Committee) have gone astray precisely because of an undue concentration on changes in interest rates to the neglect of the underlying demand-supply changes in securities and money markets that implement the rate changes.

There is purpose in adopting this "ideal type" for monetary policy. Note that, here, monetary policy consists in increases and decreases in interest-bearing national debt held outside the central bank.

Debt Issue Versus Taxation

The intent of introducing these two "ideal types" can now be made clear. I can, through this device, present the fiscal policy and the monetary policy alternatives quite starkly, and in such a way that the distinctions between the two are openly revealed. Fiscal policy reduces to changes upwards and downwards in tax rates. Monetary policy reduces to changes upwards and downwards in interest-bearing national debt held outside the public sector. In comparing these two instruments we may, therefore, examine the differences between increasing taxes and increasing debt on the one hand, and, on the other, between decreasing taxes and retiring national debt.[1]

Again, let us look at the simple politics of the matter. Governments are assumed to be responsive to the desires of the electorate and to seek either to minimize citizenry displeasure or to maximize citizenry satisfaction through their choices of policy instruments. Given that assumption, it takes no sophisticated analysis to indicate that public debt will be issued in lieu of in-

---

1. I am concerned with *primary* effects here. Both instruments will generate *secondary* effects through the multiplying effects on deposits generated by changes in bank reserves. Nevertheless, if the same degree of expansion or contraction is assumed to be achieved by fiscal or by monetary means, these secondary effects can be roughly identical as between the two instruments.

creasing taxes and, for the same reason, on the down side, taxes will be reduced in preference to debt retirement.

This rather simple explanation of the asymmetry seems "plausible" and "realistic." I propose, however, to bring this plausibility out into the clean and open air, for the underlying analysis requires explicit discussion. When this step is taken, it will be seen that the "theory" or "principle" of public debt that emerges is wholly at odds with that which dominates modern economic orthodoxy. Indirectly, therefore, the observed asymmetry in the choice of fiscal and monetary policy instruments over the cycle provides some positive evidence that the "classical" or "old-fashioned" notions about public debt remain correct after all, and despite the onslaught of the post-Keynesians. This allows me to bring up yet another defence of these classical principles of public debt, additional to those already presented in my recent book, *Public Principles of Public Debt* (1958).

Classical Principles of National Debt

If our simple political model has any relevance, it suggests that there is less intensive public reaction against restrictive monetary policy (the issue of public debt) than there is against restrictive fiscal policy (tax increases). And, on the other side of the cycle, that there is more intensive "relief" provided through tax reduction (expansive fiscal policy) than there is through debt retirement (expansive monetary policy). This seems certainly to be true, but I want to ask why. Why does an increase in interest-bearing debt arouse less antagonism on the part of the public than a tax increase designed to accomplish roughly the same objectives?

The answer is, I submit, a very old and a very simple one, and one that has been understood by sensible men for centuries. The issue of national debt allows the real costs of the restrictive measures to be postponed in time, to be shifted to individual taxpayers in future accounting periods. Actually, there should be little point in discussing this elementary principle of debt, public or private, were it not that the great weight of modern intellectual opinion comes down heavily on the side that denies its validity.

If this basic classical principle of public debt is accepted, the explanation we seek has been located. Those who must pay current taxes are members of the electorate at the moment when the policy action is taken. These taxpayers exist in the here and now, and their opposition to increases in tax rates can be heard. By contrast, who can arise to oppose an increase in tax rates in future periods, which an issue of public debt must embody? Current taxpayers will, of course, offer some reaction in anticipation of their expected future liabilities, but, when confronted with any choice between these and current tax increases their preferences are not hard to predict. By and large, and with few exceptions, modern governments will find debt issue less unpopular than taxation.

The Modern Theory of Public Debt

As I have noted above, however, this line of reasoning depends on an acceptance of the classical principle of public debt. If, instead of this, the dominant modern theory of national debt is substituted, we are left without such an explanation of the policy asymmetry which does, after all, seem so plausible. What is this modern theory of national debt which, in its current version, stems from an aftermath of the Keynesian revolution in economic thought? The heart of the argument consists in a denial of the central point of the classical theory. It is asserted that an internal public or national debt cannot involve a shifting of real costs forward in time. So long as the citizens within the economy purchase the securities sold by the government there can be no postponement of real costs, so the argument goes, because current purchasing power is given up when the debt is issued. Insofar as the national debt is internal, the method of financing cannot affect the location of real costs in time. As with taxation, all real costs are imposed immediately on the decision to borrow. The issue of public debt is, in this conception, not generically different from taxation.

Since no actual resources, in the net, are "used up" in an attempt to mop up excess liquidity during inflationary periods, either through tax increases or through the open-market sale of securities, the implication of the modern theory of debt would seem to be that no "real costs" are involved in either case. But even the most naive approach to the political process reveals the fallacy here. Surely governments that are responsible for implementing stabilization policy would be surprised to learn from the economist that tax increases, at any time and for any purpose, impose no real costs on taxpayers.

The point is that for governmental decisions thinking in terms of social aggregates and not in terms of individuals as specific taxpayers has been, and is, grossly misleading. Let us accept the weakness in the modern conception here, however, and go on to examine a second implication of this argument. Since public debt can shift no burden or cost to future periods, it is, as we have said, equivalent to taxation. Hence, there should, on the average, be no greater resistance to tax increases than to increases in the size of outstanding national debt, or so the argument implies.

At this point the theory examined here requires a closer look. With tax increases, there is no difficulty in appreciating the fact that, relatively speaking, the costs that must be involved are placed squarely on those persons who are subjected to the increased rates. Even if the sole purpose of the tax increase is that of mopping up excess liquidity, those paying the additional taxes "suffer" relative to those in the group who, presumably, gain from having an effective anti-inflationary policy introduced. But where are the equivalent costs when the alternative policy instrument—national debt issue—is employed for the same purpose?

Recall that, in this modern view that we are discussing here, these costs cannot be shifted forward to taxpayers in future periods. Suppose that the excess liquidity is mopped up by open-market sales of government securities. Who suffers the effects of this restriction in the primary sense, in the same way that the taxpayer suffers? Clearly, it is not the persons who purchase the securities, since they make a simple, voluntary, market transaction. Yet these are the only persons who, directly, give up current purchasing power—liquidity—in the whole process. They do so, however, because they are provided with a promised interest return in future periods; their sacrifice of current command over resources is a voluntary one. But, since theirs is the liquidity that is mopped up, no other members of the social group suffer any direct "stabilization burden" comparable to that imposed on the taxpayer. Under this theory, therefore, it is to be wondered that governments ever impose taxes at all, since public debt is wholly burdenless.

The theory is, of course, nonsense; it may be, quite legitimately, called the modern economists' version of the perpetual motion machine. The difficult thing to explain is the dominance that it has achieved over good minds. Any careful consideration of the elementary logic of decision-making leads inexorably to an acceptance of the classical principles of public finance, at least in their broad essentials. The difference between taxation and public debt is that the first imposes current period costs, the second postpones these costs to future periods.

Some Necessary Qualifications

As is usual in such discussions as these, certain qualifications in the argument must be introduced lest critics pounce. In the commentary above, I do not imply the complete absence of cost or burden when restrictive monetary policy is implemented. Interest rates, generally, will rise, and prices of old bonds will fall. Potential borrowers will be disappointed, and potential lenders gratified. These effects are essentially *secondary*, and they are similar to the secondary effects that would be produced by a similarly restrictive policy, implemented by the alternative method of raising taxes. In addition, such effects as these are *indirect*, and to a large extent the gainers balance off against the losers so that no net impact on the decision process could readily be predicted.

Also, as noted above, given the fractional reserve basis for deposits in commercial banks, either restrictive fiscal or restrictive monetary policy will work itself out through the operation of the deposit multiplier. A contraction in bank reserves will generate a multiple contraction in deposits, and, in the process, some borrowers will suffer a real burden. This particular effect should, however, be essentially the same whether it is due to a tax increase or to open-market sales, provided that the same degree of net liquidity is taken out of the system in each case.

These second-order effects could be discussed in some detail, but such discussion may have been, in itself, a source of confusion. Too much concentration on second-order and indirect effects tends to conceal from view the sharp distinction between the *primary* impact of the two policy alternatives. And it is these primary effects that I emphasize here.

Tax Reduction Versus Debt Retirement

Most of the discussion has been about restriction. The comparison is, if anything, simpler in the case of expansion, but since most of the points made apply in reverse order the analysis need not be elaborated in great detail.

In this case governments will choose, on the average, that policy instrument which generates the most favourable response, on the part of the public, which gives the most obvious "relief." In tax reduction, as with tax increase, the predicted incidence is straightforward. Individuals who find their current tax obligations reduced experience a real, and non-illusory, increase in real income. The incidence of debt retirement (monetization), on the other hand, is not nearly so clear. The government will, in this case, be purchasing bonds from the public with new currency, with cheques drawn on its own account in the central bank, cheques that will, of course, add directly to commercial bank reserves. Those individuals who sell bonds to the authorities receive an increment to current purchasing power but they give up, in exchange, a claim against future interest income. Their wealth is not markedly changed in the process.

The genuine beneficiaries here are those who would otherwise have had to pay taxes to meet these interest payments in future periods. With less debt outstanding their future tax liabilities are reduced. A debt retirement or monetization process removes, once and for all, a real burden from their shoulders. Since, however, this "relief" is not so clearly understood, and, in any case, is deferred, the reaction will not be equivalent to that to be expected from current tax reductions.

As in the anti-inflation case, there will, of course, be all sorts of secondary effects. But, again, these should not be allowed to obscure the basic facts of the matter. These are that the primary incidence of anti-recession *monetary* policy rests with those who pay taxes later, while the primary incidence of anti-recession *fiscal* policy rests with those who pay taxes now (or receive the benefits of expanding public services if this variant is allowed).

Implications

The observed asymmetry between the choice of monetary and fiscal instruments of policy over the cycle has been "explained" through the use of a simple model and the classical principles of public finance. But we explain only to improve, so we must ask the important question, How can the behaviour of governments be modified?

Continuation of the asymmetry over long periods is clearly undesirable on many grounds. Interest rates will be pushed ever upwards, and budget deficits will seldom, if ever, be matched by budget surpluses. This result should be condemned on ethical grounds, since it tends to place the costs of stabilization policy squarely on the shoulders of future taxpayers while concentrating the benefits in the here and now. Apart from the ethics of the matter, this pattern of policy runs directly counter to that which might be suggested if rapid economic growth should come to be accepted as an explicit aim of policy. Even if it serves no other purpose, the analysis here should suggest some of the political roadblocks that must be surmounted before a policy combination aimed explicitly at promoting growth could be introduced. As Professor Paul Samuelson and others have urged for the United States, such a policy would require that the asymmetry discussed here be replaced by that of "easy money and tight budgets."

Admitting the undesirability of the demonstrated practice does not suggest an alternative. One such might be the placing of fiscal policy back in its pre-Keynesian box, as circumscribed by the rule of the annually balanced budget, with the sole responsibility for stabilization falling on monetary policy. This alternative may seem superficially attractive to some who long for the revival of effective political controls of fiscal pressures. But myths once exploded are not easily reconstituted.

In any case, sole or primary reliance on monetary policy to achieve stabilization objectives involves an over-dependence on one market or set of markets to generate changes in a whole economic structure. This concentration inhibits the effectiveness of policy on the one hand, while subjecting those who operate in that market or set of markets to an "unfair" share of the stabilization task.

A second alternative, and one that was implied in the memoranda submitted by several economists to the Radcliffe Committee, would be the placing of sole or primary reliance on fiscal policy as the instrument of stabilization. This never-never land of "functional finance" ignores political facts altogether and assumes the presence of an all-wise, benevolent economic czar or commissar who moves tax rates and spending programmes up and down in complete indifference to the reactions of ordinary citizens. If we accept the fact that democratic process is worth preserving, the introduction of this model into practice will surely generate secular inflation due to the bias previously discussed. And even the present asymmetry in policy seems preferable to continual inflation, despite its undesirable features.

The growth in importance of the automatic fiscal stabilizers offers some measure of improvement. Insofar as these can become effective, the bias in fiscal policy is reduced. However, as has long been recognized, automatic stabilizers can, at best, help to correct cyclical swings, not to prevent them.

Improvement in governmental decision-making can come, over the long run, only as a result of the establishment of a new set of rules for behaviour, "rules" that will be rigid enough to influence the behaviour of politicians even in the face of constituency pressures. The analysis here suggests the importance of such possible rules. Symmetry should be preserved, over the cycle, in the employment of *each* of the policy instruments. That is to say, the budget should be balanced over the cycle, and open-market sales by the central bank should be balanced by open-market purchases, again over the cycle. If the trends in the economy justify a growth in the money supply, either or both of these rules may, of course, be slightly modified. However, only by a rather rigid adherence to both these rules can the natural political tendencies discussed in this paper be prevented from producing the distortions noted.

These rules are sophisticated ones, and democratic decision-making is not. But perfection should not be expected, and, above all, we should be tolerant of the politicians and critical of the economists. Only after the latter have succeeded in reformulating and securing acceptance among themselves of a new set of "principles for sound finance" can the politicians be called to task.

Notes for an Economic
Theory of Socialism

Economists have devoted considerable attention to the effects generated by market or private organization of the supply of goods and services that embody collective-consumption characteristics. Analysis of these effects makes up much of the content of modern public-goods theory. Rarely do we find the analysis turned on its head, so to speak, toward prediction of the effects generated by governmental organization of the supply of goods and services that are largely if not wholly "private," that is, fully divisible into separate and distinguishable units of consumption. When this relatively straightforward step is taken, the consequences of governmental or collective organization are readily demonstrable. The analysis is on all fours with its converse.

More than this, however, the analysis permits a satisfactory treatment of the relevant practical cases that involve the comparative efficiencies of pri-

Public Choice 8 (Spring 1970): 29–43. Reprinted by permission of the publisher, Kluwer Academic Publishers.

This paper was directly stimulated by Yoram Barzel's recent contribution in this journal. Barzel's paper, in turn, is based on a model initially discussed by Gordon Tullock. See Yorum Barzel, "Two Propositions on the Optimum Level of Producing Collective Goods," *Public Choice* 6 (Spring 1969), 31–38, and Gordon Tullock, "Social Cost and Governmental Action," *American Economic Review* 59 (May 1969), 189–97. Tullock's model is more completely developed in his *Private Wants—Public Means* (Basic Books, forthcoming). This paper may be interpreted as a generalization of the Tullock-Barzel construction in the context of a more restricted model than either of these authors considered.

I am greatly indebted to Armen A. Alchian, University of California, Los Angeles, and to Charles Goetz, Virginia Polytechnic Institute, for helpful discussions during the critical stages of the development of my argument.

vate and government (market and political) organizational alternatives when goods and services possess both "publicness" and "privateness." Conceptually, the trade-offs between jointness efficiencies derived from collective consumption and the distributional efficiencies made possible by market-like quantity adjustments can be measured. More importantly, the analysis points toward quite specific policy norms with respect to the organization of the supply of partially divisible goods and services.[1]

The apparent reason for the neglect of this type of comparative analysis is found in economists' continuing but implicit assumption about the nature of collective or governmental organization. With little or no consideration of the implications of this assumption for the decision-making process itself, economists' standard models allow governments to distribute benefits unequally and at will. When politically supplied goods and services are privately divisible or partitionable among beneficiaries or consumers, no constraints are imposed on distribution.[2] Governments are assumed to be able, without cost, to distribute these among ultimate users in precisely the market pat-

1. In a recent paper, J. G. Head and C. S. Shoup classify goods into three distinct categories depending on the relative efficiency of market and nonmarket modes of provision. Their analysis is primarily classificatory, but they appear to compare the two organizational modes as mutually exclusive alternatives. They neglect the mixed alternatives treated in this paper. As I shall indicate, a broad three-part classification also emerges from my construction. The central difference between their approach and my own stems from their emphasis on the effects of inframarginal cost-sharing schemes. If this is neglected, as I have done in this paper, the analysis of Head and Shoup suggests that the relative efficiency of the different organizational forms would depend only on cost differentials; that is, on the presence or absence of jointness efficiencies. This would, in turn, imply that all goods for which such gains from joint consumption arise can be more advantageously provided as collective-consumption goods, income effects apart. Head and Shoup seem to neglect the distributional inefficiencies arising from collectively imposed uniformities in consumption. See J. G. Head and C. S. Shoup, "Public Goods, Private Goods, and Ambiguous Goods," *Economic Journal* 79 (September 1969), 567–72.

2. Professor Armen Alchian has suggested that the terms "partition" and "partitionable" be used to refer to the separation of consumption units of a good or service among persons. This allows the terms "division" and "divisibility" to retain their orthodox economic-theory meaning in reference to an absence of lumpiness in some physical-quantity dimension. While there is much to be said for this suggested terminology on grounds of semantic efficiency, the usage of the terms "divisibility" and "indivisibility" in public-goods theory seems to have been so widely adopted as to make such a change confusing at this stage. Ambiguity will, of course, continue to be present unless the precise context in which "divisibility" or "indivisibility" is introduced is specified.

tern. Under this assumption, potential distributional inefficiencies of political organization are totally neglected.

In the models introduced here, *consumption uniformity* is postulated under political or collective provision, regardless of the descriptive characteristics of the goods and services provided. That is to say, once the provision of a good or service is politically organized, all persons in the political group share equally in the consumption benefits. This condition is necessarily satisfied when a good or service embodies technological characteristics that make divisibility among consumers impossible. One means of defining the polar case of a purely collective good is to say that no distributional problem is faced.[3] An alternative definition of the polar extreme states that consumption units to additional persons may be provided at zero cost. Note that, in this second definition, nothing is implied about the possibility or impossibility of divisibility. In effect, the analysis of this paper accepts the second definition in that full divisibility is assumed to be possible in all cases. In other words, distributional uniformity among consuming users is not imposed by the technological characteristics of the goods themselves. Instead, such uniformity tends to be produced as a consequence of the political decision-making process, at least so long as democratic structure remains ultimately in being. Democratic socialism, in any meaningful practical sense, is "about equality," and equal sharing is its centrally descriptive feature. The models of this paper do little more than to incorporate this feature systematically in efficiency comparisons among alternative organizational structures. In such comparisons, distributional inefficiencies arise when goods and services which could be differentially provided to consumers are uniformly provided unless, of course, individual preferences should be identical.

Illustrative examples may be helpful. If the pickup of garbage is politically organized, each resident of the community will tend to be provided with the same quantity of service (measured in number of pickups per week), regardless of his own quantity preferences. If education is governmentally organized, each family will be allowed access to the same quantity-quality of service independent of its own preferences.

---

3. For an elaboration of this point, see my *Demand and Supply of Public Goods* (Chicago: Rand McNally, 1968), Ch. 9.

I

Consider a two-man community. Individuals A and B find themselves under a market-like organization that supplies the good X. In Figure 1, the demand curves are shown by D_a and D_b. The price confronted by each man is P, and individually attained positions of equilibrium are shown at E_a and E_b. Each person attains equilibrium by adjusting quantity purchased to accord with his own preferences.

The problem is to examine the possible gains or losses from a shift to a

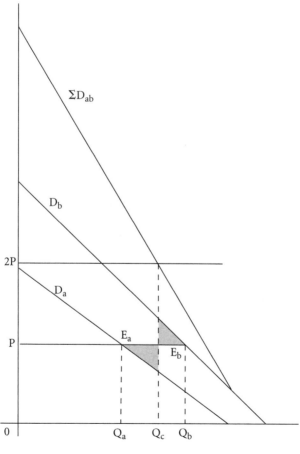

Figure 1

collective organization for the supply of X. It is assumed that X is fully divisible in consumption as between A and B. By this is meant only that there is no spillover, externality, or nonexclusion in the consumption of X. It is also assumed that neither person is interested in either the other's consumption of X or in the level of utility attained by the other. Uniformity in consumption is postulated under political or collective provision. Both A and B must consume the same quantity of X. If A is provided with one unit, then B must, and simultaneously, be provided with one unit. Trading or retrading outside the collective organization is assumed to be strictly prohibited.

The comparison lends itself to geometrical tools if the proper constructions are introduced. The collective good can be considered to be a two-component bundle containing two units of the market good X, with one being distributed to each person. Hence, the quantity dimension for examining demand-supply is two-unit bundles. The cost of providing such a bundle is now 2P which, as with the market good, is assumed to be unchanging over quantity. This dimensional conversion allows the individual market demand curves, D_a and D_b, to be treated as marginal evaluation curves for the collective good, now designated as XX, provided that income effect feedbacks are ignored.[4] In this way, A's evaluation of the two-unit bundle, XX, becomes equivalent to his evaluation of the one-unit good that he secures privately under the alternative market arrangements, since, of course, he secures only one unit in either case.[5]

If we now assume that there exists an omniscient and benevolent despot who is fully informed in modern welfare economics, and if we allow him to select the optimal collective "solution," he will add the two marginal evaluation curves vertically and set quantity at the point of intersection between the summed evaluation curve and the marginal cost curve.[6] In Figure 1, this

4. This essentially Marshallian escape route greatly facilitates straightforward presentation of the central argument without undermining its content. To the extent that income effects are relevant in determining the optimally preferred quantities of good at the margin, the ordinary market demand curves must be replaced by specific marginal evaluation curves that are, in turn, functionally related to the particular sharing arrangements assumed to be in force.

5. A similar sort of dimensional shift was used previously in my paper "A Public Choice Approach to Public Utility Pricing," *Public Choice* 5 (Fall 1968), 1–18.

6. Without the income-effect assumption made above, this solution is not unique but depends on the sharing arrangement over inframarginal units.

is shown at Q_c. As the construction indicates, there is a *welfare loss* in the shift from market to collective organization of supply. This loss is measured by the area of the two shaded triangles in Figure 1, given the constraints of the model as defined. This welfare loss is exclusively distributional. It stems from the fact that A and B are required to consume uniform quantities of the good despite their differing evaluations placed on the good at the margins. If we assume that all demands are to be met jointly under these institutional arrangements, the conditions for optimality seem to be satisfied, but the construction demonstrates that it remains more efficient in the large to allow for independent quantity adjustment. Note also that the welfare loss remains regardless of the cost-sharing arrangements, which have not been specified here.[7]

The demonstration that in this model there are excess costs of the collectivization of polar private goods suggests that offsetting cost-reducing elements must be present and sufficiently large to overcome the distributional inefficiencies before this organizational alternative becomes desirable. The cost-reducing element suggested is, of course, some departure from the polar case of zero advantage from joint consumption. Once this assumption is dropped, there may be possible gains to be secured from *joint* rather than separate consumption. The geometrical construction allows us to depict conceptually the degree or extent of "publicness" that is required to warrant organizational changes toward meeting demands jointly under the restrictive conditions outlined.

II

Consider Figure 2, which duplicates Figure 1 in several essential features. The cost of producing the two-unit bundle, XX, is now defined to be lower than double the cost of a one-unit bundle, X, by an amount R per unit, or to be $(2P - R)$. Independently considered, the technological improvement secured from joint supply involves a net welfare gain which may be measured

7. The welfare loss can best be seen by considering that under political organization each person pays an equal share in the cost of each unit supplied. The measure of the welfare loss by the two shaded triangles under other sharing schemes is more tedious to prove geometrically, but under the restrictions of the model such proof always remains possible.

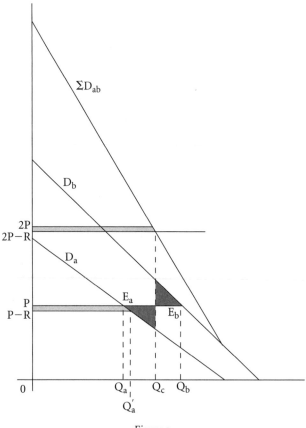

Figure 2

by the upper shaded area in Figure 2. If this gain exceeds the area of the two triangles previously shown to measure the net welfare loss, the shift from all-market to all-governmental supply of the good is socially efficient under the restrictive conditions postulated. As the construction of Figure 2 is designed to show, however, if only these polar organizational alternatives are considered, the market *may* remain the more efficient of the two, even when some jointness efficiencies exist. As Figure 2 shows by inspection, there can be net losses in shifting from market to political provision. The "publicness" gains need not be sufficient to offset the distributional losses.

This result seems to embody a paradox of sorts, since institutional means should surely exist for exploiting fully all technological advantages, including those arising from jointness in consumption. The possibility that any attempt to exploit such advantages may involve welfare losses seems at odds with the economist's professional intuition. As previously noted, the result emerges because of the uniform consumption constraint. When this source of the paradox is recognized, there is suggested a search for institutional arrangements that will allow both the technological advantages of joint consumption and the distributional advantages of individual quantity adjustments to be secured.

Assume now that the benevolent despot instructs the two-person group to consume jointly the quantity Q_a'. Over this initial range of supply-demand, the full advantages of joint consumption are exploited, and there are no distributional costs. Assume further that the despot instructs B to pay a price of P per unit for this quantity, Q_a'. This guarantees that A will secure the full measure of society's gains over the initial range of joint consumption. This is indicated by the elongated lower shaded area below PE_a. Assume further that B is allowed to purchase supplementary quantities of *one*-unit bundles of the good as he desires through market-like arrangements for supply. Under these conditions, B will extend his consumption purchases to E_b. At equilibrium, he will be securing Q_a' under joint supply arrangements with A and the additional amount, $Q_a'Q_b$, through a market. It is evident that, under this new institutional arrangement, B will find himself in precisely the same position as he is under full market organization. Since A will be better off, it must be concluded that the partial collectivization with market supplements is the best of the three alternative organizational arrangements examined to this point.

This solution also represents the most efficient organizational arrangement that is possible. There exists no means through which the remaining technological gains from jointness in consumption may be secured without incurring larger distributional losses. This conclusion may continue to contain apparent elements of paradox, however, because if considered uncritically it appears to involve the violation of the familiar necessary marginal conditions for efficiency in providing bundles of goods and services containing uniform consumption components for each user. At Q_a', the point at which joint consumption ceases, the summed marginal evaluation, shown by ΣD_{ab}, exceeds the marginal cost of production of the two-unit bundle, shown by $(2P - R)$. The familiar Samuelson requirement appears to suggest that joint consumption should be expanded to Q_c. However, when it is recognized that B can individually *supplement* the jointly supplied quantity through market arrangements at a price of P per unit, a generalization of the statement for the necessary marginal conditions can be shown to be satisfied only at Q'_a. Joint consumption of the quantity Q_c clearly violates rather than satisfies the general necessary marginal conditions for Pareto optimality.

To demonstrate this violation, it is useful to assume that individual A is the actual producer of both one-unit bundles of X and the two-unit bundles of XX. We continue to assume that these are produced at constant cost per unit of X.[8] Further assume that because of his strategic position as producer, A can choose the type of bundle; he can produce for either joint consumption or for independent private consumption. For purposes of analytical simplicity only, further assume that individual A is able to secure all gains from the possible advantages of joint provision. At Q'_a, the marginal cost of producing a two-unit bundle of XX is $(2P - R)$. The marginal cost to A, the producer, is, however, less than the marginal production cost because he, too, shares in the consumption. The supply price, or marginal cost of the two-unit bundle to B, the demander, is $(2P - R)$ less the evaluation that A himself places on this bundle. At Q'_a, this evaluation is equal to $(P - R)$. The marginal supply price to B at Q'_a is, therefore, $(2P - R) - (P - R)$, which is, simply, P. The marginal requirements met at Q'_a are that $D_b = P$, which is precisely the market equivalence. At Q'_a, the minimal supply price at which A will provide two-unit bundles is P. Beyond this quantity, however, A's own marginal evaluation becomes less than $(P - R)$. Therefore, the supply price of a two-unit bundle, as faced by B, will be higher than the supply price of a one-unit bundle provided exclusively for B's consumption which remains at P. Since we have assumed that A is the supplier here who can also secure the

8. The constant-cost assumption is required here because we allow one person to become the supplier. In a more general context, we need assume only that the actual production of the good or service, whether supplied-sold to governmental units, to subgovernmental collective groups, or to private individuals, is made available to them in such a manner as to insure that they remain price takers. That is to say, variations in quantities demanded cannot modify price-per-unit, either within a fixed or changing composition of consuming groups.

full gains from joint consumption if these exist, B's demand beyond Q'_a will be met by A's selling him one-unit rather than two-unit bundles.

The results do not depend on the particular assumption made about the sharing of the total gains from joint consumption. Individual B rather than A could have been allowed to secure all of the gains over inframarginal ranges of quantity. At the margin, however, optimality requires that the person who places the lowest evaluation on the good secure the full advantage of joint consumption. In all cases, efficiency requires that some critical quantity less than Q_c be provided for joint consumption and that the additional demands of B be met from supplementary private purchases.

III

The two-person geometrical construction may be extended to allow for any degree of jointness efficiency. It will be useful initially to consider the polar case of the purely collective or public good defined in the second sense noted earlier. Such a good is one for which the advantages of joint consumption are complete. The cost of supplying consumption units to *all* persons simultaneously is no higher than the cost of supplying consumption units to any one person individually or privately. Consider Figure 3. It is assumed that the demand (marginal evaluation) curves remain the same as in the previous figures. Under the pure collective goods assumption, the cost of producing the two-unit bundle, XX, remains the same as the cost of producing the one-unit bundle, X; that is, P.

In this setting, efficiency requires that two-unit bundles be provided in the amount Q'_c. As the construction shows, neither person has an incentive to supplement this collective provision through his own independent or private purchases if these should be possible. And, more significantly, there are sizable welfare gains in shifting from market to collective provision in this instance.

The construction in Figure 3 enables a limit to be determined for those situations in which joint consumption should be utilized in meeting *all* demands. In the two-person case depicted, assume now that the unit cost of supplying the one-unit bundle remains at P. If the gains from the simultaneous or joint provision of consumption units to both A and B are such that

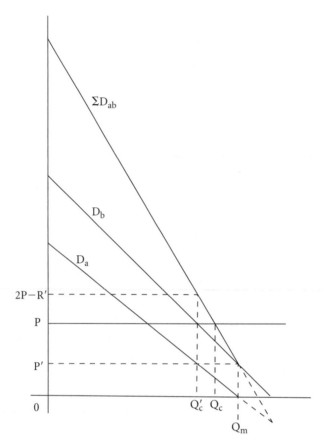

Figure 3

the two-unit bundle can be supplied at $(2P - R')$ or below, then *all* demands can be most efficiently met through joint consumption. Geometrically this limit is determined by the intersection of both D_b and P and ΣD_{ab} and $(2P - R')$ at the same quantity. The curve D_b must cut the line drawn horizontally from P at or to the left of the quantity Q'_c. In somewhat different terms, if individual B's preferred market purchase quantity does not *exceed* the optimally efficient joint-provision quantity, all demands can best be met jointly.

This general conclusion can be extended to show that there may be cases in which some demands should be met independently and nonjointly *even* when the jointness is complete in a technological sense. Instead of P, assume now that the one-unit bundle can be produced at a cost of P' per unit and that the advantages of jointness are complete so that $(2P - R') = P'$. Assume that the demand curves remain as before. In this case, note that the condition defining the limit is met. D_b and ΣD_{ab} are coincident at the intersection with the horizontal drawn from P'. At any cost per unit (equivalent for one-unit and two-unit bundles by assumption here) below P', an amount Q_m should be supplied jointly with the additional quantity desired by B being met from independent provision. This result stems, of course, from the constructed extension of D_a into the ranges of negative evaluation. Beyond Q_m, B's demands should be met privately even in the case of a purely collective good because only in this manner can A's negative evaluations be avoided or made unnecessary.

IV

The next stage in the analysis is the obvious one of generalizing the results attained with the simplified two-person model to an *n*-person setting. The problem is more complex than the familiar one of stating the necessary marginal conditions for optimality or efficiency under assumed institutional or organizational invariance. The problem here is to include within a statement of the necessary conditions for efficiency some criterion for organizational form.

This may be done by stating a generalized rule that involves an either/or criterion:

The quantity of good or service provided jointly to all members of a group of *n* persons should be extended to the *minimal* amount that satisfies *either* (1) or (2) below:

$$MC_{x_{1,2,\ldots n}} = \sum_{i=1}^{n} ME_{x_i} \qquad (1)$$

$$MC_{x_{1,2,\ldots n}} - MC_{x_{1,2,\ldots s}} = \sum_{i=1}^{n} ME_{x_i} - \sum_{i=1}^{s} ME_{x_i}, \qquad (2)$$

where $MC_{x_{1\ldots n}}$ indicates the marginal cost of supplying a single multi-component "production unit" that contains *n* separate and equal consumption units, X, one of which is provided to each person in the inclusive group of size n.[9] The right-hand term in (1) indicates the marginal evaluations for a unit of X summed over all persons in n. In (2), S designates any group of persons of size smaller than n, including one-person groups.

If (1) is met, and if cost functions and utility functions are normal, then, at that quantity,

$$MC_{x_{1,2,\ldots n}} - MC_{x\ldots s} \leqslant \sum_{i=1}^{n} ME_{x_i} - \sum_{i=1}^{s} ME_{x_i}, \qquad (1A)$$

which reduces to

$$MC_{x_{1,2,\ldots s}} \geqslant \sum_{i=1}^{s} ME_i. \qquad (1B)$$

The statement (1B) indicates that no subgroup less than the whole membership in n finds it economically advantageous to supplement privately or through independent purchase the jointly provided quantity at which (1) is satisfied. All demands are met jointly under the efficient organizational arrangements.[10]

If, however, the rule is met by the satisfaction of (2) at the *minimal* quantity, it is implied that at such quantity

$$MC_{x_{1,2,\ldots n}} < \sum_{i=1}^{n} ME_{x_i} \qquad (2A)$$

9. In the polar extremes of a purely private good, as defined here,

$$MC_{x_{1,2,\ldots n}} = MC_{x_1} + MC_{x_2} + MC_{x_3} + \ldots + MC_{x_n}.$$

In the other polar extreme where jointness efficiency is complete,

$$MC_{x_{1,2,\ldots n}} = MC_{x_1} = MC_{x_2} = \ldots = MC_{x_n}.$$

The notation here is a simplified form of that introduced in my paper "Joint Supply, Externality, and Optimality," *Economica* 33 (November 1966), 404–15. See, especially, page 406, Footnote 1.

10. This position has properties that are analogous to those that characterize a solution in the core of an *n*-person game. For an effort to relate public-goods theory to the concept of the core, although in a setting different from that of this paper, see Mark Pauly, "Clubs, Commonality, and the Core," *Economica* 34 (August 1967), 314–24.

and that

$$MC_{x_{1,2,\ldots s}} < \sum_{i=1}^{s} ME_{x_i}. \tag{2B}$$

The statement (2B) implies that independent or subgroup action on the part of some persons supplementary to the joint-provision quantity for the *n*-person group as defined by (2) is efficient. The necessary conditions for efficiency in the supplementary extension for the subgroup, which may itself be a collectivity, can be defined in a manner precisely equivalent to those laid down above for the more inclusive group. The subgroup s should provide the extended quantity jointly to the minimal limits where *either* (11) or (22) is satisfied,

$$MC_{x_{1,2,\ldots s}} = \sum_{i=1}^{s} ME_{x_i} \tag{11}$$

$$MC_{x_{1,2,\ldots s}} - MC_{x\ldots t} = \sum_{i=1}^{s} ME_{x_i} - \sum_{i=1}^{t} ME_{x_i}, \tag{22}$$

where t is any group of persons less than s, including one-person groups.

This procedure can, of course, be extended to smaller and smaller groups. As the analysis clearly suggests, the most efficient organizational mix need not be either collective or joint provision for the whole group of *n* persons, some mixture of this and single-person supplements through the market, or all persons purchasing from the market. The most efficient organizational arrangement might well be that *some* part of total demand be met by joint provision of consumption units to all *n* persons simultaneously, *some* part of total demand be met by joint provision of consumption units to all members of one or more subgroups of differing sizes, and *some* part of total demand be met by private or individualized purchases by single buyers. In the limit, of course, the conditions defined by (1) and (2) collapse to the same statements for the one-person subgroup.

V

The rules for stating the necessary conditions for both the optimal quantity of good and for the optimal organizational arrangement for its provision allows us to classify all goods and services into three mutually exclusive categories. If, for any good or service, condition (1) above is satisfied at a quantity below that which might satisfy (2), the good or service should be provided jointly for the simultaneous consumption of *all* persons in the community of *n* persons. If for all groups larger than one person membership, the equivalent of condition (2) is met at a quantity below that which meets the equivalent of condition (1), efficiency requires that all demands be met through private and individualized purchases from some market-like source, with independent quantity adjustments. Between these polar organizational extremes, there can be varying mixes among collective, cooperative, and private organizational arrangements that satisfy the efficiency norms outlined.

Since the size of the inclusive political community, n, is assumed to be exogenously determined here, it is evident from the analysis that a different classification will emerge in different-sized communities. If cost conditions are equivalent, the proportion of goods-services falling in the first category, where all demands are best met through joint provision to all members of the inclusive political community, will decline as n increases.

VI

The comparative analysis of organizational forms has relevance for policy choices. Since the restrictive requirement suggesting that all demands be met through joint provision for all members of the group in any given political community is not likely to be met in many cases, the efficiency argument for collective or governmental provision of *minimal* quantities of those goods and services that possess joint-consumption characteristics is strengthened. This conclusion applies particularly to those goods and services that are recognized to be partitionable among separate users, in whole or in part. Examples are educational services, health services, sanitation services.

There is an asymmetry in the analysis which should be explicitly recognized. It is assumed that individuals or subgroups smaller than the total membership of the political community can supplement the consumption provided by the larger unit through independent or market-like sources more efficiently than similar groups could dispose of collectively provided consumption units through independent or market-like outlets. This assumption seems acceptable on the basis of empirical observation. Private or cooperative supplementing of collective consumption can take place at reasonably low transactions costs; private or cooperative disposition of collectively supplied consumption units may involve prohibitive transactions costs. (In Los Angeles, private firms sell services that consist of removing garbage cans from back alleys and placing them on front streets where public pickups are made. It is not easy, however, to sell the services of half-empty garbage cans, and no such market is to be observed.)

Finally, I should emphasize that the whole analysis of this paper is based on the assumption that collective decision-making is itself ideally efficient. This amounts to saying that the comparison is among pure organizational alternatives. It can plausibly be argued that individuals and small groups adjust quantities to their own preferences with a high degree of efficiency. By no stretch of the imagination can a similar argument be advanced for collectively organized groups. Individual preferences are not revealed except through behavior, and the costs of securing multi-person agreement are sufficient to prevent effective groping toward collective efficiency. Decision rules must be adopted at some "constitutional" stage, and the working out of these rules may generate significant departures from efficient collective outcomes. Recognition of this tends to strengthen the argument of this paper. It has been demonstrated that, even when collective decision-making is assumed to be ideally efficient, the most advantageous organizational arrangements for the provision of many goods and services embodying collective-consumption characteristics involve collectivization of only *some* part of the total supply along with the private or voluntary group supplementation of this supply from ordinary market sources. When the predicted inefficiency of collective decision-making is taken into account, the argument for encouraging the maximal feasible usage of private or voluntary quantity adjustment becomes stronger. At a minimum, the analysis tends to undermine any arguments in favor of political prohibition of supplemental provision of goods and services, as witness the United States Postal System.[11]

---

11. I am indebted to Yoram Barzel, University of Washington, for this point.

Tax Rates and Tax Revenues in Political Equilibrium
Some Simple Analytics

James M. Buchanan and Dwight R. Lee

Introduction

Our purpose in this paper is to analyze the tax rate–tax revenue relationship that figured prominently in the supply-side economics discussion which dominated macropolicy argument in the early 1980's, and to use standard utility-maximization to define the conditions for both taxpayer and political equilibrium. In order to simplify our exposition, we ignore the serious complexities involved in conceptualizing a single rate-revenue relationship in a tax system that incorporates many separate bases for taxation, along with many rates, including progressive rates on important sources. What is *the* rate of tax in the United States? We simply assume that this question may be satisfactorily answered.

In order to bring the analysis to the simplest possible level, we shall assume that there is only one well-defined base for taxation, and, further, that there is a single uniform rate of tax imposed on the generation or use of this base. We shall use a demand-theory construction throughout the analysis. We consider the behavior of the potential taxpayer as a potential "demander" of the tax base. This construction is self-evident if we think of the

From *Economic Inquiry* 20, no. 3 (1982): 344–54. Reprinted by permission of Oxford University Press.

We are indebted to our colleagues, Geoffrey Brennan, Nicolaus Tideman, Robert Tollison and Gordon Tullock for helpful suggestions on an earlier draft.

base as an ordinary commodity, say, beer. It is less familiar, but nonetheless fully appropriate, to think of the taxpayer as demanding units of income when he supplies resource inputs. With an income base for tax, it is, of course, possible to examine the taxpayer's behavior in supplying labor or other resources to produce the base. Most of the analysis of taxpayer response has taken this supply-side approach.[1] The two constructions are reciprocals of each other; they describe the same behavior and yield identical results.[2] Our demand-side approach, however, will enable us to draw on familiar propositions in orthodox demand theory that tend more readily to be overlooked when the supply-side approach is taken.

The first objective is to examine carefully the possible relationships between tax rates and tax revenues. There will be a direct and proportionate relationship when the base is invariant with changes in rate. In terms of familiar Marshallian coordinates, the direct and proportional rate-revenue relationship exists when the elasticity of the demand for base is zero throughout the range of possible tax rates.

In all normal conditions, we should expect that the "demand curve" for the base would be downsloping throughout the range of possible rates, thereby generating nonlinear relationships between rates and revenues.[3] With a pretax price assumed constant over quantities, the rate-revenue

1. Specifically related to the Laffer-curve relationship, see D. Fullerton, "On the Possibility of an Inverse Relationship Between Tax Rates and Government Revenues," Working Paper no. 467, National Bureau of Economic Research, April 1980. By contrast, in their recent book, "The Power to Tax" (Cambridge: Cambridge University Press, 1980), Brennan and Buchanan utilize demand-theory construction throughout their analysis.

2. For a discussion of the reciprocal nature of the demand and supply relationship, see J. M. Buchanan, "The Backbending Supply Curve of Labor: An Example of Doctrinal Retrogression?" *History of Political Economy* 3 (1971): 383–90.

3. In our construction, we apply the rate of tax directly to the base, with base defined in units of ultimate consumable "goods," whether a single commodity like "beer" or the bundle of commodities and services that the taxpayer might purchase with post-tax income units. This procedure allows us to convert the percentage rate of tax readily into an increment to pretax price, and to utilize orthodox demand analysis straightforwardly. Note, however, that this construction differs from the standard definition of a tax "rate" under income taxation, which involves applying a percentage rate to the generation of base, *inclusive* of tax. In terms of a simple numerical example, if the pretax price of a unit of consumable goods is $1, a 10 percent tax, in our construction, becomes equivalent to a 10 cent addition to pretax price. In order to generate $1's worth of final consumable

Public Choice and Public Expenditures

curve becomes fully analogous to the price-revenue curve derived from the standard downward sloping demand curve. Commencing with a zero tax rate, and then allowing this rate to increase incrementally, we can trace a range over which total tax revenues increase, reach a maximum, and then a range over which revenues decrease, until at some rate, revenues fall to zero. For simplicity in exposition throughout, we shall use linear relationships between price (including tax) and quantities demanded.

The second objective is to analyze the behavior of those who make decisions on rates of tax with the purpose of predicting the "equilibrium" position or location along the rate-revenue function. In particular, we seek to determine whether or not rational rate-setting behavior could generate a location characterized by an inverse relationship between tax rate and tax revenue.

II. A Model of Government

For our purposes, we do not need to choose among alternative public-choice models of governmental decision-making (median voter, bureaucratic dominance, agenda setter, benevolent despot, monopolist surplus maximizer, etc.). We require only that government's utility function contain two arguments, expenditures (revenues), and tax rates with expenditures (revenues) considered as "goods," and tax rates as "bads." Clearly, this minimal requirement fits the objective function of all governments. The ideal position would be one of being able to make expenditures, either to finance public goods and services or to secure private-personal gains (or some combination) without, at the same time, having to levy taxes on a recalcitrant

---

goods, the taxpayer would have to generate $1.10's worth of income including tax, to which a "rate" of 9.09 percent would be applied to secure the 10 cents. Hence, a rate of 10 percent, in our construction, is equivalent to the lower rate of 9.09 percent on the inclusive base.

The distinction here is important with respect to the dimension in which responses to changes in rate are measured. Invariance in the generation of base, net of tax, in our construction, necessarily implies a positive relationship between rate and generation of base, defined gross of tax. More generally, and as our analysis in the text indicates, any range of adjustment over which the demand for base, net of tax, is inelastic definitionally implies a positive relationship between rate and base, gross of tax.

citizenry. The worst possible position, by contrast, would be that in which governments found it necessary to levy onerous taxes without securing the advantages of the revenue collections from which to make public expenditures.

The second characteristic of our model for governmental behavior is somewhat more restrictive than the first, although it is surely realistic. We postulate that governmental decisions are made on the basis of a limited time perspective.

If politicians in office could, at the end of their tenure, effectively realize the capital value generated as a consequence of their decisions, the necessary uncertainty of political tenure need not affect the time horizon. Without marketability of the capital value (generated, for example, by a record of fiscal prudence) politicians have little motivation to consider consequences that extend beyond the expected period of tenure. Furthermore, and somewhat paradoxically, expected tenure actually may be increased by focusing on short-run considerations. The rational ignorance of voters makes it unlikely that they will understand the long-term consequences of current decisions or be able to assign political responsibility for these consequences once they arrive. The politicians who push for policies that generate near-term benefits probably increase their chances for reelection even if the long-run effects of these policies are decidedly negative. This short-sighted bias is intensified by the fact that the immediate advantages of policy often accrue to specific constituencies while the eventual costs are spread over an entire taxpaying public. When providing benefits for his constituency the politician is in much the same position as the exploiter of a common property resource. Not only will he and his constituents not pay all of the cost of exploiting the political process for their immediate gain, but if they refrain from this exploitation they cannot expect to gain a preferential claim on future benefits in exchange. The politician, much like the harpooner of blue whales, sees little advantage in taking a long-run perspective.

In the analysis to follow, we do not need to specify in any precise way what the time horizon of the political decision-maker is. We require only that this horizon be shorter than that period of time that is necessary for taxpayers to make their full behavioral adjustments to changes in the rates of taxation.

III. The Rate-Revenue Analytics

We introduce a highly simplified geometrical construction, depicted in figures 1(a) and 1(b). The abscissa is drawn at the level of the pretax price, which for a money-income base is simply $1. In figure 1(a), the heavily drawn curve D_L is defined as the truncated long-run demand curve for the base with "long-run" being specifically defined to be a period sufficiently long to allow for full behavioral adjustment to each rate of tax on base, and for the attainment for the full institutional equilibrium subsequent to such

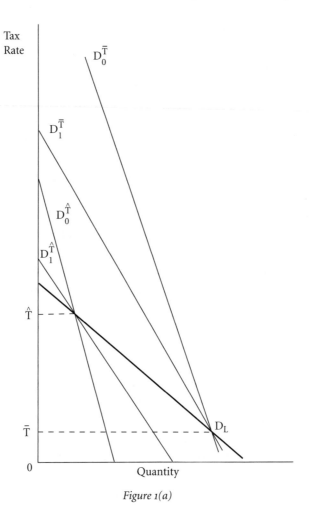

Figure 1(a)

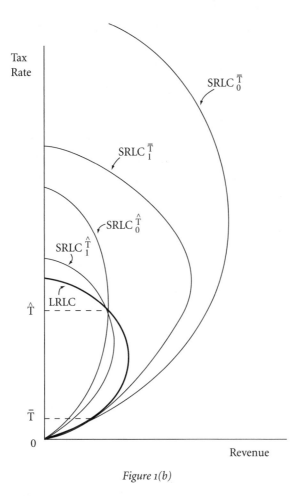

Figure 1(b)

behavioral adjustment. In his work on the Swedish tax structure, Stuart has suggested that the calendar length of such a period, for Sweden at any rate, may be up to ten years.[4] The short-run–long-run distinction clearly seems more important in the tax-adjustment context than it does when we are considering demands for ordinary commodities, in part at least because governments tend to levy taxes on those bases that are relatively immune to easy

---

4. C. Stuart, "Swedish Tax Rates, Labor Supply, and Tax Revenues," Natisnalokomiska Institutionen Lunds Universitet, Meddelande, 1979, 64.

adjustment by potential taxpayers (as indeed they are advised to do by orthodox normative tax theorists).

The same relationship as that shown in the demand curve (heavily drawn) in figure 1(a) is traced out in figure 1(b) by the heavily drawn curve, $LRLC$, with total tax revenues being measured along the abscissa. The two end points of this curve correspond to the origin (at zero tax rate) and to the intercept of the demand curve in figure 1(a), at which point the tax rate becomes sufficiently high that, given time for complete adjustment, no base is demanded at all. If prices are converted to percentage rates, this intercept value may lie close to 100 percent, although it may readily fall below or even go above this level.

The heavily drawn demand curve in figure 1(a) and the heavily drawn rate-revenue curve (Laffer curve) in figure 1(b) depict taxpayer responses to alternative rates of tax after full adjustments have been made to each rate. In other words, these curves are necessarily long-run if taxpayer adjustments to rates are postulated to take time. Indeed, these curves define a unique relationship between rate and base, or rate and revenue, only if the full-adjustment stipulation is made. If we restrict taxpayer response to any period of time shorter than that required for full adjustment, it becomes necessary to date the functional relationship between rate and base, or rate and revenue, and, in addition, to fix the initial rate to which full adjustments are assumed to have been made.

On figures 1(a) and (b), assume that taxpayers have fully adjusted their behavior to the rate shown by $\overline{T}$. There will be a whole family of demand curves [figure 1(a)] and Laffer curves [figure 1(b)], that may be drawn through the initial position of taxpayer equilibrium, each one of which will incorporate a different period of adjustment that must be specifically defined. In figure 1(a), the demand curve labeled $D_0^{\overline{T}}$ depicts the current-period adjustment to alternative rates of tax, given that taxpayers have fully adjusted to $\overline{T}$ before any change. The demand curve, $D_1^{\overline{T}}$, depicts the adjustment after a single period of time. The Laffer curves, $SRLC_0^{\overline{T}}$ and $SRLC_1^{\overline{T}}$, are, of course, alternative depictions of the same relationships. Only two short-run curves are drawn although any number could be included.

The same exercise could be carried out for any initial rate to which taxpayers might be assumed to have been fully adjusted. One additional rate, $\hat{T}$, is included in figure 1. Note that at all rates of tax above that for which behavioral adjustments have been completed, more revenues will be generated in the short-run than in the long-run, whether revenues will increase in both cases, whether short-run revenues will increase and long-run revenues decrease, or whether both short-run and long-run revenues will decrease. Conversely, for all rates of tax below that for which behavioral adjustments have been completed, more revenues will be generated in the long-run than in the short-run, whether revenues will decrease and long-run revenues increase, or whether both short-run and long-run revenues increase.

IV. Political Equilibrium

To derive the necessary conditions for political equilibrium, we must introduce the utility function for government itself, restricted by the stipulation that revenues are "goods" and taxes are "bads." This restriction allows us to depict government's preferences with ordinary indifference mapping on the same dimensions of figure 1. We do this in figure 2.

The rate-revenue relationship defines the constraints within which governmental fiscal decisions are made. But it is necessary to specify carefully which particular rate-revenue relationship is relevant here. As noted earlier, the location of the rate-revenue function will depend on the initial tax-rate equilibrium to which taxpayers have adjusted and on the length of the time horizon incorporated in governmental decisions. The long-run or full-adjustment rate-revenue or Laffer curve will become the relevant constraint only if political decision-makers adopt the long-term perspective. In all other cases, this long-run curve is irrelevant to decision-making by government, although it continues to describe the locus of equilibrium positions for taxpayers, and, through this means, to constrain the ultimate location of the position that defines equilibrium both for government and for taxpayers.

The equilibrium conditions for the politicians will be defined by the equality of the trade-offs between tax rate and tax revenue in the government's utility function on the one hand and in the appropriate rate-revenue function on the other. If this equilibrium is also to represent the long-run equilibrium adjustment for the taxpayer, it must lie on the long-run Laffer curve. One such equilibrium position is that shown at E^* in figure 2. At E^*, with tax rate, T^*, political decision-makers are in the required tangency po-

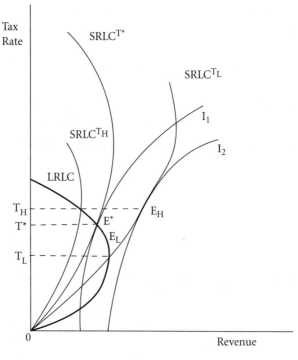

Figure 2

sition; they have no incentive to increase or to decrease tax rates. Taxpayers, on the other hand, have fully adjusted to the tax rate, T^*; they will not modify their behavior further as time passes.

Note that government could, if it desired, increase revenues in the short-run; the relevant short-run rate-revenue curve is upsloping at E^*. (It is assumed that only one short-run curve is relevant between a change in the tax rate and full adjustment to that tax rate.) If government should be strictly revenue-maximizing, E^* would not, of course, be a position of political equilibrium. In this case, political equilibrium would be attained only where the relevant rate-revenue curve becomes vertical at its intersection with the long-run curve.[5]

---

5. In a forthcoming elliptical note, we develop the analysis of equilibrium in this lim-

As the geometrical construction in figure 2 indicates, the position of equilibrium may be located either on the upsloping or the downsloping portion of the long-run rate-revenue curve. Only by chance would the position be at the maximum revenue position on the long-run relationship, and there is no analytical reason to predict precisely where the equilibrium position will be located. Note, however, that the equilibrium will always be below the maximum-revenue point on the short-term rate-revenue curve, so long as taxes are "bads" in government's utility function.

Consider the case where the tax rate to which long-term adjustment has been made is T_L, the rate which does generate maximum revenues per period after all taxpayer adjustment has been completed. Finding itself at E_L government will seek to increase the tax rate to T_H in order to attain position, E_H, on the short-run curve, $SRLC^{T_L}$, that passes through E_L and which defines the appropriate adjustments over the period of the government's planning horizon. The position, E_H, cannot be attained for longer than the short period so defined because it is not consistent with long-term taxpayer equilibrium. As time passes, and as adjustments are made, both in taxpayer behavior and in tax rates, government will (assuming convergence) shift to the position of sustainable equilibrium, E^*, with tax rate, T^*.

With different configurations of the indifference curves or the rate-revenue curves, equilibrium could, of course, be located somewhere along the upsloping portion of the long-run Laffer curve. We do not analyse this sort of equilibrium diagrammatically since the relevant necessary conditions are fully analogous to the position depicted in figure 2. We should note, however, that regardless of where sustainable equilibrium is located, the tax rate will be *above* that which would be chosen by a government whose time horizon is as long as the period required for taxpayers to make full adjustments to rate changes. It should also be evident that the longer the time horizon of government, even within the constraint that it remain shorter than the time for full adjustment, the closer will be the equilibrium tax rate to that which would characterize the rational behavior of the genuinely far-seeking government. We may summarize much of our analysis by stating that so long as

---

ited revenue-maximizing case. See J. M. Buchanan and D. R. Lee, "Politics, Time, and the Laffer Curve," *Journal of Political Economy*, forthcoming, 1982.

government is short-sighted it will always seek to exploit to some degree the vulnerability of the taxpayer over the period between the change in tax rate and the attainment of full individual and institutional adjustment.

V. Convergence and Stability

The emphasis to this point has been to define the conditions for taxpayer and government equilibrium. We have simply presumed that the equilibrium will be attained, and we have neglected any analysis of the process through which the final position might be reached as well as the whole question as to whether convergence takes place at all. Without going into a detailed analysis of the dynamic features of the model and the stability conditions, some general observations can be made.

Assume that the government can adjust the tax rate once each period, and further that the government's concern is only with the current period while full private adjustment to a tax rate is not complete until the beginning of the period following its imposition. In this case it can be shown that the tax rate will oscillate around the political equilibrium rate, T^*, if the objective is simple revenue maximization (the indifference curves are vertical with respect to the horizontal axis).[6] When the tax rate enters the utility function as a bad, tax rates may oscillate around T^* early on, but will not necessarily continue to oscillate as T^* is approached. It is clear, for example, from the discussion of figure 2 in section IV that if the initial rate is below T^* at T_L, then the next period's rate will be above T^* at T_H. Once full adjustment to rate T_H has been made and the government is contemplating a new rate, $SRLC^{T_H}$ is the relevant short-run Laffer curve. It is reasonable to assume that the slope of $SRLC^{T_H}$ will be less positive (or more negative) at each tax rate than will the slope of any short-run Laffer curve to its right, and vice versa.[7] But one also expects that at each tax rate the indifference curves become steeper as we move left, reflecting a willingness to increase the tax rate more

6. This has been established and the conditions for convergence worked out in J. M. Buchanan and D. R. Lee, "The Simple Analytics of the Laffer Curve," Working Paper, Center for Study of Public Choice, Virginia Polytechnic Institute and State University, Blacksburg, Va., September 1981.

7. This will be true of all short-run Laffer curves when the short-run demand curves are vertically parallel to each other.

in return for a given increase in revenue when revenue is low than when it is high. Therefore the point of tangency between $SRLC^{T_H}$ and an indifference curve can occur either above or below T^*.[8] The possibilities for developing a general characterization of the tax-rate time path appear limited and will not be attempted here.

VI. Expectations

A more critical restriction on the analysis involves our neglect of expectations. We have implicitly assumed that taxpayers respond to rate changes in a passive sense; they expect any rate to be permanent. They do not, themselves, model the behavior of government in imposing these rates. The introduction of taxpayer expectations into the analysis has several interesting results that are apparently relevant to current tax policy debates.

If taxpayers model the tax-setting behavior of government correctly and if both taxpayers and government have available the same data on rate-revenue relationships, taxpayers will be able to predict the position of equilibrium and make their own behavioral adjustments accordingly. The possibly long sequence of adjustments through which response to rate changes take place will be foreshortened dramatically. Suppose, however, that in a rational expectations equilibrium, described by some position like E^* in figure 2, government should want to take on a longer-time perspective than that which has characterized its previous behavior and which had been incorporated in the model of government held by taxpayers. Suppose government recognizes the additional revenue potential, in a long-run sense, available to it from tax-rate reduction, and that it seeks to exploit this. To government, this clearly should seem to be a net gain, since it should be able to secure additional revenues which will allow it to make additional outlays, while at the same time, rates of tax on the citizenry are reduced. Taxpayers should, seemingly, welcome this move toward rate reduction, since excess burdens would be lowered without any sacrifice in benefits available from public outlays.

---

8. It is possible that a tangency occurs at the point where $SRLC^{T_H}$ intersects $LRLC$ and thus there will exist multiple political equilibria. This multiple equilibria possibility does not exist in a strict revenue-maximizing model.

The government may, however, find it difficult to move from E^* along the long-run Laffer curve in the manner that seems indicated. So long as taxpayers continue to model government as a short-run maximizer, they will not respond fully to a tax rate below T^*. Rather, they will incorporate only short-run considerations into their calculus and respond along curve $SRLC^{T^*}$ in figure 2. Taxpayers will reason that, if they respond fully to the rate cut below T^*, they will leave themselves again vulnerable to short-term exploitations as government returns to T^* or above. Therefore, a rate reduction will put the government on a lower indifference curve for a period that extends beyond the short-run, and even a relatively far-sighted government will be unable to move down the long-run Laffer curve, $LRLC$ in figure 2, from position E^*.

In order to generate shifts along the long-run Laffer curve, even in the long-run, the government must convince taxpayers that tax-rate reductions are permanent; in other words, they must, simultaneously with cuts in tax rates, get taxpayers to change their model of governmental behavior. If, however, taxpayers construct their model of governmental behavior on the basis of a developing historical record, there may be no readily available means of escape from the high tax dilemma. The straightforward shift in time perspective of government is not sufficient; government must, somehow, bind or commit itself in such fashion that taxpayers become convinced that a "new deal" has, indeed, arrived. It is at this point that the argument for *constitutional* commitment on rates of tax, or on other forms of fiscal limits, comes into force. The promised results of "Reaganomics" might, indeed, become possible with constitutional rate reductions; they seem unlikely to emerge in the expectational setting of 1982 when taxpayers remain highly skeptical of the willingness of government, in future years, to keep real tax rates at promised levels.

VII. Conclusions

Our purpose in this paper has been almost exclusively analytical rather than empirical. We have shown how equilibrium positions along the "wrong side" of the rate-revenue relationship may be attained, without any violation of rationality precepts on the part of governmental decision-makers, and, further, we have indicated why escape from the genuine dilemma that such positions represent might prove difficult. The analysis is, however, helpful in assessing the attempts to locate empirically the position of the United States fiscal structure in the early 1980's. It seems clear that, in the debates of 1981, those supply-side economists who argued in terms of Laffer curve effects were implicitly adopting a long-time perspective, whereas those economists who argued that location along the downsloping portion of the Laffer curve was highly unlikely were, again implicitly, thinking in terms of some short-time Laffer relationship.

The empirical studies that have been attempted have been largely based on studies of the elasticity of input response to changes in net returns. Much of this work seems inconclusive in judging the long-run impact of a tax cut on revenues. For example, in an effort to address this impact, Fullerton makes use of thirteen empirical investigations of labor supply elasticities.[9] Of the thirteen studies all were cross-sectional except two, leaving inconclusive any means of assessment concerning the completeness of the adjustments. All thirteen studies generated estimates based on uncompensated responses to changes in the return to labor. This is reasonable when, as is the case in most of the studies, the response of particular subsets of the labor force is being investigated. However, when the response of the aggregate labor force is to be estimated, as it necessarily must be when considering the results of a general tax change, the more reasonable assumption is that at least some compensation takes place. What workers gain (lose) from a tax reduction (increase) will be offset to some degree by a reduction (increase) in benefits from governmental service.[10] To ignore this offset is to understate labor supply elasticity when leisure is a normal good.

It is also true that input supply elasticities will generally be smaller than the output elasticities that are of ultimate concern. The positive effect of an increase in the return to labor may not come primarily from the motivation it provides to work more hours, but from the motivation to work more productively. Labor supply elasticities fail to pick up the output effects that flow from human capital increases induced by an additional return to labor. This

9. Fullerton, "On the Possibility of an Inverse Relationship."

10. For a theoretical investigation of this consideration, see A. Lindbeck, "Tax Effects Versus Budgets Effects on Labor Supply," Seminar Working Paper no. 148, Institute for International Economic Studies, Stockholm, Sweden, July 1980.

output effect is further enhanced through the symbiotic interaction that exists between a growing stock of human and physical capital.

The definitive empirical work remains to be done. Not only does such work call for the estimation of long-run input elasticities (where long-run may extend to a decade or more), but also for the inclusion of these elasticities into a model that recognizes the dynamic interactions and feedbacks that exist between inputs in the generation of measured output. The simple analytics we have presented in this paper offer the challenges to those who would either refute or corroborate the claims of the Lafferites.

The thrust of the analysis does not depend at all on the empirical findings concerning the location of the United States tax structure on the long-run Laffer curve. As we have noted, so long as government makes its fiscal decisions on the basis of a time horizon shorter than that period required for full taxpayer adjustment to tax rate changes, observed tax rates will be higher than those that a far-seeking or "enlightened" government would impose. The "high tax trap" is only one of several critically important policy dilemmas that arise when there is an obvious discrepancy between the government's rate of discount and that rate that would be "efficient" in some long-run sense. Fortunately, economists are rapidly coming to be aware of the central features of these dilemmas and are now shifting their attention to the analysis of *rules* that will restrict the operations of ordinary politics.[11]

11. The "high tax trap" analyzed in this paper is closely analogous to the "inflationary trap" generated by discretionary monetary policy in a setting where there is a recognized short-run trade-off between unemployment and inflation. Governments that respond rationally in the face of this short-run trade-off are led to policies that generate inflation which is undesired within the long-term perspective. And the difficulties involved in any escape from this inflationary trap are in many respects identical to those analyzed in this paper. On the inflationary trap, see F. E. Kydland and E. C. Prescott, "Rules Rather Than Discretion: The Inconsistency of Optimal Plans," *Journal of Political Economy* 85 (1977): 473–91, and R. J. Barro and D. B. Gordon, "A Positive Theory of Monetary Policy in a Natural-Rate Model" (University of Rochester and National Bureau of Economic Research, 1981, mimeographed).

Name Index

Subject Index

administrative-decision model: extension of neutral allocation theorem to, 307–11

auction method: of assigning ownership rights, 257–62; circumstances when not applied, 261; efficiency-based argument for, 260

bargaining: Coasian solutions, 358–59, 367 n. 14; in private response to externalities, 358–59

behavior. *See* individual behavior

bequests: as transfers of value, 265

bureaucracy: behavior of politicians and bureaucrats in, 11–13, 62–70; modern theory of, 47–49; organizational behavior, 12; theory of, 48, 62–69

bureaucrats: acting in public choice role, 120; acting in self-interest, 12; acting under allocational neutrality theorem, 308–9; behavior in bureaucratic hierarchy, 63–70; in Coase's model of the state, 312; motivation of, 48–49, 65–66; in Pigovian model of the state, 312

business cycles, political: in public choice theory, 51–52

buyers: producers and sellers as consumers and, 389–91; in two-dimensional market space, 230–31; in vote market, 214–26

capitalism: ethics of, 151

cartel coalitions: costs and political effectiveness of formation of, 390–96; costs to members of individual industry, 396–97; limited range of sizes for, 403

cartels: interindustry interaction, 343–44; internal decision-making rules, 340–42; market sharing, 339–40; new entry problems, 342–43; output restriction, 339–40; players in formation game, 404–5; price fixing, 339–40

cartels, advertising-marketing: effect of formation of, 339–40; of firms in specified categories, 338–44

catallactic perspective: applied to politics, 18–21; approach to economics, 16–17, 20–21

charity: economics of, 34

choice: differences in consumer and voter, 162–69; electoral, 293–95; of individual in constitutional politics, 405; instances of free choice, 68; linked to individual preferences, 162–67; minimax principle of, 122, 124; private distinct from public choice, 29–30; social, 43–44; utility maximization as logic of, 116. *See also* collective choice; individual choice; political choice; public choice; public choice theory

Christian hypothesis, 33–34

This book is set in Minion, a typeface designed by Robert Slimbach specifically for digital typesetting. Released by Adobe in 1989, it is a versatile neohumanist face that shows the influence of Slimbach's own calligraphy.

This book is printed on paper that is acid-free and meets the requirements of the American National Standard for Permanence of Paper for Printed Library Materials, z39.48-1992. ∞

Book design by Louise OFarrell, Gainesville, Fla.
Typography by Impressions Book and Journal Services, Inc., Madison, Wisc.
Printed and bound by Sheridan Books, Inc., Chelsea, Mich.